Irish Nationalists and the Making of the Irish Race

Professor emeritus of history
at Dartmouth College

International
Irish soldiers ½
East India company

580

Irish Nationalists and the Making of the Irish Race

Bruce Nelson

PRINCETON UNIVERSITY PRESS
PRINCETON AND OXFORD

Copyright © 2012 by Princeton University Press
Published by Princeton University Press, 41 William Street, Princeton, New Jersey 08540
In the United Kingdom: Princeton University Press, 6 Oxford Street, Woodstock, Oxfordshire
OX20 1TW

press.princeton.edu

Library of Congress Cataloging-in-Publication Data

Nelson, Bruce, 1940–
Irish nationalists and the making of the Irish race / Bruce Nelson.
    p.   cm.
Includes bibliographical references and index.
ISBN 978-0-691-15312-4 (hardcover : acid-free paper) 1. Ireland—History. 2. National
characteristics, Irish. 3. Irish—Ethnic identity. 4. Race—History. I. Title.
DA925.N45 2012
320.5409415—dc23   2011047701

British Library Cataloging-in-Publication Data is available

This book has been composed in Minion Pro

Printed in the United States of America

10 9 8 7 6 5 4 3 2 1

FOR DONNA

For so many reasons, and
in memory of Joan (1931–2007)

Contents

Illustrations

Acknowledgments

WHEN I FINISHED MY LAST BOOK, which was published in January 2001, I vowed that the next one would be shorter and would be published much more quickly than its predecessor. Now it's a decade later, and I'm just completing that next book. But I try to look at the bright side. Over a period of ten years, I have made many friends and accumulated many debts. Now I can finally take the opportunity to thank some of the people whose kind assistance along the way has been indispensable.

For someone who was trained in U.S. history and who has written two books on American labor history, this has been a bold but risky undertaking. I wandered onto someone else's terrain, and the good news is that I have been welcomed by some of the very best historians in the field of Irish history. I must begin with my friend and mentor Kevin Whelan, who is one of the most brilliant scholars and generous individuals I have met in my lifetime. It would take up too much space to enumerate the ways large and small in which Kevin has facilitated the evolution of this book. But I must try—however inadequately—to express my gratitude.

Perry Curtis has also been a generous ally and friend. His *Apes and Angels*, first published in 1971, remains the starting point for studying the evolution of English stereotypes of the "wild" and "savage" Irish. Perry has read many of my chapters with great care and critical acumen; he has also shared many a story over our semiregular get-togethers at the Dirt Cowboy Café in Hanover, New Hampshire. It's nice to have one of your most knowledgeable critics as a neighbor.

I owe a word of thanks to a number of other colleagues and friends as well. For nearly two decades Alex Bontemps has taken on the task of reading just about everything I have written, and his friendship and critical insight have been a special gift. David Brody, my mentor in American labor history, read several chapters and offered a number of critical suggestions that I probably should have taken on board more than I did. Leslie Butler provided detailed and very astute criticisms of my chapters on Ireland, slavery, and abolition. Tim Meagher read several chapters and challenged me on an important point of interpretation. In retrospect, I'm grateful that he stood his ground. Brian Hanley and I have shared many meals, ideas, and resources ever since we first met in Dublin in the summer of 2002. Irene Whelan's generosity and her unrelenting belief in my work have provided great comfort and reassurance at critical moments along the way. Thanks also to the staff of Notre Dame's Keough-Naughton Irish Studies Centre in Dublin for their unfailing warmth and generosity; to Seamus Deane, Luke Gibbons, Joe Cleary, and Breandán MacSuibhne; and to Abby Bender, Bob Bonner, Vincent Comerford, David Gleeson, Robert A. Hill, Ely Janis, Kevin Kenny, Joe Lee, Mic Moroney, Angela Murphy, Orla Power, Matthew Stout and the Byrne Perry Summer School, Paul Townend, and Clair Wills.

In writing this book I ventured onto the terrain of South African history and found a great tutor in Ben Carton of George Mason University. In reading and commenting on my two South Africa chapters, Ben went far beyond the ordinary obligations of collegiality. I am also grateful to Lindsay Braun, of the University of Oregon, who patiently has tried to walk me through the complex and contextual meanings of such elementary terms as "Boer" and Afrikaner" and even "black" and "white" in nineteenth-century South Africa.

One of the most enjoyable benefits of working in the field of Irish history has been the opportunity to spend substantial amounts of time in Ireland for the last decade. When it comes to the generous hospitality I encountered there again and again, I must offer a special word of thanks to Andrew Pilaro. In 2003 Andrew gave me a place to stay in Dublin at a point when I was ramping up my research on this project. The opportunity to spend weeks at a time in the city's indispensable research libraries, and to have a comfortable place to come home to every night, was a great gift. I will be forever grateful to Andrew, and also to Anita Whelan, who helped me out of many a jam during my sojourns in Georgian Dublin. A word of thanks, as well, to Tony Pilaro and Robert Binswanger, whose initiative helped to make it all possible.

I must also express my gratitude to Dermot and Ann Keogh in Cork city for their unfailing kindness and generosity. Dermot, the head of the history department at University College Cork, arranged for me to spend the autumn of 2002 at UCC, where I often had the opportunity to share a meal with the Keogh family. While I was in Cork, Gillian Smith (now Gillian Doherty) became a good friend, and she made sure that I never lacked for things to do in my spare time. Through Gill I was able to meet Gabriel Doherty, and David and Anne Smith, who are every bit as warm and generous as their daughter.

And then there is my cousin Mary Rodgers, who lives in Ballynahinch, County Down. I have visited Mary (and, until 2002, her brother, Pat) more times than I can count by now, and always there is a cup of tea, a good meal, a comfortable place to sleep, and more family stories. I'm grateful to Mary for being there for me and for many other family members as well.

It is a pleasure to thank the staffs of a number of research libraries—first and foremost the National Library of Ireland in Dublin, which became a kind of home away from home for me. It was always a privilege to work in the NLI's main reading room and manuscripts reading room and to take advantage of the innumerable resources that are available at both sites. I must also thank the staff at the British Library, in London, where I spent many productive and enjoyable days during the autumn of 2003, and again in the fall of 2008. The British

Library also became a kind of home away from home, and desk number 3094 in Humanities 2 proved to be an amazingly congenial workplace. Thanks also to the staffs of the Manuscripts and Archives Research Library, Trinity College Dublin; the University College Dublin Archives; the Manuscripts and Archives Division, New York Public Library; and the Chicago Historical Society.

For indispensable assistance with illustrations, I am most grateful to Dennis Grady at the Dartmouth College Library; Berni Metcalfe at the National Library of Ireland; Seamus Helferty at the University College Dublin Archives; Sharon Sutton and Ellen O'Flaherty at Trinity College Dublin; Moira Fitzgerald at the Beinecke Rare Book and Manuscript Library, Yale University; Anne Moore at the Special Collections and University Archives, W.E.B. Du Bois Library, University of Massachusetts Amherst; Sean Casey and Jane Winton at the Boston Public Library; Michael Foight, Special Collections and Digital Library Coordinator, Falvey Library, Villanova University; and Jeffrey B. Perry.

For research fellowships, I am especially indebted to the John Simon Guggenheim Memorial Foundation, which made it possible for me to spend the autumn of 2002 in Cork and much of the spring of 2003 in Dublin, where I delved into a rich array of research materials. Thanks also to Dartmouth College and to Carol Folt, who was then dean of the faculty at Dartmouth, for a senior faculty research grant in 2007.

For research assistance, I must thank Wesley Clark, Abigail Johnson, Peter Kenseth, Victoria McGrane, Kathleen (Katie) Nunan, Julian Saltman, Elizabeth Teague, Nicole Valco, Rachel Zeile, and Allen Zhang, all of whom are now Dartmouth graduates. Individually, each of them proved willing to go beyond the call of duty; together, they provided me with a steady (and sometimes overflowing) stream of research materials.

For editorial guidance and technical assistance at Princeton University Press, my thanks to Clara Platter, Sarah Wolf, Dimitri Karetnikov, Leslie Grundfest, Brigitta van Rheinberg, and my excellent copyeditor, Dalia Geffen. Many thanks also to the two anonymous readers who evaluated my manuscript for the press and offered many constructive criticisms and suggestions.

Finally, I dedicate this book to my wife, Donna Nelson, and to the memory of my sister, Joan Lindgren. Joan was a brilliant poet and translator, a lover of all things Irish, and so much more. Her death in 2007, eighteen days after she was diagnosed with cancer, came as a great shock and left a void that cannot be filled. Fortunately, I have a wonderful daughter, Ellen, and son, Chris, who, together with their spouses and children, have done much to enrich my life and keep me focused on what matters most—including, above all, our six grandchildren. And what better person to share all of this with than Donna? After more than forty-eight years together, I can't begin to list all that she has meant to me and done for me. So let me say, simply: this book is for Donna, for so many reasons.

PERMISSIONS

Portions of chapters 3 and 4 appeared in "'My Countrymen Are All Mankind,'" *Field Day Review* 4 (2008), 260–73, used here with permission.

Portions of chapter 3 appeared in "'Come out of such a land, you Irishmen': Daniel O'Connell, American slavery, and the making of the 'Irish race,'" in *Éire-Ireland* 42 (Spring/Summer 2007), 58–81, with permission of the Irish American Cultural Institute.

Portions of chapters 5, 8, and the epilogue appeared in "Irish Americans, Irish Nationalism, and the 'Social' Question, 1916–1923," *boundary* 2, vol. 31 (Spring 2004), 147–78. Copyright 2004, Duke University Press. All rights reserved. Reprinted by permission of the publisher.

Portions of chapter 5 appeared in "'From the Cabins of Connemara to the Kraals of Kaffirland': Irish Nationalism, the British Empire, and the 'Boer Fight for Freedom,'" in David T. Gleeson, ed., *The Irish in the Atlantic World* (Columbia: University of South Carolina Press, 2010), 154–75. Copyright 2010, University of South Carolina Press. Reprinted by permission of the publisher.

PART 1

The Making of the Irish Race

Prologue: Arguing about (the Irish) Race

> All is race; there is no other truth.
>
> —Benjamin Disraeli, 1845

> The truth is that there are no races.
>
> —Kwame Anthony Appiah, 1992

THIS BOOK IS ABOUT RACE.[1] Therefore it must begin with the acknowledgment that few subjects have proven more contentious in the last several decades.[2] It was not so long ago—certainly in my "growing up" years, the 1950s—that race appeared to be not only a social phenomenon of major importance but also a fixed and immutable category. Then you were either white or black—or perhaps red, yellow, or brown. But mostly the poles were black and white, and there was little room in that binary for "in-between" people whose objective reality and subjective identity could not be captured by one designation or the other. I can't remember when I first learned about Walter White, the long-time executive secretary of the NAACP, who actually *looked* white but *chose* to be black. "I am a Negro," White declared in his autobiography. "My skin is white, my eyes are blue, my hair is blond. The traits of my race are nowhere visible upon me." *Then how could he be a Negro?* I would have asked myself in those days. I would have found Cyril V. Briggs equally anomalous. Briggs, who features prominently in these pages, was born in the British Leeward Islands in 1888; he immigrated to the United States in 1905 and soon became a leading figure in the New Negro Manhood Movement that developed among African Americans in the early twentieth century. Like Walter White, Cyril Briggs looked white and chose to be black; indeed, one black newspaper editor characterized him as an "angry blond Negro."[3]

It is significant that White and Briggs chose blackness. It is also significant that they did not choose—and could not have chosen—an "in-between" status, or racial hybridity.[4] There were mulattoes in the United States and in the islands of the Anglophone Caribbean, to be sure; but especially in the United States, lightness of skin was not a ticket to in-between status for "colored" people. A few mulattoes passed for white; some chose to be black; most recognized that they had no choice because others had chosen for them. They resided in a world where the lines between whiteness and blackness were sharply drawn and where to be black was to be a second-class citizen, subject to all-encompassing discrimination, humiliation, and, all too often, violence.

Since then our understanding of race has changed dramatically. Even during my growing-up years, it had been changing in ways that were not yet reflected in popular culture or, for that matter, in the historical profession. As early as 1942, in the context of Nazi racism and the early stages of the Holocaust, anthropologist Ashley Montagu had characterized the "fallacy of race" as "man's most dangerous myth," and geneticists were in the process of discrediting—indeed, demolishing—the body of work that had long been regarded as the "science of race."[5] Today race no longer appears to be fixed, unchanging, immutable. On the contrary, it is, in Kerby Miller's words, "subjective, situational, and variable," and racial "in-betweenness" has become not only a possibility but a definitive marker of the human condition for millions of people, in the United States and all over the world.[6]

The new status of race, its lack of objective definition, has led some intellectuals to argue that race is ephemeral, even "illusory."[7] "How can you write a book about race?" an Irish friend asked me recently. At the very least, he argued, race lacks precise meaning, and thus to study it is to enter a "black hole" of subjectivity. Better to focus on something real, like . . . "Like what?" I asked. What could be more real than the crushing weight of centuries of white supremacist ideology or the persistence of deeply rooted structures of inequality that were (and at times still are) justified with appeals to racial difference and incapacity?

At the level of consciousness, my friend was light-years removed from Benjamin Disraeli's insistence, in 1845, that "all is race, there is no other truth." Few historians would make such a claim today. Not because race is unimportant, but because we have come to recognize that it is not and has never been an absolute category that can be understood apart from the historical contexts that have nurtured, and altered, it. Beginning as early as the fifteenth century, race derived much of its meaning from the rise of European colonialism, plantation agriculture, and chattel slavery in the emerging Atlantic World. Ironically, the eighteenth-century revolutions, above all in Britain's North American colonies, served not only to sharpen the dichotomy between freedom and slavery but also to compel the founders of the new American nation to use race as a means of justifying the persistence of involuntary servitude in a society devoted to the expansion of liberty. Just as slavery required a cheap and abundant labor supply, "blackness" justified slavery, and blackness was about far more than skin color. It implied a set of racial characteristics—laziness, irrationality, congenital irresponsibility, and lack of self-control—that sharply differentiated the unfree from the free. Many slaveholders and their apologists argued that because of these characteristics the Negro was inferior, perhaps innately so, and thus fit only for servitude.

This is the terrain of race that is familiar to many of us. But to better understand the history of race discourse, we must return to Benjamin Disraeli's proclamation that "all is race, there is no other truth." When he made this statement,

Disraeli was not referring to skin color. Rather, he was giving voice to another discourse of race that focused on relationships among Europeans dating from the days of the Roman Empire. His fictional character Sidonia declared that "all is race" in the context of a discussion of the "faculties" of the people of Italy, Spain, Germany, France, and England. For the intensely patriotic Disraeli, it was self-evident that England was flourishing while other European nations were declining or, at best, struggling in vain to keep pace with the "Saxon race." "Is it the universal development of the faculties of man that has rendered an island, almost unknown to the ancients, the arbiter of the world?" Sidonia asked and immediately answered, "Clearly not. It is her inhabitants that have done this; it is an affair of race. A Saxon race, protected by an insular position, has stamped its diligent and methodic character on the century."[8]

England, then, was led and populated mainly by a Saxon race that had given the nation its essential character. In this statement Disraeli was content to define England's character as "diligent and methodic," but others were prepared to go far beyond such prosaic references in accounting for its glorious achievements. Disraeli's political and literary careers paralleled the emergence of an Anglo-Saxon school of English historiography that flourished throughout much of the nineteenth century. In his pioneering book *Anglo-Saxons and Celts*, published more than forty years ago, Perry Curtis identified Anglo-Saxonism as "the notion that the Anglo-Saxon people or race . . . had a peculiar genius for governing themselves—and others—by means of a constitutional and legal system that combined the highest degree of efficiency with liberty and justice." Nineteenth-century historians of widely divergent political views could agree that (in John R. Green's words) "we must look far away from England itself" to discover "the fatherland of the English race." Green and his contemporaries were reaching back to an imagined "Teutonic antiquity" in the "free forests" of Germany, where "the infant genius of our liberty was nursed." According to these historians, it was the westward migration of Teutonic and Saxon peoples in the fifth and sixth centuries that laid the foundation of the traditions of self-government that represented the crowning achievement of the Anglo-Saxons—above all in England, but increasingly in its white settler colonies as well.[9]

For Anglo-Saxonists, it was axiomatic that the true "English-speaking peoples" constituted a superior race that was destined to achieve dominion over much of the world. Perhaps this axiom was a necessary corollary of colonialism. But it was rendered far more insidious by the premise of the new science of evolution, namely that the process of natural selection inevitably contributed to "the Preservation of Favoured Races in the Struggle for Life."[10] Increasingly, science, history, and literature facilitated the construction of an informal hierarchy of races based on the argument that racial traits were either in the blood, and therefore innate, or inculcated by centuries of cultural evolution until they became almost irreversible. Thus Alfred Milner, Britain's high commissioner in South Africa, could claim that "the white man must rule, because he is elevated by many, many steps above the black man; steps which it will take the latter centuries to climb." "It is quite possible," Milner added, that "the vast bulk of the black population may never be able to climb [these steps] at all."[11]

In this smug affirmation of hierarchy, inequality, and (congenital) inferiority, the toxicity of race as a subject of cultural and political discourse in the nineteenth century becomes painfully evident. But it's important to acknowledge from the outset that, in Matthew Frye Jacobson's words, "the term 'race' was highly unstable and was applied with a staggering imprecision."[12] "Race" could be synonymous with "nation"—the distinction was seldom clear; or it could apply to a family of nations, notably the Celts, who together were said to compose a single race, albeit with some allowance for geographic variations.[13] "Race" often implied innate characteristics but sometimes suggested that a people could be redeemed, usually through a process of "Anglicization" designed to make backward races more like the English. Although race often created a sharp dichotomy between two peoples, it routinely strayed farther afield and brought third parties into the mix. Thus, in demonizing the Irish, English observers often compared them to the "savages" of North America and sometimes to the "Hottentots" of South Africa, who were "commonly seen as the 'lowest' of the savage races."[14]

Racial discourse *could* be sympathetic; more than a few Englishmen and -women believed that the Anglo-Saxon's habit of diligence and method should be complemented by the Irish penchant for sentiment and spirituality. Perry Curtis and others, notably Michael de Nie and Steve Garner, have demonstrated that English representations of the Irish varied, depending on the political and social conditions of the moment.[15] In times of relative peace and tranquillity in Ireland, more-benign views predominated. But given the long history of conflict between "native" and "stranger" in Ireland, English critics could and did draw on a vast reservoir of hostile and demeaning views of the "Irishman by nature." In fact, they had been doing so since at least the twelfth century.[16] Few politicians exceeded Disraeli in this regard. He sometimes expressed the belief that governance with a firm hand, combined with a capacity for sympathetic understanding, would pacify the Irish and make them loyal and obedient citizens of the United Kingdom. But more often he tended to regard the Irish as the antithesis of the English. The Irish, he wrote in 1836, "hate our free and fertile isle. They hate our order, our civilisation, our enterprising industry, our sustained courage, our decorous liberty, our pure religion. This wild, reckless, indolent, uncertain and superstitious race have no sympathy with the English character. . . . Their history describes an unbroken circle of bigotry and blood."[17]

Like Disraeli, many members of England's educated and governing class defined themselves over against the "wild," "indolent," and "superstitious" Irish race. Irish vice made them all the more certain about English virtue, and the propagation of an Anglo-Saxonist creation myth only added to their certainty. According to Curtis, the ethnocentric—or racial—prejudice of English

Anglo-Saxonists had the effect of "reduc[ing] the Irish Question . . . to an apparent conflict between two fundamentally incompatible races."[18]

For well over a century this discourse of race as national (and sometimes multinational) character coexisted with the more familiar discourse of race as color. Scientists, ethnologists, and anthropologists developed an extensive literature that attracted a wide readership and, increasingly, defined the parameters of scholarly and popular thought about the definition and meaning of "race." One of the most famous of these tracts was by the Scottish anatomist Robert Knox, whose book *The Races of Men: A Fragment* was published in 1850. "The object of this work," Knox boldly declared, "is to show that the European races, so called, differ from each other as widely as the Negro does from the Bushman; the Caffre from the Hottentot; the Red Indian of America from the Esquimaux; the Esquimaux from the Basque." Knox believed that although different races could coexist within nations, "nationalities, however strong, could never in the long run overcome the tendencies of race." Nations came and went, whereas races had existed for many centuries, "unaltered and unalterable."[19] Knox's successors—notably, John Beddoe in England and Madison Grant in the United States—offered variations on his basic themes, but what stands out about their work is the preoccupation with race as national or multinational character rather than with race as color.[20]

Remarkably, this tendency—so foreign to our own understanding of race—continued well into the twentieth century. Thus, in 1944, the American novelist Wallace Stegner wrote an article entitled "Who Persecutes Boston?" which appeared in the *Atlantic Monthly*. In the article he used the words "race" and "racial" fifteen times without ever referring to Negroes or blacks or whites. Stegner, who was teaching literature at Harvard at the time, was deeply concerned about the violent conflict between Irish Americans and Jews in Boston during World War II. Much of the violence was concentrated in Dorchester, where the population was overwhelmingly Jewish; most of it was aimed at Jewish youths, who were being assaulted by Irish gangs from Roxbury and South Boston.[21] Stegner could have characterized the conflict in Boston as ethnic or even religious, since it appeared that the assailants were Irish and Catholic in virtually every case. But he chose the word "racial" to identify the nature of the violence, and he appeared to operate within the discourse of European races—albeit without accepting the invidious assumptions about superiority and inferiority that were at the heart of the narrative constructed over more than a century by its most notorious practitioners.

In retrospect, it would seem reasonable to suggest that Stegner's frame of reference in "Who Persecutes Boston?" was outdated, even anomalous. After all, nearly half a century earlier, the African American intellectual W.E.B. Du Bois and a small coterie of black activists from around the world had met in London to declare, all too presciently, that "the problem of the twentieth century" would be "the problem of the colour line."[22] By 1944, moreover, black migration to the cities of the North and West had accelerated dramatically, and the diverse threads of black protest—in the streets, the courts, and the workplace—were converging to create the modern civil rights movement. But even among scholars who were navigating the rapidly expanding terrain of conflict along the color line, the preoccupation with the "races of Europe" and their alleged characteristics proved to be stubbornly persistent. The distinguished anthropologist Ruth Benedict offers a fascinating case in point. In a pamphlet entitled *The Races of Mankind*, first published in 1943, Benedict and her coauthor, Gene Weltfish, argued that "no European is a pure anything" and that "Aryans, Jews, [and] Italians are *not* races."[23] There were, she now maintained, only three races of humankind: the Caucasian, the Mongoloid, and the Negroid. But in a conciliatory gesture toward a familiar paradigm devised by scholars such as the Harvard economist William Z. Ripley and nativist intellectuals such as Madison Grant, Benedict reaffirmed that the "Caucasian Race" was subdivided into Nordics, Alpines, and Mediterraneans. Once again, references to "fair-skinned, blue-eyed, tall, and long-headed Nordics," to Alpines who were of "in-between skin color, often stocky, [and] broad-headed," and to slender, darker-skinned Mediterraneans entered the discourse of race. According to Nell Irvin Painter, Benedict could not resist the temptation to "place herself and her presumptive readers squarely in the Nordic column." In doing so, however, she embraced the Irish as "our blood brothers" and declared unequivocally that "we of the white race, we of the Nordic race, must make it clear that we do not want the kind of cheap and arrogant superiority the Racists promise us."[24]

As for Wallace Stegner, a year after writing "Who Persecutes Boston?" he and the editors of *Look* magazine coauthored a book entitled *One Nation*. In the face of the dislocation and social conflict that had accompanied World War II, the book's emphasis was on creating a nation characterized by "liberty and justice for all." In this instance, Stegner did not—and for the most part could not—concentrate mainly on conflict among European races in the United States. Rather, his principal focus was on the persistence of discrimination based on color. He readily acknowledged that African Americans were the "Pariahs of the American Caste System"; he also discussed the plight of Asian Americans (Chinese, Filipinos, and Japanese), Mexican Americans, and Native Americans. But in tracing the record of discrimination in the United States, he included Jews and Catholics, which opened the door to a focus on nativist prejudice against "Irish, Polish, French, Italian, and other [European] peoples" who had immigrated to America in the previous hundred years. As much as Filipino immigrants, Mexican Americans, or even American Negroes, he argued, Catholics and Jews were "minority groups" who had been victimized by discrimination because they lived on the wrong side of the "wall down the middle of America." On one side of that wall, Stegner asserted, "is the majority of our people—white, Protestant, and gentile, with social,

white supremacy?

economic, and religious patterns of behavior derived from Anglo-Saxon and North-European ancestors. On the other side are people who because of color, religion, or cultural background are not allowed to be full citizens of the United States."[25]

The problem for Stegner was that facts on the ground were undermining his complex and multifaceted definition of "minority groups" and were propelling Jews and Catholics of European descent into the camp of besieged "white people." In the context of wartime migration and black demands for equal access to housing, jobs, and schools, northern cities such as Detroit and Chicago became cauldrons of racial conflict—not between Protestants and Catholics or Nordics and Mediterraneans, but between whites and blacks. In particular, "white ethnics" asserted the validity of their hybrid identities as Irish-, German-, and Polish-Americans and aggressively claimed whiteness as the basis for access to their communities. "White people built this area," declared the *South Deering Bulletin* in Chicago, and "we want no part of this race mixing."[26]

The parallel languages of race as color and race as character actually had much in common. Skin color was rarely a neutral marker; it almost always implied character. To be black was to be marked as lazy, irrational, childlike, and destined for servitude. Increasingly, in the northern United States, free blacks were perceived as an anomaly. They had no place in the emerging social and political order; they belonged in Africa. This perception became so widespread that even European immigrants quickly learned its coda and corollaries. "I met with an Irishman a few weeks ago," Frederick Douglass reported to an antislavery audience in New York City in 1849. "He had scarcely shed the feathers of 'ould Ireland,' and had the brogue still on his lips. And that man, newly imported to this country, gravely told me that it was his deliberate opinion that the coloured people . . . could never rise here, and ought to go to Africa."[27]

That Irishman, with "the brogue still on his lips," was not untypical of Hibernian immigrants to the United States in the mid-nineteenth century. The Irish presence in the urban North engendered considerable anxiety and hostility. Irishmen and -women often took up residence in poor neighborhoods, where they lived side by side with free blacks and competed with them for jobs, but also, on occasion, embraced them as "desirable companions and lovers."[28] In the eyes of wealthy Protestants who claimed the right to construct hierarchies of race and nationality—in England and Ireland as well as the United States— the Catholic Irish were the bearers of cultural characteristics that made them *like* blacks. They too were perceived as indolent, irrational, childlike. Some observers speculated that their historical roots were racially ambiguous or even African; others compared them to gorillas and chimpanzees.

In *Apes and Angels*, a study of "the Irishman in Victorian caricature" and an even more innovative and important book than *Anglo-Saxons and Celts*, Perry

Curtis demonstrates how, in the course of the nineteenth century, images of the Irish in English newspapers and periodicals were gradually transformed. Over time, the bumptious "Paddy" of cartoon caricature became a "dangerous ape-man or simianized agitator"; the object of good-natured contempt became the object of fear and loathing. Curtis is less interested in the "darkening" of the Irish Celt and the linking of the Green with the Black than he is with the representation of Irish Repealers, Fenians, and Land Leaguers as subhuman—especially as monkeys and apes—in the age of Darwin. But the effect was the same. Somehow, even those Englishmen and -women who professed sympathy for the beleaguered and much-maligned Irishman were inclined to regard him as stubborn, as feckless, and, ultimately, as the "eternal Paddy" who had many traits in common with members of the world's inferior races.[29]

Is it not entirely comprehensible, then, that the Irish would have needed to claim the mantle of whiteness for themselves—that they would have had to *become* white to earn the respect of other races and nationalities?[30] Like blackness, whiteness was about far more than skin color; it was about laying claim to a set of cultural characteristics that made one respectable and capable of exercising the rights of citizenship. The Irish came to understand that to gain acceptance in American society, they had to build a wall between themselves and Negroes, whether free or enslaved; they had to demonstrate that the two races did not share the same characteristics. Like the Italians who followed them across the Atlantic and settled in the industrial cities of late nineteenth and early twentieth-century America, "they had to look with loathing on everything the native whites loathed," including, especially, African Americans. But the Irish did not merely imitate the native whites. They became white largely on their own terms (albeit with considerable help from powerful institutions such as the Democratic Party and the Catholic Church). And in doing so they strenuously rejected the notion that to become white meant to join the ranks of the Anglo-Saxons, or "Anglomaniacs," who, according to *Irish World* editor Patrick Ford, were seeking to reduce the United States to a British colony. "The one enemy of the honor of the Republic on American soil," Ford charged, "is the presumptuous and intolerant Anglo-Saxon."[31]

The need to claim the mantle of whiteness as a badge of citizenship and testament to one's humanity was especially urgent in the United States, where the economic and institutional weight of slavery and the presence of millions of Africans and their descendants played so prominent a role in shaping culture and society. But even in Ireland, where by the mid-nineteenth century the black population was very small indeed, race as color was present in the consciousness of many of its citizens. Its presence stemmed in part from the cartoon caricatures of a simianized Paddy that appeared in the pages of weekly journals of news and opinion; from the growing popularity of blackface minstrelsy as a form of mass entertainment; from the rise of a discourse of "white slavery" that privileged the suffering of Irish peasants over that of Negro slaves; and from

the experience of Irishmen who served in the British army and, according to
W.E.B. Du Bois, proved unusually willing "to 'kill niggers' from Kingston to
Delhi and from Kumasi to Fiji."[32]

The Irish quest for national identity and racial vindication was marked to a
significant degree by this inheritance. Many historians have portrayed Irish nationalism as a force that was turned inward, preoccupied overwhelmingly with
"Ourselves," expressing little, if any, interest in parallel movements for emancipation in other parts of the world. Indeed, for many Irish nationalists, the belief
that Ireland's "true destiny lay in cultivating her national distinctiveness as as-
siduously as possible" became sacrosanct.[33] At the same time, the Irish were a
dispersed people.[34] More than four million of them emigrated permanently between the Great Famine and the Great War, and by the 1880s nearly 40 percent
of those born in Ireland were living somewhere else—most often in the United
States, but also in Britain, Canada, Australia, New Zealand, South Africa, and
other countries. This made Ireland (in Timothy Guinnane's words) "an extraordinarily outward looking society."[35] Even in the most remote and insular parts
of the country, Irish people were connected to family members abroad and often depended for their very existence on the remittances that came regularly in
the famed "American letter."[36] Dependence on family in the United States and
elsewhere made Irishmen and -women keenly aware of developments in other
countries. In his sojourn on the Aran Islands, John Millington Synge found that
the Spanish-American War of 1898 was "causing a great deal of excitement.
Nearly all the families have relations who have had to cross the Atlantic, and all
eat of the flour and bacon that is brought from the United States," he reported,
"so they have a vague fear that 'if anything happened to America' their own
island would cease to be habitable."[37]

But if the Irish at home were an outward-looking people, it was equally true
that members of the Irish race who lived abroad looked back at an "idealized
'holy Ireland,'" often with a sense of sadness and loss.[38] Many thought of themselves as involuntary exiles from the land of their birth and cherished memories
of the society they had left behind, reimagining it in ways that served their
psychic needs in their adopted homes. No one nurtured this tendency more
compellingly than the famous Irish tenor John McCormack, who, singing to
adoring audiences in overflow concerts throughout the world, celebrated Ireland as a "land of love and beauty" and a "perfect loving mother" whose "exiled
children" would remain eternally devoted to her.[39]

This kind of sentimentality formed only a part of the diasporic imagination. Many Irish exiles maintained close ties to nationalist groups at home and
claimed an integral place for themselves in the ongoing movement to free Ireland. Contemporary observers often expressed admiration for their intense
emotional investment in all things Irish but amazement and apprehension at
their unrelenting antagonism toward England. The American Irish became especially notorious for the "white-hot intensity of [their] hatred." They donated

large amounts of money to nationalist organizations in Ireland and provided indispensable material and moral support to the Fenians, who were determined to use every weapon at their disposal to overthrow British rule in Ireland and build an independent Irish republic.[40]

For many Irish nationalists, the very purity of their hatred of England meant a singular preoccupation with Ireland's grievances that precluded sympathetic engagement with other reform and revolutionary movements. As early as 1869, Friedrich Engels lamented the apparent fact that Ireland was "the *sacra insula,* whose aspirations may not he lumped together with the profane class struggle of the rest of the sinful world."[41] This condition was attributable in large measure to the extraordinary power of a Catholic Church whose hierarchy propagated "the twin gospels of respectability and resignation" among the faithful; to the absence of a sizable industrial labor force and formidable trade union movement throughout most of Ireland; and to the long shadow cast by the experience of famine and emigration on men and women throughout the Irish diaspora.[42] "Of all the world's peoples," David Emmons has written, "the Irish of the second half of the nineteenth century were arguably the most unsettled and insecure." The implication is that emigrants from Ireland were driven not to seek radical change but to find "steady work" and to create an "Irish enclave" that, as much as possible, replicated the "social and cultural patterns" of the old country.[43]

The Making of the Irish Race

My task in the pages that follow is to open up and complicate this history by focusing on the evolution of Irish nationalism (and Irish racial identity) in the context of powerful global phenomena such as slavery and abolition, the British Empire, and the class and national struggles of the late nineteenth and early twentieth centuries. My goal is to interrogate the stereotype of Ireland as a self-contained "Holy Island" by focusing on elements of the nationalist movement that turned outward to a global arena of suffering and struggle and affirmed that "[our] sympathy with distress . . . extends itself to every corner of the earth."[44]

Chapters 1 and 2 trace the English (and British) construction of the Irish race from the twelfth century to the twentieth—a process that must be seen in the context of conquest, colonization, and Anglicization. It's true that the Irish responded in diverse ways to the English presence in their country, and that some Irishmen and -women readily adapted to English mores and sought to build a better life for themselves and their families within the system that the newcomers imposed. It's also true that there were periods of relative calm in the relations between Irish and English, tenant and landlord, native and stranger. But when taking the long view, what stands out is not only the failure of British governance in Ireland but also the extent to which the English blamed the Irish for this failure and argued that something in the Irish *nature* made the Irish people uncivilized, savage, and dangerous to peace and order.

[margin note: Irish Savage People?]

IRELAND, SLAVERY, AND ABOLITION

This is the necessary backdrop for examining the trajectory of Irish nationalism in the nineteenth and early twentieth centuries. The rest of the book concentrates on how the Irish made themselves (although not under conditions of their own choosing). Chapters 3 and 4 examine Irish nationalism in the context of the debate over slavery and abolition, especially in the 1830s and 1840s. They revolve around the larger-than-life figures of Daniel O'Connell and Frederick Douglass. O'Connell was by reputation Ireland's Liberator; he certainly was the most authoritative and charismatic voice of the emerging Irish Catholic nation of the early and mid-nineteenth century. He was also an outspoken opponent of slavery—in fact, one of the most powerful antislavery voices in all of Europe. He insisted that members of the rapidly growing Irish community in the United States stand with him, and with Anglo-American abolitionists, in opposing slavery. When they refused, he issued one of his most famous jeremiads, calling on his countrymen to "come out of such a land, . . . or, if you remain, and dare countenance the system of slavery that is supported there, we will recognize you as Irishmen no longer."[45] Of course, his countrymen and -women did not "come out of such a land." Rather, they continued to emigrate to the United States in ever-larger numbers, especially in the context of a great famine that took the lives of a million people and led to the emigration of many more. Seeing the White Republic, and Irish Americans, through O'Connell's eyes requires us to explore the complex circumstances that confronted Irish immigrants in the United States and to understand why they would not—and to some degree could not—embrace his antislavery views. What is perhaps most remarkable about O'Connell, though, is not his success or failure in this regard but his attempt to construct an Irish identity that required opposition to slavery and other forms of oppression as one of its essential components.

[margin note: Jeremiad]

Even more than O'Connell, Frederick Douglass was one of the great antislavery voices of the nineteenth century. But unlike the Liberator, who was born into an affluent and well-connected Irish Catholic family, Douglass was born a slave, and he came to Ireland as a fugitive from American slave catchers. Ironically, he arrived on the eve of the Great Famine and was deeply disturbed by the poverty and suffering he encountered there, even before famine-related starvation and mortality became apparent. But for the most part Douglass experienced Ireland as a place where his spirit soared, where his sense of dignity was markedly enhanced, where he could be *free*. Just as I will examine the United States through O'Connell's eyes, so I will examine Ireland through Douglass's eyes and try to understand why and how he failed to come to terms with some of the fundamental realities of Irish society. Unlike O'Connell, Douglass was unable—at this stage of his life—to combine a strong sense of nationality with opposition to slavery and other forms of oppression. "I have no love for America, as such; I have no patriotism. I have no country," he announced from speakers' platforms in Ireland, Britain, and the United States.[46]

IRELAND AND EMPIRE

Chapters 5 and 6 examine Irish nationalism in the context of the British Empire and its rapid expansion in the second half of the nineteenth century. In a nation plagued by massive emigration, the empire offered employment to tens of thousands of Irish young men. But to many critics of British policy, the empire symbolized Britain at its most rapacious and unjust. Irish nationalists developed a strong sense of affinity with the Boers of South Africa and with the two Boer republics, the Orange Free State and the Transvaal, which were menaced by British subterfuge and outright aggression at the end of the nineteenth century. In the context of the "Boer War," which began in October 1899, South Africa became a major outlet for the energies and organizing efforts of Irish nationalists and a crucial site in shaping their understanding of themselves and their adversaries. Chapters 5 and 6 focus mainly on two individuals, Michael Davitt and Erskine Childers, who were participants in the South African War. Davitt, who was nearing the end of his life at this time, became a bitter opponent of British foreign policy and a war correspondent for American and Irish newspapers. He had long been committed to an essentialist discourse of Anglo-Saxon versus Celt that required the demonization of the Saxon for his manifold sins. He claimed that the "national characteristics" of the Irish race "greatly differ[ed] from Anglo-Saxonism, with its purely materialistic spirit and aims." He called England "a nation without faith, truth or conscience" and accused the English people of "incurable hypocrisy. . . . They profess Christianity," he charged, but "believe only in Mammon."[47] While we cannot forget that Davitt became justly famous for his opposition to anti-Semitism and support for the aboriginal peoples of Australia and New Zealand, we must also recognize that in romanticizing the Boers as heroic victims of British imperialism he allowed himself to demonize their black African adversaries in ways that not only distorted historical reality but also reflected the intense racism of his time.

Erskine Childers, a much younger man than Davitt and a graduate of Trinity College Cambridge, participated in the South African War as a volunteer member of an artillery company that augmented the regular British military forces. The son of an English father and an Irish mother, he entered the war as a British patriot but in its aftermath became a pro-Boer and, soon thereafter, an Irish nationalist. As we shall see, he had much in common with the white South African Jan Christian Smuts, who was also a Cambridge graduate and a participant in the war as a political and military leader of the Boer republics. Both men were deeply concerned with the place of the white settler colonies, or dominions, in the emerging British Empire-Commonwealth. But ultimately they went in markedly different directions. Smuts became an eloquent advocate of dominion status for the Union of South Africa (and for Ireland); Childers chose Irish republicanism and, with exceptional courage and grace, accepted the consequence—in his case, death at the hands of a Free State firing squad. More, perhaps, than any other Irish republican, he spoke the language of white entitlement and identified Ireland as "the last unliberated white community on the face of the globe."[48]

IRELAND AND REVOLUTION

Chapters 7 and 8 focus on Ireland's relationship to the revolutionary movements that developed in the context of World War I and its volatile aftermath. Irish historians disagree about whether the struggle for Irish independence that crested in the years from 1916 to 1921 merits being called a revolution.[49] But for many contemporaries who identified themselves as revolutionaries of one stripe or another, there could be no doubt. Ireland was a vanguard nation pointing the way forward toward emancipation from colonial domination and, some dared to believe, from capitalist exploitation as well. Chapter 7 focuses on the strong attraction that Ireland held for Afro-Caribbean and African American intellectuals and activists such as Marcus Garvey, Cyril Briggs, Claude McKay, Hubert Harrison, W.E.B. Du Bois, and A. Philip Randolph. With the exception of Garvey, all of these men identified themselves as socialists at some point in their lives, and all of them (again, with the exception of Garvey) struggled to reconcile the competing demands of race and class. The Afro-Caribbean activists, in particular, took inspiration from the "Irish Revolution." References to the Irish Parliamentary Party, Sinn Féin, and the Irish Republican Brotherhood dotted their newspapers and broadsides, as did the names of Irish revolutionary heroes such as Terence MacSwiney and Eamon de Valera. Insofar as they embraced black nationalism, they pointed to the Irish preoccupation with "Ourselves," which they translated as "Race First." But even those who chose socialism could celebrate Ireland's "epic" struggle for freedom.[50] Some African American intellectuals, above all Du Bois, were more circumspect about the Irish. They were keenly aware of the antagonism that for generations had marked the relationships between blacks and Irish immigrants in the United States. And yet even for Du Bois "Bleeding Ireland" became an irresistible symbol of the human capacity for suffering and regeneration.

Chapter 7 focuses mainly on the "Black Atlantic" and its relationship to Ireland. Chapter 8 is situated within the framework of the "Green Atlantic" and its relationship to socialism and black nationalism. New York City became a world capital of insurgent movements during and after the Great War.[51] The experience of Irish nationalists in New York during this critical decade in Ireland's history—above all, the experience of the Irish Progressive League—further complicates the narrative of Ireland as "*sacra insula*" and of Irish emigrants as narrowly conservative. The Irish Progressive League was founded in 1917 for the express purpose of supporting the mayoral candidacy of Morris Hillquit, a well-known leader of the Socialist Party who was running for mayor of America's largest city against two Irish Catholic candidates. The league established the goal of reaching out to progressives and socialists and winning their support for Irish independence. In its three years of existence, it proved to be a remarkably active force within the Irish nationalist movement, with a remarkably eclectic assemblage of activists—ranging from socialists and feminists to labor radicals and racial liberals to cultural nationalists and "Sinn Féiners." The league also played a critical role in launching one of the most remarkable episodes of Ireland's war for independence—the Irish Patriotic Strike, which took place in New York Harbor for three weeks in August and September 1920. It was a rare moment—when Green and Black came together in a common struggle—but it was followed by Eamon de Valera's public lament that "Ireland is now the last white nation that is deprived of its liberty."[52]

No matter how great his stature in the nationalist movement, it would not be fitting to give de Valera the last word here. For in the Irish Progressive League we see a vision of the Irish nation that was turned outward as well as inward, that was open to socialism and to other progressive currents that were so much in the air during the war and postwar years, that reached out to black nationalists and spoke, gingerly, of a common struggle for liberty. The league put it simply and directly in declaring that "the Irish are for freedom everywhere." But no one put it more emphatically than Liam Mellows, a leader of the Easter Rising living in exile in New York, who declared, on Saint Patrick's Day 1918, "We will be rebels [not only] to England [but also] to any form of injustice in any country the world over."[53]

Of course, this merging of nationalism and internationalism, and of the national and social questions, was not the principal tendency within Irish nationalism, which is embodied in Cathal Brugha's emphatic statement "We, of the Republic . . . should have . . . but one objective . . . to get the English out of Ireland . . . [and] nothing should be allowed to distract us from that paramount purpose."[54] Brugha's words have been taken as reflective of a broad consensus within the leadership and membership of the revolutionary movement, and revisionist historians have tended to airbrush other currents out of the picture altogether, or at best to treat them as of little consequence. The goal of this book is to wield a different kind of brush, to offer a different angle of vision on the nationalist movement and its arduous work of making race and nation, and to focus on those Irishmen and -women who were prepared to affirm that "the cause of human freedom is as wide as the world."[55]

CHAPTER ONE

"The blood of an Irishman"

THE ENGLISH CONSTRUCTION OF THE IRISH RACE, 1534–1801

> From the later sixteenth century, when Edmund Spenser walked the
> plantations of Munster, the English have presented themselves to the world
> as controlled, refined and rooted; and so it suited them to find the Irish hot-
> headed, rude and nomadic, the perfect foil to set off their own virtues.
> —Declan Kiberd, 1995

IN RECENT YEARS scholars from a wide range of academic disciplines have noted
that for the architects of empire, the process of identity formation seems to
require the creation, and demonization, of a colonized Other whose vices serve
to highlight the virtues of the colonizer. Apparently, no matter what our station
in life, we need to imagine the Other in order to envision ourselves not only as
literal, flesh-and-blood creatures but also as bearers of a set of characteristics—
above all, a set of virtues—that define the collective entity we call the nation
and the race. In *Inventing Ireland,* Declan Kiberd has identified a process that
many have called the racialization of the Irish—the reduction of a culturally
and biologically diverse people to a monolithic whole and the designation of
their racial or national characteristics as the antithesis of Anglo-Saxon virtue.
Kiberd locates this process in the late sixteenth and early seventeenth centuries,
but its roots go back much further, at least to the twelfth century, when the
Paris-trained cleric Giraldus Cambrensis (Gerald of Wales) reported to the
English king Henry II that the Irish were

> a people living off beasts and like beasts; a people that yet adheres to the most
> primitive way of pastoral living. For as humanity progresses from the forests to the
> arable fields, and thence towards village life and civil society, this people, spurning
> agricultural exertions, having all too little regard for material comfort and a positive
> dislike of the rules and legalities of civil intercourse, has been able neither to give up
> nor abandon the life of forests and pastures which it has hitherto been living.

Cambrensis had ventured across the Irish Sea as a servant of the English
Crown, and, increasingly, the purpose of his treatises was to justify English
conquest. Thus it became necessary to present the native inhabitants of Ireland
in the worst possible light. In his *Topographia Hibernica*, he characterized the
Irish as incorrigibly savage and barbaric. "This people," he concluded, "is a . . .
truly barbarous one, . . . being not only barbarous in their dress, but suffering

their hair and beards to grow enormously in an uncouth manner. . . . Indeed, all their habits are barbarisms." Cambrensis also gave voice to what became an indelible impression of the Irish as fundamentally devious and untrustworthy in their relations with the Norman adventurers who had come to civilize them. He concluded that "one must fear their craftiness far more than their warfare; their quietude more than their fieriness; their sweet talk more than their invective; malice rather than pugnacity; treason more than open war; hypocritical friendliness rather than contemptible enmity."[1]

Over the centuries there was also a quite different tendency—to exoticize the Irish and give expression to a kind of premodern primitivism that saw in the lifestyle and folkways of the Gael an attractive, even compelling, alternative to the way of life that prevailed in England and within the Anglicized Pale of Settlement in Ireland itself. Whereas Cambrensis had condemned Irishmen for "suffering their hair and beards to grow enormously in an uncouth manner," others found the self-presentation of the Gael alluring, symbolizing a state of noble savagery. It was evident not only in men's dress and hairstyles, but also in the frank and seemingly reflexive sensuality that was said to characterize Irishwomen. Indeed, it could extend even to as controversial a figure as the Gaelic chieftain Shane O'Neill, one of the most ruthless and effective adversaries of the English military in Ireland, who was denounced by a late nineteenth-century biographer as "a glutton, a drunkard, a coward, a bully, an adulterer, and a murderer." In 1562 O'Neill was granted an audience at the court of Queen Elizabeth, where his presence created quite a stir. Unlike his father, who had submitted to Henry VIII in 1542 wearing English clothes and accompanied by English noblemen, Shane came dressed in native garb, surrounded by a retinue of Scots mercenaries, all of them displaying "bare heads, ash-coloured hanging curls, golden saffron undershirts, . . . loose sleeves, short tunics, and shaggy lace." According to a seventeenth-century chronicler, "The English nobility followed [all of this] with as much wonderment as if they had come from China or America."[2]

A fascination with the more exotic dimensions of "Irishness" would remain a secondary countercurrent of the English discourse on Ireland and the Irish for centuries. It was most likely to surface during periods of relative calm in the relations between colony and metropole, and it found a distinctive outlet in the celebration of the "grandeur" and "sublimity" of the Irish landscape that flourished during the late eighteenth and early nineteenth centuries.[3] For the most part, however, when the English needed to extend their authority, control more territory, and lay claim to more arable land, then the barbarism and savagery, even the alleged paganism, of the Irish became a justification for policies of brutal suppression.

A pivotal moment in this process of development was the sixteenth century, especially after 1534, when the Tudor monarch Henry VIII broke with Rome and created a Protestant kingdom that was increasingly at odds with the

Catholic powers on the European continent. Henry and his successors feared England's vulnerability to attack by France and Spain and saw Ireland not only as a stepping-stone to the English heartland but as a nation whose stubbornly Catholic population might be willing, even eager, to collude with England's enemies. Ultimately, perceiving a land and a people in desperate need of re-formation, they decided to bring all of Ireland under English control.[4]

In simplest terms, the government's goal was to extend the reach of the Pale, the region around Dublin where the English language, English common law, and English land-use patterns had long prevailed. In the longer term, the hope was that all of Ireland could be brought from "a state of savagery to a state of civilisation."[5] Undeniably, many English observers experienced culture shock when they encountered the native, or Gaelic, Irish in areas characterized by traditional ways of living. It seemed to these observers that the Irish "live[d] brutishly . . . more like beasts than men"; that they were "licentious" and "given to idleness"; that some of them were "half naked" for want of clothes to cover them," and others wore loose-fitting garments and allowed their hair to cover their eyes in order to conceal their devious designs. As Cambrensis had noted in the twelfth century, they continued to follow their cattle and obstinately re-fused "to descend to husbandry . . . or to learn any mechanical art or science." Insofar as they had a system of law, it appeared to be a form of lawlessness, for it was decentralized, seemingly arbitrary, and administered by men (brehons) who, in English eyes, were "unlearned and barbarous." Worst of all, perhaps, Irishwomen demonstrated a freedom from constraint that was dangerous to the maintenance of civil society and civilization itself. Because divorce was readily accessible under brehon law, the Irish could move easily from one part-ner to the next—hence the frequent charge of "incest" in Irish sexual relations. At best, then, the Irish appeared to be "a people altogether stubborn and un-tamed"; at worst, they were "wild, barbarous and treacherous."[6]

The goal of re-forming the Irish led to policies that alternated between con-ciliation and coercion—or, in Jane Ohlmeyer's more provocative phrasing, between "assimilation" and "annihilation."[7] Insofar as the latter is concerned, some historians have charged that the Irish themselves, above all the Gaelic lords and chieftains who ruled the lands beyond the Pale, were prone to grue-some acts of violence, and that the instability created by their constant fratri-cidal warfare played a vital role in drawing the Tudor monarchy into Ireland in the first place.[8] According to Kenneth Nicholls, however, "The crown's commit-ment to military intervention helped to change Ireland from a country suffer-ing from an excess of violence into one utterly devoured by it." The devastation that accompanied the government's scorched-earth campaigns in southwest Munster and in Ulster became especially notorious, thanks in large measure to the chilling but unapologetic testimony offered by English chroniclers such as Edmund Spenser and Fynes Moryson. In southwest Munster, from 1569 to 1573 and again from 1579 to 1583, the "systematic burning of the people's corn,

the spoiling of their harvests and the killing and driving of their cattle" created famine conditions that—over a six-month period in 1582 alone—may have
taken more than thirty thousand lives. According to Spenser, the "Prince of Poets in his tyme" and the author of *A View of the Present State of Ireland*, "in short
space . . . a most populous country suddenly [was] left void of man or beast."[9]

A similar policy of conquest was applied in Ulster, where the forces of the
Crown set out to subdue the Gaelic lords, above all the O'Neills, the preeminent symbol of the power and culture of Gaeldom. Actually, Hugh O'Neill, England's most charismatic and effective adversary in the Elizabethan era, had
tried to "remain loyal to the crown for as long as possible and . . . was amenable
to aspects of royal policy in Ulster."[10] But O'Neill's determination to keep his
lordship intact, and to enjoy the political and military power that flowed from
it, brought him into irreconcilable conflict with the government. During the
latter stages of the Nine Years' War (1594–1603), the government again pursued a draconian policy that involved the burning of crops, the killing of cattle,
and the starving of the population in order to undermine the base that sustained O'Neill's resistance. When peace finally came, it was, in David B. Quinn's
memorable words, "the peace of death and exhaustion." Although no accurate
estimate of the loss of human life is possible, Ulster was, to a significant extent,
depopulated.[11]

For many Englishmen, the Catholicism of the Irish became definitive proof
of their inferiority as a nation and a race. But others were not convinced that
the Irish even qualified as Catholic. Their worship and devotional life seemed
to embody more primitive forms of religious practice—something much closer
to paganism than to any variant of Christianity. This accusation derived in large
measure from the fact that Irish religious observance, especially in the rural
areas beyond the English Pale of Settlement, incorporated many pre-Christian
practices and continued to reflect the intertwining of a folk religion attuned to
the rhythms and wonders of the natural world with normative Catholicism.
"They are all Papists, by their profession," Spenser acknowledged, "but . . . so
blindly and brutishly informed for the most part . . . that you would rather
think them atheists or infidels."[12] The English military commander Sir Arthur
Chichester agreed, calling the Irish "the most treacherous infidels in the world,"
while his superior officer, Lord Deputy Mountjoy, expressed the opinion that
"even the very best of the Irish people were in their nature little better than
devils."[13] These characterizations were way stations on a slippery slope that led
to the very depths of degradation. After comparing Shane O'Neill to "Huns and
Turks," one English official went even further and called him "that cannibal."
Others repeated Cambrensis's characterization of the Irish as "a people living
off beasts and like beasts." If indeed they were "little better than devils," and
even "like beasts," then the moral precepts that placed limits on indiscriminate
killing did not apply to them.[14] Thus Chichester could report from County Tyrone in 1601, "We have burned and destroyed along . . . Lough [Neagh] even

within four miles of Dungannon where we killed man, woman, child, horse, beast and whatever we found."[15]

If the sixteenth century was a time of "incomplete conquest," in the next century the process was completed. By the 1690s the English had constructed the foundations of an enduring and multifaceted Protestant Ascendancy.[16] The seventeenth century was marked by two major—and appallingly destructive—wars, one of them lasting more than a decade. It was also marked by successive waves of dispossession, which ultimately meant that almost all Catholics east of the River Shannon ceased to be landowners. Increasingly, it appeared that Ireland was a nation defined by a fundamental antagonism between Irish Catholics and English (and Irish) Protestants. The events that played the key role in consolidating this perception were the Catholic rebellion of 1641 and the Cromwellian invasion of 1649. The rebellion, which began in Ulster, occurred after several decades of relative calm, during which the "plantation" of much of that province appeared to have won the acquiescence, if not the enthusiastic support, of the native Irish population. The suddenness of the rising, and the fury that accompanied it, served only to reinforce Protestant perceptions of the Catholic Irish as treacherous and innately savage. On the other side of the religious divide, Oliver Cromwell became a byword for English cruelty and injustice, and the "curse of Cromwell" assumed a prominent place in Irish legend.

The uprising of 1641 actually began as a limited engagement, initiated by eminent Catholic landowners, notably Hugh O'Neill's grandson Sir Phelim O'Neill, whose objectives were also limited—mainly, to secure their property and win greater freedom to practice their religion. But O'Neill and his associates quickly lost control of the rebellion, as much of the Catholic population rose up and turned on Protestant settlers, who, in many cases, had displaced and exploited them. A lively pamphlet literature developed immediately after the first reports of atrocities reached London, and in 1646 Sir John Temple published *The Irish Rebellion*, which soon took on iconic status and was reprinted regularly over the centuries whenever Protestant rule in Ireland appeared to be in jeopardy.[17] Temple and other chroniclers of the rebellion claimed that as many as three hundred thousand Protestants were murdered, even though in 1641 the Protestant population of Ulster probably did not exceed thirty-four thousand.[18] According to Temple, "Jesuits, friars, and priests told the Irish that the Protestants were heretics and were 'not to be suffered any longer to live among them: that it was no more a sin to kill an English-man, than to kill a dog.'"[19]

For more than a decade, war ravaged much of Ireland. It reached a crescendo with the Cromwellian invasion in August 1649. Oliver Cromwell spent forty weeks on Irish soil, and during that time he and his forces captured twenty-five fortified towns and castles. But he became most famous—or infamous—for the siege of Drogheda (and to a lesser extent the siege of Wexford), which resulted in thousands of deaths and enduring images of cruelty and barbarism. John Morrill estimates that at least thirty-five hundred people were killed by Cromwell's forces at Drogheda, including large numbers of civilians. In perhaps the most infamous act of the siege, the governor and three hundred of his soldiers were executed in cold blood soon after they had surrendered with assurances that their lives would be spared. The governor, an English Royalist, "had his 'brains beat out' with his own wooden leg." According to Morrill, Drogheda "was a massacre . . . without . . . parallel in seventeenth-century British and Irish history. . . . There was nothing which matched it in scale or in the range of its brutalities."[20]

In the aftermath of a decade of war, the victorious Cromwellians imposed a thoroughly repressive regime on the defeated Irish Catholics. Among its essential features were the dispossession of Catholic landowners in three of Ireland's four provinces and their removal to Connacht; the wholesale expulsion of soldiers, priests, and vagrants; and the ban on "popery." The Act of Settlement of 1652 mandated that "all 'priests and Jesuits' involved in any way in the rebellion were to forfeit their lives." Some were executed, but many more, perhaps a thousand, went into exile, mostly in Catholic Europe.[21] The central issue was land. The more radical elements of the new regime envisioned a society of small agricultural holdings owned and worked by a pious Protestant yeomanry. Their goal was to cleanse much of Ireland of its Catholic population. But as in the Ulster plantation scheme earlier in the century, their plans ran afoul of reality. It soon became evident—at least to the larger Protestant landowners—that the continued presence of Catholic "earth-tillers and herdsmen" on their estates was essential. Nonetheless, the overall trend was clear. Catholics owned 59 percent of the land in 1641, even after the plantations of the early seventeenth century. By 1660 their holdings had been reduced to 22 percent of the total, and much of that was in Connacht, where an uprooted and often traumatized Catholic community was hemmed in between the Shannon and the sea.[22]

The remainder of the seventeenth century offers abundant evidence to bear out David Hayton's assertion that although Ireland's early modern history was one of conquest and colonization, it proceeded by "fits and starts."[23] The restoration of the monarchy in 1660, and the return of Charles II to the throne, led to a period of relaxation after two decades of upheaval and to renewed opportunities for Catholics in politics and society. This development took a major leap forward with the accession to the throne of Charles's brother James II in 1685. James, a convert to Catholicism, was determined to restore freedom of religion and the rights of citizenship to his Catholic subjects.[24] But while his supporters triumphed for the moment in Ireland, he was under siege in England, where less than 1 percent of the population was Catholic and the majority was fiercely hostile to "popery." James fled London in December 1688, on the same day that his Dutch son-in-law, William of Orange, entered the city and prepared to succeed him as king of England.

James II
secret
Catholic

What followed was a war on Irish soil that mobilized troops from seven European nations. William defeated James at the famed Battle of the Boyne in July 1690. The decisive battle came a year later, at Aughrim in County Galway, where the Williamites won a decisive victory on what one historian has called "the bloodiest day in Irish history." The Treaty of Limerick, which ended the war, appeared to guarantee that "the Roman-Catholics of this Kingdom" would be free to "exercise . . . their Religion."[25] But vengeful Protestants made sure that the terms of the treaty were never honored. Acting through an Irish parliament cleansed of its Catholic members, they created what Hayton has called "a savage code of discriminatory legislation" aimed at the definitive, and permanent, subjugation of Ireland's Catholic community.[26]

The penal, or popery, laws further circumscribed Catholic ownership of land (which fell to 14 percent of the total by 1703 and slipped even further later in the eighteenth century). They also placed sweeping constraints on the institutional life of the Catholic Church and the freedom of Catholics to practice their religion. Catholics were excluded from Parliament by an English statute passed in 1691 but did not finally lose the right to vote until 1728. Some historians have argued that the penal laws were unevenly enforced and have demonstrated that priests and bishops were able to operate "freely, if discreetly, in most areas" by the 1720s. Nonetheless, for more than a century, Irish Catholics felt the oppressive weight of a Protestant Ascendancy that was founded on their dispossession and seemed to require their demonization.[27]

In spite of the magnitude of their victories at the Boyne and Aughrim, and their success in crafting draconian penal legislation, few Irish Protestants could forget that they constituted a small island in a vast sea of "popery." Indeed, fear of the malevolent—even murderous—intentions of the Catholic majority became integral to the Protestant psyche. Jonathan Swift, the Anglican dean of Dublin's Saint Patrick's Cathedral and the author of *Gulliver's Travels*, put the matter succinctly in 1729, lamenting that "it is almost impossible [to find] a country gentleman . . . who does not live among his own tenants in continual fear of having his plantations destroyed, his cattle stolen, and his goods pilfered." But Swift was well aware that by 1729 there had been no Catholic rebellion against Protestant governance in Ireland in nearly forty years. Thus, while commenting on the "Rapine, Sloth, Ignorance, as well as Poverty of the Natives," he denied that the Catholic population represented a significant threat to the survival of the Protestant Ascendancy. "The Papists are wholly disarmed," Swift concluded. "They have neither Courage, Leaders, Money, or Inclinations to Rebel."[28]

The relative absence of tension in the relations between Protestants and Catholics for much of the eighteenth century helped to facilitate a new appreciation not only of the majesty of the Irish landscape but also of the culture and educational achievements of the ancient Gaels. As early as 1716, in her *Irish Tales*, the mysterious Sarah Butler reminded her readers that "once *Ireland* was esteem'd one of the Principal Nations in *Europe* for Piety and Learning."²⁹ The distinguished agricultural reformer Arthur Young, who traveled and worked in Ireland in the late 1770s, found virtue not only in the ancient Irish but also in their descendants. Although accepting some of the timeworn stereotypes of the "common Irish" as dirty, lazy, and uncivilized, he nonetheless constructed an idealized portrait of a vibrant and praiseworthy people characterized by "vivacity and a great eloquent volubility of speech," combined with "hospitality to all comers, be their poverty ever so pinching."³⁰

These positive portraits—and there were many of them in the eighteenth century—competed with but were ultimately overwhelmed by the more traditional and hostile representations of the Irish. Dean Swift earnestly searched for ways to wean "this uncultivated people from that idle, savage, beastly, thievish manner of life, in which they continue sunk" to a degree that it was almost impossible for his proverbial "country gentleman" to employ "a servant of human capacity, or the least tincture of natural honesty." Swift wondered if banning the use of the Irish language "would, in a great measure, civilize the most barbarous among them, [and] reconcile them to our customs." His fellow churchman Bishop George Berkeley offered a similar view. He asked in print "whether there be upon earth any Christian or civilized people so beggarly, wretched, and destitute as the common Irish," and "whether their habitations and furniture are not more sordid than those of the savage Americans." The controversial Scottish historian John Pinkerton injected a biological element into this age-old discourse on Irish savagery, asserting that the Celts "are savages, have been savages since the world began, and will forever be savages while a separate people; that is, while themselves and of unmixed blood."³¹ Pinkerton's introduction of blood into the equation anticipated nineteenth-century scientific speculation on the nature of the races of mankind, but his objection to the Celts as a "separate people" also harked back to Edmund Spenser and other colonizers of the Tudor and Stuart eras who believed that the Irish could overcome their savagery only when they ceased to be Irish.

As deeply rooted as these cultural polarities were, Ireland was not immune to the revolutionary currents emanating from France and the North American colonies. In the course of the eighteenth century, many Irish Protestants had come to resent the restrictions on trade imposed by the British government and the subordinate status of the Irish legislature relative to the British Parliament at Westminster. They also took offense at "the large numbers of Englishmen being appointed to desirable positions in the Irish civil, military, and ecclesiastical establishments."³² These accumulating resentments helped to precipitate a major sea change in the identity of many Protestants. In the 1770s "patriotism"—a new sense of Irishness and a staunch commitment to the defense of Irish interests—emerged as a vital force in Irish political life, and a Patriot party in the Dublin Parliament offered an increasingly formidable challenge to the status quo. Irish patriots saw the American Revolution as a "mirror-image" of their own struggle for self-government.[33] In the context of Britain's imperial crisis, they won major victories—the right to trade freely with the American colonies in 1779 and the right to "legislative independence" in 1782. But for the most part the patriot phenomenon failed to transcend the sectarian definitions of self and society that had long permeated Ireland. "The patriot conception of the Irish nation was an exclusively Protestant one," Ian McBride has argued, and Jim Smyth has pointed out that "support for legislative independence proved contingent on the maintenance of Protestant Ascendancy."[34]

Presbyterians, who had succeeded in transforming Counties Antrim and Down into a kind of "Scottish nation" in the north of Ireland, had an ambivalent relationship to the Protestant Ascendancy. Knit together by shared origins, they were also united by their anger at legislation that sought to limit the rights of Dissenters in Irish society. As one Presbyterian clergyman complained, members of his family had "assisted in conquering the Roman Catholicks, and [then] were reduced to the same servitude." Over the course of the century, Ulster Presbyterians' grievances against the established order continued to fester, and they in turn were widely regarded as a "turbulent, disorderly set of people whom no people can govern or no God please."[35] Many of them would come to believe that the exercise of economic, political, and religious liberty in Ireland required the severing of the British connection and the establishment of an independent republic. But they arrived at that conclusion only after seeking to achieve parliamentary reform and religious liberty within the existing system. Their instrument was the Society of United Irishmen, founded in Belfast and Dublin in 1791. Their preeminent spokesman was Theobald Wolfe Tone, an Anglican and graduate of Trinity College who prepared for a legal career at the Middle Temple in London but soon grew "sick and weary of the law" and turned to politics and pamphleteering. From the very beginning of his engagement with the political issues that inflamed the 1790s, Tone flirted with separatism; as early as July 1791 he asserted that separation from Britain "would be the regeneration of this country." A month later he published *An Argument on Behalf of the Catholics of Ireland*, which, according to Thomas Bartlett, remains "the most famous pamphlet in Irish history." In it Tone argued that "not only were Catholics capable of liberty but that there could be no liberty for anyone in Ireland until 'Irishmen of all denominations' united against the 'boobies and blockheads' that governed them."[36]

Tone made Catholic Emancipation, and the complete revocation of the penal laws, central to his political agenda, and the United Irishmen concurred—in principle. But many of those who became committed republicans found it difficult to countenance the empowerment of Ireland's Catholic majority and the unshackling of "popery." After all, they had long believed that Catholic doctrine was sharply at odds with true religion and Enlightenment ideals, and that the message preached by Catholic priests represented the antithesis of reason and toleration. Tone himself shared the widespread perception that the institutional power of the Catholic Church was in decline. He even made mocking references to the "rusty and extinguished thunderbolts of the Vatican."[37]

Few, if any, "thunderbolts" had emanated from the Catholic hierarchy in Ireland during the eighteenth century. Its leaders had conducted themselves with remarkable restraint and proclaimed their loyalty to the British state at every opportunity. But as Britain's imperial crisis accelerated, many members of the Catholic middle class assumed an aggressive stance in pursuing the goal of full Catholic Emancipation. By the 1790s, they were prepared to challenge the hierarchy and its allies for leadership of the movement, and they "succeeded in mobilising virtually the entire Catholic adult male population" in the process. The result was a significant step toward full emancipation, as a legislative enactment of 1793 gave Catholics the right to vote and to hold most, but not all, civil and military offices.[38]

In spite of these gains, or perhaps to some degree because of them, Ireland remained a profoundly divided society in the 1790s—one in which issues of land, religion, and the rights of citizenship continued to polarize the Irish people—and rival forces at the grassroots level prepared for armed confrontation. By the spring of 1798, after years of intense government repression, members of the Society of United Irishmen had become convinced that the time was ripe to strike a decisive blow for liberty. Many remained optimistic that a successful nationwide offensive was possible; many also believed—or hoped—that a French landing was imminent, and that it would provide the spark and the resources the movement so badly needed. As it turned out, there was no nationwide offensive, and the French landing did not take place until August, in County Mayo, where it was easily suppressed.[39] In the meantime, counties along Ireland's eastern seaboard, from Antrim in the north to Wexford in the south, had become the site of a historic but failed rebellion. It began on May 23 in Counties Dublin, Meath, and Kildare; from there it spread to Wexford and belatedly moved north to Antrim and Down, which should have represented the insurgents' best hope for a decisive military victory. These two counties—disproportionately literate, prosperous, and Presbyterian—had been the great bastions of republicanism. But when the moment of truth arrived, northeast Ulster proved to be the scene of bitter failure and defeat.[40]

Wexford—or the area of the county north and east of the River Slaney, along with parts of north Carlow and south Wicklow—presented an altogether different picture.[41] The fighting in Wexford lasted more than six weeks, and for three of those weeks the rebels were able to construct the rudiments of a Wexford republic, the first and only republican regime on Irish soil before the Easter Rising of 1916.[42] But Wexford also witnessed grisly acts of sectarian violence that provided Protestant polemicists with the ammunition they needed to portray the uprising—in Wexford and elsewhere—as a massive Catholic assault on Protestants: "1641 renewed."[43]

In recent years, however, historians such as Louis Cullen, Kevin Whelan, and Daniel Gahan have called into question the enduring mythology of an uprising that was essentially sectarian.[44] They have pointed out that Catholics and Protestants shared the leadership of the movement in Wexford and mingled amicably among its rank and file. But they have also acknowledged the moments of sectarian horror, above all at Scullabogue, a townland in the southern part of the county where rebel forces slaughtered "well over a hundred" loyalists. Most of them were burned to death in a barn by guards who set the building on fire and prevented their captives from escaping. Although the victims at Scullabogue were mostly Protestants, they apparently included about twenty Catholics, and there were Protestants as well as Catholics in the ranks of those who carried out the killings.[45] Although the evidence needed to flesh out the full story of this atrocity is largely absent, we do know that any sectarian atrocities, no matter what the source, represented a clear violation of the policies of the United Irishmen, who sought to overcome, not exacerbate, the religious divisions that were a part of Wexford's ethnocultural geography.

Overall, according to Thomas Bartlett, "Around ten thousand rebels (including a high proportion of non-combatants), and about six hundred soldiers [were] slain, and large areas of the country [were] effectively laid waste."[46] Many United Irish leaders were tried in courts-martial, found guilty, and executed. Others from the ranks who survived the uprising fell victim to the counter-revolutionary onslaught that followed it, most notably in Wexford, where a self-styled "Black Mob" of militant loyalists "sought to carry out a 'White Terror.'"[47]

But the most vigorous and important campaign that followed the rebellion was more literary than military, as a host of commentators burst into print with contrasting interpretations of the uprising and the factors that had caused it. Much of the British press was remarkably conciliatory, as were elements within the British government. Many observers believed that the rebellion had been an act of desperation by a minority within Irish society, not a rising of the Irish people. Some expressed a new respect for the Catholic hierarchy, which had demonstrated its loyalty throughout the crisis. And many pointed first and foremost to the culpability of revolutionary France and the deleterious effect of the "French disease." Soon after arriving in Ireland, the newly appointed viceroy, Lord Cornwallis, noted "the folly which has been too prevalent in this quarter of substituting the word Catholicism, instead of Jacobinism, as the foundation of the present rebellion."[48]

Cornwallis was strongly opposed by a conservative faction of Irish Protestants who were determined to defend the Protestant Ascendancy and, in the service of that objective, to portray the rebellion as "a popish plot to extirpate all Protestants." Their strident claims were hardly new; they built on a traditional narrative centered on the trauma of 1641 and exploited a recurring fear that Catholics were always and everywhere on the verge of launching another round of atrocities directed at their heretical enemies.[49] In addition, the growing commitment of the British government to Catholic relief and to the elimination of most, if not all, of the penal laws proved deeply unsettling to Irish Protestants. The government's commitment grew out of a pragmatic calculation that with the fires of rebellion burning in North America and Jacobinism convulsing France, the loyalty of Ireland's Catholic population was absolutely vital to Britain's security. For Protestant conservatives, this was more than disorienting; it was outright betrayal, but a betrayal that could be reversed. In this regard, the uprising of 1798 was a godsend. Insofar as it could be portrayed as a *Catholic rebellion* whose ultimate goal was the annihilation or expulsion of Irish Protestants and the separation of Ireland from Britain, perhaps the Protestant Ascendancy could be restored.

In constructing such a narrative, its proponents had to explain away many inconvenient realities. After all, Protestants had played the leading role in the rebellion in Ulster and had been present among the leadership and rank and file in Wexford. The Society of United Irishmen, the organization that planned and led the rebellion, was widely recognized as predominantly Protestant. And then there was the unequivocal opposition of Ireland's Catholic hierarchy to the uprising. How could all of this be written out of the script? The person who came to the fore in taking on this monumental task was Sir Richard Musgrave, a devout Anglican, member of Parliament for Lismore, County Waterford, grand master of the Orange Order in the county, and, according to Jim Smyth, "Ireland's premier conspiracy theorist of the late eighteenth and early nineteenth centuries." For Musgrave and his conservative allies, it was axiomatic that Catholics were by nature untrustworthy. To conceal their evil designs, they might resort to Jesuitical argument, or they might simply lie. But the fruits of their labors were inscribed in history: in France, the massacre of the Huguenots on Saint Bartholomew's Day in 1572; in England, the Gunpowder Treason Plot of 1605; in Ireland, the atrocities of 1641; in Scotland, the Jacobite rising of 1745; in Ireland again, the agrarian disturbances of the late eighteenth century, with their appearance of sectarian antagonism; and, finally, 1798. Three years later Musgrave published his *Memoirs of the Different Rebellions in Ireland*. According to Smyth, "Every aspect of the book, its argument and digressions, the structure of the narrative, the piling up of page after page of blood-stained detail, the value-charged language and strident invective, is calculated to serve as a warning that Catholics can never be trusted and that their demands must always be resisted."[50]

Although Musgrave claimed to believe that popery was always and everywhere the same, he also argued that "no parallel can be drawn between the popery of Ireland and that of any other country in Europe." Emphasizing the congenital savagery and disloyalty of Irish Catholics, he characterized the rural poor of Munster as "but one step above animal instinct" and the rebels in Connacht as "vermin . . . whose object is blood." Harking back to centuries-old schemes aimed at pacifying and cleansing Ireland, he recommended the creation of exclusively Protestant towns and the immediate expansion of the number of Protestant clergymen, for, as the London Hibernian Society reasoned, "the hope . . . that the Irish will be a tranquil and a loyal people . . . must be built on the anticipated reduction of popery."[51]

Musgrave's *Memoirs* became one of the canonical texts of conservatism in nineteenth-century Britain. But ultimately the book's utility went well beyond a particular religious denomination or political party, for whenever the Irish Question flared up in ways that frightened, outraged, or even amused a broad swath of British public opinion, Musgrave's argument that the perversity of the Irish was rooted in an inextricable mix of Roman Catholicism and native savagery achieved a new resonance. Even among those who professed sympathy for "unhappy Erin," there remained a fundamental, and seemingly eternal, question. "Is there anything particular in the blood of an Irishman that disposes him to shed that of his fellow men?" *Bell's Weekly Messenger* had asked in October 1798. If not, then "where are we to seek for the everlasting barbarism and brutality by which Ireland is disgraced?"[52]

CHAPTER TWO

Celts, Hottentots, and "white chimpanzees"

THE RACIALIZATION OF THE IRISH IN THE

NINETEENTH CENTURY

> With me, race, or hereditary descent, is everything; it stamps the man.
> —Robert Knox, 1850

> Too much, no doubt, has been made of the influence of race. Yet the
> Teuton is a Teuton and the Celt is a Celt.
> —Goldwin Smith, 1905

> The Irish problem is a problem of the Irish *race*, and is neither a
> byproduct of politics nor of environment, but is rooted in the racial
> characteristics of the people themselves.
> —Captain Hugh Pollard, 1922

THE NINETEENTH CENTURY created new imperatives in the relationship between England and Ireland. Once again, an Irish rebellion had been suppressed, and this time Ireland had been incorporated into the Union, with a hundred seats in the House of Commons at Westminster and thirty-two in the House of Lords. From the standpoint of British capital, the need to modernize Irish agriculture and discipline the Irish labor force became more urgent in the first half of the century. Perhaps inevitably, given the extraordinary disparity of wealth and population between the two countries, British needs dictated which crops were grown for export, and British manufactured goods flooded Ireland's domestic market and pushed many small-scale producers of textiles and linens into an already swollen agricultural labor force. Increasingly it appeared that there were two Irish economies—"a highly commercialized export sector . . . alongside an impoverished subsistence economy." The latter was populated by small farmers and agricultural laborers who may well have constituted half of the population by the 1840s. They were largely dependent on the potato as a food source, and the combination of poverty, overreliance on a single crop, and rapid population growth foreshadowed a disaster of epic proportions.[1] Even before the coming of the Great Famine, visitors to Ireland were stunned by the level of deprivation they encountered. In 1839 the French reformer Gustave de Beaumont noted that "misery, naked and famishing, . . . covers the entire country. It follows you everywhere, and besieges you incessantly."[2]

Numerous English observers inquired into the root causes of Ireland's misery. At the heart of the matter, many of them alleged, was the contrast between English industry and Irish indolence. Thus *Fraser's Magazine* could declare without hesitation that "the English people are naturally industrious—they prefer a life of honest labour to one of idleness," whereas the Irish "will not work if they can exist without it." Addressing the issue in explicitly racial terms, the *Times* declared that "by the inscrutable but invariable laws of nature, the Celt is less energetic, less independent, less industrious than the Saxon." In the same vein, the Edinburgh anatomist Robert Knox argued that "in the ordinary affairs of life, [the Celts] despise order, economy, cleanliness; of to-morrow they take no thought; regular labour—unremitting, steady, uniform, productive labour—they hold in absolute horror and contempt." The polarity, then, was clear: whereas industry, and "a life of honest labour," defined the Englishman, sheer laziness defined his Irish counterpart. "Even here in London," *Fraser's Magazine* claimed, "the Irish labourers are the least satisfactory people in the world to deal with." In Ireland itself growing reliance on the potato led to widespread accusations that the Irish were an "incorrigibly lazy people" who were content to subsist on a "lazy" crop.[3]

English observers also argued that the Irish were guided more by passion than reason, more by sentiment than calculation. In short, they were deemed irrational and therefore childlike and feminine as a race. In his book of essays *The Poetry of the Celtic Races*, the French philosopher Ernest Renan characterized the Celts as melancholy and emotional and concluded that "if it be permitted us to assign sex to nations as to individuals, we should have to say without hesitance that the Celtic race . . . is an essentially feminine race." The English poet, essayist, and cultural critic Matthew Arnold, who was influenced by Renan, also identified a "Celtic genius" that was essentially feminine, with "sentiment as its main basis, with love of beauty, charm, and spirituality for its excellence." Much as Arnold admired these characteristics, he nonetheless believed that the Irish lacked the attributes that would have qualified them to govern themselves. "The skillful and resolute appliance of means to ends which is needed both to make progress in material civilization, and also to form powerful states," he concluded, "is just what the Celt has least turn for." The historian James Anthony Froude agreed. He viewed the Irish as "passionate in everything—passionate in their patriotism, passionate in their religion, passionately courageous, passionately loyal and affectionate." But like Arnold, he concluded that "they are without the manliness which will give strength and solidity to the sentimental part of their dispositions." Here "manliness" meant neither courage nor a willingness to resort to violence, but a capacity for reason and self-control and, therefore, a capacity to govern self and society. In their passion, Froude implied, the Irish were feminine, whereas the Anglo-Saxons' unsentimental disposition made them masculine and fit to rule others.[4]

It was precisely the passionate nature of the Irish that made them so dangerous, for passion could easily spin out of control and lead to violence. Until the rise of Fenianism in the 1860s and the notorious bombing campaigns in England that made the term "Fenian" a synonym for terrorism in British eyes, relations between Britain and Ireland in the nineteenth century were relatively peaceful.[5] There was, to be sure, Robert Emmet's abortive uprising in 1803 and Young Ireland's "Cabbage Patch" rebellion in 1848. Of even greater significance were the recurring waves of agrarian protest, led by secret societies such as the Whiteboys, Rockites, and Molly Maguires, which horrified English public opinion and reinforced the image of Ireland as a place where violence stalked the land.[6] Many Englishmen had already convinced themselves that to revel in chaos, anarchy, and violence was an essential marker of "Irishness." "The very name [of Ireland] forces to our recollection images of shillelaghs, and broken heads, and turbulence of every kind," declared one observer in 1834. According to another observer, the Anglo-Irish antiquary Thomas Crofton Croker, "When not driven by necessity, [the Irish] willingly consume whole days in sloth, or as willingly employ them in riot." But when mere riot gave way to purposeful violence, aimed at land grabbers, policemen, and the British state itself, the commentary lost its levity and took on a tone of hysteria. "The aboriginal inhabitant of Ireland," the *Spectator* argued, "appears to [be] the sole instance in modern and civilised Europe, of an animal in human form that avowedly exults in ferocity, malevolence, and the love of blood," Robert Knox spoke for many of his fellow Saxons when he concluded that "[bayonet government] seems to be the only one suitable for the Celtic man."[7]

These portrayals of the Irish as lazy, irrational, and prone to violence came together in a particularly lethal way in the Great Famine, which devastated Ireland from the mid-1840s to the early 1850s.[8] The potato blight *phytophthora infestans*, which first appeared in 1845, and the disease and starvation that followed, caused unimaginable suffering. In a nation of eight and a half million people, more than a million—nearly one-eighth of the total population—perished; close to two million emigrated over the course of a decade, and hundreds of thousands of cottiers and agricultural laborers were evicted from their small holdings and cast adrift.[9] The *Limerick and Clare Examiner* protested in 1848 that "nothing, absolutely nothing, is done to save the lives of the people—they are swept out of their holdings, swept out of life, without an effort on the part of our rulers to stay the violent progress of human destruction."[10]

Actually, in the early stages of the crisis, there was a significant outpouring of concern in Britain. The Religious Society of Friends made a heroic effort to relieve the massive suffering, and even the Whig government of Lord John Russell pledged to use "the whole credit of the Treasury and the means of the country . . . to avert famine and to maintain the people of Ireland." But government policies often served to make matters worse—ultimately, much worse—and "donor fatigue" reduced contributions from the British public. A consensus soon emerged that the responsibility for the crisis lay with the Irish themselves. A "local problem" required local solutions, and Ireland, allegedly an integral part of the United Kingdom, was thrown back on its own rapidly diminishing resources.[11]

To many British observers, the problem at the root of the famine was poverty, and they believed that Irish poverty was the fault of the Irish themselves. For centuries visitors had commented with amazement on the extent of deprivation in Ireland, which made it appear that its inhabitants "form[ed] a different race from the rest of mankind." It was even more disturbing to these commentators that in the midst of their suffering, the Irish seemed to "wear the appearance of content." If only they had been willing to labor with discipline and regularity, Ireland *could* have been a thriving country, Yorkshire writ large. Instead, the Irish preferred to depend on the charity of others. "The Irish peasant had tasted famine and found that it was good," said the *Times* in September 1846, just as the potato crop was about to fail for the second year in a row. The *Economist* chimed in with the observation that "the Irish must pray for famine every year."[12] As the situation continued to deteriorate, policymakers and pundits convinced themselves that the massive evictions, along with the rapidly escalating pace of emigration and even the relentless march of disease and death, were a providential sign that "the soil of Ireland [was now] open to industrial enterprise and the introduction of new capital." And who better to provide that enterprise and capital than a new generation of planters from England and Scotland? Once again, it appeared that the redemption of Ireland, especially the west of Ireland, required the cleansing of the Irish from the land. Lord Clarendon, who served as lord lieutenant from 1847 to 1852, believed that it had "become necessary to 'sweep Connaught clean' through the removal of some 400,000 people"; and the popular magazine *Punch* went so far as to exclaim, "The old Irish cry of 'Ireland for the Irish' will soon be heard no more; for if emigration keeps up its present enormous rate, there will soon not be a single Irishman in Ireland, and the cry must be changed to 'Ireland for the English.'"[13]

An even more extreme statement came from Robert Knox, who claimed in 1850 that in spite of justifiable criticisms of English misrule in Ireland,

> the source of all evil [there] lies in *the race*, the Celtic race of Ireland. . . . The race must be forced from the soil; by fair means, if possible; still they must leave. England's safety requires it. I speak not of the justice of the cause; nations must ever act as Machiavelli advised: look to yourself. The Orange [Order] of Ireland is a Saxon confederation for . . . clearing the land of all papists and jacobites; this means Celts.

Knox argued that the Encumbered Estates Act, which the British Parliament passed in 1849, "aims simply at the quiet and gradual extinction of the Celtic race in Ireland," and he seems to have embraced a policy of ethnic cleansing, even "extinction," with equanimity. Perhaps the always flamboyant and often controversial Knox was too far from mainstream British opinion to be taken as representative in his views. But the distance between extreme and mainstream perspectives on the Irish Question during the later stages of the famine may not have been that great. After all, influential politicians and public intellectuals, Whig and Tory alike, envisioned a "new plantation," of Connacht in particular, and argued that at the very least Irish proprietors should be supplanted by enterprising newcomers from England and Scotland. Although relatively few Britons may have been willing to endorse a policy aimed at the wholesale removal of the Irish from their own country, a prominent Englishman noted in 1848 that the dominant sentiment in London was "disgust . . . at the state of Ireland and the incurable madness of [her] people."[14]

Even in their moment of greatest need, it was not only the "incurable madness" but the "savagery" of the native Irish that came to the fore in British commentary. This tendency was magnified by the outbreak of food riots, agrarian agitation, and other acts of violence in parts of the country as the effects of the famine intensified. Ireland witnessed the killing of seven landlords and at least ten middlemen in the winter of 1847–48—most notably, the assassination of Denis Mahon, a major in the British Lancers and heir to a massive estate in County Roscommon. Major Mahon had evicted three thousand tenants in recent months, but he had paid the fares of nine hundred of them to emigrate to North America. Tragically, one of the vessels carrying his former tenants became a prototype of the infamous "coffin ships." Nearly 160 of its passengers died at sea, and many others were condemned to death in the fever hospitals at Grosse Isle, Quebec. Among his own kind, however, Major Mahon was regarded as not only an "improving" landlord but also a benevolent patriarch who was solicitous of the well-being of those who lived on his vast holdings. Thus the outcry that greeted his assassination in November 1847 was predictable. Upon hearing the news, Queen Victoria lamented in her diary that the Irish "are a terrible people, & there is no civilized country anywhere, which is in such a dreadful state, & where such crimes are perpetrated!" Lord Clarendon bemoaned the apparent fact that in Ireland "every man is in favor of the criminal: law and order have no friends."[15] A month later the *Bristol Mirror* charged that "the Indians with their tomahawks and scalping knives are a much nobler set of savages than the murderers of Limerick and Tipperary."[16]

The comparison of the Irish with the "savages of America" was familiar enough; it dated from the seventeenth century. But there was a dramatically new development in the second half of the nineteenth century, a time when Darwinian science posited an evolutionary chain of being in which humans were descended directly from African apes. In this context, British commentators created a "simianized," or apelike, Paddy whose likeness to the "backward" races of Africa was inescapable. Perry Curtis has traced this development in *Apes and Angels*. He notes that the Rising of 1798 led British cartoonists to develop images of a preternaturally ugly Paddy whose appearance was far more ominous and repellent than that of the bumptious but relatively harmless stage Irishman who had predominated for much of the eighteenth century. Some of these cartoon characters were given porcine features, but until the 1860s the cartoon Irishman remained largely human. It was with the coming of Darwinian evolution, and the reemergence of violent Irish republicanism in the guise of Fenianism, that the transformation of the stereotypical Paddy really took off with the publication of cartoon caricatures such as "The Irish Devil-Fish" (a massive octopus with simian facial features) and the even more notorious "Irish Frankenstein," with his dagger dripping blood. According to Curtis, "In a biological sense, Paddy had devolved, not evolved, from a primitive peasant to an unruly Caliban, thence to a 'white Negro,' and finally he arrived at the lowest conceivable level of the gorilla and the orangutan."[17]

There were at least four major historical factors at work in Paddy's devolution. They can be encapsulated in the words "empire," "Fenianism," "emigration," and "science." The nineteenth century witnessed a dramatic expansion of the British Empire. Especially in the later decades of the century, Britain's leading role in the seizure and exploitation of African colonies sharpened the racial identity of the British people and their awareness of racial difference. The second half of the century also saw major developments in Irish nationalist consciousness and in the organizations that became the embodiment of Irish aspirations. Although land agitation and the demand for home rule provoked widespread fear and opposition in England, the rise of Fenianism played the most important role in reinforcing apprehension about the racial character of the Irish people and about their relationship to England and the empire. The Fenians, with headquarters in Dublin and New York, were a transatlantic movement, committed to the overthrow of British rule in Ireland by physical force. Although an attempted uprising in March 1867 fizzled out, the movement's underground cadres provoked a "Fenian panic" in Britain with the killing of a police sergeant during a jail break in Manchester and the subsequent dynamiting of London's Clerkenwell Prison during another attempted breakout. The Clerkenwell bombing resulted in 12 deaths, 120 injuries, and massive devastation in one of London's poorest neighborhoods. According to a British reformer, it was "calculated to destroy all sympathy [for Ireland], and to evoke the opposition of all classes."[18]

And yet Fenianism appeared to have many sympathizers among the large number of Irish emigrants who settled in British cities in the mid- and late nineteenth century, clustering together in ethnic ghettos, maintaining their allegiance to the Catholic Church, and clinging to the belief that rapacious Irish landlords and heartless British politicians had forced millions of Erin's sons and daughters into a life of exile. Even larger numbers of Irish emigrants went to the United States, where they nursed the same grievances and offered encouragement, manpower, and monetary support to the Fenians. "The Greater Ireland is

2.1. "The Fenian Guy Fawkes" (Punch, Dec. 28, 1867; courtesy of Dartmouth College Library)

on this side of the Atlantic," declared the émigré newspaper editor Patrick Ford from his headquarters in New York City. "This is the base of operations. We in America furnish the sinews of war."[19]

All of these developments were interpreted in racial terms, in part because of major innovations in the realm of science. Well before the emergence of Darwinism, physicians, anthropologists, and others who claimed a unique professional expertise weighed in on "the races of men" and sought to embed them within a larger hierarchy of human and animal species. The work of Charles Darwin and his many imitators served to accelerate the burgeoning sense that life was a struggle in which only the fittest species, races, and individuals would survive. Although overshadowed by Darwin, the Edinburgh anatomist Robert Knox was one of the most prominent theorists of race and racial difference in the nineteenth century. Knox boldly declared that "race is everything in human history," and he believed that neither environment nor education—nor, for that matter, the passing of centuries—could alter the essential characteristics of a particular race. Because he offered the imprimatur of science to the claim that the "fair" races were inherently superior to their "dark" counterparts, Knox is widely regarded as one of the founders of modern racism.[20] But his ideas are not reducible to the advocacy of "white" over "black" (terms he seldom used). The son of a Freemason who claimed family ties to John Knox, Scotland's greatest Protestant Reformer of the sixteenth century, he was an outspoken critic of organized religion and an antimonarchist who dared to envision the day when the republican "tri-colour flag may wave over the United States of Great Britain and Ireland."[21] He was also a critic of European colonialism, which he characterized as a plot to seize territory "by fraud and violence" and to hold it "by deeds of blood and infamy." He was particularly scornful of British imperial policies in Africa, and in India, where "the doings . . . are said to be without a parallel in history."[22]

Knox spent three years in South Africa as a British army surgeon, and his observations of the "Hottentot" and the "Caffre" became the foundation of his theories of race. But his most famous publication, *The Races of Men: A Fragment*, focused mainly on European races, including the Saxon and the Celt. Knox regarded himself as a Saxon, along with the Lowland Scots from whom he was descended. He portrayed the Saxons as "a tall, powerful, athletic race of men; the strongest, as a race, on the face of the earth. They have fair hair, with blue eyes, and so fine a complexion, that they may almost be considered the only absolutely fair race on the face of the globe." Even more important, he argued, they "[are] democrats by their nature, the only democrats on the earth; the only race which truly comprehends the meaning of the word liberty." Knox also claimed to have the "highest regard and esteem" for the Celt, who was "an admirer of beauty of colour, and beauty of form, and therefore a liberal patron of the fine arts. . . . Most new inventions and discoveries in the arts may be traced to him." But these innovations were then "appropriated by the

Saxon race, who apply them to useful purposes." Here, again, was the starkly drawn contrast between the rational Saxon and the irrational Celt, between the Saxon's capacity for self-government and the Celt's utter inability to "comprehend the meaning of the word liberty." Insofar as Celts had praiseworthy attributes, it was the French who embodied them. "The Celtic race presents the two extremes of what is called civilized man," he wrote; "in Paris we find the one; in Ireland, at Skibbereen and Derrynane, the other. Civilized man cannot sink lower than at Derrynane."[23]

In spite of his often-expressed belief that the science of race was at an early stage and that much remained unknown about the races of men, Knox allowed himself the luxury of sweeping generalizations about various races. On occasion, he engaged in what can only be called literary tirades, as when he summed up the "Celtic character" as marked by "furious fanaticism; a love of war and disorder; a hatred for order and patient industry; no accumulative habits; restless, treacherous, and uncertain." Even in regard to France, the citadel of Celtic achievement, he observed that the country's "vast Moorish population" was "superior in all respects to the lazy, worthless Celt."[24]

Knox's elevation of the dark-skinned Moor above the Celt is a vivid example of the slippage that often occurred in racial discourse about the Irish. Even relatively sympathetic observers resorted to characterizations of Irish Celts that linked them to darker races and, sometimes, to apes. Frances Power Cobbe, a journalist, suffragist, and humanitarian crusader who was born in Dublin to an English mother and an Anglo-Irish father, is representative of this tendency. She was not formally trained in anthropology, but her article "The Celt of Wales and the Celt of Ireland" employed many of its tropes in identifying the racial characteristics of the Irish. Cobbe retailed venerable stereotypes of the Irishman's penchant for drunkenness and violence, but she also argued that "the whole mental machinery of the Welsh and Irish seems better oiled than that of the Saxon." This no doubt would have drawn a howl of protest from Robert Knox, but he would have been much more comfortable with her observation that the Irish Celt "has managed to introduce (or preserve?) in the human countenance a mouth scarcely improved since the much remoter date when we were apes."[25] Similarly, the English anthropologist John W. Jackson waxed lyrical about the Irish on occasion, even predicting that Ireland would be "the darling of the future; the spiritual complement to England's material power; the intuitive supplement to Scotland's coercive logic; the fecund mother of sages and poets, painters and composers." But Jackson also ruminated on the "Iberian character" of the Irish peasantry, raising the familiar specter of southern origins, Moorish blood, and intimations of darkness and savagery. Referring specifically to the peasants of the west and south of Ireland, he reported that "an absolutely negroid type has been occasionally detected by keen observers," which meant that "inferior and non-Aryan racial elements are clearly perceptible in the population of the sister isle."[26] Jackson's fellow anthropologist Hector

MacLean concurred and identified a racial type, also with Iberian characteristics, that was "very prevalent in the west of Ireland. . . . The stature is generally low," he claimed, "with dark skin and complexion; the head is long, low, and broad; the hair black, coarse, and shaggy; the eyes black or dark brown, or grey, with fiery lustre; forehead receding, with lower part of face prominent."[27] To those who were predisposed to believe them, reports of this kind served to reinforce elite and popular perceptions of the Irish as akin to "the negro," "the savage," and even "the ape."

One of Knox's more esteemed successors in the scientific study of race made an even larger contribution to the process of darkening the Irish Celt. The English physician and anthropologist John Beddoe devoted more than thirty years to observing and recording the physical features of the peoples of Britain, Ireland, and western Europe.[28] He was deeply interested in color, especially the color of his subjects' hair and eyes, and at times he was prone to using these traits to explain intelligence and character. But in important respects he was far less rigid than Knox. Whereas the Edinburgh anatomist identified a relatively small number of races and argued that they had resisted any meaningful change in their essential characteristics over many centuries, Beddoe saw numerous races and acknowledged that most of them had been reshaped over time through migration and intermarriage. Whereas Knox saw Ireland as a land divided between Celts and Saxons, Beddoe believed that the very use of the word "Celt" was misleading, and he discovered numerous racial gradations in Ireland. Thus, "In the county of Wexford, and in the city and neighbourhood of Waterford," he found "a tall fair race, which extends, with some modification, up the northern bank of the Suir, across the Golden Vale of Tipperary, into the county of Limerick." He reported that "the Wexford men, among whom countenances quite Norwegian are pretty numerous, have the reputation of being peaceable and industrious, but bold and fierce when aroused." A "tall fair race" whose members were "peaceable and industrious" hardly sounds like popular, or scholarly, portrayals of the Irish in the nineteenth century. And, indeed, where Beddoe found such racial characteristics, he attributed them to English, or perhaps Norwegian, ancestry. More broadly, he expressed the belief that "in our own islands, . . . it is safe to say that men of distinction are in large proportion natives of the more blond areas."[29]

To locate the "real" Irish, then, one had to go to the west and southwest of the country, where there had been less immigration and therefore less mixing of blood. To be sure, in fishing villages on Galway Bay and in the Aran Islands, Beddoe found significant examples of intermarriage, and thus of racial hybridity. But for the most part, the west was the home of "swarthy" and "dark-complexioned aborigines," many of whom had dark eyes and even darker, sometimes "coal-black," hair. By themselves, hair and eye color did not indicate skin color, and for the most part Beddoe acknowledged that he was dealing with whites, although he did record that in the mountains between Sligo and

Roscommon he had encountered "the swarthiest people I have ever seen." He also created an "Index of Nigrescence" to measure the range of hair and eye color from one racial type to another, and like virtually all of the anthropologists of his generation, he could not help but speculate on the relationship between racial classification and intelligence and temperament. "There is an Irish type . . . which I am disposed to derive from the race of Cro-Magnon," he reported. "In the West of Ireland I have frequently seen it. Though the head is large, the intelligence is low, and there is a great deal of cunning and suspicion." He also discovered a tendency toward "prognathism" among people in England, Wales, and Ireland, with Ireland as its "present centre." Venturing onto very slippery terrain indeed, he speculated that "most of its lineaments are such as to lead us to think of Africa as its possible birthplace, and it may be well, provisionally, to call it Africanoid."[30]

Beddoe did not always follow the apparent logic of his own conclusions. He argued in *The Races of Britain* that "the points of likeness to the anthropoid apes are distributed variously among the different races of mankind, . . . [and] none of them can be taken in themselves to imply intellectual or moral inferiority." But by creating an index of nigrescence, and constructing a prognathous physical type in Ireland that he identified as "Africanoid," he provided openings for others who were far more determined to assert the racial inferiority of the Irish and to see them as a race that had not achieved the salient characteristics commonly associated with "whiteness." In the early twentieth century, especially in response to the polarization and violence of the Irish War of Independence, a new generation of scholars and pseudoscholars was determined to portray the Irish as a people whose many negative attributes were rooted in a suspect racial past. In 1919 two Harvard geneticists claimed that the Irish were "principally the product of the mingling of two savage Mongolian tribes," and in 1922 two equally zealous Hibernophobes found a "strain of negro blood" in the Firbolgs, or Attacotti, the ancient race that had invaded Ireland and allegedly waged a war of extermination against its "fair-haired and clean-skinned" rivals on the island.[31]

These developments in the realm of science were reflected in a wider, more random discourse through which elite and popular commentators linked the Irish with black Africans and African Americans in a shared stereotype that alleged laziness, irrationality, and an incapacity for self-government as essential characteristics of both races. By the mid-nineteenth century or soon thereafter, the tendency to portray the Irish as apelike creatures who were laughably crude and lamentably violent was becoming a commonplace in the United States as well as Britain. In a meditation on the "Celtic physiognomy," the American magazine *Harper's Weekly* commented on the "small and somewhat upturned nose [and] the black tint of the skin," while *Punch* characterized the "Irish Yahoo" who populated "the lowest districts of London and

2.2 "The Ignorant Vote" (Thomas Nast, *Harper's Weekly*, Dec. 9, 1876; courtesy of Dartmouth College Library)

Liverpool" as "a creature manifestly between the Gorilla and the Negro," a "climbing animal [who] may sometimes be seen ascending a ladder with a hod of bricks."[32]

These stereotypes continued long after segments of the Irish immigrant community had begun to achieve a modicum of middle-class respectability. During a tour of the United States in 1881–82, Edward Augustus Freeman, an avowed Anglo-Saxonist and the regius professor of modern history at Oxford, wrote to a friend back home that America "would be a grand land if only every Irishman would kill a negro and be hanged for it." There were those who dissented from this statement, he acknowledged, "most commonly on [the] ground that, if there were no Irish and no negroes, they would not be able to get any domestic servants." In 1882, in the American journal *Puck*, Frederick Opper rendered the Irish peasant as "The King of A-Shantee," a subhuman, distinctly simian creature. In his play on the word "Ashanti," Opper linked Irish Celts to black Africans. A decade later, while honeymooning in Dublin, the Fabian socialists Sidney and Beatrice Webb reported that "the Irish people are charming but we detest them as we should the Hottentots—for their very virtues. Home Rule is an absolute necessity in order to depopulate the country of this detestable race." As late as 1927, Britain's secretary of state for the dominions and colonies would declare that "a curse hangs over Ireland." Understanding its source would be difficult, if not impossible, Leo Amery acknowledged. But "I fear the starting point is a fault in the blood, some element of ape-like savagery which has survived every successive flood of settlers."[33]

What comes through in so many of these observations is the racial "in-betweenness" of the Irish in the eye of the beholder.[34] Although *Harper's Weekly* did comment on the "black tint of the [Irish] skin," few observers were willing to argue that the Irish were "black" or "coloured," no matter how high they registered on Beddoe's index of nigrescence. Instead, in the age of Darwin, Irishmen and -women were portrayed as "white chimpanzees," as "creature[s] manifestly between the Gorilla and the Negro," and as "more like a tribe of squalid apes than human beings." Charles Kingsley, an Anglican clergyman and regius professor of modern history at Cambridge, was "haunted by the human chimpanzees" he encountered during a holiday in Ireland in 1860. "To see white chimpanzees is dreadful," he confided to his wife; "if they were black, one would not feel it so much, but their skins, except where tanned by exposure, are as white as ours." Thomas Carlyle, the Scottish writer and polemicist, did not doubt that the Irish had "a white skin" and even "European features," but they were "savages" nonetheless. "The Celt[s] of Connemara," he wrote in the 1840s, "are white and not black; but it is not the colour of the skin that determines the savagery of a man" or of a race. "He is a savage who in his sullen stupidity, in his chronic rage and misery, cannot know the facts of this world when he sees them; [who] . . . brandishes his tomahawk against the laws of Nature." Carlyle exempted the "Teutonic Irish" of Ulster from his censure, but he charged that the chronic laziness of the Celtic Irish, and their refusal to accept that for the foreseeable future their role must be to labor for others, made them akin to the black ex-slaves of Jamaica, for whom he recommended a return to the "beneficence" of involuntary servitude. As for Kingsley, he informed a friend that the "harsh school of facts" had cured him of any illusions about equality between the races. "I have seen," he wrote, "that the differences of race are so great, that certain races, e.g., the Irish Celts, seem quite unfit for self-government."[35]

Other observers also believed that the racial characteristics of the Irish made them seem more like blacks and less like bona fide "white men." When James Bryce wrote of the Negro that "his intelligence is rather quick than solid, and . . . shows the childishness as well as lack of self-control which belongs to primitive peoples," he could just as easily have been describing the Irish as far as many readers were concerned.[36] During the Great War, it was not uncommon for those who witnessed or worked with Irish recruits in the British army to characterize them as "hardy and brave," but also as prone to "displays of unnecessary bravado" that resulted in excessive casualties on the battlefield. Even a British officer who had "great sympathy" for the Irish troops he led confided to his wife that "his men came from 'an extraordinary and inexplicable race' and that Ireland must be an 'island of children with the bodies of men.'" These are nearly the same terms that French observers applied to the black soldiers who were recruited from France's West African colonies. They too displayed a "wild impulsiveness" and "fierce ardour for hand-to-hand combat" that made them ideal "shock troops." But there were also frequent allegations that they lacked discipline and cohesion, that, like the Irish, they were a race of "children," albeit "wonderful children, with generous hearts."[37]

For the Irish, racial in-betweenness was a condition they could ill afford at a time when European and American conceptions of race were narrowing, from the belief in a "multiplicity of nations, races, and religions" to the fulsome embrace of a simple binary division between "white" and "nonwhite." In *Drawing the Global Colour Line*, Marilyn Lake and Henry Reynolds have traced the emergence of "white men's countries" in the context of imperialism, labor migration, and the growing danger that colored nations and races appeared to represent in the late nineteenth and early twentieth centuries. To some degree, this insistence on the hegemony of whiteness reflected the confidence of statesmen such as Theodore Roosevelt and academics such as Edward A. Freeman that the Anglo-Saxon race and the "English-speaking peoples" were not only destined to circumvent the globe but to rule—and reshape it. The American historian John Fiske fantasized that the work the "English race began when it colonized North America is destined to go on until every land on the earth's surface . . . shall become English in its language, in its political habits and traditions, and to a predominant extent in the blood of its people." Freeman, who believed that "history [was] a science which recorded the data of racial progress just as natural science tracked the laws of natural evolution," chimed in with the confident assertion that "the Aryan, be he Greek, Roman, or Teuton, could no more escape the burden of ineluctable progress than a sunflower seed could escape its destiny as a sunflower."[38]

But as labor migration escalated and became global in scope, the growing presence of Chinese and Indian immigrants in places such as California, British Columbia, Australia, and South Africa made the discourse of "Anglo-Saxon races" and "English-speaking peoples" largely irrelevant for hard-pressed Europeans working on the frontiers of industrial capitalism, who were increasingly likely to see their world as divided between "white men" and "coolies." The Irish could not claim to be either Anglo-Saxons or Teutons; in fact, Irish cultural nationalists ridiculed the very notion that the Celt had anything in common with the hated Saxon. But at the same time the laborers who made up the most numerous component of the Irish diaspora could feel no sense of affinity with the Chinese, whom they regarded as intruders who threatened to undermine their standard of living and rob them of their manhood. In California, Irish workers, led by Irish-born agitator Denis Kearney, played a leading role in the successful campaign to prohibit Chinese immigration to the United States. Nonetheless, globe-trotting academics, journalists, and politicians such as Charles Dilke implied that "Chinamen" and "Irishmen" were *both* "cheap races," and that both were a threat to the living standards of native-born workers in the countries they "invaded."[39]

Dilke was a graduate of Cambridge, where he studied with Charles Kingsley. He was also a Liberal politician, a widely published author, and a racial imperialist whose main concern was not the supremacy of British capital but the triumph, on a global scale, of English institutions and values. The great impediment to this accomplishment, he believed, was the migration of the "cheaper races" to English-speaking countries such as the United States and Australia. "In America," he wrote in *Greater Britain: A Record of Travel in English-Speaking Countries during 1866 and 1867*, "we have seen the struggle of the dear races against the cheap—the endeavors of the English to hold their own against the Irish and the Chinese." But the threat these races posed was not only to the standard of living of the Saxons and their descendants but to civilization itself. He warned of "the danger to our race and to the world from Irish ascendency." For if the Celt, his religion, and his "fierce" temperament prevailed, then the Englishman and his way of life would be eclipsed and the "freedom of mankind" would be jeopardized.[40]

In tracing the evolution of anti-Irish stereotypes and polemics, then, from the sixteenth century through the nineteenth and into the twentieth, one comes face to face with a process of racialization rooted in conquest, colonization, and Anglicization. It was a process that sometimes engendered violence on a horrific scale and one that by means of the stage Irishman, the cartoon caricature, and the condescension and ridicule inherent in the "Paddy joke" did enormous damage to Irish self-esteem.[41] We have seen how the native Irish were portrayed as heathens, savages, and even wild animals; we have seen, too, how Paddy was constructed as feckless, lazy, riotous, and, sometimes, dangerous to the peace and tranquillity of England as well as Ireland. Perhaps by way of summary it is appropriate to turn to the *Kentish Gazette*, which in February 1847 sought to identify the essential ingredients of the Irish character and to offer up a solution to the Irish Question. During one of the most devastating months of the Great Famine, the *Gazette* commented editorially that "the system of agitation, of midnight plunder, of open-day assassination, of Hottentot ignorance, superstition, idolatry, and indolence must be eradicated, removed, abolished by the strong arm of the law."[42] "Idolatry" and "superstition" were, of course, code words for Catholicism; indolence was, allegedly, the preferred pastime of the Irish people; assassination and midnight plunder were the staples of Irish politics; and Hottentot ignorance linked the Irish to African people who were widely regarded as primitive and backward, thus completing the process of racialization.

But it bears repeating that English attitudes toward the Irish were not uniformly negative. Perry Curtis has identified a female icon that became an important counterweight to the "ape" in Victorian portrayals of the Irish. In the interchangeable figures of Hibernia and Erin, English cartoonists created a character who was sometimes defenseless, but at other times resolute, sometimes frightened and in tears, but always loyal to "Mother England" and prepared to affirm, "Ah, sure thin, Misther Bull, I'll never lave ye, and I don't want to be Home Ruled at all." Hibernia reminded the English of their virtue and reaffirmed the conviction that theirs was a civilizing mission, in Ireland as well as Africa. Hibernia's creators fashioned a compelling melodrama in which the strong and the masculine invariably rescued the weak and the feminine and thwarted the dastardly Irish ape-man in the process.[43]

Michael de Nie has gone a step further than Curtis and has exhaustively mined the British press for representations of the Irish, from the Rising of 1798 to the Land War of 1879–82. De Nie has found many sympathetic portrayals of the Irish across a wide spectrum of newspapers and has argued that "competing and often disparate visions of Ireland and the Irish were continually offered," often within the pages of a single publication. Thus it was common for British newspapers to call for a recognition of the legitimacy of Irish grievances and, soon thereafter, to insist that the British government and people bore no responsibility for Ireland's unfortunate condition. Above all, when discord prevailed in the relations between Britain and Ireland, and a policy of conciliation did not lead to the anticipated outcomes, "The British press invariably cited one overriding cause—Irishness." Clearly, much of the British public understood Irishness in racial terms and ultimately saw it as the antithesis of Anglo-Saxon virtue.[44]

This was an important part of the context in which Irish nationalists created their own sense of racial identity and destiny. Perhaps inevitably, they too resorted to the binary of English versus Irish and Anglo-Saxon versus Celt. But in doing so, they altered the familiar categories and created a new set of polarities. The Irish became a uniquely spiritual people, in opposition to the crass materialism of the English. They became proudly rural and agricultural, in contrast to the urban character of England and the degradation that the proliferation of "dark Satanic mills" had meant for its inhabitants. They became chaste, God-fearing, and, by definition, Catholic. Catholicism, wrote James A. Froude, was "in the granules of [their] blood." As such, they were fiercely devoted to a traditional culture rooted in family, faith, and fatherland, but a culture that appeared to be menaced everywhere by the seductive but degrading influences of secularization and Anglicization.[45]

As early as the sixteenth century, a small coterie of Irish scholars, many of them Catholic churchmen living in exile, had launched an ambitious campaign to disprove the slanders of Giraldus Cambrensis and his latter-day imitators and to recover the historical record of an Ireland that had distinguished itself "in valour, in learning, and in being steadfast in the Catholic faith."[46] But it was in the middle of the nineteenth century, with the emergence of Young Ireland, that Irishmen and -women in the vanguard of the nationalist movement sharpened their insistence on the fundamental cultural differences that separated England and Ireland. Ironically, many of the leaders of Young Ireland were Protestants; some were the descendants of Cromwellian settlers. But increasingly they asserted that "no character is so unlike the Irish as the English, and none so unfit for the Irish to follow." Lamenting the spread of the English language and of a broader, more insidious process of Anglicization, they warned that "Ireland must be un-Saxonised before it can be pure and strong."[47] This became a common refrain among nationalists of widely varying political persuasions. Thus the Fenian leader John O'Leary warned that "if Irishmen are to save their honour, they must keep aloof from everything English," and the Gaelic Leaguer Douglas Hyde, a cautious moderate in politics, insisted that "we must create a strong feeling against West-Britonism, for . . . if we give it the least chance . . . [it] will overwhelm us like a flood."[48]

These statements from diverse sources are reflective of a cultural nationalism that gained rapid momentum in the Ireland of the late nineteenth and early twentieth centuries. For many cultural nationalists, the necessary tasks were to fend off "West-Britonism," to restore the Irish language to primacy in the cultural life of the nation, and to turn inward and focus on "Ourselves." W. B. Yeats's collaborator Lady Augusta Gregory, a vital force in the Irish Literary Revival in her own right, put it succinctly: "Whatever I have written that is . . . 'worth while' has come from my own surroundings, my own parish, my own home." Douglas Hyde, who like Gregory was an Anglo-Irish Protestant, put the matter in explicitly racial terms. In his famous speech "The Necessity for De-Anglicising Ireland," he declared that "we must strive to cultivate everything that is most racial, most smacking of the soil, most Gaelic, most Irish, because in spite of the little admixture of Saxon blood in the northeast corner, this island *is* and will *ever* remain Celtic to the core."[49]

Some Irish nationalists were reluctant to accept Yeats, Lady Gregory, John Millington Synge, and other Protestants as authentic participants in the nationalist movement. D. P. Moran, the fiercely polemical editor of the "Irish Ireland" journal, the *Leader*, called them "resident aliens."[50] Moran was especially hostile to Yeats, the Anglo-Irish poet, playwright, and devotee of the occult who sought to cultivate an Irish spirituality that was distinctively pagan. Not only did Yeats "write poetry which no Irishman understands," Moran charged, but "he is a bigot who thinks he is broadminded; a prig who thinks he is cultured; he does not understand Ireland." More generally, Moran coined the term "Sourfaces" to describe Irish Protestants. He allowed that they could *become* Irish, but only by accepting the fact that Ireland was a Catholic and Gaelic nation, and he insisted that "the Gael must be the element that absorbs." According to his biographer, "Moran was a bigot who helped to inflame existing religious bitterness." But he was less inflammatory, and less bigoted, than a number of lay and clerical voices that gave expression to a deeply rooted paranoia about the impact of modernity on the cohesion and moral fiber of Irish society.[51]

One of Moran's rivals for the leadership of Irish Ireland was Arthur Griffith, the principal architect of Sinn Féin. The son of a Dublin printer, and a printer and journalist himself, Griffith played an increasingly important role in the nationalist movement beginning in March 1899, when he founded the *United Irishman*, until his death of a cerebral hemorrhage in August 1922. In comparison with the mystical flights of fancy that characterized Yeats's Celtic spirituality, Griffith's nationalism was eminently practical and programmatic, focused on the nuts and bolts of nation building and on concrete plans for economic regeneration. When Yeats declared that "the work of Ireland is to lift up its voice for spirituality, for ideality, for simplicity in the English-speaking world," Griffith retorted, "We believe nothing of the kind. The work of Ireland is to uplift itself, not to play the missionary nation."[52] This single-minded preoccupation with "Ourselves" would become one of the hallmarks of Griffith's nationalism. He resisted any efforts to dilute the purity of the nationalist agenda by linking it to the quest for social reform. He was especially hostile to socialism and to the militant trade unionism of "Big Jim" Larkin, both of which he saw as English imports designed to derail the struggle for Irish self-government. When his friend Frederick Ryan, an active and articulate socialist, died in 1913, Griffith paid homage to his extraordinary personal integrity but attacked his "cosmopolitan heresy," above all his belief that "the suffering Egyptian had not less claim on him than his own countrymen." Ryan, he argued, was not a bona fide Irish nationalist, for "the man who declared he wanted National freedom in order to promote social reform, did not know the meaning of the nation."[53]

Griffith lived in the Transvaal (formally known then as the South African Republic) for eighteen months in the late 1890s. While there he became deeply enamored of the Boers' struggle to maintain their independence and more convinced than ever that "God Almighty had not made the earth for the sole use of the Anglo-Saxon race."[54] In the Boers he saw the embodiment of his own values. They were, by his lights, chaste, chivalrous, deeply religious, and hardworking, essentially a self-reliant agrarian people who wanted to be left alone to live their own lives. In the Boers' resistance to British imperialism, Griffith saw a Manichaean struggle between good and evil, between virtue and vice, between a transcendent nobility and a narrow, vulgar materialism. Some of the capitalists, large and small, who sided with the British in the mining regions of the Transvaal were Jewish, and the presence of Jews at the heart of this conflict intensified Griffith's anti-Semitism, all the more so because the South African War of 1899–1902 coincided with a crisis that was engulfing France in the aftermath of the court martial of Alfred Dreyfus, the Jewish artillery captain in the French army who was accused of passing military secrets to the Germans. The *United Irishman* charged that by supporting Dreyfus, the Jewish press was undermining the French army and thereby weakening the "Grande Nation," which had been Ireland's "most faithful and powerful friend" in her struggles against England.[55]

The anti-Semitism that found expression in the pages of the *United Irishman* reached a crescendo in the issue of September 23, 1899, when Frank Hugh O'Donnell, a regular contributor to the journal, identified "the Three Evil Influences of the century" as "the Pirate, the Freemason and the Jew." "United they stand in Europe against France," he declared.

> United they stand in Africa against the Transvaal Republic. The swarming Jews of Johannesburg, who have gained for the mining town the nickname of Judasburg, are the staunchest, though not the most valiant, snarlers in the Uitlander pack. The Jews, who swarmed from their London Ghetto into Hyde Park on Sunday, to rave out obscene insults against the French Army, were the loving comrades of a whole mob of blethering English agitators, Nonconformist tubthumpers, and Radical ranters, who howled against France and the French Generals with a low ferocity truly Anglo-Saxon. It was a sorry gathering. Some thirty thousand Jews and Jewesses, mostly of phenomenal ugliness and dirt, had come out of their East End dens at the summons of their Rabbis. If they hated France, it was also evident that they detested soap and water still more acutely.[56]

O'Donnell was a controversial figure whose highly charged verbal assaults on other nationalists ranging from Michael Davitt to W. B. Yeats earned him an increasing measure of notoriety. (Yeats would later characterize him as "half genius, half sewer rat.")[57] Griffith eventually denied him further access to the pages of the *United Irishman*, but in the meantime he somehow found it possible to deny that O'Donnell's splenetic rants could be characterized as anti-Semitic.[58] As for Griffith himself, he continued to speak out, in contradictory ways, about Jews, their presence in Ireland, and the increasing power of Zionism in the Jewish Diaspora. During the Limerick pogrom of 1904, he defended the infamous Father John Creagh, the Redemptorist priest whose sermons helped to stir up anti-Semitic fervor in the city's Catholic population. He did so, he said, not because of Jews' religious beliefs but because of their "business practices." At the same time, he also expressed admiration for Zionists, "those honest and patriotic Jews who desire the reestablishment of the Hebrew nation in Palestine."[59]

In 1913 Griffith wrote the preface to a reissue of John Mitchel's famous *Jail Journal*, one of the sacred texts of Irish nationalism. Mitchel was a leading voice in the Young Ireland movement of the 1840s, a leading rebel in 1848, an escapee from forced exile and imprisonment in Australia, and an outspoken apologist for chattel slavery in the United States and for the Confederacy in the American Civil War. Griffith viewed Mitchel as "the greatest man in Irish history" and as a kindred spirit who had performed the same essential task that Griffith saw himself performing—namely, severing "the case for Irish independence from theories of humanitarianism and universalism." "Against all effort . . . to sew onto the doctrine of Ireland's national independence a tale of obligation to the world at large," Griffith wrote, "John Mitchel is the superb protest." To those who felt compelled to apologize for any of Mitchel's ideas or actions, Griffith had only contempt. "Even [Mitchel's] views on slavery have been deprecatingly excused," he scolded, "as if excuse were needed for an Irish nationalist declining to hold the negro his peer in right."[60] When the Great War erupted in August 1914, he charged that the employment of "coloured" troops on the Allied side was a "betrayal of the white race." (The British forces in Europe included Gurkhas and Sikhs, and the French made use of Senegalese and North Africans.) Griffith called Europe "the white man's land" and wrote that the "introduction of savage Asiatics and Africans into Europe in a war between civilised powers is unparalleled in European history since anno domini."[61]

The prolific writings of Griffith and Moran have provided abundant ammunition for historians who point to the ethnocentric and even racist dimensions of Irish nationalism in its heyday. Thus, in his book on nationalist propaganda during the era of the Great War, Ben Novick refers to "the general racism that imbued Irish nationalist thought," and then he asserts: "Irish nationalist ideology was xenophobic and moralistically insular. Racism, anti-Semitism, and xenophobia all played a part in propaganda long before the war began, but the outbreak of the Great War caused this sort of propaganda to take on a new dimension."[62] Novick is building on a foundation constructed by scholars such as Conor Cruise O'Brien and Tom Garvin, beginning in the 1970s. They have been joined by an impressive coterie of revisionist historians, journalists, and novelists for whom the "pieties" of the nationalist tradition have become anathema.[63] The portrait they have painted over the years is one of a nationalist movement that was in large measure sectarian and ethnocentric, backward-looking and stubbornly antimodern, unrelenting in its opposition to the intrusion of the "social question" into the national struggle. Moreover, they contend, especially in the critical years from the Rising of 1916 to the conclusion of the civil war in 1923, leading elements within the movement proved to be antidemocratic and militarist in their politics and their vision of the Irish Republic.[64] In this sense, the reemergence of republican militarism at the end of the 1960s, and the bloodletting that convulsed Northern Ireland for the next three decades, represented not a departure from Ireland's nationalist tradition but a continuation of it. To a remarkable degree, O'Brien and others have argued, the "ancestral voices" of the dead past have been able to exert their authority over the living generations, to the great detriment of modern Irish society.

The remainder of this book will, for the most part, paint a quite different portrait of Irish nationalism, or at least of Irish nationalists who do not fit easily within the paradigm created by O'Brien, Garvin, and a generation of revisionist historians.[65] I will focus mainly on how Irish nationalists defined themselves in relation to the many other movements for emancipation that coexisted, and sometimes intersected, with the struggle for Irish freedom in the nineteenth and early twentieth centuries. I will also identify the ideological and cultural boundaries that sometimes entrapped Irish nationalists within the confines of a racial discourse that was ethnocentric and white supremacist. We have seen already that Arthur Griffith proudly represented one major tendency within the movement. He believed that an important part of his task was to resist all efforts to "sew onto the doctrine of Ireland's national independence a tale of obligation to the world at large." As the founder of Sinn Féin, he is often credited with turning the focus on "Ourselves" into a doctrine of "Ourselves Alone." But although Griffith played a major role in the evolution of Irish nationalism, there was no iron-clad consensus that his stance must eclipse all others. The very fact that he felt compelled to speak out forcefully against socialism and internationalism suggests that other forces within the movement were offering a formidable challenge to his perspective.

The alternative to a narrow, insular expression of Irish nationalism had begun to take shape long before Griffith was born. It was first articulated by the United Irishmen of the 1790s, who were deeply influenced by the American and French revolutions and who sought, in Wolfe Tone's famous words, to "unite the whole people of Ireland, to abolish the memory of all past dissensions, and to substitute the common name of Irishman in place of the denominations of Catholic, Protestant and Dissenter."[66] It found expression, too, in the person of Daniel O'Connell, who was Europe's leading antislavery advocate in the first half of the nineteenth century. By the time of his death in 1847, O'Connell had become anathema to Irish republicans, who were repelled by his unrelenting commitment to the "British connection" and by his unwillingness to concede that violence could be a means to achieve Irish self-government. But far more than many of his critics, O'Connell sought to merge the Irish people's quest for emancipation with broader struggles for freedom and justice beyond Ireland's borders. He called on Irishmen and -women, in the United States as well as Ireland, to join hands with the abolitionist movement, and he argued that his nation's refusal to be "tainted with slavery" had in important respects shaped the Irish people and defined their national character. In an era of increasingly intense and narrowly focused nationalism, O'Connell helped to lay the foundations of a different kind of national sensibility, one that sought to transcend nationalism's exclusions and to create instead an Irishness that was generous, inclusive, rooted in Ireland's native soil, but global in its sympathies and sense of obligation.[67]

Later in the nineteenth century, the politics and vision of Michael Davitt and Patrick Ford were also rooted in this sensibility. Ford was the editor of the *Irish World and American Industrial Liberator*, the most influential Irish weekly in the United States. Davitt, a former Fenian who served seven years in a British prison for gunrunning, became a prominent leader, and the most compelling symbol, of the movement for land reform in Ireland. Even as they focused their energies on the quest to transform the system of land ownership in their native country, Davitt and Ford repeatedly reaffirmed their commitment to "Universal Justice and the Rights of Humanity." Davitt's biographer Carla King has stated that over time "he became more and more concerned with injustice and oppression in the world—against the Boers, the Aborigines in Australia, the Maoris in New Zealand, the Jews in Kishinev and in Eastern Europe generally, and the prison population and the poor everywhere. The world's oppressed and dispossessed became his parish."[68]

Even William Rooney, whose name is closely associated with Arthur Griffith's, can stand as an important alternative to Griffith's nationalism. Rooney founded the Celtic Literary Society in 1893 and later cofounded the *United Irishman* with Griffith. He was the son of a Fenian and Land War prisoner, and his commitment to Ireland's cultural and political independence rivaled, and even exceeded, his father's. Educated by the Christian Brothers, he left school at the age of twelve and became a junior clerk in a solicitor's office. Informally, he continued his education, learning Irish and becoming an early proponent of the language revival. Griffith regarded Rooney as a close friend and mentor, and after Rooney's death from tuberculosis at the age of twenty-nine, he declared that "no man could have led [Ireland] more truly than Rooney, had not his passion burned out his life."[69] What stands out most about Rooney in retrospect is the fact that although he had a strong commitment to the Gaelic Revival, he was a civic nationalist who sharply criticized the ethnocentric nationalism of D. P. Moran. Moreover, unlike Moran (and far more than Griffith), he was an anti-imperialist who was prepared to reject any offer from Britain to "rob the nations of the East and South under the protection of the British flag." He was also an internationalist who, remarkably, envisioned an independent Ireland whose shores would become a haven "for the oppressed of every race *and colour.*"[70] Whereas Griffith lived and became famous as an embodiment of Irish nationalism, Rooney died in 1901 and was wrongly regarded thereafter only as a more charismatic and articulate forerunner of Griffith's ideas and policies.

Those who sought ways to combine nationalism and internationalism, and the social and national questions; those who believed in racial equality and the "brotherhood of man"; those who opposed imperialism and offered the hand of friendship and solidarity to nationalists in India and Egypt, were an eclectic lot. Some, like James Connolly, came from the poorest segments of the working class; others, like Countess Markievicz, were to the manor born. Some, like Robert Lynd, were Protestants; others, like Connolly, were lapsed Catholics who ultimately found Ireland's Catholic ethos irresistible and returned to the fold—in Connolly's case, on the eve of his execution in 1916. Some, like Connolly and Big Jim Larkin, were born to emigrant parents in cities such as Edinburgh and Liverpool but migrated to Ireland and made its quest for freedom the centerpiece of their lives. A few, like Helen Merriam Golden, were not Irish at all, but nonetheless committed themselves unreservedly to the cause of Irish independence. And one, Roger Casement, was a servant of the British Crown for more than two decades who was honored—and ultimately knighted—by the government for the extraordinary service he had rendered—first in exposing the genocidal crimes of King Leopold's regime of superexploitation in the Belgian Congo, and then for a similar exposé in the Putumayo River region of Peru. Casement was a Protestant Ulsterman who, as a teenager, had developed a keen awareness of the legacy of conquest, violence, and dispossession that had destroyed the Gaelic world of his native province in the sixteenth and seventeenth centuries. As an adult, in the British consular service, he came to believe that there was an intimate connection between the history of Tudor and Stuart Ireland and the horrors of the Congo. "Up in those lonely Congo forests where I found Leopold," he wrote to his friend Alice Stopford Green in 1907, "I found also myself—the incorrigible Irishman" who looked at the tragedy of the Congo "with the eyes of another race, of a people once hunted themselves." It was as Sir Roger Casement that he was executed for treason in 1916 because of his campaign to gain German material and military support for the Easter Rising. Of the many individuals and groups that pleaded with the British government to spare his life, perhaps none captured the character and reach of his nationalism more poignantly than the Negro Fellowship League, which reminded Casement's executioners that "there are so few heroic souls in the world who dare to lift their voices in defence of the oppressed who are born with black skins." "Because of [his] great service to humanity, as well as to the Congo natives," said the league, "we feel impelled to beg for mercy on his behalf."[71]

As extraordinary as these men and women were, however, they lived in a particular historical context and sometimes reflected it in ways that later

2.3. Roger Casement and John Devoy, 1914 (Joseph McGarrity Collection, Digital Library, Villanova University)

generations can only find disquieting. The second half of the nineteenth century and the early years of the twentieth were an era marked by imperialism and virulent racism, a historical moment when science became the handmaiden of white supremacist ideology and anthropologists, public intellectuals, and politicians fantasized about the superiority of Anglo-Saxon, Teutonic, and Aryan races. In such a context, it is hardly surprising that even the most progressive Irish nationalists became entrapped in an essentialist discourse that required the exaltation of the Celt and the demonization of the Anglo-Saxon. Leading separatists and republicans sometimes combined a relentless critique of British imperialism and sympathy for its victims with an uncritical embrace of Britain's main rival, Germany, and a tendency to give expression on occasion to the anti-Semitism and racism that surrounded them. As World War I loomed on the horizon, Casement praised "the honesty and integrity of the German mind, the strength of the German intellect, the skill of the German hand and brain, the justice and vigour of German law, the intensity of German culture, science, education and social development," and concluded, grandly, that "the world of European life needs to-day, as it needed in the days of a decadent Roman world empire, the coming of another Goth, the coming of the Teuton."[72] This became a common theme among Irish nationalists during the Great War. Even James Connolly, who was a far more consistent anti-imperialist than Casement, succumbed to the same temptation, praising Germany and damning England's ally Russia in words that echoed the discourse of civilization versus barbarism that had been used for centuries to demonize the Irish. "If we had to choose between strengthening the German bully or the Russian autocrat," he wrote in the *Irish Worker* in the first month of the war, "the wise choice would be on the side of the German. For the German people are a highly civilised people, . . . whereas the Russian Empire stretches away into the depths of Asia, and relies on an army largely recruited from amongst many millions of barbarians who have not yet felt the first softening influence of civilisation."[73]

Nonetheless, when viewed from the vantage point of their own times, as they must be, what stands out about most of the Irish nationalists who are the focus of this book is their insistence on linking the quest for Irish independence with the struggles of "the oppressed of every race and colour." Although they seldom represented a majority viewpoint, these men and women were not marginal figures within the movement. Davitt was widely revered as the founding father of the Land League; Patrick Ford was, for part of his career at least, the preeminent voice of Irish America. Connolly, for all the controversy he generated as a labor organizer and tribune of socialism, was respected in the councils of advanced nationalism and was among the leaders and martyrs of the Easter Rising. Liam Mellows was widely admired within the movement for his courage and unrelenting commitment to the Irish Republic; and Peter Golden worked closely with Eamon de Valera during Dev's eighteen-month sojourn in the United States. As secretary of the New York–based Irish Progressive League, he and his wife, Helen Merriam Golden, labored tirelessly to persuade progressives and socialists in the United States to support the struggle for Irish independence.

These examples help explain why revolutionary nationalists, from Jamaica to India and beyond, along with labor radicals in Britain and the United States, insisted on viewing the war for Irish independence as an inspiration, even as a model, for their own struggles for emancipation. Thus the Scottish socialist John Maclean could state in the summer of 1920 that "Ireland's victory is obviously the undoubted prelude to Labour's triumph throughout the world,"[74] and Cyril Briggs, the Afro-Caribbean émigré who created the African Blood Brotherhood in conscious imitation of the Fenians, could hail the Irish Revolution as "the greatest Epic of Modern History."[75] Although these euphoric statements cannot withstand the scrutiny of later generations and the certainty that hindsight brings, they nonetheless serve as a reminder of the complexity and broad appeal of Irish nationalism, especially at the moment when it stood on the threshold of its greatest victory.

PART 2

Ireland, Slavery, and Abolition

CHAPTER THREE

"Come out of such a land, you Irishmen"

DANIEL O'CONNELL, AMERICAN SLAVERY, AND THE
MAKING OF THE IRISH RACE

> No man, in the wide world, has spoken so strongly against the soul-drivers of this land as O'Connell.
>
> —William Lloyd Garrison, 1842

> Over the broad Atlantic I pour my voice, saying, "Come out of such a land, you Irishmen, or, if you remain, and dare countenance the system of slavery that is supported there, we will recognize you as Irishmen no longer."
>
> —Daniel O'Connell, 1843

> The opposition of Irishmen in America to the colored man is not so much a Hibernianism as an Americanism.
>
> —Black abolitionist William C. Nell, 1847

CHARLES LENOX REMOND, an African American from Salem, Massachusetts, first met Daniel O'Connell in 1840, at the World Anti-Slavery Convention in London and was overwhelmed by the encounter.[1] "For thirteen years have I thought myself an abolitionist," he reported to a friend, "but I had been in a measure mistaken, until I listened to the . . . fearless O'Connell." Only then was Remond "moved to think, and feel, and speak" as a true abolitionist thought and felt and spoke. William Lloyd Garrison, the preeminent voice of radical abolitionism in the United States, was no less impressed. He told his wife, Helen, that the Irishman's words at the convention were "received with a storm of applause that almost shook the building to its foundations. The spectacle was sublime and heart-stirring beyond all power of description on my part." The plain-living, plain-spoken Garrison was no respecter of persons; he vowed to be "as harsh as truth, and as uncompromising as justice." But he could not help but tell his wife, with obvious pride, "I have shaken hands with O'Connell repeatedly."[2]

Although O'Connell's fame stretched from Ireland to Britain to the European continent, and from there to the Americas, his reputation derived first and foremost from the campaign for Catholic Emancipation he led in his native country in the 1820s. It was, Donal McCartney writes, "the first mass movement of organised democracy in Europe." Catholics made up approximately 80 percent of Ireland's population by this time, and O'Connell used the parish structure and clerical leadership of the Catholic Church as the foundation stone of his movement. Through skillful agitation and mass mobilization, he gradually raised the temperature of protest until Tory leader Robert Peel reluctantly conceded that he could not "see the smallest chance of ever turning [Ireland] to any good for the empire at large but by settling [the Catholic question]." When the victory came, in 1829, the Protestant archbishop of Limerick acknowledged that "an Irish revolution has in great measure been effected." It was O'Connell's revolution; he had emerged as Ireland's Liberator.[3]

The campaign for Catholic Emancipation prefigured a second major initiative, for repeal of the Act of Union, which O'Connell led under the umbrella of his Loyal National Repeal Association. To stoke the fires of this campaign, he ultimately resorted to a series of "monster meetings," which attracted huge crowds that enthusiastically supported his demand for the return of self-government to Ireland through the restoration of an Irish parliament in Dublin. According to the legend of O'Connell, what stood out about these meetings was not just their size—which allegedly approached a million on several occasions—but the respect, even reverence, the assembled masses showed the "Immortal Dan." Surely, the historian Thomas Babington Macaulay declared, "The position which Mr. O'Connell holds in the eyes of his fellow-countrymen is a position such as no popular leader in the whole history of mankind ever occupied."[4]

With O'Connell, however, things were seldom as simple as such plaudits implied. The fact that he earned "innumerable tributes of personal devotion" while also provoking a "frenzy of hatred" suggests that he was a man of enormous complexity who embodied many of the contradictions of Irish society in his own persona. The unrivaled symbol of Irishness and Irish aspirations for autonomy, he declared that Catholics were "ready to become . . . West Britons if made so in benefits and justice." The leader of a mass movement for Repeal, who demanded justice for Ireland here and now, he was also a machine politician and parliamentary horse trader who subordinated Repeal to the British Whigs' agenda year after year and, according to his adversaries, "says one thing one day & just the contrary the next." The sincere advocate of religious toleration, he made nationalism synonymous not only with Catholicism but also with the parochial agenda of the Irish Catholic hierarchy. The architect of peaceful protest and zealous advocate of the compelling power of "moral force," his monster meetings, with their polarizing rhetoric, created a mass of seething energy that—his critics charged—teetered on the edge of anarchic violence.[5]

Historians have generally agreed that O'Connell was, first and foremost, a pragmatic reformer whose most salient characteristics were flexibility, opportunism, and a determination to "avoid or prevent social revolution" at all costs.[6] His belief in nonviolent moral force as the only legitimate foundation of political mobilization, and his commitment to home rule rather than national independence for Ireland, made him something of an embarrassment, even a pariah, for subsequent generations of radical nationalists, from John Mitchel to Arthur Griffith and James Connolly. However, placing him in the context of the bitter conflict between pro- and antislavery forces in the Atlantic World renders some of these hallowed generalizations deeply problematic. His commitment to the immediate abolition of slavery, even when it threatened to cost him the allegiance of important segments of his mass political base, made him anything but a pragmatist on that issue, and his unyielding embrace of the cause of racial equality pulled him toward an enduring alliance with a transatlantic network of Protestant reformers that many of his political allies and rivals in Ireland viewed with distrust, even contempt.[7] Like most of his contemporaries, he was a racial essentialist, one who was fond of exclaiming that "[the Irish] people are foremost in every physical and social quality" and renowned in Europe and America for their "intellectual capacity" as well.[8] But in spite of a penchant for such outbursts, O'Connell's essentialism usually propelled him outward toward a wider world, not inward toward racial chauvinism. Indeed, he articulated a conception of Irish history and identity that made Irishness synonymous with opposition to oppression "wherever it rears its head." This essentializing project was at the root of an outlook that was at once nationalist and internationalist, an outlook that allowed (even compelled) him to choose internationalism over nationalism at critical moments in his career.

O'Connell clearly believed that the Irish people possessed certain racial and national characteristics and that anyone who deviated from these essential traits could not claim to have the "genuine feelings of Irishmen." In this regard he was operating within the framework of a highly contested intellectual discourse that often represented racial and national characteristics as fixed and immutable. Many educated British commentators portrayed Ireland as a country with two nations (the Catholic and the Protestant) and three races (English, Scottish, and native Irish). They assumed that the English and Scottish conquest and settlement of Ireland had been a case of civilization triumphing over barbarism and that racial difference and unequal racial capacities were largely responsible for the ongoing problems and polarities of Irish society. So pervasive, and galling, was this perception that no less a figure than Dublin-born Edmund Burke was moved to complain that the English regarded his countrymen as "a race of savages who were a disgrace to human nature."[9]

In leading the campaign for Repeal, O'Connell took it upon himself to stand the dogma of Catholic inferiority and native Irish savagery on its head and to offer a sustained rebuttal to the claims of Sir John Temple, Sir Richard Musgrave, and other Protestant polemicists. His principal instrument for the accomplishment of this monumental task was his *Memoir on Ireland: Native and Saxon*, which sought to demonstrate how grievously Ireland had suffered from centuries of "English misrule." O'Connell's purpose was to acquaint Queen Victoria (to whom the volume was dedicated), and through her the British people, with "the confiscations, the plunder, the robbery, the domestic treachery, the violation of . . . the sanctity of treaties, the ordinary wholesale slaughter, the planned murders, the concerted massacres, which have been inflicted upon the Irish people by the English Governments." Throughout the *Memoir*, he buttressed his own arguments with abundant testimony from a wide range of English Protestant observers to support his claim that "no people on the face of the earth were ever treated with such cruelty as the Irish."[10] Not surprisingly, he focused at length on the seventeenth century, when Irish Catholics had suffered the sustained trauma of settlement, conquest, dispossession, and the systematic denial of citizenship rights. Even in 1641, he argued, when the uprising of the native Irish had allegedly caused the slaughter of tens of thousands of English and Scottish Protestants in Ulster, it was Irish Catholics who were the real victims of hatred and violence. And this was not merely a feature of the remote past. "Even the present administration," O'Connell concluded in 1843, "is popular in England in the precise proportion of the hatred they exhibit to the Irish people."[11]

Remarkably, for someone who frequently asserted his commitment to the "British connection," and thus to the British Empire, O'Connell had long been a critic of British colonization. He was, after all, an "Aborigine" himself, and he "therefore felt a personal sympathy for the native inhabitants of every other country." In a speech to members of the Aborigines' Protection Society in 1840, he lamented the "misery," "guilt," "suffering," "crime," and "devastation of nations" that had been the "consequence of the spread of colonization, and of the extensive occupation of countries heretofore uncivilized." "No other human event," he believed, "[had] led to evils so multitudinous." To be sure, this was not all Britain's doing. But as the world's most powerful empire, it was disproportionately responsible for the crimes that inevitably flowed from colonization. As an Irishman, he had seen his own nation colonized and his people, the native Irish Catholics, brutalized and dispossessed. That England had failed to "exterminate the Irish nation" was due far more to Irish courage and tenacity than to English virtue. Looking farther afield, he asked, "What had Britain done in New South Wales? . . . She had annihilated the Aborigines there, either by destructive violence or by the force of her institutions." He feared that "if some protection were not given to the natives [of New Zealand], they [too] would soon be counted among the people that were forgotten, and a new chapter would be added to the history of those crimes which had taken place under the rule of Great Britain."[12]

Explicitly in his *Memoir*, and implicitly in much of his private correspondence, O'Connell configured the "Irish nation" and the "Irish people" as, by definition, Catholic. In 1826 he had declared publicly that "the Catholic people of Ireland are a nation." Thirteen years later, in a letter to his friend Archbishop

John MacHale, he acknowledged that in developing his campaign to repeal the Act of Union, "my object would be once again to organise all Catholic Ireland in an effort of resistance to all our enemies"—not only the Tories, his historic adversaries, but also the Whigs, his allies in the cause of reform. Ultimately, his nationalist perorations—above all, his *Memoir on Ireland*—were a classic example of defining the collective self—in this case, the Irish Catholic nation— over against English (and, for good measure, Scottish) Protestants. The *Memoir* was full of extravagant praise for the "faithful, brave, long oppressed, but magnanimous people of Ireland." In a typical passage, O'Connell announced his obligation to conclude from the evidence he had marshaled that "the people of Ireland . . . stand superior in their national characteristics to the inhabitants of any other country on the face of the globe."[13]

Although he sought to employ his Manichaean reading of Irish history as a weapon in the campaign to restore self-government to Ireland, in practice O'Connell continued to defend the civil rights of Protestants and called on them to join with Catholics in a "communion of benevolent affection, and genuine Irish patriotism."[14] Likewise, he never ceased to hope that his alliance with the Whigs could be reconstituted, for Ireland's benefit and for the sake of the liberal causes he had long espoused. Nor could he forget that the British people and their government had abolished slavery in the empire, emancipating eight hundred thousand enslaved Africans in the Anglophone Caribbean. In recalling that heady triumph, he gave the lion's share of the credit to the "genial softness of the British heart."[15]

Most of all, O'Connell was never willing to turn his nationalism in upon "Ourselves Alone." On the contrary, he had long believed that "Ireland and Irishmen should be foremost in seeking to effect the emancipation of mankind" precisely because "the Irish people . . . had themselves suffered centuries of persecution." "I feel that I have something Irish at my heart which makes me sympathize with all those who are suffering under oppression," he declared at a meeting of the British India Society in 1839. Perhaps the most eloquent affirmation of his commitment to "universal man" came in September 1845, at a Repeal meeting in Dublin, with the African American abolitionist Frederick Douglass in the audience. It was there he declared:

> Wherever tyranny exists, I am the foe of the tyrant; wherever oppression shows itself, I am the foe of the oppressor; wherever slavery rears its head, I am the enemy of the system. . . . My sympathy with distress is not confined within the narrow bounds of my own green island. No—it extends itself to every corner of the earth. My heart walks abroad, and wherever the miserable are to be succored, and the slave to be set free, there my spirit is at home, and I delight to dwell.[16]

O'Connell had begun to come to terms with the issue of slavery in 1824, when the Liverpool Quaker merchant James Cropper visited Ireland to muster

3.1. Daniel O'Connell, 1844 (courtesy of the National Library of Ireland)

support for a proposal to alleviate Irish poverty and undermine West Indian slavery by developing a network of cotton manufactories in the Emerald Isle that would sell Irish textiles to India in return for the sale of East Indian sugar to Ireland. It was a complex and visionary scheme, and for the most part it went nowhere. But it planted a seed of ethical concern in O'Connell that would blossom into decades of outspoken abolitionism. In his early years in Parliament he played a leading role in marshaling Irish—and other—votes on behalf of the elimination of slavery in the British Empire.[17] Even before that was finally accomplished, he turned his attention to slavery in the United States. The abolitionist movement there divided into a number of competing organizations and tendencies over the years. O'Connell had an especially volatile relationship with the Garrisonians, the most zealous and uncompromising antislavery partisans, who were characterized by a hostility to politics, a loathing of compromise in any form, and a proudly Protestant devotion to various antinomian heresies. Nonetheless, it was sweet music to their ears when he declared publicly in 1831, "I am an Abolitionist. I am for speedy, immediate abolition. . . . I enter into no compromise with slavery."[18]

For all of his reputation for legal sophistication and political savvy, O'Connell's opposition to slavery was based on simple affirmations that were grounded in his conception of the law and his view of Ireland's history and national character, but above all in his religious faith.[19] He was, to be sure, a utilitarian, but as Joseph Lee has argued, his utilitarianism was "essentially ethical rather than doctrinal." First and foremost, he was a Catholic moralist, although it is important to emphasize that his stance on slavery flowed from *his* Catholic moralism, not that of the institutional church, which in Ireland remained largely silent on the greatest of all nineteenth-century controversies and in America often took the side of the slave owner. O'Connell insisted that no constitution—indeed, no law of any kind—could "create or sanction slavery," which was "repugnant to the first principles of society" and "contrary to the law of God." "What the law of God forbids," he declared, "no human law can sustain or countenance." He believed, deeply and viscerally, that "we are all children of the same Creator, heirs to the same promise, purchased by the blood of the same Redeemer." Thus it was axiomatic that "slavery is opposed to the first, the highest, and the greatest principles of Christianity."[20]

It was common among Europeans and white Americans to employ a universal language of redemption and rights while taking it for granted that the words did not apply to people of color, above all to black Africans and their descendants. But O'Connell followed the language of Christianity and the Declaration of Independence to its logical conclusion; he believed in racial equality. The American Declaration, he argued, "does not limit the equality of man . . . to the white, to the brown, or to the copper-colored races; it includes all races—it excludes none." Like all men and women, people of African descent were "beings for whom the Son of God offered up his blood." Thus "it is our duty to proclaim that the cause of the negro is our cause" and to insist upon removing "the stain of slavery . . . from the face of the whole earth."[21]

When O'Connell turned his attention to slavery in the United States, he launched a sustained diatribe against the White Republic that was as sweeping and audacious as it was politically risky. White Americans were inclined to think of themselves as God's chosen people and to regard their government as the "model government in the earth." But O'Connell believed that slavery had polluted the very soil of the United States and undermined its claim to preeminence among the nations. As early as 1829 he had declared that "of all men living, an American citizen, who is the owner of slaves, is the most despicable; he is a political hypocrite of the very worst description." American slave owners were "felons to the human race," "traitors to liberty," "blasphemers of the Almighty," even "monsters in human shape." But it was not just the slave owners. Because they tolerated slavery, the "freemen of America"—that is, the vast majority of white Americans—were "hypocrites, tyrants, and unjust men" who were entirely unworthy of their claim to cherish liberty and equality. "Liberty in America means the power to flog slaves, to work them for nothing," he exclaimed. Although he did not attack republicanism as such, he implied that it engendered a "sentiment of pride" and a "feeling of self-exaltation" that, in the case of the American republic, urgently needed unmasking. "Let us tell these republicans," he counseled, "that instead of their being the highest in the scale of humanity, they are the basest of the base, the vilest of the vile." At the World Anti-Slavery Convention, he announced that he would "recognize no American as a fellow-man, except those who belong to anti-slavery societies." Turning to the Garrisonian delegation, led by Garrison himself, he declared, "I wish for no higher station in the world; but I do covet the honor of being a brother with these American Abolitionists." Apart from them, however, white Americans were not only debased but also condemned to divine retribution. "America!" he warned, "no matter what glory you may acquire beneath [your star-spangled banner], the hideous, damning stain of slavery rests upon you, and a just Providence will sooner or later avenge itself for your crime."[22]

O'Connell acknowledged that for years he had longed to visit the United States. But slavery had contaminated the new nation and rendered it unclean. "So long as [America] is tarnished by slavery," he declared in 1833, "I will never pollute my foot by treading on its shores." Instead, "armed with the lightning of Christian truth," he would make his voice heard across the broad Atlantic.[23] He believed he had a special responsibility to address the rapidly expanding community of Irish immigrants in the United States, and at first many of them were predisposed to revere him. In the 1820s the emerging Irish commercial and professional classes in cities such as New York, Philadelphia, and Charleston had enthusiastically supported his campaign for Catholic Emancipation, and with the coming of the mass movement for Repeal in the early 1840s, much of Irish America mobilized to march in step with the Liberator once again.[24]

For O'Connell, for Irish America, and for American society, this was an especially volatile moment—when the United States and Britain were engaged in a contest for dominance in the breakaway republic of Texas and for sovereignty over the Oregon territory; when antiabolitionist mobs were assaulting his allies and friends, destroying their printing presses, and, on occasion, murdering those who dared to demand the eradication of slavery; when Irish emigrants, by the hundreds of thousands, were seeking to escape poverty and hunger by taking refuge in the proverbial land of liberty across the sea. All of this created difficult terrain for the Liberator. In opposing the westward expansion of slavery and denouncing the U.S. annexation of Texas as "robbery," he appeared to be taking the side of Britain against the United States. In reaffirming his support for the embattled abolitionists and calling on Irish immigrants to do the same, he was asking his exiled countrymen to play with political and social dynamite. In siding with the abolitionists, moreover, he solidified his alliance with Protestant reformers and radicals—many of whom were regarded by Catholic churchmen as "fanatics and bigots" who "entertain a virulent hatred and unchristian zeal against Catholicity and the Irish."[25]

American abolitionists nonetheless continued to believe that the Irish were coming to the United States in ever-larger numbers to "escape from the chains of British tyranny," and they assumed that resistance to tyranny in Ireland required opposition to oppression abroad. "Nine tenths of the Irish, are at heart, thorough going abolitionists," Garrison's friend and ally John A. Collins declared hopefully. Thus it was exhilarating but hardly surprising to learn that O'Connell, Father Theobald Mathew, Ireland's legendary "Apostle of Temperance," and sixty thousand other Irishmen and -women had signed the "Address of the Irish People to Their Countrymen and Countrywomen in America." This famous document, which came to be known as the Irish Address, forthrightly called upon Ireland's exiled sons and daughters to "unite with the abolitionists, and never . . . cease your efforts, until perfect liberty be granted to every one of [America's] inhabitants, the black man as well as the white man."[26]

The Irish Address emerged from the combined efforts of Irish and American abolitionists. At the conclusion of Charles Lenox Remond's antislavery lecture series in Ireland in the summer and fall of 1841, one Irish enthusiast reported, "We held a meeting at the Royal Exchange, at which an address was agreed to most warmly and enthusiastically—to be signed by 1,000,000, or by millions, if we have patience to collect so many names." The writing of the address fell to some combination of Richard Allen, Richard Davis Webb, and James Haughton, the leaders of the Dublin Quaker reform circle, who had begun developing a warm and enduring relationship with Garrison and his associates at the World Anti-Slavery Convention a year earlier. Members of the predominantly

Protestant Hibernian Anti-Slavery Society played the leading role in circulating the address for signatures, along with agents of O'Connell's overwhelmingly Catholic Repeal Association.[27] When Remond returned to the United States in December 1841, he brought the Irish Address with him.[28]

With great fanfare, the Garrisonians called a mass meeting at Boston's Faneuil Hall on the evening of January 28, 1842, to publicize the address and unveil the massive document, with its sixty thousand signatures. It was, Garrison reported, a "great and glorious meeting," with perhaps as many as four thousand people present, including "very many Irishmen." Remond and the soon-to-be-famous Frederick Douglass both spoke. But the meeting's most euphoric moment came when the veteran Quaker abolitionist James Cannings Fuller addressed the Irishmen and -women in the audience and elicited "tremendous applause" in response.[29] According to the *Liberator*, Fuller was a man with the warm and generous "heart of an Irishman, the arms of whose philanthropy embrace the whole human race." In Faneuil Hall, he presented himself as an "old countryman" who was overcome by emotion at the sight of so many of his exiled compatriots, to whom he declared, "I know what feelings and sufferings bring an Irishman to America. . . . OPPRESSION drove you here, . . . you came for universal liberty!" For that very reason, he warned, "see to it that none of you bows down to th[e] deadly influence of slavery." "In the beloved name of the country of your birth, and the country of your adoption, go on, till you have driven the curse of slavery from the American soil."[30]

The Irish Address was couched in the language of the most militant—and controversial—advocates of reform in American society. It directly challenged the core belief of the vast majority of white Americans that theirs was a republic of divinely ordained virtue. "What a spectacle does America present to the people of the earth!" the address declared. "A land of professing christian republicans, uniting their energies for the oppression of three millions of innocent human beings, the children of one common Father." As long as this "curse" afflicted the United States, it could not be "a land worthy of your adoption." Rather than embrace America in its current state, the address called upon Irishmen and -women to "treat the colored people as your equals, as brethren. By all your memories of Ireland, continue to love liberty—hate slavery—CLING BY THE ABOLITIONISTS—and in America you will do honor to the name of Ireland."[31]

But could the majority of Irish immigrants have followed this advice? At the very moment the Irish Address was written, the vast majority of Americans were moving toward a fuller and more insistent embrace of white supremacist ideology and practice. The mobbing of abolitionists, the disfranchisement of free blacks in northern states, and the hysterical denunciations of "amalgamationism" led Garrison to admit that "when we first unfurled the banner of the *Liberator*, . . . it did not occur to us that nearly every religious sect, and every political party would side with the oppressor."[32] Richard Robert Madden, an

Irish visitor to the United States, offered an equally bleak assessment. "The inhabitants of the free states of the North[,] in which slavery has been abolished," he observed,

> detest the people of colour and their descendents, who are now free, with a degree of rancorous animosity that is almost incredible. Though slavery has been done away with in the State of New York, still negroes are not suffered to associate with white people, to eat or drink or travel with them, or even to sit side by side in the same church or theatre: and, in short, are treated in the public streets and in all places of resort with insolent contumely and frequently with brutal violence.[33]

In this context, to ask Irish immigrants to "treat the colored people as your equals, as brethren," was to ask them to go directly against the American grain, to link them even more closely with a despised and powerless race, to condemn them to the margins of the society they had chosen as their home.

Quite apart from the pressures that pushed Irish immigrants toward the holy grail of white identity, there were important class and cultural differences that stood in the way of an alliance between the Irish and abolitionism in the United States. The antislavery vanguard was, in the words of the patrician Edmund Quincy, "chiefly made up of persons of small but independent means"; "farmers, mechanics, teachers and persons of small capital, scattered over the country towns." The Irish, in stark contrast, were largely poor urban laborers who were, according to Quincy, "too ignorant and degraded to be abolitionists." Even Wendell Phillips, who professed to believe that Irish immigrants would be "fit for great things" with the right leadership, was repelled by the "low," "mean," "demagogical" politics at an Irish nationalist meeting he attended. "Never shall I do it again," he wrote to Richard Allen in Dublin. "O'Connell never could have breathed there unless his electricity had been able to purify the air." Allen and his fellow Dublin reformers "would have fainted." As for Phillips himself, "The mouth tasted bad for days after." The meeting's tone, its lack of decorum, even—apparently—its smell was "so unlike [an] abolition meeting."[34]

But in the immediate aftermath of the "indescribably enthusiastic" unveiling of the Irish Address, the Garrisonians dared to hope for the best. "Until I am compelled to believe otherwise by evidence which it would be folly to dispute," Garrison reported, "I shall cling to the opinion that the great body of our Irish fellow-citizens mean to be found on the side of the oppressed (for is not Ireland oppressed?) the world over." Garrison had been nurtured in the bosom of radical Protestantism, with its belief that American society—including the entire spectrum of its religious denominations—was mired in the swamp of compromise and betrayal, thus obligating the true believer to follow the promptings of the spirit and "come out" of corrupt institutions. Increasingly, he concluded that the necessary corollary of this belief was that abolitionists must seek to "come out" of the Union that bound Northern liberty to Southern slavery. Hoping to strengthen the ties between Irish nationalism and the abolitionist

3.2. William Lloyd Garrison at age thirty (courtesy of the Trustees of the Boston Public Library / Rare Books)

movement, he announced his support for O'Connell's campaign to repeal the Act of Union. "For my own part," he wrote in March 1842, "I avow myself to be both an Irish Repealer and an American Repealer. I go for the repeal of the union between England and Ireland, and for the repeal of the union between the North and the South."[35]

Only a few months later, however, Garrison appeared ready to concede that the battle for the allegiance of Irish America was already lost. "I do not wonder that you blush, and hang your head," he wrote to Richard Allen, "to see the unkind and insolent reception which the Irish Address has met with, on this side of the Atlantic, at the hands of your exiled countrymen. It is now quite apparent that they will go *en masse* with southern men-stealers, and in opposition to the anti-slavery movement." He believed that the Irishmen and -women who attended the Faneuil Hall meeting had "acted out their natural love of liberty" on that occasion. But since then their leaders—"crafty" priests, "unprincipled political demagogues," and equally demagogic newspaper editors—had poisoned their minds to the point where "they have wholly kept aloof from us." Alas, he lamented, "So much more potent is the influence of American slavery over their minds, than that of Father Mathew and Daniel O'Connell combined!"[36]

Why were Irish emigrants, of all people, likely to "join the pro-slavery ranks after crossing the Atlantic"?[37] The question confounded the abolitionists, and it continues to preoccupy historians of race and ethnicity a century and a half later. Was it because Irish peasants were "essentially conservative" and therefore hostile to the radicalism that the antislavery vanguard appeared to represent? Was it because of the influence of the Catholic Church, which sanctioned slavery and was relentlessly critical of abolitionism? Was it because of the ethnocentrism and anti-Irish prejudice of many activists in the abolitionist movement? Or was it, as many observers have maintained, a result of intense job competition between free blacks and desperately poor Irish immigrants in the labor markets of northern cities such as Boston, New York, and Philadelphia?[38] All of these factors contributed to the growing antagonism between Black and Green on American soil. But it's worth emphasizing that the most common explanation—labor market competition—is also the least satisfactory. Nearly a million Irish men, women, and children entered the United States in the thirty years between 1815 and 1845, and in the decade after 1845 about a million and a half Irish exiles left their homeland for America. Their impact on the cities where they settled was enormous. Their sheer numbers alone would have made it so. But in addition, their poverty, their unfamiliarity with urban living, their Catholicism and clannishness—in short, their very Irishness—marked them as different, in ominous ways. Hence the legend of "No Irish Need Apply" and the long-standing belief among Irish immigrants that they faced real and persistent discrimination in the labor market. Patrick Ford, who emigrated from Galway to the United States in 1845, recalled "finding constantly that the fact that I was Irish and a Catholic was against me" when he searched for work in Boston.[39] Indeed, there was virulent anti-Irish sentiment in many quarters in the middle third of the nineteenth century, especially in New England, where Anglo-Protestant identity, and prejudice, was most strongly entrenched. In the mid-1850s the nativist backlash spread from coast to coast, and in 1854 Know-Nothing candidates—who were aggressively, often hysterically, anti-immigrant and anti-Catholic—won the mayoral elections in Boston, Philadelphia, Chicago, and San Francisco and the governors' races in Massachusetts and California.[40]

For the most part, whether because of employer discrimination or their own lack of "human capital" or some combination of the two, the Irish were disproportionately concentrated in the lower echelons of the urban labor market. The men worked in a wide swath of unskilled (and a relatively few skilled) occupations, and the women labored mainly as dressmakers, laundresses, and domestic servants. The Irish were also disproportionately represented among the sick and the incarcerated. According to Cormac Ó Gráda, they accounted for "71 per cent of all admissions" to New York City's public hospital between 1846 and 1858, and in a single year (1858) more than half of those lodged in the city's prisons were Irish-born. Overall, Ó Gráda concludes, "While life in America in the 1850s almost certainly marked an improvement on conditions in Ireland . . . , Irish immigrants fared poorly in terms of occupational mobility or wealth accumulation."[41]

But over time the Irish were to become victors, not victims, in the labor market, and relative to African Americans they were the victors early on.[42] To be sure, as late as the 1850s and early 1860s, some Irish immigrants shared residential neighborhoods and unskilled jobs with free blacks—notably, in Manhattan's infamous "Five Points," which had become, by reputation, the "world's most notorious slum." At a time when the fear of "amalgamation" was nearly pervasive among whites, the evidence of interracial sexual liaisons and even intermarriage between Irish and African American residents of the area served only to accentuate its notoriety.[43] But most Irish immigrants were quick to learn the elementary lesson that acceptance in American society would require the creation of distance, not intimacy, between Black and Green, and the sheer number of Irish job seekers, and their tendency to flood the lower echelons of the labor market, contributed significantly to the displacement of African Americans from jobs they had held for generations. As early as July 1838, an anonymous African American complained that "impoverished and destitute [foreigners], transported from the trans-atlantic shores, are crowding themselves into every place of business and of labor, and driving the poor colored American citizen out." Fifteen years later, Frederick Douglass sounded the same theme but offered a more detailed bill of particulars. "Employments and callings, formerly monopolized by us, are so no longer," he declared in 1853. "White men are becoming house-servants, cooks and stewards on vessels [and] at hotels. They are becoming porters, stevedores, wood sawyers, hod-carriers, brick-makers, white-washers, and barbers, so that the blacks can barely find the means of subsistence."[44]

So there was job competition. But over time it was much more likely to pit Irish workers against German or native-born workers, even Corkmen against Kerrymen, than it was to pit Green against Black.[45] The numbers tell much of the story. By 1855 there were 21,749 Irish-born laborers and porters in New York City, compared with 702 black laborers and porters. In Boston the disparities were equally stark: 7,007 Irish-born laborers in 1850, but only 115 black laborers; 2,292 Irish-born domestic servants, but only 48 black servants. The truth is that the free African American community was simply too small, too marginal, and too grievously victimized by the rising tide of white supremacy to provide effective competition for employment.[46]

The overall population statistics serve only to reinforce the underlying reality. In Boston the city's small black community increased by only 200 (from 1,800 to 2,000) between 1830 and 1850, whereas by the latter year, the 46,000 Irish-born people living in Boston accounted for one-third of the city's population. In New York the Irish population more than doubled between 1845 and 1860, whereas its black population, which had reached an antebellum high of 16,358 in 1840, actually declined during this period. By 1860 New York had 203,740 Irish-born residents—more, apparently, than Dublin.[47]

Beyond the economic arena, one can discern the emergence of a distinctive Irish American outlook, nurtured by the Democratic Party, the Catholic Church, and the larger ideological currents and geopolitical realities that were reshaping American society in the antebellum era. The Democrats played a major role in welcoming Irish immigrants to America and teaching them the values and mores of the White Republic. They also forged a broad cross-class alliance that brought wage laborers in northern cities and wealthy southern planters together in a dynamic political movement dedicated to the maintenance of white supremacy and intersectional unity. In embracing the Democratic Party, Irish immigrants imbibed its intense Negrophobia and reflexive hostility to the "mad and fanatical abolitionists."[48]

On a day-to-day basis the Catholic Church and its increasingly Irish hierarchy played an even greater role in socializing the American Irish and training them to be obedient Catholic communicants and loyal citizens of their adopted country. Church leaders argued that the United States was preeminently the land of the free, that its Constitution was the world's great charter of liberty, that the most ominous threat to liberty came not from slavery but from the radical abolitionists who fanned the flames of sectional conflict and denounced the Constitution as an "agreement with hell." To the members of the Catholic hierarchy, it was self-evident that America had long served as a blessed haven of refuge for a people driven from their homeland by hunger and oppression. To criticize the American republic was to jeopardize the well-being of Irish immigrants in their new home.

O'Connell called on the American Irish to "cling by the abolitionists," but to many Catholics it appeared that antislavery sentiment was synonymous with Protestant bigotry. Indeed, some abolitionists, in Ireland and the United States, were unashamedly anti-Catholic. Ireland's leading Garrisonian, the Dublin Quaker Richard Davis Webb, was at best ambivalent about O'Connell, whom he once characterized as a "double tongued pleader" and "unscrupulous liar." Like the vast majority of Irish Protestants, Webb opposed O'Connell's Repeal campaign because he feared it would lead to a Catholic Ascendancy in Ireland, or, as he put it, "the ascendancy of the most intolerant of sects" and "the most bigotted[,] priest ridden form of Christianity." When O'Connell addressed the

Cork Anti-Slavery Society, he found that his audience was "implacably opposed to his politics and had besides strong anti-Catholic prejudices." As he looked abroad, moreover, O'Connell was compelled to acknowledge that the ranks of American abolitionism included "wicked and calumniating enemies of Catholicity and of the Irish." Although the Garrisonians actively supported the cause of Irish freedom and went out of their way to disavow nativism and anti-Catholicism, even Garrison's *Liberator* allowed the publication of a screed that poked fun at "the ridiculous expression that was said to come over O'Connell's face as he crossed himself before dinner."[49]

In retrospect, it is hardly surprising that many abolitionists gave conscious and unconscious expression to a worldview that was reflexively Protestant and therefore, in the context of the nineteenth century, at least covertly anti-Catholic. Most members of the antislavery vanguard had been nurtured in religious denominations that were deeply influenced by evangelical and pietistic strains of Protestant belief. They were the inheritors of a dynamic view of history that saw the spread of liberty as the unfolding of a divine plan that had its roots in the Protestant Reformation. A corollary of this belief was the premise that chattel slavery and Roman Catholicism were both relics of an authoritarian and irrational past and that freeing the Irish from their "enslavement to Rome" was as worthy an endeavor as freeing Africans from the clutches of plantation slavery. Thus Massachusetts congressman Anson Burlingame argued that slavery and Catholicism were "in alliance by the necessity of their nature—for one denies the right of a man to his body, the other the right of a man to his soul. The one denies his right to think for himself, the other the right to act for himself."[50]

On the Catholic side of the religious divide, the church had always accepted the existence of slavery—as a necessary evil, rooted in original sin, and as an institution sanctioned by secular regimes. But in 1839 Pope Gregory XVI roiled the waters of the Atlantic World when he issued *In Supremo*, an Apostolic Letter that unequivocally condemned the slave trade and appeared—to some readers—to identify the institution of slavery as equally "unworthy of the Christian name."[51] Abolitionists seized on the letter's vehement admonition "that none henceforth dare to subject to slavery . . . Indians, negroes, or other classes of men" as decisive proof that the pope had sided with them. In fact, *In Supremo* issued no injunction to free any of the millions of men, women, and children who were already enslaved. The American Catholic hierarchy quickly mounted a counteroffensive aimed at demonstrating that "His Holiness condemns what our own laws condemn as felony—the slave trade"—and that his letter had no bearing upon "domestic slavery as it exists in the southern states and in other parts of the Christian world." Speaking on behalf of the American bishops, the *United States Catholic Miscellany* argued that "our theology is fixed." The church had "repeatedly . . . testified" over the centuries that "she regarded the possession of slave property as fully compatible with the doctrines of the gospel."

Some American bishops actually owned slaves, as did a number of the religious orders in the American South—notably, the Maryland Province of the Society of Jesus, which held nearly four hundred slaves in the 1820s.[52] At the same time, spokesmen for the American church were careful to stress that "negroes . . . are members of Jesus Christ, redeemed by his precious blood," and thus entitled "to be dealt with in a charitable, Christian paternal manner." So successful were Catholic slaveholders in implementing this injunction—Bishop John England of Charleston argued—that "I have known many freedmen who regretted their manumission."[53]

What made American Catholicism most distinctive on the question of slavery, though, was its uncompromising hostility to abolitionism. "There is no danger, no possibility . . . that Catholic theology should ever be tinctured with the fanaticism of abolition," declared the *United States Catholic Miscellany*. "No one would be recognized as a Catholic who would utter the expressions we have heard from the lips of American abolitionists." While the antislavery vanguard succeeded in dividing a number of the most important Protestant denominations in the United States, its effect on the Catholic Church was exactly the opposite. The growing power of "immediatism" served to unite the church hierarchy across sectional lines and—in practice, if not in principle—to push many Catholic spokesmen into the proslavery camp. Increasingly, they denounced the Garrisonians as "bloody-minded sectarians" and "bigots of the most despicable character." "We charge them with treason to the country," the *Boston Pilot* declared in 1839, "as conspirators against the peace of society—and as a class of tyrants of the most dangerous and treacherous character." Church leaders were eager to contrast their own patriotism and allegiance to the laws of the United States with the abolitionists' descent into lawlessness and anarchy. "Obey the public authorities," the bishops counseled the faithful; "show your attachment to the institutions of our beloved country by prompt compliance with all their requirements."[54]

In response to the Irish Address and its triumphant unveiling at Faneuil Hall, spokesmen for Irish America at first questioned the document's authenticity. Bishop John Hughes of New York, a native of County Tyrone and a rising star in the American hierarchy, declared at first that it must be a forgery. If it was not, he said, then it became "the duty of every naturalized Irishman to resist and repudiate the address with indignation." Why? Because it "emanated from a foreign source."[55] The *Natchez Free Trader*, a Mississippi newspaper with strong Irish immigrant connections, called the very idea that O'Connell and Father Mathew were associated with the Irish Address a "foul slander." Instead, the paper blamed it on "Dr. Madden."[56] Richard Robert Madden, an Irish Catholic medical doctor, author, and abolitionist, was indeed a prominent signer of the address. He had served the British government in Jamaica and Cuba in the 1830s and would do so again, in West Africa and Australia, in the 1840s. He had also developed a well-deserved reputation in Cuba, Jamaica, and the United States as a friend of the Negro and enemy of slavery and had been especially effective in puncturing the myth of slave life and labor in Cuba and other Spanish colonies as singularly benign.

After his sojourn in Cuba, Madden came to the United States and at the urging of American abolitionists became the star defense witness in the famed *Amistad* case, which led to the freeing of forty-nine captive Africans who had mutinied against the crew of their slave-trading ship and were in danger of being sent to Cuba as chattel property.[57] Although the *Natchez Free Trader* was wrong in denying O'Connell and Father Mathew's association with the Irish Address, the newspaper had picked an auspicious target in Dr. Madden, whom it called "an Irishman who has sold himself to England and his soul to Satan." In a refrain that would become increasingly prominent in Irish American political discourse, the editor charged, "Abolition is a British, not an Irish doctrine," and he refused to believe that there was a "single Irish abolitionist" in the United States.[58]

When it became clear that O'Connell *had* signed the Irish Address, other Irish Americans rushed to warn him about the reckless course he had chosen and to deplore the company he was keeping. "I pray you to leave to Americans the control of their own institutions," the corresponding secretary of the Irish Repeal Association of Louisiana wrote in April 1842. He pointed out that "even in the Northern States, where slavery does not exist, Irishmen have no feelings in common with abolitionists." Rather, "They look upon them as a band of dangerous disorganizers" whose goal was to undermine the "fabric of freedom" that Washington and other Revolutionary patriots had created. Irish emissary Thomas Mooney counseled the Liberator that "the friends of Ireland [in the United States] must be conciliated, and their efforts in your behalf must be kindly and attentively appreciated and acknowledged."[59]

O'Connell was keenly aware of the material support that Irish America could provide his Repeal campaign, but, at the same time, he could not be silent about his abhorrence of slavery. For about a year, he sought to effect a workable compromise, vowing that he would accept financial contributions from American supporters, even from southern slave owners, as long as it was understood that "while [slavery] existed, he would be its most determined enemy, whatever . . . the consequence." On occasion, however, he was downright effusive in his praise of American supporters of Repeal and, more broadly, of the American people. In February 1843 Robert Tyler, the son of the proslavery president of the United States John Tyler, made an "impromptu speech" at a meeting in Washington, DC, that not only endorsed Repeal but also concluded with a testament to the rebels of 1798 and to the violent methods they had employed in seeking their freedom. The fame of Tyler's remarks spread so rapidly that O'Connell felt compelled to respond. At a Repeal meeting in Dublin, he reiterated his long-standing commitment to nonviolence, saying that he would "not accept any political change . . . at the expense of one drop of human blood." He also vowed that "while I live, the connection with England shall not be broken." But mostly he praised Robert Tyler and his father, both of whom were slave owners, and used the occasion to emphasize "our affectionate gratitude for the sympathy of the American people. We want their sympathy and encouragement," he said, "and shall gladly receive their contributions whenever they are sent. What is my object . . . in looking for American sympathy? It is the pleasure and satisfaction it gives me to have men of intelligence, and of purity of principle and high-mindedness, joining in the struggle to which we are devoted."[60]

"Purity of principle and high-mindedness" among slaveholders? Could this be the Daniel O'Connell who had denounced the "freemen of America" as "hypocrites, tyrants, and unjust men," the "basest of the base" and "vilest of the vile"?[61] The abolitionists were distraught. Wendell Phillips, who only recently had offered effusive praise of the Liberator in public, now dismissed him privately as the "Great Beggarman." Others descended to sectarian bigotry—mocking his Catholic piety as mere "superstition" in one case, denouncing his alleged enthusiasm for "clerical domination" in another. Garrison, who printed these jibes in his paper in the name of free speech, was more principled. He acknowledged that O'Connell continued to avow "his uncompromising hostility to slavery" but expressed keen disappointment that "while he does not hate slavery less, he loves Repeal more." In a private letter, O'Connell's Irish friend James Haughton was much less circumspect. An indefatigable campaigner for abolition and temperance as well as Repeal, Haughton virtually begged the Liberator to put an end to "the unholy alliance between Irishmen and slave-dealers in America" and warned, "Do not lose your moral power . . . by the acceptance of further sympathy or aid from American 'soul-drivers.' The work of your life will be marred and destroyed by such an unholy contamination."[62]

Stung by the barbs of his American critics and sensitive to the frequent accusation by Catholic churchmen that the Garrisonians were fanatical disturbers of social order, O'Connell sought, momentarily, to distance himself from radical abolitionism. At a Repeal meeting in Dublin, he went so far as to criticize Garrison for being "something of a maniac" on "religious subjects." Ultimately, though, he took Haughton's exhortations to heart. Upon reflection, he concluded that his willingness to accept financial contributions from slave owners and to praise the likes of Robert Tyler and his father was incompatible with his core beliefs. His change of direction was occasioned by a letter from the Pennsylvania Anti-Slavery Society to the Loyal National Repeal Association, offering a point-by-point response to the apologia for slavery that was becoming a defining feature of many Irish American newspapers and Repeal associations. When the Pennsylvania letter was presented at a Repeal meeting in Dublin in May 1843, O'Connell declared, "I never heard anything read in my life that imposed more upon my feelings, and excited a deeper sympathy and sorrow within me." Remarkably, the man whom Garrison had once praised for

speaking out against the "soul-drivers of this land" more strongly than anyone "in the wide world" now exclaimed that "I never before, in fact, knew the
horrors of slavery in their genuine colors." Nor, he said, did the Irish people
know "the real state of slavery in America." But how could his countrymen and
-women who had crossed the Atlantic in search of liberty allow themselves to
become apologists for an institution that represented the complete negation of
liberty? Such a stance was not only unthinkable, it was also incompatible with
any authentic expression of Irish nationality. In one of his most poignant—but
ultimately futile—jeremiads, the Liberator called on his benighted countrymen
in America to "come out of such a land, or if you remain, and dare countenance
the system of slavery that is supported there, we will recognize you as Irishmen
no longer."[63]

Here, again, O'Connell was deploying his essentialist conception of Irishness
on behalf of a universal ideal. He reminded Irish Americans that their native
land had a long and distinctive, even unique, history of opposition to slavery. It
was "the first of all the nations of the earth that abolished the dealing in slaves."
It "never was stained with negro slave-trading," "never committed an offense
against the men of color," "never fitted out a single vessel for the traffic in blood
on the African coast." He rejoiced that at a time when Liverpool was crowded
with slave ships and thus "tainted with slavery," "not a single slaver ever sailed
from Dublin, or Drogheda, or Belfast, or Waterford, or Cork, or any other port
in Ireland." This proud history had shaped the Irish "heart"; it had entered the
Irish "blood"; it had even, in important respects, defined the Irish "nature." By
O'Connell's lights, the very air Irishmen and -women breathed should have
filled them with the elixir of freedom and reinforced their determination to
end oppression in all its forms.[64]

Actually, O'Connell was wrong (although no doubt unwittingly so) in making at least some of these claims. He was right in his assertion that slave ships did
not sail from Irish ports during the heyday of the African slave trade, although
that apparently owed more to restrictions the British Parliament imposed than
to moral qualms among Irish merchants. But he was wrong in his assumption
that Irish society remained untouched by slavery. The fact that, beginning in
the seventeenth century, Irishmen and -women were swept up in the emigrant
stream to North America and the islands of the Anglophone Caribbean made
it inevitable that Ireland would be affected by the development of the peculiar
institution. Although most Irish emigrants in the seventeenth century began
their working lives abroad as indentured servants and free wage laborers, by the
eighteenth century immigrants to the Caribbean were more likely to become
overseers or small planters—even large planters on occasion. Nicholas Tuite,
the son of an Irish emigrant from County Westmeath, accumulated a hundred
acres of land and forty-one slaves on Montserrat but found even greater opportunity as a merchant and shipowner, carrying slaves and provisions from island
to island. Ultimately, he concentrated his energy and resources on the Danish

island of Saint Croix, where by 1766 he "owned seven plantations . . . and was part owner of seven others." Antoine Walsh, who died on Saint Domingue in 1763, was even more successful. The son of a Dublin-born merchant who emigrated to France and became involved in the slave trade, Walsh lived most of his life in the ports of Saint Malo and Nantes, where he was a leading member of France's prosperous Irish community. He eventually became an *armateur*, or outfitter of ships that sailed to Africa to buy slaves. Nini Rodgers, the preeminent historian of Ireland, slavery, and abolition, estimates that he purchased more than twelve thousand Africans for export to the plantation societies of the Americas.[65]

To what extent was Irish society affected by the activities of men such as Nicholas Tuite and Antoine Walsh? Rodgers readily acknowledges that "not much in the way of slave trade profits trickled back to Ireland," but she also emphasizes that the provision trade with the West Indies—the sale of butter, salted beef and pork, and other agricultural products—had an "enormous impact" on Munster and a significant impact on Connaught as well. As the Irish at home gradually developed a taste for tobacco and sugar, they became connected, at some level, to the plantation economy and its slave labor system. By the middle of the eighteenth century, sugar had become Ireland's most valuable import, and two-thirds of its sugar supply was refined in Dublin. "Sugar fuelled the rise of the Catholic middle class," Rodgers argues, and the Catholic middle class became the foundation stone of O'Connell's campaign for Catholic Emancipation and Repeal of the Union.[66]

Nonetheless, when members of the Cincinnati Repeal Association entered the fray in the summer of 1843 with a letter that constituted a sustained apologia for American slavery, O'Connell denounced them as "pseudo Irishmen." The Cincinnati repealers acknowledged at the outset that slavery was an "evil of the highest magnitude." But they argued that it was sanctioned by the American Constitution and therefore could not be abolished; that any attempt to eradicate it would be impractical and might well imperil the survival of the Union; that "the vast majority of slaves in this country are happy and contented with their bondage"; and that the real enemy of American liberty was not chattel slavery but the abolitionists. They also repeated the familiar argument that immediate abolition was unthinkable because people of African descent were "inferior as a race[.] Slavery has stamped its debasing influences on the African," they claimed, "and between him and the white almost a century would be required to elevate the character of the one and destroy the antipathies of the other. The very odour of the negro is almost insufferable to the white; and, however humanity may lament it, we make no rash declaration when we say that the two races cannot exist on equal terms under our government and our institutions."[67]

O'Connell insisted on setting aside an entire meeting of the Repeal Association to address the Cincinnati letter. He argued by way of response that neither the American Constitution nor any other could sanction slavery, and that all Catholics must be aware that their church had condemned "slave-holding, and especially slave-trading." While he acknowledged that there were "many wicked and calumniating enemies of Catholicity and of the Irish" among the abolitionists, he counseled that the way to deal with their failings was to outdo them in seeking to abolish slavery. As for the argument that Negroes were "naturally inferior," he dismissed it as a "totally gratuitous assertion" and ridiculed the claim that the "odour of the negroes" was "insufferable." He agreed that Negroes "have not as yet come to use much . . . eau de Cologne," but reminded his exiled countrymen that it was all too common for white men—slave owners—to have sexual relations with black women. Clearly, the "odour" of female slaves had not been a deterrent to these liaisons, which continued to produce "multitudes of . . . children."[68]

Ultimately, though, his basic argument was that "genuine Irishmen" could not possibly *think* as these "pseudo Irishmen" thought. "How can the generous, the charitable, the humane, the noble emotions of the Irish heart have become extinct among you?" he demanded.

> How can your *nature* be so totally changed? . . . It was not in Ireland you learned this cruelty. Your mothers were gentle, kind, and humane. Their bosoms overflowed with the honey of human charity. Your sisters are probably, many of them, still amongst us, and participate in all that is good and benevolent in sentiment and action. How, then, can you have become so depraved?[69]

When he uttered these words in October 1843, O'Connell was approaching seventy, and his health was beginning to fail. He was also facing other challenges—in Ireland, Britain, and Irish America—that would soon diminish his power and reputation. At home a new generation of Irish nationalists was beginning to contest his leadership and his hitherto-sacrosanct principles. In Britain the Tory government was determined to use the tried-and-true methods of repression to thwart his demand for Repeal, first by outlawing his monster meetings and then by imprisoning him. In Irish America, O'Connell seems to have taken it for granted that his status as the leader of his people was secure and that he could bend his exiled countrymen and -women to his will. But the same middle-class elements—the merchants, professionals, and "strong" farmers—who had been the bedrock of his support in Ireland were refusing to conduct the struggle for Repeal on his terms in America. In the South, especially, these men were Protestants as well as Catholics; many of them had achieved positions of affluence and respect in their local communities; some were slave owners. By now, they understood all too well that breaking with the proslavery consensus that reigned supreme among southern whites would jeopardize not only their economic interests but also their status as free men who were worthy of the blessings of liberty. Thus members of the Baltimore Repeal Association resolved that they would "repel, with feelings of disgust and

abhorrence," the call to throw themselves into the arms of the abolitionists—
"those desperate fanatics, who, to abolish negro servitude, would wreck and
crush a world of freedom." In Charleston the leaders of the Repeal Association
went even further and announced that they were dissolving their organization,
for one reason: O'Connell's denunciation of slavery in the United States and his
assault on the character of American slaveholders, particularly the Irish among
them. When the Liberator insisted that they choose between loyalty to their
state and allegiance to his Repeal Association, their response was unequivocal:
"We say South Carolina forever."[70]

For the moment at least, most repealers, in the South as well as the North,
refused to see a contradiction between Irish nationalism and American patriotism. But insofar as O'Connell compelled them to choose, many of them has-
tened to affirm that they would "never forsake" the United States. Surely a politician as flexible and opportunistic as O'Connell was alleged to be would have
reconsidered his course as he became aware of the turmoil he had caused in the
Repeal movement, including the dissolution of Repeal associations in Charleston; Natchez, Mississippi; and Milledgeville, Georgia. Instead, even though his
relationship with Irish America hung in the balance, he persisted in his assault
on American slavery.[71]

The issue of slavery and abolition, and its ramifications for O'Connell's leadership in Ireland and Irish America, became even more volatile in 1845. In December of that year the U.S. government annexed the breakaway republic of
Texas as a slave state, and then—beginning in 1846—it invaded Mexico and
seized more than half a million square miles of its territory. A decade earlier,
rebellious Texans, most of them settlers from the United States, had declared
their independence from Mexico and defeated the armed forces of Mexican
president Antonio López de Santa Anna. Inevitably, the fate of Texas became
intertwined with the issue of slavery. The Mexican constitution of 1835, which
abolished the institution, had been one of the factors that led to the Texans' declaration of independence, and by 1840 Negro slaves made up about 20 percent
of the Lone Star Republic's population. Mexico warned that any attempt by the
United States to annex its "stolen" territory would mean war. Britain, meanwhile, actively sought to pull Texas into its orbit and hoped to use its influence
to achieve the abolition of slavery there. The specter of English interference on
terrain that "rightly" belonged to the United States served to intensify American Anglophobia. The governor of Mississippi denounced Britain as "a wily
nation that has never failed to do us injury" and as the "national personifica-
tion [of] stealthily advancing" abolitionism. Ashbel Smith, Texas's emissary in
London, warned that Britain's "ultimate purpose" was "to make Texas a refuge
for runaway slaves from the United States, and eventually a negro nation, a
sort of Hayti on the [North American] continent." Abolitionists appeared to
validate this apprehension with declarations—such as the urgent plea of former

president John Quincy Adams— that "the freedom of this country and of all mankind depends upon the direct, formal, open, and avowed interference of Great Britain to accomplish the abolition of slavery in Texas."[72]

Together, the annexation of Texas and the Mexican War became an especially volatile arena for working out a racialized sense of American Manifest Destiny. Many Anglo-Americans regarded the dark-skinned, "mongrelized" people of Mexico as racially inferior and believed that their allegiance to the Catholic Church left them in a state of "Ignorance, Superstition, Idolatry and Vice." Some opposed the incursion into Mexico for that reason; others claimed that the westward march of American power would mean the spread of Protestantism and the triumph of the Anglo-Saxon race. The reality was more complex. Britain, the quintessential symbol of Anglo-Saxonism, supported Mexico (while refusing to provide military assistance to its besieged ally). Irish Americans largely ignored the talk of importing "English blood" and the Protestant religion into Texas and, in most cases, became strong supporters of the war. They saw it as an opportunity to assert their allegiance to the United States and as a means of enhancing American power at the expense of Britain. "The hatred of the Irish population among us toward England is of a bitter and most implacable type," Garrison reported in 1845, "and it all goes in favor of the annexation of Texas." Almost half of the soldiers who fought in the U.S. forces that invaded Mexico were foreign-born. Many of them chafed under the harsh regimen that nativist officers imposed, and there were unusually large numbers of desertions. Some Irish recruits went over to the other side and fought for Mexico as members of the famed "San Patricios," or Saint Patrick's Battalion. Robert Ryal Miller has confirmed the names of forty San Patricios, most of them deserters from U.S. Army units, who were born in Ireland. But there were thousands of Irish immigrants in the ranks of the U.S. Army, and many of them fought valiantly for their adopted country.[73]

Sensing widespread discontent among American soldiers, the Mexican government sought to appeal to Catholic enlistees and to the Irish in particular. "Irishmen!" a leaflet from General Santa Anna implored. "Listen to the words of your brothers, hear the accents of a Catholic people. . . . Is religion no longer the strongest of human bonds? Can you fight by the side of those who put fire to your [churches and convents] in Boston and Philadelphia?" The leaflet concluded by reminding the Irish that "you were expected to be just because you are the countrymen of that truly great and eloquent man, O'Connell, who has devoted his whole life to defend your rights."[74]

O'Connell threw his full support behind the "colored" "half-Indians" of Mexico. Although he was keenly aware of the complex religious and racial dimensions of the conflict, it was the issue of slavery that determined his allegiance. He mocked the pretensions of self-proclaimed "Anglo-Saxon civilizers," pointing out that the "Papists" of Mexico "have abolished negro slavery, while the sublime religionists of Texas . . . have introduced, and perpetuated . . . that most abominable and unchristian practice." To counteract the designs of the "marauding" Texans, he sought to sponsor a "powerful colony" of free blacks and escaped slaves on territory ceded by the Mexican republic, "either subject directly to the British Crown or . . . under the protection of the British flag" and dedicated to helping "persons of colour . . . become purchasers of the soil." Failing in that endeavor, he implored Britain to intervene directly to block the further extension of slavery in North America. Ironically, at the very moment he was telling friends at home that the British people's "hatred [of] Ireland and Catholicity" made it necessary to mobilize Catholic Ireland to fight—on its own—for Repeal, he was declaring that "the British people must be roused" in the fight against the westward expansion of slavery. Once they understood the stakes in Texas, he declared, "British humanity would . . . rally and support the oppressed." Ultimately, his hope was that "Anglo-Saxon" Britain would unite with "Papist" Mexico against "Anglo-Saxon" America, and he offered the allegiance of Catholic Ireland as a large part of the prize. Speaking in Dublin in March 1845, he declared, the British "can have us[;] . . . the throne of Victoria can be made perfectly secure—the honor of the British empire maintained— and the American eagle, in its highest pride of flight, be brought down. Let them but . . . give us the Parliament in [Dublin's] College Green, and Oregon shall be theirs, and Texas shall be harmless."[75]

O'Connell had, in a sense, come to the end of the road. Few of the forces he counted on were prepared to stand with him in defending Mexico and seeking to thwart the westward expansion of slavery. Insofar as he implied that Irishmen, including Irish immigrants in the United States, would take up arms in support of Britain's efforts to check American territorial aggrandizement, he was—as a growing chorus of critics pointed out—deluding himself. In a typical Irish American response, the members of the Norfolk and Portsmouth (Virginia) Repeal Association expressed shock and disappointment that "Mr. O'Connell . . . is ready to aid and assist the British nation in the destruction of this free and happy country," and they resolved that "as American citizens, whether native or adopted," they would "cheerfully and steadfastly support and protect the American eagle, in its onward and upward flight, against *every* foe."[76]

Even the British people, apart from the ranks of their most zealous anti-slavery advocates, were hardly disposed to interfere in the internal affairs of a powerful nation thousands of miles from the heart of the empire. Nor was their government prepared to risk war—at this time and on this terrain—in an effort to obstruct the self-proclaimed Manifest Destiny of the United States. Moreover, in continuing to speak the language and promote the agenda of abolitionism, O'Connell was not only shattering the bonds that linked him to his countrymen across the Atlantic but also opening the door to challenges from other elements in the nationalist movement at home. Thus the *Freeman's Journal*, a Catholic and nationalist "repeal newspaper" that had strongly endorsed the Liberator's critique of American slavery, now supported the U.S. annexation of Texas and welcomed the prospect of war between Britain and the United States because, its editors reasoned, England's difficulty might well become Ireland's opportunity.[77]

Speaking through the pages of the *Nation*, the men and women of Young Ireland went much further than any of the Repeal newspapers in developing a thoroughgoing critique of the Liberator's politics.[78] They chafed at his allegiance to the agenda of the Irish Catholic hierarchy. They became increasingly restive in the face of his stubborn reliance on moral force as the only legitimate means to win his objectives. They were embarrassed by his unfailing—and, some argued, obsequious—gestures of allegiance to the British monarchy. Gradually, some of them dared to imagine an agenda that went far beyond Repeal to the quest for an independent Ireland, achieved by physical force. However, their criticism of O'Connell's stance on American slavery and its relationship to Irish nationalism was essentially narrow, opportunistic, and conspicuously amoral. Like most de facto apologists for the peculiar institution, they began by condemning slavery, but they also characterized it as a "minor and external subject" insofar as Ireland was concerned. They denied that their country had a "Quixotic mission to address all the wrongs of humanity"—certainly not in America, where "the men of the southern states must not have their institutions interfered with, whether right or wrong." Increasingly, as a famine of unprecedented magnitude devastated Ireland and its people, they reaffirmed their belief that the "abolition of *white* slavery" must take precedence over any external task.[79]

A few Young Irelanders—notably, the insurrectionist John Mitchel and his close friend and ally the Catholic priest Father John Kenyon—went even further and emerged as unashamed apologists for chattel slavery. Father Kenyon was becoming one of the new nationalism's most ardent, and useful, polemicists. As a Catholic, he challenged the perception that Young Ireland was essentially Protestant in outlook and agenda. Indeed, through the pages of the *Nation* and other publications, he wielded his pen in explicit opposition to what he characterized as "Quaker fancies" and Protestant "fanaticism." His goal was not only to undermine O'Connell's esteemed place within the nationalist movement but also to associate the Liberator of Catholic Ireland with Protestant heresy. He argued that the Bible did not condemn slavery as a crime, nor had the Catholic Church ever "defined it to be such." He attacked O'Connell's commitment to moral force and his refusal to countenance the shedding of blood to achieve his objectives. "No law, natural or revealed, makes bloodshedding a crime," he argued. He warned that O'Connell's doctrine of moral force, if taken to its logical conclusions, was "subversive of all government" and "a proposition . . . only on the side of fanaticism."[80]

It is undeniable that O'Connell's quest to win Irish America for the cause of abolition was a near-complete failure. In spite of his exalted reputation and long record of leadership in his own country, he was unable to mobilize the

American Irish beneath his antislavery banner. Indeed, the "blasts" from his "bugle" served mainly to unite them in opposition to his interference in the internal affairs of their adopted country. As George Potter put it, "They heeded his words on an Irish issue. They told him to go to the devil on an American issue."[81]

The sources of his failure were many. They were rooted in his unyielding commitment to principle and in his ego—notably, his insistence that leadership rightly belonged in his hands and in those of his increasingly sclerotic entou- ~sclerotic rage. But they were rooted, above all, in the circumstances that overwhelmed him at a moment when his physical vulnerability and impending death only reinforced his growing incapacity. In the name of Christianity, and in fidelity to his own vision of the essential meaning of the Irish nation, he asked his countrymen and -women to embrace a number of interrelated phenomena that many of them—especially in the United States—saw as alien to their interests and incompatible with their evolving sense of identity. He implored Irish emigrants not only to reject chattel slavery but also to embrace the Negro and the cause of racial equality. He declared himself an abolitionist and called on Irish America to stand with these "mad" and "fanatical" creatures. After writing his *Memoir on Ireland: Native and Saxon* and declaring that the "savages" of the most uncivilized portions of the earth "never were, nor could have been, guilty of such barbarities, as were the monsters who administered the English Government in Ireland," he nonetheless asked the Irish people to unite with Britain in contesting the westward expansion of slavery on the North American continent.[82] He did so at a time when Anglophobia was spreading like wildfire in the United States and charges that abolitionists were willing instruments of Britain's attempt to subvert America's Manifest Destiny were increasingly common.

His embrace of perfidious Albion became even more problematic in the light of events at home. Less than six months after his effusive declaration that Britain "can have us," the failure of much of Ireland's potato crop signaled the coming of an unprecedented catastrophe that would allow Young Ireland's John Mitchel to argue persuasively that "the Almighty, indeed, sent the potato blight, but the English created the Famine."[83] Together with a succession of British policies that served to magnify the scale of the suffering, the wholesale destruction of a way of life based on potato cultivation caused the death of more than a million Irish and—over the course of a decade—the emigration of many more. In this appalling context, O'Connell could do nothing to reverse the tide. Acknowledging that Ireland was starving, he could only ask, "What is to be done?"[84] Like the health of the nation whose destiny he saw as synonymous with his own aspirations and leadership, his physical condition rapidly deteriorated. He died in Genoa, during an aborted pilgrimage to Rome, in May 1847.

While acknowledging O'Connell's failure, it is also necessary to recognize the boldness of his vision and the existential logic of his manifold allegiances. Father Kenyon may not have been altogether wrong in implying that the Liberator thought and sounded like a Protestant "heretic." Of course, he was a staunch and devout Catholic—the leading Catholic layman in all of Europe. But his commitment to the abolition of slavery came from the deep wellsprings of his Christian faith, not from the institutional church. He was driven by an inner light, by a compulsion to bear witness on behalf of his beliefs, that was reminiscent of John Woolman, perhaps even Martin Luther. Whereas the Catholic Church in Ireland remained largely silent on the question of slavery, and the church in America became an outspoken defender of the institution's compatibility with the "doctrines of the gospel," O'Connell felt compelled to declare, "Slavery, I denounce you wherever you are! Come freedom, come oppression to Ireland—let Ireland be as she may—I will have my conscience clear before my God."[85]

This is what led him into the ranks of radical abolitionism. True, in 1843 he denounced the radicals and singled out Garrison for a special gesture of contempt. But his language, his choice of allies, and in important respects his view of the world—all kept leading him back to the Garrisonians. Like them he was a "disorganizer" and a "come-outer" where slavery was concerned. (Garrison claimed him as a fellow "disorganizer" as early as 1831.)[86] The Garrisonians felt obligated to come out of corrupt institutions and went so far as to call upon the North to come out of the Union with the South, to renounce the American Constitution in the name of a higher, divinely ordained law. O'Connell called on the Irish in the United States to "come out of such a land"—if not out of the United States, then "out of the councils of the iniquitous, and out of the congregation of the wicked, who consider man a chattel and a property, and liberty an inconvenience." He was a Garrisonian also in his opposition to violence and his belief that unrelenting agitation could create a public opinion and a moral force that would transform the world. "We are engaged in a strife not of strength but of argument," he wrote to the American abolitionist and women's rights advocate Lucretia Mott. "Our warfare is not military; it is Christian. . . . We rely entirely on reason and persuasion . . . and on the emotions of benevolence and charity which are more lovely and permanent amongst women than amongst men." No wonder that by 1845 Garrison was again hailing him as the "incorruptible Liberator of Ireland."[87]

What stands out most about O'Connell's relations with Irish Americans is the boldness and willful indiscretion of his harsh and unrelenting critique of the hubris of their adopted home. For him, no country that condoned the enslavement of human beings had the right to celebrate its commitment to liberty. He came to believe that the "air of America" engendered not a love of freedom but an attachment to slavery; not the validation of the stirring words of the Declaration of Independence but, rather, the unimpeachable evidence of Americans' hypocrisy and moral depravity. In preaching to his countrymen and -women across the Atlantic, he turned America's republican discourse upside down. For him, it was axiomatic that not only the experience of oppression but also the "natal air" of the Irish people made *them* the friends of humanity. Thus they were obligated to "cling by the abolitionists," to embrace the Negro as friend and fellow citizen, and thereby to honor their native land and its core principles as he defined them. "Wherever the Irish are known throughout the world," he insisted, "they are known as the friends of humanity." How could it be, then, that "those who are humane everywhere else [are] cruel in America"?[88]

Clearly, O'Connell's Ireland was in part the creation of his imagination; it was, in some respects, far removed from the complex realities of Irish history and of his own times. But in important respects, too, he had the charisma and the power to make his vision of Ireland become a major component of the contested discourse of Irish nationalism. At Repeal meetings in Dublin, his audiences burst into applause and cheered when he announced his unconditional opposition to slavery; they *knew* that as the leader of the Irish nation, he was also "the friend of liberty in every clime, class, and color." Irishmen and -women wrote to friends and family in America asking how it was that they could oppose O'Connell's criticism of the "enemies of liberty," how it was that they had ceased to be Irish.[89]

At times O'Connell pitted his commitment to the abolition of slavery against his obligations to Ireland and, remarkably, chose the former. He recalled a moment, early in his career in Parliament, when the West India interest offered to support him on Irish issues if he would remain silent on slavery. He responded, "May my right hand forget its cunning, and my tongue cleave to the roof of my mouth, if to save Ireland—even Ireland, I forget the Negro one single hour."[90] But mostly he simply assumed that identification with the cause of suffering humanity flowed naturally and inevitably from the historical experience of the Irish people and the shaping of their character over the centuries. As Irishmen and -women departed from their homeland in ever-larger numbers, he envisioned the emigrants as a new generation of "Wild Geese," fighting not for the Catholic monarchies of Europe in this instance but against slavery and every form of oppression, wherever it existed. Unlike Hungary's Louis Kossuth and a new generation of European nationalists who came of age in the 1840s, he refused to trim his sails on questions of human liberty, refused to come, hat in hand, before the councils of the mighty American Republic and turn a blind eye to slavery and systemic racial inequality. "We are struggling for liberty ourselves," he declared, "and we would not deserve to be free, if we countenanced [slavery's] existence in any other part of the world."[91]

CHAPTER FOUR

"The Black O'Connell of the United States"

FREDERICK DOUGLASS AND IRELAND

> Behold the change! . . . Instead of a democratic government, I am
> under a monarchical government. Instead of the bright blue sky of
> America, I am covered with the soft grey fog of the Emerald Isle. I
> breathe and lo! the chattel becomes a man.
>
> —Frederick Douglass, January 1846

> In America the slave is called a slave—he is black, and is flogged. In
> Ireland he is called a labourer—he is white, and is only starved.
>
> —Irish abolitionist Ebenezer Shackleton, 1840

UNTIL HIS DEATH IN 1847, and for a generation thereafter, O'Connell remained a revered international symbol of the antislavery movement.[1] No matter how much Irish immigrants disappointed them, the Garrisonians could take ample consolation from their belief that the Liberator was the voice of Ireland.[2] Indeed, for them O'Connell *was* Ireland; they created the green isle of their imaginations out of his stirring words and larger-than-life persona. Garrison hailed the Irish Address as a "noble gift of Ireland to America" that "strengthen[ed] her claim to be the 'first flower of the earth, and first gem of the sea.'" John A. Collins persuaded himself that "O'Connell and all the Irish of Ireland are abolitionists"; those who were not, Garrison argued, must be "bastard Irishmen" who "cannot have a drop of genuine Irish blood running in their veins."[3]

As the antebellum era unfolded, more and more American reformers had the opportunity to visit the Emerald Isle. Among black abolitionists, in particular, the contrast between the near-pervasive racism they encountered in the United States and the warm reception they received abroad proved to be a pivotal—and, for some, a transformative—experience. Charles Lenox Remond reported that during his sojourn in England, Scotland, and Ireland, "there had been no show of disrespect, no brutal taunts, no scornful looks," nothing to "grieve his soul" or cause him to flee in search of a more congenial environment. On the contrary, he was "hailed as a man—cherished as a brother—caressed as a friend." Frederick Douglass recalled that on this terrain he first "breathed an atmosphere congenial to the longings of his spirit, and felt his manhood free and unrestricted."[4] Here, too, he met the great O'Connell. Douglass maintained that as a boy in Maryland,

"I heard his denunciation of slavery, I heard my master curse him, and therefore I loved him." He loved O'Connell all the more when they shared the stage at a Repeal meeting in Dublin and the Liberator introduced him to the throng at Conciliation Hall as "the Black O'Connell of the United States." He basked in the glow of the comparison and marveled as the Immortal Dan proceeded to speak out against American slavery with singular passion and eloquence. It was on this occasion that O'Connell made his famous declaration that "wherever tyranny exists, I am the foe of the tyrant; wherever oppression shows itself, I am the foe of the oppressor; wherever slavery rears its head, I am the enemy of the system. . . . My sympathy with distress . . . extends itself to every corner of the earth."[5]

The black abolitionists' sense of comfort and security in Ireland undoubtedly derived in part from the fact that during their sojourn there they lived largely within the confines of a sympathetic community that sought to be attentive to their every need. But even among wider sections of the Irish people, the simple fact of their presence—and complexion—would not have marked them as altogether novel. Historian William A. Hart has estimated that more than two thousand Africans and people of African descent were in Ireland during the second half of the eighteenth century. A few blacks were musicians and actors; some were drummers in British regiments; most were domestic servants; and for much of the eighteenth century at least some of these servants were slaves. Hart argues that in retrospect "there is no disguising the existence of slavery in Ireland at this time, nor that it was restricted, in practice, to black people from Africa and the East Indies." Insofar as there was slavery, however, its boundaries were porous; the path from slave to indentured servant to free wage laborer was, in relative terms, easily traveled, and there was no Irish legislation relating to slavery. Newspaper references to blacks as slaves virtually disappeared in the early 1770s, at about the time of Britain's famed Somerset case.[6]

As "Africans" sojourning in a European society, Remond and Douglass had some distinguished predecessors in Ireland—most notably, the ex-slave, best-selling author, and abolitionist icon Olaudah Equiano, who spent eight months there in 1791. His remarkable autobiography, *The Interesting Narrative of the Life of Olaudah Equiano*, went through nine English-language editions in six years. The fourth edition, which was printed in Dublin, eventually sold nineteen hundred copies in Ireland, nearly as many as Thomas Paine's *Rights of Man*.[7] Equiano was a convert to Christianity, and his vivid portrayal of his conversion experience was bound to resonate with the literate Protestant population of the north of Ireland, where he spent much of his time. But he was also sympathetic to the secular, radical currents that were circulating in the Atlantic World, and in Belfast he developed warm relations with members of the Society of United Irishmen such as Samuel Neilson, whose friends nicknamed him "the Jacobin," and Thomas McCabe, who called himself the "Irish Slave."[8]

Remond and Douglass had a quite different predecessor in the itinerant preacher John Jea. Like Equiano, Jea was a man of wide experience; indeed, both of them were citizens of the Atlantic World and pioneers of the Black Atlantic.[9] Jea was born in southern Nigeria. In the early 1770s, when he was two years old, he, his parents, and his siblings were forcibly transported to the North American mainland aboard a slave ship. He grew up in a Dutch household in rural Kings County, New York, in a family that belonged to the conservative Dutch Reformed Church. According to his own recollection, he had a conversion experience at the age of fifteen and learned to read the Bible, in "the English and Dutch languages," by the medium of miraculous literacy. His conversion led to his deliverance—not only from sin but also from slavery. By the 1790s he had become an electrifying preacher, and when he signed on for an ocean voyage as a ship's cook, he felt called to carry the good news of the Gospels far and wide.[10]

In his published autobiography, *The Life, History, and Unparalleled Sufferings of John Jea, the African Preacher,* Jea reported that he arrived in Ireland in 1803 and stayed for two years, taking an Irishwoman as his wife before departing on his next mission. Fortuitously, he lived there on the eve of Irish Protestantism's "Second Reformation," which aimed to overcome the "falsehood and folly" that Protestants deemed inherent in the Catholic faith by converting the benighted Irish masses to "true" Christianity.[11] The Second Reformation was evangelical in its inspiration and leadership, and although it mobilized segments of virtually every Protestant denomination, it found an especially congenial home among Irish Methodists. Jea was, by denominational affiliation, a Methodist, but his theology and religious practice verged on Pentecostalism, and his ministry derived its authority only from the power of his preaching. He had no church, and there is little or no evidence that any clergymen, of any denomination, cooperated in his work. But he claimed that in Limerick, where he spent most of his time while in Ireland, "the brethren and sisters in Christ gladly received me." Indeed, "the prosperity of the work of the Lord in this place was . . . like unto Pentecost," and "the fame of my preaching spread through the country, even from Limerick to Cork." Jea also testified that he had engaged in a series of polemical exchanges with "Roman" clergymen, and that after one of these encounters, they "went out full of rage and fury, and determined to lay in wait for my life."[12]

Although Jea was too idiosyncratic and isolated to fit comfortably within the institutional framework of the Second Reformation, his preaching clearly reflected one of its most salient characteristics—namely, the linkage between the evangelical Protestant impulse and a deeply rooted anti-Catholicism.[13] This became an important subtext of the evolution of abolitionism in Ireland, which developed first among members of the Religious Society of Friends in the 1780s and then, in the late 1820s and early 1830s, among evangelical Protestants from a number of religious denominations.[14] Numerically, the Religious Society of Friends was a small sect. In the early nineteenth century, it had about 4,500 adherents in Ireland, with perhaps 650 of them living in Dublin. Many of its members were descended from veterans of Cromwell's army who, in the aftermath of their ruthless suppression of the Irish Catholic uprising of the 1640s, settled on confiscated lands, renounced war, and built a religious community that was set apart from the world and yet deeply engaged with it.[15] The Quakers became legendary for their economic success, and their commitment to philanthropic endeavor earned them widespread respect. They were also part of an international network that linked them closely to their coreligionists in England and North America. Through these affiliations, they emerged as leaders of a movement to abolish slavery that encompassed much of the Atlantic World.

The Quakers' position within Ireland's polarized religious landscape was unique. In the words of one of their own, they formed a "third party, not quite the same as either Catholics or Protestants," and to a remarkable degree, they were able to work with both.[16] But by the late 1820s a new force was germinating on Irish soil, as zealous evangelicals from a number of Protestant denominations turned their attention to slavery and began to address it in their own distinctive way. In 1829 evangelical Protestants took the lead in founding the Dublin Negro's Friend Society, and several of the society's organizers began a tour of Irish cities and towns that engendered an unprecedented commitment to immediate abolition. Many of the society's mass meetings were held in Protestant churches—most often, in Methodist meetinghouses. In fact, the leadership and membership of the Dublin (soon to be Hibernian) Negro's Friend Society overlapped to a significant degree with that of the Hibernian Bible Society, which was notoriously anti-Catholic in ethos and intent.[17]

The other major pillar of the evolving antislavery movement in Ireland was O'Connell himself. Without asking permission of anyone in the hierarchy of the Catholic Church, he identified Catholicism with the cause of abolition and adopted the evangelical trait of "looking at Slavery as a Sin, wherever it exists, and . . . declaring war against it, over the whole globe."[18] It is a testament to the depth of O'Connell's commitment to abolition that he increased his own involvement in the movement at the very moment when evangelical antislavery was taking off, even though he was keenly aware of the "Orange" coloration of the Second Reformation and believed that the Wesleyan Methodists, in particular, were the determined enemies of Catholicism and of the religious liberty he cherished. "In the long struggle the Catholics of Ireland made for the abolition of the laws that infringed freedom of conscience," he reminded them, "*you* never gave us any assistance. On the contrary, you were found in the adverse ranks, active, persevering, virulent!"[19]

Charles Lenox Remond was the first of the nineteenth century's growing cadre of black abolitionists to visit Ireland. A native of Salem, Massachusetts, he was the oldest son of John Remond, an immigrant from Curaçao in the Dutch West Indies. For the first twelve years of his life, John Remond was a slave in Curaçao. In 1798 he arrived in Salem aboard a merchant vessel and, over time, achieved remarkable success—as a businessman, leader of the black church and the wider black community, and member of the Federalist Party. He was also one of the first African Americans to take out a life membership in the New England Anti-Slavery Society. Along with Charles's maternal grandfather, who had been a landowner in nearby Newton and a patriot during the Revolutionary War, John Remond offered his son an unusually firm foundation upon which to take his stand in life. But far more than his father, who had lived the liberating transition from slavery to freedom and had achieved a modicum of economic success and security, Charles experienced the increasing racial oppression and exclusion that made his childhood home a place that was "almost fatally infected with prejudice against the African color." As a white antislavery activist recalled, "Respectable, intelligent, well-dressed, well-behaved colored people . . . were . . . insulted and outraged . . . [whenever] they presumed to exercise the plainest, most simple of the inalienable rights of humanity."[20] Remond responded by becoming an abolitionist. He heard Garrison speak as early as 1831 and soon joined the ranks of his closest and most trusted black supporters. In 1838 he was the first African American appointed to the position of traveling lecturer by the American Anti-Slavery Society. Described as "small," "spare," "neat," and "genteel in his personal appearance," he gave unstintingly of himself to the cause and became, by reputation, "one of abolition's most effective speakers." Indeed, the *Liberator* reported that his manner of speaking was "peculiarly dignified," his language was "pure and chaste, and his enunciation . . . perfect."[21]

Remond accompanied Garrison to England in 1840 to attend the World Anti-Slavery Convention and remained abroad for seventeen months. In England and Scotland, he defended the cause of Garrisonian abolitionism at a time when much of the British antislavery movement had turned against Garrison and his allies, who were now, in George Thompson's memorable words, "despised, disparaged, and everywhere spoken against."[22] One of the key weapons in the assault on Garrison was a widely circulated letter by the Reverend Nathaniel Colver, a Baptist minister in Boston, who charged that the editor of the *Liberator* "so identifies himself with *every infidel fanaticism* which floats, as to have lost his hold on the good." In these daunting circumstances, Remond tried mightily to stem the tide of defections from the Garrisonian camp. During one thirty-day period, he spoke so often that he virtually collapsed from "loss of voice and strength."[23]

He arrived in Ireland in May 1841 and stayed for nearly six months. Far more than in England and Scotland, he encountered "receptive and overflowing crowds," not only in Dublin but also in Wexford, Waterford, Limerick, Belfast, and other cities and towns. Richard D. Webb reported that the American visitor addressed six meetings in Dublin, four at the Friends' Meetinghouse and two at the Presbyterian Church. All of them were well attended, and at one, in particular, "The room was crowded almost to suffocation, but the attention and zeal of the audience could not be surpassed." From Dublin, Remond journeyed

4.1. Charles Lenox Remond (courtesy of the Boston Public Library / Prints Department)

south to Wexford in the company of Richard Webb's brother James, where they held three crowded meetings. In nearby Waterford, he spoke to a large and enthusiastic audience at the town hall. Altogether, he delivered five lectures in Waterford, a place Richard Webb had characterized as "apathetic," but in fact the number of people clamoring to hear Remond was so large that his hosts finally had to begin charging admission to keep the attendance manageable. Then it was on to Limerick, where he gave three lectures, to a bigger audience each time. Richard Webb reported that the last of these gatherings was the "most crowded and the most attentive meeting I ever attended."[24]

Toward the end of the summer, Richard Webb took Remond on an outing to the coast of County Clare, in Ireland's wild and scenic west. Webb was a sober Quaker, well-to-do printer, and descendant of Cromwellian settlers who nonetheless regarded himself as one of the "hot-headed, excitable Irish."[25] His description of their adventure together must rank as one of the most extraordinary reports from Ireland ever to appear in the pages of the *Liberator*. Their travels took them from Loop Head, on the southwestern tip of the Clare coast, where the mighty Shannon River emptied into the Atlantic, to the Cliffs of Moher, which Webb described as "some of the highest ocean cliffs in Ireland, or perhaps in the world." Here, Webb marveled, the "wild waves of the Atlantic . . . fret and fume, and swell, and roar, and foam, and thunder, and gnaw, and dance," and "keep up an everlasting tumult." This was Ireland's land- and seascape at its most romantic, and also a place where much of the population was more quintessentially "wild Irish" than anything Remond could have encountered in Dublin or Waterford or, for that matter, in nearby Limerick. Accompanied by a bagpiper who added soul-stirring music to the mix, the dark-skinned Remond's meeting with the pale-faced "primitives" of Ireland's remote west was an event that no one could have scripted in advance.

> Men, women, and children followed us along the cliffs, along the roads, and into the cabins—for there are no houses. The people are chiefly remarkable for beautiful hazel eyes, fairly divided among both sexes—and a great profusion of lovely faces among the women—bare legs, tattered garments, great poverty, wonderful good humor, and original simplicity and ignorance of the rest of the world. . . . How the music set them going! They ran, and jumped, and laughed, and showed their fine white teeth, that might drive a dentist to despair. They crowded round us—stared and chattered in Irish . . . as intelligibly to us as the lingo of the New Zealanders was to Captain Cook when he first landed among them. . . .
>
> Remond agreed he had never seen more poverty, a denser rural population, or so many laughing eyes and pleasant faces, as he witnessed yesterday. The cheerfulness and light-hearted gaiety of all these poor people is wonderful.

Webb concluded that "such a wild halloo as [the piper's] music and Remond's [complexion] set up in the primitive district we travelled, nobody could conceive."[26]

In the arena of antislavery proselytizing, the American visitor's labors continued to yield a rich harvest. In the company of Richard Allen, he journeyed to Belfast, where the antislavery movement had been "in great measure asleep." But "at no place in Ireland were there greater meetings, than at Belfast," Allen reported; "at no place did greater enthusiasm prevail." Thanks to Remond's efforts, contributions even came from "places inland," away from the major coastal cities and towns, where, according to Allen, "we hardly thought the anti-slavery cause was known; but the fame of Remond's advocacy has spread far and wide, and enlisted the sympathy of thousands for the slave."[27]

Four years later, Frederick Douglass embarked on a tour of Ireland that was even more of a triumph. Although he was born a slave and did not achieve legal emancipation from slavery until his twenty-ninth year, Douglass was, undeniably, "one of the giants of nineteenth-century America." Perhaps his most remarkable feature was his unerring capacity to create and sustain an authentic sense of selfhood in a society that insisted on regarding him as less than fully human.[28] Born on Maryland's Eastern Shore, probably in February 1818, he barely knew his slave mother and never knew his father, although the combination of rumor and the boy's color made it clear that his father was white. Raised by his maternal grandmother, Betsy Bailey, and given the name Frederick Bailey as a child, Douglass was at first shielded from the harsh regimen of slave life. But as he matured in age and physical stature, he went from house servant in Baltimore to field hand on a Maryland plantation, where the notorious "nigger-breaker" Edward Covey flogged him regularly as a means of crushing his spirit and conditioning him for slave labor. Characteristically, Douglass refused to be broken. Instead, in his first great act of self-creation, he struck back at his tormentor and bested him in a desperate struggle that lasted, he later recalled, for "nearly two hours." It was a major step on young Frederick Bailey's road to freedom, which took him back to Baltimore, where, dressed as a merchant seaman, he escaped to New York City in September 1838. From there, he journeyed to Massachusetts and found work as a day laborer on the wharves of New Bedford.[29]

With its strong abolitionist presence and sizable community of free blacks, New Bedford was—in William McFeely's words— "the best city in America for an ambitious young black man."[30] Douglass's life there was marked by hard work on the docks, but also by active involvement in the black church and a growing attraction to the movement led by the charismatic William Lloyd Garrison. When, at several abolitionist meetings, Douglass rose from the audience to denounce the scheme to return American slaves to Africa, and to describe his own experience of the horrors of chattel slavery, the Garrisonians recognized that they had stumbled on an unusual resource in this young and uncommonly gifted black man. At first the relationship was one of mutual admiration. The Massachusetts Anti-Slavery Society hired Douglass as a lecturer in 1841, thus allowing him to hone the skills that would make him one of the great orators of the nineteenth century. Often his hearers were stunned by the combination of his regal physical presence and "highly melodious and rich" voice. He was, wrote a correspondent to the *Liberator*, "chaste in language, brilliant in thought, truly eloquent in delivery." But he was also a black man in a world where even the most uncompromising white abolitionists found it difficult to accept people of African descent as equal and fully autonomous human beings. When Douglass and Remond upbraided a white lecturer for focusing more on the "crime" of private property than on the evils of slavery, they were reprimanded by the Anti-Slavery Society's leadership. One white member accused them of "monkeyism" and called them a "disgrace to abolition" for their "unwilling[ness] to be directed by others."[31]

Once again, it was time for Douglass to declare his independence. He did so by taking time off from the lecture circuit to write the *Narrative of the Life of*

4.2. Young Frederick Douglass (courtesy of the National Park Service and Frederick Douglass National Historic Site, FRDO 2169)

Frederick Douglass, the first of his three autobiographies, and by looking eastward across the Atlantic, where, in city after city, large and sympathetic audiences would strengthen his claim to full freedom—even preeminence—in a movement that had both created and constrained him. Ironically, there was another, more ominous consideration that pointed him eastward as well. The appearance of his *Narrative* in June 1845 made Douglass a prime target for the "slave catchers" who were eager to return escaped chattel to their masters in the South. "To avoid the scent of the blood hounds of America," he set sail for Liverpool several months after the book's publication. From there it was but a short journey to Ireland.[32]

Douglass delivered "more than fifty lectures" in most of Ireland's largest cities and towns. His audiences included mayors, clergymen, and "a large company . . . of 'highly intelligent and influential people.'" Those who heard him speak were pleased that he bore himself with the "ease and grace of a gentleman"; they described his oratorical skills as a matter of "admiration" and even "astonishment." And yet at least some of his hearers were relieved to find that there was "little, if anything, in his features of that peculiar prominence of lower face, thickness of lips, and flatness of nose, which peculiarly characterize the true Negro type."[33]

The goal of his visit to Ireland, Douglass said, was to "encircle America with a girdle of Anti-slavery fire." To build that fire, he unrelentingly exposed the horrors of chattel slavery—not only the reign of the boot, the lash, and the branding iron but also the invisible scourge that cast men and women "into the depths of moral and intellectual degradation." But always he returned to the physical cruelty, and invariably his audience responded with murmurs of sympathy and, sometimes, gasps of horror. "I stand before you with the marks of the slave-driver's whip, that will go down with me to my grave," he told an audience in Cork. Even worse, "I saw one poor woman . . . who had her ear nailed to a post, for attempting to run away, but the agony she endured was so great, that she tore away, and left her ear behind." The journalist who transcribed his speech reported that the audience responded with "great sensation," "great applause," and "tremendous cheers."[34]

For someone who only recently had been a slave himself, this reception was overwhelming. "Seven years ago I was ranked among the beasts and creeping things," Douglass told another audience in Cork; "to-night I am here as a man and a brother." In his correspondence, he went much further, contrasting the omnipresence of racism in the United States with the "total absence of all manifestations of prejudice against me, on account of my color," in Ireland. "I can truly say, I have spent some of the happiest moments of my life since landing in this country," he wrote to Garrison on January 1, 1846.

> In the Southern part of the United States, I was a slave, thought of and spoken of as property. . . . In the Northern States, a fugitive slave, liable to be hunted at any

moment like a felon, . . . doomed by an inveterate prejudice of color to insult and outrage on every hand. . . . But now behold the change! . . . Instead of a democratic government, I am under a monarchical government. Instead of the bright blue sky of America, I am covered with the soft grey fog of the Emerald Isle. I breathe and lo! the chattel becomes a man. I gaze around in vain for one who will question my equal humanity, claim me as his slave, or offer me an insult. . . . I find no difficulty here in obtaining admission into any place of worship, instruction or amusement, on equal terms with people as white as any I ever saw in the United States.[35]

In fact, Douglass encountered a far more complex and fractured society than this euphoric portrait suggests, and his valiant attempt to negotiate Ireland's dense thicket of contradictions and divisions reveals much not only about Douglass himself but also about the fragility of the relationship between the rapidly evolving Irish nationalist movement and transatlantic abolitionism. The Ireland he experienced was marked by at least four conundrums that would confound even those reformers who came to the fray armed with the noblest of intentions. First, there were the stark class inequalities and the massive deprivation that—as much as its shimmering green hills and valleys—characterized the Emerald Isle and inevitably raised questions about the relative weight of American slavery and Irish poverty on the scale of human suffering. Second, there were the sectarian divisions that constituted another of the nation's major fault lines, pitting Catholics against Protestants and shaping the abolitionist movement and the network of relationships that sustained Douglass in Ireland in ways he could not fully understand. Third, there was the question of Ireland's relationship to Britain (and, by implication, to America as well). Should she remain a loyal component of the United Kingdom, as most Protestants insisted, or seek a greater measure of self-governance, as the Catholic majority increasingly demanded? More than that, could Britain (and British-inspired reform movements) be Ireland's ally and friend, or did the very name of Britain signify danger and betrayal? Finally, there was the closely related question of the meaning of the Irish nation and the character of Irish nationalism. Was O'Connell right to insist that because they had suffered centuries of persecution, the Irish "should be foremost in seeking to effect the emancipation of mankind"? Or were his critics right to argue that the regeneration of the Irish nation and the freeing of its people from their humiliating oppression was the only foundation on which a legitimate Irish nationalism could be constructed?

Douglass unhesitatingly took an extreme position in this particular debate. Even more than O'Connell and his Quaker allies in Ireland, he was an internationalist, and he freely stated, "I have no nation." For most Irish nationalists, this placed him well beyond the pale—not only of the good but also of the imaginable. How could a man with no country construct a viable foundation on which to stand and find his bearings? How could an American disavow the nation that served as the cradle of republican liberty, the haven for Irish emigrants, the necessary counterweight to British power in the world? Douglass had a ready answer. "America only welcomes me to her shores as a brute," he claimed. "She . . . would not receive me as a man." But his stance served only to reinforce the chasm that separated many Irish nationalists, and their countrymen in the United States, from the abolitionists and their allies in the battalions of radical reform.[36]

From the standpoint of his own personal and political development, Douglass was entirely correct to claim that his visit to the Emerald Isle was a triumphant moment, full of rich and vivid memories that he would treasure for the rest of his life. But from the standpoint of the development of abolitionism in Ireland, his visit offers an illuminating vantage point on a movement that was peaking—or perhaps had already peaked—and was about to enter a long phase characterized by decline and marginalization. Douglass did not cause that decline; unforeseen circumstances that were far beyond his control played the principal role. But his experience highlights some of the contradictions that were endemic to the abolitionist movement and that played out in distinctive ways in Ireland.

One thing that was crystal clear from the start was the indescribable poverty that assaulted his senses every day. Douglass's arrival in Dublin coincided almost exactly with the destruction of a substantial percentage of the nation's potato crop in September 1845. The infamous "potato blight" would strike again a year later, this time destroying virtually the entire crop and leading directly to the Great Famine.[37] But even before the onset of famine, signs of the "greatest wretchedness" were everywhere. Dublin's streets were "almost literally alive with beggars," Douglass reported, "some of them mere stumps of men, without feet, without legs, without hands, without arms—and others still more horribly deformed, with crooked limbs, down upon their hands and knees, . . . [or] laid upon their backs, pressing their way through the muddy streets and merciless crowd." Most heartrending of all were the little children he encountered "at a late hour of the night, covered with filthy rags, and seated upon cold stone steps, . . . fast asleep, with none to look upon them, none to care for them." Somewhat ruefully, Douglass acknowledged that he was confronted with men, women, and children "in much the same degradation as the American slaves." Whose advocate, then, should he be? Whose cause should he espouse when Ireland's poor were *more* wretched than he had been as the chattel property of his master in the United States? "I see much here to remind me of my former condition," he reported to Garrison, "and I confess I should be ashamed to lift up my voice against American slavery, but that I know the cause of humanity is one the world over."[38]

This generous affirmation of humanity's oneness was at the heart of the abolitionists' vision, but in speaking out against American slavery, Douglass had to confront the increasingly insistent argument that the Irish needed to focus all of their sympathy on the "white slaves of Ireland." "When we are ourselves free," the *Waterford Freeman* editorialized in September 1845, "let us then engage in any struggle to erase the sin of slavery from every land. But, until then, our own liberation is that for which we should take counsel, and work steadily."[39] Increasingly, over the years that spanned the Repeal campaign and the horrors of the famine, this argument was radically reconceptualized by those who, mimicking a wide range of proslavery voices in the United States, argued that the "slavery" of the Irish peasant and agricultural laborer was far worse than that of the Negro slave in America. No one, not even John Mitchel, made this argument in greater detail or with more fervor than the American polemicist John C. Cobden. "For centuries the Irish nation has groaned under the yoke of England," he would write in 1853.

> Seldom has a conquered people suffered more from the cruelties and exactions of the conquerors. While [the famed British abolitionists] Clarkson and Wilberforce were giving their untiring labours to the cause of emancipating negro slaves thousands of miles away, they overlooked a hideous system of slavery at their very doors— the slavery of a people capable of enjoying the highest degree of civil and religious freedom.

The corollary, of course, was that, unlike the Irish, Negroes, enslaved or free, were not "capable of enjoying the highest degree of civil and religious freedom." But this was secondary to Cobden's basic argument that Ireland continued to endure

> a cruel system of slavery, for which we may seek in vain for a parallel. . . . If the Irish master took his labourer for his slave in the American sense, he would be compelled to provide for him, work or not work, in sickness and in old age. Thus the [Irish] master reaps the benefits, and escapes the penalties of slave-holding. He takes the fruits of the labourer's toil without providing for him as the negro slaves of America are provided for. . . . In no other country does the slaveholder seem so utterly reckless in regard to human life as in Ireland.[40]

Douglass assured Garrison that "I cannot allow myself to be insensible to the wrongs and sufferings of any part of the great family of man."[41] But he drew the line at the argument that there was slavery in Ireland, a form of slavery even worse than that in America. "If slavery existed here," he answered, "it ought to be put down, and the generous of the land ought to rise and scatter its fragments to the winds." But in fact "there was nothing like American slavery on the soil on which he [Douglass] now stood. Negro-slavery consisted not in taking away any of the rights of man, but in annihilating them all—not in taking away a man's property, but in making property of him." To those who refused to understand the qualitative difference between oppression and suffering on the one hand and the reduction of a human being to a "marketable commodity, to be . . . sold at the will of his master," on the other, Douglass offered no quarter. And, for the most part, his hosts agreed with him.[42]

Who were his hosts? Douglass acknowledged with pride that most of them were eminently respectable men of the rising commercial and professional elites, especially in cities such as Cork and Belfast. But the dynamic heart of abolitionism in Ireland was Dublin, where a small but extraordinary group of Quaker activists remained indefatigably committed to the cause of antislavery and to a host of other reforms as well. The formation of the Hibernian Anti-Slavery Society in 1837 had marked the reemergence of Quakers at the center of the movement, most notably in Dublin, where three men stood out from the rest: the merchant Richard Allen, the printer and bookseller Richard Davis Webb, and the merchant James Haughton, who came from a Quaker family but converted to Unitarianism as an adult. Alfred Webb, the oldest of Richard and Hannah Webb's five children, recalled that for years, at least until the Great Famine and the events that accompanied it,

> my father, Richard Allen, James Haughton, Uncles James and Thomas Webb, and others in Dublin were the centre of a general movement for reform, and the amelioration of the ills of humanity in every direction. . . . Slavery, temperance, British India, anti-opium, anti-capital punishment, anti-corn law, mesmerism, cold-water cure—everything was taken up. . . . But temperance and slavery were the central interests.[43]

Beginning with their experience at the World Anti-Slavery Convention, which Richard Webb's sister-in-law Maria Waring celebrated as "grand and glorious beyond expression," the Dublin reformers developed especially close ties with the abolitionist movement in the United States and remained faithful to the embattled Garrisonians, above all to Garrison himself, through thick and thin. Waring described Garrison as "one of God's nobility" and believed she had never before seen "such an angelic, holy looking face." Webb himself, who was usually more inclined toward choleric criticism than euphoric affirmation, admitted that upon meeting Garrison, "my admiration and veneration were raised to . . . as high a pitch as they could be towards any man." "I seem to breathe a freer air when you are with me," he wrote to his hero in September 1840. "I never longed to see anyone so much as thyself." The Garrisonians, in turn, were deeply moved by their Dublin friends' broad vision and steadfast faith. "Though his heart is Irish," said Maria Weston Chapman of Richard Allen, "it beats for all the world. Though a staunch Orthodox Quaker, . . . neither sect, nor party, nor geographical boundary confines the sphere of his efforts for the happiness and welfare of his fellow-men."[44]

In spite of their reputation for plain living, dress, and speech, the small band of Dublin Quakers became legendary in the transatlantic reform community for the warmth and generosity of their hospitality. "That visit to Dublin!" in the summer of 1840, Garrison exulted to Hannah Webb several years later. "To be so cordially entertained by strangers, being a 'foreigner' [myself]—to be welcomed to their firesides and their hearts . . . my heart has ever since . . . been welling over with the crystal waters of gratitude." Nathaniel P. Rogers, a Boston abolitionist who accompanied Garrison to the World Anti-Slavery Convention and from there to Dublin, was even more effusive in his praise. "We had a great-souled time with the Webbs, the Allens, . . . the Haughtons," and other members the Dublin circle of reformers, he recalled. "But only for three days. I marvel we came away so soon. . . . We ought to have stayed three months. I never met with such a circle as that Dublin one, and never expect to again."[45]

Beneath the aura of good fellowship and transatlantic solidarity, however, all was not well with the Quaker commitment to antislavery. What went wrong? First, the transatlantic Quaker community had experienced a series of internal crises of identity and direction over the years, which had ended in the "disowning" of numerous individuals (James Haughton's father, for example, for his refusal to accept the new emphasis on scriptural authority) and had caused larger schisms that saw whole clusters of individuals—such as the "Hicksite" Quakers in the United States—depart as a group. At a time when the majority of Quakers were moving toward the embrace of normative Protestant doctrine, the Hicksites insisted on the priority of the inner light, the "eternal divine spirit made manifest in the souls of men."[46] Within Ireland, moreover, many Quakers were apprehensive about the increasing political assertiveness of Ireland's Roman Catholic majority. One Quaker response to the mass campaigns for Catholic Emancipation and Repeal of the Union was to call on the faithful to reaffirm their status as a people apart by avoiding improper engagement with "public or political questions." Was antislavery public and political, and therefore a subject to be avoided? Increasingly, some Quakers answered in the affirmative, especially when the radical abolitionism of the Garrisonians began to make inroads in Dublin. Richard Webb hailed "Garrison's reformation" as more important than Luther's, and his wife, Hannah, believed that Garrison was seeking "a world in which there would be no slavery, no king, no beggars, no lawyers, no doctors, no soldiers, no palaces, no prisons, no creeds, no sects, no weary or grinding labor, no luxurious idleness, . . . no restraint but moral restraint, no constraining power but love." Caught between the demand for Repeal, which appeared to threaten a Catholic Ascendancy, and Garrison's radicalism, which seemed bent on undermining all human institutions, the majority of Irish Quakers became more conservative and more resistant to engagement with anything that deviated from the purest and least political forms of philanthropy.[47]

Even before Douglass's visit in 1845, the chill in the air was painfully evident to those who remembered the Quaker community as one marked by a high degree of harmony and good fellowship. James Cannings Fuller, the transatlantic activist who had helped orchestrate the unveiling of the Irish Address at Faneuil Hall in January 1842, returned to Ireland a year later and was shocked by what he encountered among a people he had long regarded as his spiritual kin. When he attended the yearly meeting in the spring of 1843, he found that "with the exception of three or four families of friends who are interested in the anti-slavery cause, there were very few houses to which I was welcomed." Fuller understood all too well that it was his "anti-slavery character," above all his affiliation with the Garrisonians, that stood between him and the "hospitality which members of our society are so apt to exhibit towards each other."[48]

Matters finally came to a head in September 1845, when the Dublin Monthly Meeting decided to deny Frederick Douglass further use of its meetinghouses because he failed to offer his critique of American slavery, and of those who aided and abetted it, "in a sufficiently gentle spirit." In response, Richard and Thomas Webb wrote a long letter to the Monthly Meeting registering their emphatic dissent. In his lecture at the Friends Meeting House on Eustace Street, Douglass had especially offended the Methodists with his stinging denunciation of the shortcomings of their brethren in the United States. The Webbs expressed amazement that "those who have been nurtured in the lap of ease, who have never experienced cruelty, hunger, or the midnight of the mind which is the fate of the bondsman, [would ask] a slave to speak in silken terms of Slavery." Turning the focus of criticism away from the Methodists, they pointed to the failings of their own denomination, in Ireland and America, and declared that an "occasional address" and a "gently breathed whisper across the Atlantic" were of little use in confronting the inertia of their fellow Quakers. In a separate letter to Garrison, Richard Webb charged that Friends in both countries were "timid people" who, in "seeking to dwell in the quiet," had virtually nothing in common with the men and women whose unflinching witness had brought the Religious Society of Friends into being. It was the beginning of the end for the Webb brothers. Richard, in particular, turned most of his attention to antislavery and became one of the leading Garrisonians in the British Isles. Although he did not sever his formal ties with the Friends until 1851, the process of separation had begun much earlier. As a true Garrisonian, he, too, was a come-outer, one who could acknowledge cheerfully: "I am generally regarded as a fanatic in these parts."[49]

Over time other Protestant denominations also became more cautious in their relationship to abolitionism. Even during Remond's visit to Dublin in 1841, where he spoke to large and enthusiastic audiences, Richard Allen reported that "we have been shut out from places which ought to have been open to us"—most notably, from Methodist churches, whose leaders claimed that they could allow lectures only on subjects that were "exclusively religious." The Garrisonians actually contributed to the problem by making a scorching critique of Christianity as it was practiced by virtually every denomination in the United States central to their message. Douglass was relentless in his condemnation of the "man-trapping, woman-whipping, slave-branding and cradle-robbing Christian[s] of America." "The American pulpit is on the side of slavery," he charged, "and the Bible is blasphemously quoted in support of it." On these grounds, he insisted that Irish Christians of every denomination sever the bonds of communion with their counterparts in the United States. "Let these American Christians know their hands are too red to be grasped by Irishmen. . . . Stand forth to the world and declare to the American Church, that until she puts away slavery, you can have no fellowship with [her]." Individual clergymen and even some congregations were willing to go along, but for the most part the leadership and membership of the churches refused to become a party to the dismembering of institutions they regarded as vital to their spiritual well-being. And so doors were closed, congregations were split, and a potential—and once active—source of support was alienated.[50]

Nonetheless, it was of major significance that in a society where 80 percent of the population was Catholic, Douglass's hosts were almost invariably Protestant. In some cities, to be sure, he interacted with Catholics as well as Protestants. He attended several temperance gatherings in Dublin and spoke at one of O'Connell's Repeal meetings at Conciliation Hall. (The constituency of both movements was overwhelmingly Catholic.) In Cork he shared the stage with the legendary Father Mathew and was a guest in his home.[51] Mostly, however, he spoke to audiences that were predominantly, perhaps overwhelmingly, Protestant. In Limerick a local newspaper criticized Douglass for lecturing at the Belford Row Independent Chapel and thus "giving a sectarian appearance to a cause that equally belongs to all."[52] He would no doubt have protested that his goal *was* to speak to all and that his outlook and intentions were entirely nonsectarian. But in the cocoon of fellowship that enveloped him during his sojourn abroad, it is unlikely that he understood the full extent of Protestant privilege and sectarian antagonism in Ireland. Alfred Webb, who became an Irish nationalist of unusually cosmopolitan sympathies, came to understand this problem all too well. "When a Protestant child is born in Ireland," he would write in 1893,

> his chances of preferment through the institutions of the country are treble at least the chances of a Catholic child. . . . Every Protestant occupies a certain position of prestige not occupied by a Catholic. This has entered into the very marrow of the Protestants of all persuasions. . . . I was brought up in a circle [that was] liberal as regards everything but Ireland. Unfortunately I imbibed the feeling that Catholics were all low and uneducated.[53]

"It was not without a wrench," Webb recalled, that he "burst these trammels of feeling" and freed himself from the deep, prejudicial reflex inculcated not only by the Protestant community in general but also by his parents, Richard and Hannah Webb, whose reputation for hospitality spanned the Irish Sea and the Atlantic. Alfred Webb recalled that whereas Garrison and Rogers, both "strangers" and "foreigners," were welcome in the Webb household as a matter of course, for an Irish Catholic "to enter our house (except as a servant) was a matter of comment."[54]

Not all Catholics were servants or impoverished peasants. There was, by this time, a substantial Catholic middle class, and there were poor Protestants. But, generally, wealth and privilege were the hallmarks of Irish Protestants, and Irish Catholics bore the stigma of poverty and degradation. Douglass did attract the "suffering poor" to some of his meetings. He offered a vivid recollection of his first meeting in Ireland—a temperance gathering in Dublin, where "more than five thousand people were assembled." This occasion triggered his observation that the "ignorant and degraded" Irish "lacked only a black skin and wooly hair, to complete their likeness to the plantation negro."[55]

But this recollection came nine years after the fact. At the time of his visit to Ireland, Douglass was much more inclined to highlight—indeed, celebrate— the fact that most of the men and women who heard him speak were "highly influential," "intelligent," and "respectable" (the adjectives themselves implied Protestant). Their presence validated him; it demonstrated how far he had distanced himself from the social death of slavery and from the stigma of color that haunted free blacks in the United States. Reflecting on the suffering that had moved him almost to tears in Dublin, he told Garrison, "The *immediate*, and it may be the main cause of the extreme poverty and beggary in Ireland, is intemperance. This may be seen in the fact that most beggars drink whiskey."[56]

Clearly, Douglass was preaching to the choir. His emphasis on the need for temperance and the virtues of hard work made him all the more attractive to his hosts. But his words also reflected the yawning chasm between abolitionism and the masses of Irish peasants and laborers. In an agricultural society where a relative handful of Anglo-Irish landlords owned most of the land, Ireland's poor and dispossessed were groaning under the weight of systemic inequality and, increasingly, drifting into some of the most dangerous and exploitative jobs in the emerging Irish diaspora—working in the textile mills of Manchester and other British cities and mining coal and building canals and railways in America. "Hire an Irishman" was the watchword on the levees of New Orleans. Let *him* succumb to malaria; slave property was too valuable for that.[57] Who, then, was the slave, and who the greater victim of the landlord and the capitalist?

Douglass was right to insist on the qualitative difference between chattel slavery and the onerous conditions Irish "wage slaves" faced in the free labor market. Moreover, in the autumn of 1845 he could not have anticipated the full impact of the Great Famine. But as he listened impatiently to the growing chorus of voices—in Ireland and Irish America—claiming that Ireland's starving people were the world's *real* slaves, he allowed himself to fall into the trap of stubbornly accentuating the difference between chattel slavery and Irish poverty, thereby diminishing the extent and significance of the latter. "The Irishman is poor," Douglass acknowledged, "but he is *not* a slave. He *may* be in rags, but he is *not* a slave. He is still the master of his own body, and can say with the poet, . . . 'The world is all before him, where to choose[?]'" He continued to emphasize, moreover, that Ireland was a free society, where "the multitude can assemble upon all the green hills, and fertile plains of the Emerald Isle—[to] . . . pour out their grievances, and proclaim their wants without molestation."[58]

Many contemporary accounts, by Irish and foreign observers, told a very different story. Indeed, if Douglass had accompanied Richard Webb to West Clare in 1850, as Remond had in 1841, he would no longer have encountered the "great profusion of lovely faces among the women" and "cheerfulness and light-hearted gaiety" among the people there. Clare was ravaged as few other Irish counties were by the famine. In the area of West Clare that Remond had visited in 1841, the watchwords by the late 1840s were "eviction," "emigration," and "death." In Kilrush Union more than 20,000 people were evicted from the land in a two-year period; the great majority of them had their homes leveled as they departed. As late as 1850, the number of deaths in the Kilrush Union workhouse reached 1,700, an average of 140 a month. Thus it is almost certain that some of the "primitives" who danced to the piper's tune and marveled at Remond's complexion on that magical summer day in 1841 later died from disease or malnutrition. Many of the survivors would have been evicted from their cabins and minuscule plots of land and compelled to fall back on the dubious refuge that the vastly overcrowded—and diseased—workhouse offered. Among those who managed to remain on the land, some would have been sick and emaciated, living, already, beneath the "famine shadow" that stalked much of rural Ireland for generations after the Great Hunger.[59]

Other contemporaries were quick to point out that those Irishmen and -women who dared to "pour out their grievances" and "proclaim their wants" increasingly met with a "molestation" that further chilled the atmosphere of a besieged—and traumatized—nation. Douglass knew well that the British government not only had prohibited the monster Repeal meeting scheduled for Clontarf (on the outskirts of Dublin) in October 1843 but had also done so with a massive show of military force. Douglass also knew that even though O'Connell had acquiesced in this decision, he was charged with seditious conspiracy and imprisoned for three months in 1844. This was but a prelude to the arrest, trial, and "transportation" of the rebels who sought to organize a national rising against tyranny and starvation in the summer of 1848. Four Young Irelanders were convicted of high treason and sentenced to death, but all were instead transported to Van Diemen's Land. Perhaps Ireland was not, unambiguously, an "enslaved country," as Young Ireland claimed. But in his zeal to demonstrate the fundamental difference between freedom and slavery, Douglass's facile assertion that Irishmen and -women were free to "pour out their grievances, and proclaim their wants without molestation," can only have struck many Irish nationalists as a gross distortion of reality.[60]

Douglass further complicated his relationship with a wide swath of Irish opinion by emphasizing—even in the midst of the famine—that he was a confirmed and unashamed Anglophile. In doing so, he was giving voice to a long-standing African American tradition. Like many blacks, he was predisposed to overlook Britain's long record of involvement in the slave trade and to focus on an altogether different history—the British government's support of emancipation for American slaves during the Revolution and the War of 1812; the rise of a popular and increasingly powerful antislavery movement, beginning in London in the 1780s; the abolition of the slave trade in 1807; and, above all, the emancipation of nearly a million West Indian slaves in the 1830s. This history convinced many blacks that Britain was the principal ally of the sons and daughters of Africa, whereas republican America, with its soaring affirmation that "all men are created equal," was in fact the enemy of black freedom. Their heroes were not slave-owning American patriots such as George Washington and Thomas Jefferson but British antislavery pioneers such as William Wilberforce and Thomas Clarkson, after whom they named their fraternal organizations. No one articulated this perspective more clearly than David Walker, the abolitionist, journalist, and forerunner of black nationalism in the United States, who declared in 1829, "The English are the best friends the colored people have on this earth. They have done one hundred times more for the melioration of our condition, than all the other nations of the world put together."[61]

As early as 1834 it had become customary for African Americans to mobilize on August 1—Emancipation Day in the Anglophone Caribbean—rather than on July 4 to celebrate and reaffirm their quest for freedom. The Anglophile tradition had taken root long before the 1830s, and perhaps nowhere more so than among black Methodists. There was a long history of intense loyalism among Methodists in Britain, Ireland, and, to a lesser extent, North America, and Methodism attracted many more African Americans than any other Protestant denomination. Equiano was a Methodist; so was John Jea. During the War of 1812, an American consul in France had called on Jea to enlist in the American navy to fight against Britain, and he had replied, "Far be it [from] me to ever fight against Old England, unless it be with the sword of the Gospel, under the captain of our salvation, Jesus Christ." To side with the United States, he argued, would be to enlist under the "banner of the tyrants of the world."[62]

Douglass's contention that Britain was the world's leading friend of freedom could only accentuate the growing gulf that separated him and the abolitionist movement from the increasingly Anglophobic nationalism of Young Ireland. "I have every reason to love England," he declared from a London podium in March 1847. "Liberty in England is better than slavery in America. Liberty under a monarchy is better than despotism under a democracy. . . . I have known what it was for the first time in my life to enjoy freedom in this country."[63] Ironically, he made these remarks at a time when the famine was reaching horrific proportions in Ireland and when large numbers of Irishmen and -women were fleeing to England for refuge, only to be greeted with apprehension, fear, and loathing as "the filthiest beings in the habitable globe." Once again, it must have appeared to the new generation of Irish nationalists that Douglass, the American slave, was welcomed, even pampered, in England, whereas the white slaves of Ireland were condemned to waste away on the mean streets of Liverpool, Manchester, and other British cities.[64]

At a moment when the United States was gearing up for war with Mexico, a war that promised a vast extension of the territory open to chattel slavery, Douglass was driven more than ever to a relentless condemnation of the base hypocrisy of the American government and the majority of its citizens. Speaking in Ireland in the autumn of 1845, he declared, "I want the Americans to know that in the good city of Cork, I ridiculed their nation—I attempted to excite the utter contempt of the people here upon them." At the end of his transatlantic sojourn, in his "Farewell to the British People," he announced, "I am going back . . . to the United States in a few days, but I go there to . . . unmask her pretensions to republicanism, and expose her hypocritical professions of Christianity." "No nation upon the face of the globe," he claimed, "can exhibit a statute-book so full of all that is cruel, malicious, and infernal as the American code of laws. Every page is red with the blood of the American slave."[65]

It is hard to imagine words that could have been less congenial to Irish nationalists at a time when the United States was sending a steady flow of famine relief to the people of Ireland. Young Ireland had always been intensely pro-American, in part as a logical corollary of its Anglophobia, which only accelerated with the famine and the wave of political repression that accompanied it. How, then, could Douglass choose Britain over America, which the *Nation* called "liberty's bulwark and Ireland's dearest ally"?[66] Worse, how could he stand on the soil of the United States and declare, as he did in May 1847, "I have not, I cannot have, any love for this country, . . . or for its Constitution. I desire to see it overthrown as soon as possible and its Constitution shivered in a thousand fragments."[67]

After Douglass's departure from Ireland, a number of events and trends converged to push abolitionism toward the margins of Irish society. The Great Famine had an unprecedented impact on Irish life. Necessarily, it dwarfed all other concerns. Although it sent more than a million of Ireland's sons and daughters into exile aboard the "emigrant ships," the famine also turned the nation's attention inward toward Ireland's own oppression. The death of O'Connell served only to reinforce this trend and to create greater space for competing voices within the nationalist movement. Even before O'Connell's death in May 1847, Father John Kenyon dared to speak publicly about slavery in ways that might have been unthinkable as long as the Liberator remained an active force in Irish society and politics.

In January 1847 Father Kenyon addressed a letter to the *Nation* that was as remarkable for its tone as for its substance. Indirectly, his target was O'Connell.

More directly, it was James Haughton, a member of the Dublin Quaker reform circle and a close associate of the Liberator in the Repeal campaign. He mocked Haughton's pious opposition to slavery and characterized his indignant refusal to accept the "bloodstained contributions" of American slave owners as "one of the notable blunders" of the Repeal Association. "If, instead of slave-holders, slave-eaters were substituted in the argument," he wrote, "I should still accept their aid, and thank them for it, to repeal this abominable Union."[68] This could only have struck home like an electric shock for Haughton, who called slavery "a system of wickedness that has no parallel in the annals of the human race." For Kenyon, however,

> the whole question [is] one whose importance is much exaggerated by fancy, per-chance by fanaticism. We are all slaves, in a thousand senses of the word—slaves to time, slaves to space, to circumstances, to the habits of our great-grandfathers on ei-ther side, and to the whims of our maternal ancestors in all their nonsensical genera-tions. . . . If to all these slaveries there be superadded one other—namely, slavery to slave-holders—I cannot see that our position will be very essentially deteriorated. . . .
>
> Let us, then, Mr. Haughton, in the name of common sense, mind, for the present, our own business. . . . If [slavery] be an evil, it is no special concern of ours; we shall not be damned for it, though we take useful coins from the evil-doers. . . . If it be an evil, may God mend it.[69]

Father Kenyon was by no means the only spokesperson for Young Ireland on these matters; even by the standards of the new nationalism, his combative personality and relentless logic led him to take extreme positions that alien-ated some of his colleagues. But he found a ready ally in John Mitchel, Young Ireland's *enfant terrible*. The son of a Unitarian clergyman from Ulster, Mitchel was a graduate of Trinity College Dublin and an early contributor to the *Na-tion*. Although he regarded Father Kenyon as "the finest fellow . . . I ever knew," neither Kenyon nor anyone else in Young Ireland could match Mitchel's liter-ary eloquence and insurrectionary fervor. He became a scathing critic of the liberalism that O'Connell cherished. Indeed, in the context of the famine, he became a political and social revolutionary. As he witnessed death and devasta-tion spreading all around him, he was moved to conclude that "if the men who plow and dig, who sow and reap, will but eat the food they raise—if they will but consent to live like Christians instead of dying like dogs, there [will be] an end of both foreign sway and domestic tyranny and treason."[70]

On virtually every point of contention between Young and Old Ireland, Mitchel became O'Connell's leading adversary. O'Connell frequently expressed his loyalty to "our most gracious and ever beloved Sovereign Queen Victoria" and affirmed that "while I live, the connection with England shall not be bro-ken." Mitchel had come to believe that England was the ultimate source of all of Ireland's misery and that complete independence from all things English was Ireland's only salvation. Whereas the Liberator insisted that moral suasion was the only legitimate means to achieve Ireland's just ends, Mitchel counseled reliance on "passive resistance" where necessary, but "above all, let the man amongst you who has no gun, sell his garment and buy one." Finally, whereas O'Connell blended Catholicism and the traditions of the Enlightenment in a commitment not only to the Irish nation but also to every reform that contributed to "the inevitable progress of man," Mitchel came to despise every pious concern with the regeneration of humanity that emanated from English soil. He saw antislavery as, at best, a diversion from Ireland's real needs and, at worst, as a mere reflection of British hypocrisy. Replicating Thomas Carlyle's deep alienation from the social order and moral universe that Britain's new industrial and political ruling class had created, he eagerly embraced the splenetic Scotsman's outlook on the "Nigger Question."[71]

Mitchel was a genuine anomaly—a revolutionary in the Irish context, but an ardent and unapologetic defender of slavery and white supremacy in the United States. He always maintained that there was no contradiction or inconsistency in taking these apparently opposite positions. In both settings, he claimed, his enemy was Britain, the British Empire, or, as he often put it, the "British system." Britain embodied the "civilization of the nineteenth century," which he despised. Although it claimed to represent the essence of progress, it had given rise not only to urbanization and the factory system but also to massive poverty, enforced idleness, and the reduction of human relations to the cash nexus. And all the while, the architects of that false civilization relentlessly propagated the insidious doctrines of political economy and trumpeted the alleged benefits of "free labor." There was more than a touch of Marx and Engels in Mitchel's critique of the emerging system of industrial capitalism. But he was no socialist. Indeed, he considered socialists "worse than wild beasts." His ideal was the Irish rural society of the eighteenth century as he imagined it. "I have always looked with a sort of veneration upon an independent farmer cultivating his small demesne," he wrote in his *Jail Journal*, "a rural *pater-familias*, who aspires to no lot but labour in his own land, and takes off his hat to no 'superior' under God Almighty."[72]

After arriving in the United States in 1853, Mitchel quickly became convinced that the American republic was made up of two warring nations. He regarded the civilization of the North as an extension of British institutions, British values, and British hypocrisy. In the South, however, he found "a special hostility to the British system; . . . founded on essential differences in the two types of human society." As he mingled with members of the South's planter aristocracy, he discovered in them the gentility and refinement, the sense of duty, and the martial spirit that he regarded as essential foundation stones of a viable social order. Always, he assured his Irish friends, "I was thinking of Ireland, and contending for the South as the Ireland of this continent."[73]

In becoming a partisan of the American South, he also became a vociferous defender of chattel slavery, to a degree that shocked even his most sympathetic

Irish friends. First, however, he felt compelled to savage one of his Irish adversaries, the venerable James Haughton. When Haughton learned that several leaders of Young Ireland had taken refuge in the United States, he wrote a letter calling on them to stand with the abolitionists in their war against slavery. Mitchel's response was scathing and unequivocal. "Let us try to satisfy our pertinacious friend, if possible, by a little plain English," he declared in his recently founded newspaper, the *Citizen*. "We are not abolitionists; no more abolitionists than Moses, or Socrates, or Jesus Christ. We deny that it is a crime, or a wrong, or even a peccadillo, to hold slaves, to buy slaves, to keep slaves to their work by flogging or other needful coercion." Haughton had warned Mitchel and his associates that their silence on slavery would make them "participators" in its wrongs. "But we will not be silent," Mitchel reassured him, "and as for being a participator in the wrongs, we, for our part, wish we had a good plantation, well-stocked with healthy negroes in Alabama."[74]

Did this stance flow organically from Mitchel's experience in Ireland? There can be no doubt that the Great Famine added immeasurably to the ferocity that usually accompanied his opinions and characterized his prose. But in Ireland his response to the issue of slavery—above all, to O'Connell's insistence on linking Repeal with abolition—had been essentially pragmatic. Along with most members of Young Ireland, he had believed that slavery was an external matter and that Irish nationalists were entirely justified in concentrating all their energy on addressing the suffering of their own people. Thereafter, during his long voyage to Van Diemen's Land as a prisoner of the British government, he had encountered Brazilian slaves in the waters off the coast of Pernambuco, and his observations were characterized by an ambiguity that was altogether absent from the proslavery stance he would later adopt in the United States. He acknowledged that until that moment he had never seen "a slave in his slavery—I mean a merchantable slave, a slave of real money-value, whom a prudent man will, in the way of business, pay for and feed afterwards." He had seen only Irish "slaves"—peasants who were of no value to Ireland's landlord class and thus were being driven from the land by means of starvation, disease, and forced emigration. In stark contrast, he argued, "These slaves in Brazil are fat and happy, obviously not overworked nor underfed, and it is a pleasure to see the lazy rogues lolling in their boats, sucking a piece of green sugar-cane, and grinning and jabbering together."[75]

Mitchel's writing was original in content and tone, but this caricature of "fat and happy" Negroes appears to bear the mark of Thomas Carlyle, who published his own scathingly irreverent "Discourse on the Negro Question" in 1849. (Driven by a characteristic need to be ever more offensive, he would reissue the article as "Occasional Discourse on the Nigger Question" three years later.) In the aftermath of the emancipation of Britain's West Indian slaves, Carlyle was deeply concerned about what he construed as the collapse of the islands' sugar economy and especially the unhappy fate of Jamaica's plantation magnates. The leading culprits, he charged, were economists and evangelists who had preached the glories of free labor and racial equality. But Carlyle's main target was "Quashee"—his name for the emancipated slave—who, refusing to work for the planters, was content to sit and devour pumpkins all day. While Ireland starved and England's laboring classes reaped the bitter fruits of the industrial revolution, he raged, "how pleasant [it is] to have always this fact to fall back upon; our beautiful black darlings are at last happy; with little labor except to the teeth, which, surely in those excellent horse-jaws of theirs, will not fail!" He threatened that if Quashee refused to abandon his indolent lifestyle, "he will get himself made a slave again . . . and with beneficent whip . . . will be compelled to work."[76]

Mitchel was deeply influenced by Carlyle. His dizzying combination of radicalism and reaction and his furious outbursts of grossly inflated prose were very much reminiscent of the Scottish critic. His characterization of Brazilian slaves as "lazy rogues" who "grinned" and "jabbered" while they sucked on a piece of sugar cane closely parallels Carlyle's word portrait of Quashee with his endless supply of pumpkins. There was, however, a significant, if momentary, difference between the two men in this regard. Mitchel actually took pleasure in watching slaves "lolling in their boats" in the coastal waters of Pernambuco. Their apparent carelessness appealed to him and led him to conclude that "the condition of slaves in any Spanish, Portuguese, or French colony is not by any means so abject as it was under the English and is under the Americans." Given his future trajectory, it is even more remarkable that at this moment he could reflect with equanimity on the fact that only recently there had been a "bloody insurrection of the slaves" in Pernambuco, and could affirm that "the moment the black and brown people are able, they will have a clear right to exchange positions with the Portuguese race."[77]

In America, however, he quickly joined the ranks of slavery's most ardent defenders. When Father Kenyon—of all people—admonished him that "to promote the system [of slavery] for its own sake would be something monstrous," he responded by arguing that slavery was no necessary evil; it was a positive good, "good in itself, . . . good [in] every way." In a letter to another Irish friend, he declared, "I consider negro slavery the best state of existence for the negro, and the best for his master; and if negro slavery in itself be good, then the taking of negroes out of their brutal slavery in Africa and promoting them to a humane and reasonable slavery here is also good." In the *Southern Citizen*, which he founded in 1857 as "an organ of the extreme southern sentiment," he proposed "the re-opening of the African slave trade in the interests of both blacks and whites." From there it was a small step to active support of Southern secession and of the Confederacy during the Civil War. He proved to be one of the most irreconcilable of the South's Irreconcilables, and—once again—he paid a heavy price for the ferocity of his commitment to his core beliefs. Two of his sons died fighting for the Confederacy—one at Gettysburg in

1863, the other at Fort Sumter a year later, and Mitchel himself was imprisoned, albeit briefly, at the end of the war. He reckoned that he was the only person who had ever been a political prisoner of both the British and the American governments, and he took a certain pride in this singular status. "These two governments, we are told, are the very highest expression and grandest hope of the civilisation of the nineteenth century," he wrote in his journal. And since "I despise the civilisation of the nineteenth century, and its two highest expressions and grandest hopes, . . . the said century sees nothing that can be done with me except to tie me up."[78]

In his commitment to social revolution in his homeland, and to slavery and white supremacy in America, Mitchel went too far for many of his erstwhile friends in Young Ireland. Charles Gavan Duffy, the Monaghan-born Catholic who was one of the founders of the *Nation*, recalled that Mitchel wanted to propagate his racist viewpoint in the pages of the paper, "but I could not permit this to be done, my own conviction being altogether different."[79] William Smith O'Brien, a son of the Protestant Ascendancy who graduated from Trinity College Cambridge and trained in the law at Lincoln's Inn, also professed to abhor chattel slavery, which, he believed, was contrary to "every noble instinct of human nature, every principle of natural and revealed religion."[80] But Duffy, O'Brien, and other members of Young Ireland who remained politically active in the 1850s were hardly abolitionists. In fact, relative to the sense of moral urgency that had permeated O'Connell's discourse on race and slavery, they sounded an altogether different note. They saw slavery as a remote issue that was of no direct concern to Ireland, and they were determined to keep it at arm's length. They were, moreover, keenly aware of the emergence of Irish America as a major player in shaping, and financing, Irish nationalism and knew all too well that their exiled countrymen would not stand for any tampering with the "domestic institutions" of the United States. O'Brien himself dismissed abolitionists and their allies in the cause of human regeneration as a "whining tribe of philanthropists" who were out of touch with the complex realities of contemporary society. Yes, slavery was an inhuman institution, but Garrisonian immediatism was a dangerous illusion, and, in any case, the interests of the slaveholders as well as the slaves had to be taken into account.[81]

O'Brien visited the United States in 1859 and, in the company of Mitchel and Thomas Francis Meagher, met with President James Buchanan, who spoke fondly of his family's roots in County Donegal. Buchanan told O'Brien that "no peasantry in Europe [was] better clothed and better fed than [American] slaves," and he encouraged O'Brien to see for himself during his impending tour of the South. O'Brien visited Richmond, Charleston, Mobile, New Orleans, and other southern cities; he even stayed on a sugar plantation owned by an Irish immigrant in Louisiana and had the opportunity to view slavery "at first hand." Like Buchanan, he concluded that American slaves were usually well treated, and they were certainly better off than the white slaves of Ireland.[82]

If there was one institution that might have built on O'Connell's abolitionist legacy and effectively countered the proslavery drift of Irish nationalism, it was the Catholic Church. As early as 1840, Richard Robert Madden had called on the church hierarchy in Ireland to take the lead not only in addressing the subject of slavery but also in making a special effort to educate the "lower classes of our countrymen" on an issue that many of them were bound to encounter as immigrants in North America. Although a Catholic himself, Madden had lived outside Ireland in the 1820s and 1830s and, according to Nini Rodgers, had become "very much the liberal rationalist." He married a Protestant and, in Britain and the United States, interacted comfortably with abolitionists who were reflexively, and often devoutly, Protestant. But of late he had become more devout in his own faith, and he was deeply distressed at the way the Catholic Church in Cuba had accommodated itself to the institution of slavery. Now, in a speech to the Hibernian Anti-Slavery Society and a letter to the members of the Irish church hierarchy on the eve of their annual synod, he issued a bold—and public—plea for Ireland's bishops to affirm that "there does not exist in nature, in religion, or in civil polity, a reason for robbing any man of his liberty, be he black or white."[83]

Based on the three trips he had made to the United States since 1834, Madden informed the bishops that "the grossest prejudices are entertained against the slaves by our countrymen" in America. "They are not only apathetic and indifferent on the subject of the emancipation of the slaves," he reported, "they are . . . strenuously opposed to those who labour in behalf of this cause." But he also pointed to an "astounding paradox"—namely, that Ireland's poverty should compel massive emigration to the United States and thereby "raise up a power in a foreign land, potent enough to influence any question of political moment that arises in it." If the Irish were to exert themselves on behalf of the abolition of American slavery, he argued, "that system could not possibly endure!" But to accomplish that end, the Irish bishops must disavow, once and for all, "the sanction which slavery has the audacity to derive from religion."[84]

Madden took considerable comfort from the fact that Pope Gregory XVI had recently issued an Apostolic Letter condemning not only the slave trade but also, he believed, slavery itself. Although Catholic churchmen in the United States would soon argue that the pope had limited his condemnation to the international trade in human beings and not to the ownership of chattel property as such, Madden was unequivocal in claiming the imprimatur of the Holy See for his antislavery perspective, and he urged the members of the Irish hierarchy to reinforce the authority of the pope's letter by endorsing and publicizing it themselves. In Cuba, he warned, "The contaminating influence [of slavery] is extended even over sacred things, and comes within the precincts of sacred places." If the Irish bishops would only speak out, they could prevent the same contamination from spreading to the Catholic Church in the United States.[85]

The Irish hierarchy did not respond to Dr. Madden's letter. Who, after all, was he? A man who publicly praised Protestant abolitionists, including William Lloyd Garrison, for their "heroic fortitude and truly Christian forbearance." A man who would soon become the leading historian of the United Irishmen, another assemblage of heretics whose enthusiastic embrace of the American and French revolutions had threatened the very foundations of Irish society and jeopardized the church's still-precarious place within it.[86]

What is more remarkable, perhaps, is the apparent unwillingness of Daniel O'Connell to approach the hierarchy in a way that complemented Madden's initiative. O'Connell stood as the symbol of Ireland and Catholicism in ways that the relatively obscure Madden could not, and he had a close relationship with many members of the church hierarchy. Indeed, he had virtually compelled the bishops to follow his lead on a number of occasions. Most famously, in 1815 he had intervened to prevent the hierarchy from accepting the Vatican's recommendation that the British government be granted a veto over episcopal appointments in Ireland. "I am sincerely a Catholic but I am not a Papist," he had declared then, and he had warned the clergy that if they became the "vile slaves" of British power, the Irish people would despise and desert them.[87] In the 1840s, however, he issued no public appeals for the clergy to join him in the crusade against slavery, and there is no indication in his correspondence that he called on any member of the hierarchy to stand beside him in this battle. Perhaps he reasoned that unlike the veto controversy, chattel slavery was an external matter, and one that pertained more to the secular than the sacred domain, and therefore it could not carry the same weight with the bishops. Perhaps, too, he reckoned that the delicate task of persuading members of the hierarchy to join the struggle for Repeal had to be his priority.

At the grassroots level, in cities and towns where the Repeal campaign had a strong institutional base, O'Connell's outspoken identification with antislavery meant that many Irish Catholics became identified with the cause as well. O'Connell's Repeal wardens played the leading role in circulating the Irish Address in the autumn of 1841, which suggests that although the infrastructure of abolitionism in Ireland—notably, the Hibernian Anti-Slavery Society—was overwhelmingly Protestant in membership and ethos, the signers of the address were mainly Catholic. Perhaps this is why Richard Davis Webb ultimately dismissed the document he had coauthored as a "farce." Viscerally anti-Catholic in spite of himself, and skeptical at best about the merits of the Repeal campaign, he declared, "How few among the tens of thousands who have already signed understand what they put their names to! Is it moral to use such machinery?" In fact, Webb ignored—or perhaps was unaware of—the fact that significant numbers of Catholic clergymen were among the signers of the address. Richard

Allen reported that in October a single individual had secured the signatures of a Catholic bishop and seventy-two priests. "How many, then," the *Liberator* asked triumphantly, "are [included] among the sixty thousand names that are appended to the Address?"[88]

But the institutional church remained silent as the controversy over slavery swirled around it. The Irish bishops were, in important respects, caught in a pincer between the growing assertiveness of the Vatican and the rapidly expanding presence and power of the Catholic Church in the United States. Their overwhelming concern was to build up the personnel and infrastructure of Irish Catholicism; to move the faithful toward more regular participation in the mass and the sacraments; and, above all, to fend off the challenge represented by the aggressive, proselytizing thrust of Irish Protestantism's Second Reformation.[89] In such a climate, they could hardly ignore the fact that their friends and compatriots in the American hierarchy—Irish-born men such as John England and John Hughes—were denouncing abolitionism not only as a danger to social order but also as quintessentially Protestant.

Surely no one symbolized the chasm between abolitionism and the Catholicism of the American Irish more vividly than John Hughes, the archbishop of the New York diocese. Hughes was born on a small farm in County Tyrone in 1797. Twenty years later he followed his father to the United States and thereafter played a leading role in building Catholicism's institutional and ethnopolitical presence in American society from his base in the most Irish of American cities. At first he expressed an abhorrence of slavery, but over time he became an apologist for the peculiar institution and a sharp critic of O'Connell's alliance with abolitionism. He was convinced that slaves in the American South (and in Cuba, which he visited in 1853) were far better off than the "starving laborers" of the urban North, and he skewered the abolitionists for championing the one while ignoring the other. He agreed wholeheartedly with the Boston-based priest who observed that Negro slaves in Maryland were "a happy lot of people compared to the poor Irish in Boston." On one occasion he went so far as to declare, "I should sooner remain in Southern bondage than avail myself of the opportunity of Northern freedom."[90]

After Bishop John England's death in 1842, Hughes emerged as the leading member of the Catholic hierarchy in the United States. He symbolized Catholicism's new preeminence as the nation's largest single religious denomination and also embodied the overwhelming Irishness of the American church. Hughes retained a special affinity for his exiled countrymen and -women and a strong commitment to the cause of Irish freedom. But he also became an American patriot who demanded that Catholic immigrants—first and foremost the Irish among them—demonstrate their unswerving loyalty to their adopted land. When the Civil War began in 1861, he flew the American flag from Saint Patrick's Cathedral and called on Catholic men to join the fight to preserve the Union. But he continued to distance himself from abolitionism.

4.3. Archbishop John Hughes (courtesy of the Library of Congress)

"The Catholics," he wrote to Secretary of War Simon Cameron in October 1861, "are willing to fight to the death for the support of the constitution, the Government, and the laws of the country. But if it should be understood that . . . they are to fight for the abolition of slavery, then, indeed, they will turn away in disgust from the discharge of what would otherwise be a patriotic duty."[91]

Soon after he penned these words, Hughes journeyed to France, Italy, England, and Ireland as a quasi-official emissary of the Lincoln administration and its campaign to build support for the Union in places where the Confederacy had become the object of sympathy. His visit to Ireland was especially meaningful to him and to his Irish hosts. In Dublin he was treated "as if he were a visiting head of state." Newspapers were keen to give voice to his opinions, and he thrilled many Irish readers when he suggested that their countrymen in America had "in many instances . . . entered into this war partly to make themselves apprentices" in the use of weapons that could later be used to liberate their homeland.[92] Such a statement could not have been welcomed by Paul Cullen, the archbishop of Dublin and architect of Ireland's Devotional Revolution. Cullen often reminded advocates of physical force that "our great Liberator" had achieved Catholic Emancipation "by peaceable means and by force of reason, without violating any law." But even Cardinal Cullen felt compelled to defer to Hughes's stature as leader of the increasingly influential American church. In July 1862 he asked Hughes to preach the sermon at the laying of the foundation stone of Ireland's Catholic University in Dublin. In what became one of the largest religious celebrations in Irish history, two hundred thousand people turned out for the event, and the procession from the cathedral to the foundation site took four hours. Tyrone-born John Hughes was at the very center of this celebration, speaking as an honored, even revered, son of Ireland to his own people and speaking also as the voice of the Irish diaspora in America.[93]

Was James Haughton right, then, to claim that the American "man-stealer may now walk unrebuked" in Ireland? Hughes was neither a slave owner nor a slave trader. But he had allowed himself to become an apologist for the "man-stealers" who still plied their trade in much of the Atlantic World and within the United States. In October 1861, only a few months before his departure for Europe, he became embroiled in a controversy with the outspoken and independent-minded Catholic convert Orestes Brownson, who had called for the immediate abolition of slavery in order to prosecute the Civil War more effectively. Hughes lashed out at Brownson with words he would later regret. In an article published in his official organ, the *Metropolitan Record*, the archbishop appeared to defend the slave trade and to adopt the reasoning of slavery's most aggressive apologists, who saw no crime in an institution "by which savage Africans have been gradually tamed and prepared for Christian civilization." Referring ominously to the state of "savagery" and "barbarism" that allegedly prevailed in Africa, he portrayed the slave trade as a form of rescue. "We of course believe," he wrote, "that no genuine Christian—no decent man— would be engaged in this kind of business; still, we cannot discover the crime, even of the slaver, in snatching [Africans] from the butchery prepared for them in their native land." Nor, he argued, "would it be a crime for humane masters to purchase them" at a reasonable sum and then "take care of these unfortunate people. Under the circumstances," he concluded, "it is very difficult to discover in the purchasers any moral transgression of the law of God, or of the law of man, where [the slave trade] is authorized."[94]

Could there have been a greater contrast with O'Connell? The demise and death of the seemingly Immortal Dan and the rise of "Dagger John," an Irishman who had become all too American in his racial attitudes, revealed, finally, how fragile a reed Ireland was as the repository of the American abolitionists' hopes and dreams. Indeed, John A. Collins's confident assertion that "O'Connell and all the Irish of Ireland are abolitionists" had never captured the complex reality of Ireland's relationship to the controversy over slavery and abolition. But while O'Connell lived and poured out his voice across the broad Atlantic, it could appear so. His eloquence and unprecedented authority, combined with his devout Catholicism, so overshadowed the silence of the Irish hierarchy that it was possible to believe that Catholic Ireland *was* virtually unanimous in its commitment to abolition. The truth was far more prosaic. As the Catholic theologian John T. Noonan has acknowledged, "Only after the cultures of Europe and America changed through the abolitionists' agency and only after the laws of every civilized land eliminated the practice, did Catholic moral doctrine decisively repudiate slavery as immoral. Only in 1890 did Pope Leo XIII attack the institution itself."[95]

Frederick Douglass finally returned home in the spring of 1847, after twenty months in England, Scotland, and Ireland.[96] It was a time of unprecedented Irish immigration to North America. Altogether, in the five years from 1847 to 1851, more than 750,000 Irish men, women, and children entered the United States through the port of New York. Although these immigrants were not the poorest of the poor, they were mainly laborers and servants who were overwhelmingly Catholic and often "Irish-speaking, and illiterate." They bumped up against free blacks on urban street corners, pushed them to the margins of the labor market, and, according to their critics, allowed themselves to be controlled by "a crafty priesthood and unprincipled political demagogues."[97] In May 1850, speaking to a raucous meeting of the American Anti-Slavery Society in New York City, Douglass complained that "the Irishman but recently landed on these shores has greater privileges than are enjoyed by us. We who dwell among you," he said plaintively, "we who have watered the soil with our tears, and fertilized it with our blood—we only ask you to treat us as well as you treat him." Douglass's words make it clear that in his mind the fate of African Americans was closely linked to that of Irish immigrants. If White America treated "us" as well as it treated "them," then Black America could hope for a measure of mobility and security. The Irish saw the same linkage but drew the opposite conclusion. In their case, it was necessary to sever the bond, to distance themselves from downtrodden blacks, to deconstruct the cultural symbolism that marked "the Irishman" and "the African" as bearers of the same disabilities.[98]

Douglass's outlook continued to evolve for nearly half a century after his return to the United States in 1847. As the leading spokesman for Black America, he remained keenly aware of the role of the Irish in American society. Of necessity, his observations about them were often critical, as when he commented on the prominent part they played in victimizing the Chinese in California. "Our Celtic brothers," he declared in 1869, "[have] never [been] slow to execute the behests of popular prejudice against the weak and defenseless," and they were doing so with a vengeance on the Pacific Coast. He also ventured the judgment that "perhaps no class of our fellow citizens has carried . . . prejudice against color to a point more extreme and dangerous than have our Catholic Irish fellow citizens."[99]

And yet, immediately, he was reminded of the great contradiction that had become so clear to him during and after his sojourn in Ireland. For as much as he was aware of Irish American "prejudice against color," he also expressed the belief that "no people on the face of the earth have been more relentlessly persecuted and oppressed on account of race and religion, than the Irish." In 1887, at a meeting in Washington, DC, on behalf of home rule for Ireland, he recalled "standing on the banks of the Liffey, side by side with the great Daniel O'Connell, [who] . . . called me then the Black O'Connell of America." And now, here was Douglass more than forty years later, declaring himself "an out-and-out Home Ruler for Ireland," but also an "out-and-out Home Ruler for every man in this Republic." Wasn't that the lesson he had learned from O'Connell, and the Webbs, and the entire circle of transatlantic reformers in which he had first "felt his manhood free and unrestricted"?[100] "There is no such thing as limiting the spirit of liberty," he told his audience. "Liberty! why it is like the sun in the heavens—it shines for all. National lines, geographical boundaries, do not and cannot confine it. It belongs to the whole world, and the whole world has a right to stand up in its behalf."[101]

PART 3

Ireland and Empire

CHAPTER FIVE

"From the Cabins of Connemara to the Kraals of Kaffirland"

IRISH NATIONALISTS, THE BRITISH EMPIRE, AND THE "BOER FIGHT FOR FREEDOM"

> From the China towers of Pekin to the round towers
> of Ireland, from the cabins of Connemara to the kraals
> of Kaffirland, from the wattled homes of the isles of
> Polynesia to the wigwams of North America the cry is:
> "Down with the invaders! Down with the tyrants!"
> Every man to have his own land—every man to have his own home.
> —"The West Awake!!!" April 1879

IN THE SECOND HALF OF THE NINETEENTH CENTURY, Irish nationalism confronted a new and radically altered world.[1] As England became the center of an increasingly large and racially diverse empire, Ireland appeared to shrink. Following the shock of the Great Famine, its population continued to decline steadily.[2] Nonetheless, British statesmen convinced themselves that Ireland remained the linchpin of empire, the brick that somehow kept the entire edifice in place. When Liberal prime minister William Gladstone offered concessions to the increasingly insistent Irish demand for home rule, a potent combination of Conservatives and Liberal Unionists expressed dread at the effect "surrender and defeat" in Ireland would have "upon our position in the world—on our moral position, on our material position, on our political position, on our imperial position." Whatever test India or Egypt or South Africa may have offered at the end of the nineteenth century, John Benyon writes, "there can be little doubt that the real and ultimate 'Test of Empire' in this period was Ireland."[3]

Irish emigration meant that Ireland itself had become a dispersed nation whose exiled people refused to let go of their Irish identity or—worse—of their enmity toward England. To be Irish was to be "not English"; more than that, to be Irish apparently meant to define oneself over against England and its empire. Particularly in the United States, Irish organizations and newspapers began to exert a disproportionate influence on the evolution of the nationalist movement at home. The American Irish became warm supporters of home rule and the Irish Parliamentary Party, but many of them also offered strong support to the Fenians and admired the memory of John Mitchel—quite apart from his stance on slavery—precisely because they shared his intense hatred of all things English. As Irish America loomed ever larger, the shapers of public opinion in Britain could not help but take note of this new and ominous phenomenon. "In former Irish rebellions," a leading Liberal politician warned in 1885, "the Irish were *in Ireland*. . . . Now there is an Irish nation in the United States, equally hostile, with plenty of money, absolutely beyond our reach and yet within ten days sail of our shores."[4]

And yet Ireland's relationship to the empire and to Britain was complex. Ireland was England's first colony and, in the eyes of some, the victim of seven hundred years of "crucifixion" at the hands of the colonizers from across the Irish Sea.[5] But many Irishmen and -women were beneficiaries of the British connection and partners—albeit junior partners—in the construction and maintenance of Britain's vast imperial frontier. Among the many historians who have addressed this apparent contradiction, perhaps none puts it more vividly than Alvin Jackson. "Ireland was simultaneously a bulwark of the Empire, and a mine within its walls," he writes. "Irish people were simultaneously major participants in Empire, and a significant source of subversion. For the Irish the Empire was both an agent of liberation and of oppression."[6]

This chapter will focus on the construction of Irish identity in the context of the mosaic of races, and the racial hierarchies, that the British Empire created. In the late nineteenth and early twentieth centuries, white settler regimes from Canada to Australasia to southern Africa aggressively demanded the right of self-determination for themselves and gradually achieved dominion status within the framework of an emerging empire-commonwealth. This process of change was accompanied by a new imperial discourse that celebrated the British as an "imperial race," embraced the white populations of the Dominions as "Britons overseas," and proclaimed that "the whole British people throughout the world constitute a great democracy."[7] But most architects of the New Imperialism had no intention of including Indians, Africans, or any other "colored race" within the parameters of the "British people throughout the world." At best, the dark-skinned races that inhabited the empire were regarded as "primitive" and "backward" peoples who could, perhaps, evolve toward the privilege of limited self-government over a period of decades, or even centuries.

These developments confronted Irish nationalists with a familiar question: what was their relationship to other peoples who were seeking liberation? Were the inalienable rights they demanded for themselves based on their claim to be a white and European people? Or were they, as Daniel O'Connell had insisted, "Aborigines," an indigenous people victimized by a settler regime, who could—on that basis—unite with the "colored races" of the empire as allies in a broader anticolonial struggle?[8] Insofar as Irish nationalists envisioned the world in terms of a mosaic of races and saw themselves as a colonized people whose land and liberty had been stolen by a voracious alien intruder, it was possible for them to develop a sense of solidarity with the people of India, Egypt, and southern Africa in a common struggle against colonialism in general and the British Empire in particular. But once they claimed the mantle of whiteness for themselves, once they based their sense of entitlement on the belief that they were a "white nation," their capacity to build broad anticolonial solidarity was significantly compromised.

In the last quarter of the nineteenth century and the first decade of the twentieth, these issues played out with compelling force in South Africa, where the "heroic Boers"—white people of European descent—took up arms to defend the liberty and autonomy they had fought for centuries to achieve, where imperial Britain cloaked its quest for global supremacy in the language of democracy and progress, and where a bewildering array of dark-skinned indigenous peoples sought to stave off the devastation and dispossession that the march of "civilization" had entailed. Inevitably, perhaps, the Boers became a vivid symbol of the festering grievances and heady aspirations that were at the very heart of Irish nationalism. Undeniably, the war between Boer and Briton that engaged the world's attention from October 1899 to May 1902 played a vital role in the regeneration of Irish nationalism as a mass movement focused squarely on the question of sovereignty in the context of empire. But the South African War also served to recast the fight for Irish freedom as part of a global struggle for the rights of "white men."[9] In doing so, it blinded even the most progressive Irish nationalists to the rights and grievances of South Africa's black majority.

The old adage about the British Empire—that "the Irish fought for it, the Scottish and Welsh ran it, but the English kept the profits"—is no doubt an oversimplification.[10] But Irishmen were disproportionately represented in the British army. Peter Karsten points out that in 1830, "no less than 42.2% of all non-commissioned officers and men throughout the British Army were Irish, a figure far out of proportion to their numbers in the United Kingdom." Two decades later, Irishmen continued to make up half of the soldiers in the army of the East India Company and perhaps 40 percent of the regular British army troops in India.[11] Protestants served overwhelmingly as officers in the armed forces and in the higher echelons of the Indian Civil Service, so much so that in the 1890s seven of India's eight provinces were governed by Irishmen and the Indian Army was under the command first of the Anglo-Irish general Frederick Sleigh Roberts and then of Londonderry-born George Stuart White.[12]

Catholics were first allowed to enlist in the British army in large numbers in the 1790s, and for more than a century thereafter tens and even hundreds of thousands of Irishmen continued to follow the increasingly well-worn path into the armed forces of the Crown. Many joined Irish regiments such as the Connaught Rangers, the Royal Dublin Fusiliers, and the King's Liverpool Regiment (popularly known as the Liverpool Irish). In some cases, their uniform jackets were green, and the insignias on their jackets included harps, shamrocks, or other distinctively Irish symbols. They marched to and from Catholic mass in military formation and were allowed special celebrations on Saint Patrick's Day.[13] Radical nationalists pleaded with them not to "take the King's [or the Queen's] shilling" and, on occasion, denounced them as "traitors to Ireland," even as the "meanest curs in creation." But especially for poor agricultural laborers and their counterparts in urban areas, the choice was often framed as "'take the shilling' or starve." Thus the Irish revolutionary James Connolly, who was born in Edinburgh to Irish emigrant parents, enlisted in the King's Liverpool Regiment at the age of fourteen and was stationed in Ireland for seven years. His oldest brother had preceded him in the same regiment and was sent to India in 1877.[14]

Irish nationalists, at home and in the diaspora, responded in diverse ways to Britain's quest for global hegemony. Many leaders of the Irish Parliamentary Party emphasized their commitment to preserving "the unity and integrity of the Empire." This was especially true of Isaac Butt. The son of an Anglican clergyman from Donegal, Butt was a product of the Protestant Ascendancy. By 1870 he had become committed to home rule or, in his words, to "a self-government which gives us the entire right to manage our own affairs." But he emphasized from the outset that home rule was fully compatible with a continuing commitment to the empire. "We have paid dearly enough" for Britain's "vast foreign and colonial possessions," he argued, and thus "we are entitled to our share in them."[15] Butt went too far, however. So great was his enthusiasm for empire, so transparent his identification with the "conquerors," that his status as a spokesman for Irish aspirations was seriously jeopardized. His rival and successor, Charles Stewart Parnell, was a far more confrontational figure. At times, especially when speaking at mass meetings in Ireland, he allowed himself the luxury of virulent anti-imperial rhetoric. But he was more careful and constrained in the House of Commons—"very strong," one of his parliamentary colleagues noted, "in NOT saying the thing which should not be said." It fell to Parnell's eventual successor John Redmond to return constitutional nationalism to a more fulsome embrace of empire. Echoing Isaac Butt, he told an English audience in 1913 that "we ask . . . to be allowed to cross the threshold into an Empire—ours . . . by right of service as well as yours."[16]

More than Butt, though, Redmond and his Irish Party lieutenants made Ireland's allegiance to the empire contingent on the granting of home rule. Ireland *wanted* to be a loyal partner in the imperial project, they argued; the denial of her quest for self-government made such loyalty difficult to muster. But "on the day Home Rule was conceded to Ireland," the Belfast MP Joseph Devlin declared, "Ireland would become in good faith the friend and supporter and co-partner with Great Britain in the perils, as well as the glories, of the British Empire."[17]

No matter what their differences, virtually all home rulers shared a deep resentment of "the Hottentot system of governing Ireland," a system rooted in the belief that the Irish, like the indigenous peoples of Africa, lacked the capacity to govern themselves. As late as 1886, the Conservative Party leader Lord Salisbury dismissed the Irish demand for home rule by comparing the people of Ireland to the "Hottentots" of South Africa, and the *Dublin Evening Mail* (a Unionist newspaper) fretted that too many Irishmen and -women were "in the moral and intellectual condition of Dahomey." For many nationalists, then, it became strategically wise and psychologically necessary to insist that like Canadians and Australians, the Irish people were a white, and European, race, entitled to home rule for precisely that reason. Redmond's lieutenant John Dillon told an audience in New Zealand that the Irish deserved self-government "because we are white men," and Redmond himself asked an English audience in 1913 why Ireland should be the "only . . . white race in the Empire that is to be denied the right to govern herself."[18]

It is tempting to argue that home rulers sought to locate Irish demands for a greater measure of self-government within the framework of white entitlement, whereas radical nationalists were more thoroughgoing anti-imperialists, willing to stand shoulder to shoulder with Indians, Egyptians, and Zulu warriors in a common struggle against the British Empire. But in fact the two nationalist traditions were far from consistent in their attitude toward the empire and the mosaic of races and nations it encompassed. Some home rulers, including Frank Hugh O'Donnell, sought to encourage close ties between Irish and Indian nationalists. O'Donnell was born in an English army barracks and educated in Galway, where he graduated with numerous honors from the Queen's College. Elected to Parliament in 1874, he played an important role in broadening the concept of home rule to include all of England's colonial possessions—above all, Ireland and India. He argued that "India has sacred claims to Irish sympathy, because it was Irish soldiers, Irish regiments, and often Irish generals and statesmen who deprived India of her native government and independence."[19] More generally, the Irish Party's role in Parliament was to serve as a persistent (if not altogether consistent) critic of British imperial policies as they applied to both white and "coloured" peoples.[20]

Radical nationalists generally expressed more hostility to the empire than their home rule rivals did. Many of them were willing to contemplate an alliance with virtually any adversary of perfidious Albion. This could include European nations such as France, Russia, and Germany or "coloured" peoples such as Afghans, Indians, and Sudanese. Such a stance did not necessarily imply a commitment to racial equality or hostility to imperialism as such. With the notable exception of James Connolly, Irish nationalism did not give rise to economic and structural critiques of empire like those produced by Vladimir Lenin and J. A. Hobson. But if systemic analysis was notably lacking, moral outrage at the empire's crimes and a strong—if not universal—sense of solidarity with other victims of British imperialism were often important components of radical nationalism.

Michael Davitt and Patrick Ford embodied this broader sense of solidarity in their own lives and articulated it with particular eloquence. Davitt was the son of peasants from County Mayo who were evicted from their home during the Great Famine. Thirty years later, from a jail cell in England's Portland Prison, he vividly recalled the trauma of an experience he had shared with significant numbers of his countrymen and women. In the summer of 1850, he wrote, "We were one morning thrown out on the roadside and our little house and home [was] pulled down before our eyes by the reigning institution; the 'Crowbar Brigade.'" Davitt was only four at the time, but he nonetheless remembered "the remnants of our household furniture flung about the road, the roof of our house falling in and the thatch taking fire," while his parents looked on with four young children, the youngest of whom was only two months old, and wept at the sight of their "burning homestead."[21]

Soon thereafter, Davitt's family emigrated to the east Lancashire textile town of Haslingden, where his parents found employment as fruit hawkers. Michael went to work in a textile mill at the age of nine and lost his right arm in a factory accident two years later. As a teenager he joined the Irish Republican Brotherhood and was sentenced to fifteen years' penal servitude for gunrunning. After his release from Dartmoor Prison in December 1877, he returned to County Mayo, where he was "greeted as a returning hero with torch-light parades and cheering crowds." His goal, he concluded, must be to lead "a war against landlordism for a root settlement of the land question." He became the "father" of the Irish National Land League, which fought to restore ownership of the soil to those who worked it. Characteristically, he also looked outward and helped to build an American Land League that established more than nine hundred branches and raised more than half a million dollars to support the struggle in Ireland. During his third tour of the United States, in 1882, he reminded the American Irish that the Land War was not only a battle for the "rights of your kindred, but for those of industrial humanity throughout the world."[22]

Although Davitt and Ford spent relatively little time in each other's company during their overlapping careers as agitators, they had much in common. Born in 1837, Ford emigrated from Galway in 1845 and settled with his family in Boston, where he came under the influence of William Lloyd Garrison. After serving in the Ninth Massachusetts Regiment during the American Civil War, he founded the *Irish World* in 1870 and quickly made it one of the leading voices of a movement for social reform that aimed at creating a "cooperative commonwealth" in the United States.[23] Although Ford was not a socialist, he embraced a wide array of reform proposals such as the income tax and the eight-hour day, and he envisioned a society in which "the wage system, competition, profit-taking, and 'distinctive classes' would all disappear." He was, moreover, a strong supporter of the Land League, in Ireland and America. Through a special Spread the Light Fund, he was able to distribute nearly half a million free copies of his newspaper in Ireland between 1879 and 1882. The effect was electric, "as if some vast Irish-American invasion was sweeping the country with new and irresistible principles of liberty and democracy." Ford's goal was to link the issues of land and labor in an international context. He declared that "the cause of the poor tenant in Donegal is the cause of the factory slave in Fall River," and he sought to unite the "Irish serf" and the English wage slave in a common struggle against a common foe.[24]

In important respects, Ford, Davitt, the renowned social reformer Henry George,[25] and a few other stalwarts became the informal executive committee of a radically democratic and internationalist Green Atlantic—focused first and foremost on Ireland, America, and Britain but committed to "Universal Justice and the Rights of Humanity."[26] In the pages of his newspaper, Ford expressed a keen sense of solidarity with oppressed peoples around the world irrespective of their color and alleged level of civilization. His associate, the *Irish World*'s European correspondent Thomas J. Mooney, became a distinctive critic of empire and defender of the oppressed in his own right. He denounced imperial expansion as the theft of land and emphasized the need to "call out boldly for the *land to the cultivator*," from Ireland to India to the Sudan.[27]

Much of Ford's agenda was anathema to "pure" nationalists, who declared it "pernicious . . . to put the claims of a class . . . above the claims of the nation." His most articulate critic was the journalist John Devoy, who had entered New York Harbor as a much-heralded Fenian exile in 1871 and quickly emerged as the most compelling voice of physical force nationalism in the United States. As early as 1878 Devoy had grasped the importance of land agitation for Irish nationalism, and he characterized landlordism as the "greatest curse inflicted by England on Ireland." But he was appalled at the direction of Ford's politics and was soon characterizing his rival as a "raving lunatic." He argued, moreover, that in Ford's "tremendous plans" for "universal social reform, Ireland has a very small place indeed." "Are we men who have undertaken to effect a great and radical change in the tenure of land that will embrace the whole world?" Devoy asked. "Do we propose a great social revolution that will alter the present constitution of human society? . . . Or are we Irishmen struggling for the welfare of our own people?" His answer was unequivocal: "We are fighting for the Irish people and for the Irish people alone."[28]

In fact, there were moments when the "Irish people" themselves expressed a strong sense of solidarity with races and nations beyond their shore. This was vividly evident during the Land War of 1879–82. What began as a local struggle and spread like wildfire to become a national movement for land reform also became a movement with international and anticolonial overtones, in part because it coincided with widely publicized campaigns by British military forces in Afghanistan and southern Africa. Land League organizers and propagandists were quick to make the connection between the history of English atrocities in Ireland and the rapacity of British imperialism. The editor of the *Nation* accused Britain of "waging a war of extermination [in southern Africa] such as they waged in Ireland in the days of Elizabeth, burning the homes of the people whose land they have invaded and hunting them down like brutes." When Davitt, Parnell, and other representatives of the Land League addressed crowds of tenant farmers, they were often greeted with sustained cheering for the Zulu king Cetshwayo and for his defiant people, who at that moment were locked in bitter combat with a British force that was invading their homeland. Although Davitt was a direct and enthusiastic participant in these expressions of international solidarity, they did not originate with him. Rather, they reflected a widespread belief—spelled out by the organizers of the historic Irishtown meeting of April 1879—that the cause was the same "from the China towers of Pekin to the round towers of Ireland, from the cabins of Connemara to the kraals of Kaffirland, from the wattled homes of the isles of Polynesia to the wigwams of North America."[29]

From a long-term perspective, it is undeniable that Davitt was one of the giants of Irish nationalism. His critics, in his own time and since, have charged that he ultimately soft-pedaled the social question and became "unflinchingly aligned to constitutional nationalism." He was elected to Parliament in 1892 as a member of the Irish Parliamentary Party. But the Irish Party and Parliament were never a good fit for him, and he resigned his seat in 1899.[30] He actually broadened the scale of his activity as he aged and became a genuine internationalist. He sympathized with India's struggle for freedom and became a relentless opponent of British imperial policy in Africa. He defended the rights of Aborigines against the predation of white Australians, some of whom were Irish immigrants or Australians of Irish descent. He spoke out forcefully against the vicious anti-Semitic pogroms in early twentieth-century Russia and supported the right of the Jewish people to a homeland in Palestine. When he died in 1906, the British socialist Keir Hardie memorialized this "one-armed friend of humanity" as "the founder and chief of the Irish Land League . . . [who] brought into Irish politics the new spirit of internationalism and of labour and social emancipation."[31]

But a closer look at Davitt in the context of the conflict between Boer and Briton at the end of the nineteenth century can shed further light on the pitfalls of constructing national identity on a foundation of binary opposition and illuminate the magnetic pull of a rights discourse grounded in white entitlement.[32] During and after the South African War, Davitt venerated the Boers and vilified the British; indeed, he created a near-perfect set of polarities—one representing the good, the other embodying evil. He declared that the Boers were "absolutely in the right in heroically defending with their lives the independence of their country," whereas Britain was committing "murder and robbery . . . for the basest of motives."[33] In constructing this binary, he allowed himself to stereotype and demonize the dispossessed indigenous peoples of South Africa who were seeking to use the chaos that war created to reclaim their land and restore a measure of their dignity.[34] But Davitt was hardly alone in this regard;

5.1. Michael Davitt, 1904 (courtesy of the Board of Trinity College Library Dublin)

his idealization of the Boers and his blindness to the just aspirations of black Africans reflected a perspective that was shared by a broad spectrum of world opinion.[35]

The Boers were the quintessential white settlers. Their Dutch ancestors had arrived at the Cape of Good Hope in the 1650s, and they were gradually joined by an influx of French and German immigrants who blended into the larger Dutch community. They spoke Dutch or, increasingly, Afrikaans, a creolized form of speech that blended various Dutch dialects with the spoken languages of several of the European, Asian, and indigenous groups who inhabited South Africa.[36] Although many Dutch settlers lived in Cape Town and its agricultural hinterland, as a people they became famous for their treks to the interior in search of better land and to escape the constraints imposed by the Dutch and British governments. In 1891 the South African novelist Olive Schreiner celebrated the "long 'trek' of the Boer peoples . . . which in its ultimate essence is a search, not for riches, not for a land where mere political equality may be found, but for a world of absolute and untrammeled individual liberty; for a land where each white man shall reign . . . over a territory absolutely his own."[37] For all of her romantic racialism, Schreiner succeeded in capturing the contradiction at the heart of the Boers' persona: they were, at once, supreme individualists (or fiercely independent family units) and a people bound together by a strong sense of common destiny.[38] In an increasingly secular world, the Boers were portrayed as devoutly religious—"simple men with only the Bible to guide them." They came to regard themselves as God's chosen people who were predestined to build an African city on a hill, but who then asked to be left alone to raise their cattle, cultivate their crops, control their native subalterns, and worship their God in their own way.[39]

In 1795, and again in 1806, the British seized the Cape Peninsula from the Dutch and gradually established sovereignty over all of South Africa. The fact that the Boers resisted Britain's imperial agenda and succeeded in constructing two independent republics—the Transvaal and the Orange Free State—made them all the more irresistible to Irish nationalists as a symbol of courage and resolve. When the discovery of gold on the Witwatersrand caused Britain to reassert its sovereignty over the Transvaal, it created a compelling David and Goliath narrative, pitting the spiritual quest of self-reliant Dutch farmers against the materialism and militarism of a bloated empire.

It is hardly surprising, then, that Irish nationalists supported the Boers and saw them as allies in their own struggle for self-government. But the Boer worldview and narrative of history were not only avowedly Christian and implicitly anti-imperialist but also deeply and reflexively white supremacist. Actually, until the nineteenth century, the color line in South Africa remained remarkably permeable. From the moment of their arrival on the subcontinent in 1652, the Dutch had been outnumbered by the "coloured" peoples they encountered: the brown-skinned Khoikhoi and San, or (in the language of white settlers) "Hot-tentots" and "Bushmen," who barely survived the Europeans' diseases, superior weaponry, and draconian labor discipline; the many Bantu-speaking African peoples, or "Kaffirs," who were concentrated in the vast interior regions that Dutch farmers coveted; and the slaves, who were imported from East Africa (Mozambique and Madagascar) and Asia (India, Ceylon, Malaya, and Java).[40] Since whites continued to be a small minority of the population, sexual liaisons across racial lines were inevitable. This created a new race of "Coloureds," who symbolized the instability of the evolving racial hierarchy. Some Coloureds, especially light-skinned young women, were able to pass into the white com-munity through marriage, for in general the Boers remained committed less to abstract notions of racial purity than to their "right" to expropriate the land and control the labor of peoples they regarded as both inferior and indispensable.[41]

British authorities sought to Anglicize the Dutch settler population through the promotion of the English language and to protect colored peoples from the harsh forms of servitude the settlers had imposed on them. The keenest defenders of dark-skinned servants and slaves were British missionaries, some of whom were closely associated with the transatlantic abolitionist movement. The Reverend John Philip, who arrived in the Cape Colony in 1819 to supervise the work of the London Missionary Society, infuriated the settlers by express-ing his belief in racial equality and by affirming that in "scattering the seeds of civilization, social order, and happiness" among Khoi, Coloureds, and black Africans, the missionaries were also "extending British interests, British influ-ence, and the British empire."[42] The final straw came when the British Parlia-ment ended slavery throughout the empire in the 1830s. It now seemed that there was "no longer any justice for the burghers, but only for the blacks." Thus thousands of Boers set out from the coastal settlements of the Cape Colony and began a journey toward the interior, where they ruthlessly suppressed the Bantu-speaking peoples whose lands they seized. In Afrikaner mythology, this became the Great Trek, and the Boers rationalized the imperative that had set them in motion in frankly racist terms. Anna Steenkamp, the niece of one of the leaders of the Great Trek, recalled in 1843 that it was not so much the fact of emancipation that "drove us to such lengths" as the realization that Africans and Coloureds were being "placed on an equal footing with Christians, con-trary to the laws of God and the natural distinction of race and religion. . . . It was intolerable for any decent Christian to bow down beneath such a yoke," she concluded, "wherefore we rather withdrew in order thus to preserve our doctrines in purity."[43]

In some respects, Steenkamp's observation is highly misleading. Even though the Boers "withdrew" and sought to place themselves beyond the reach of British authority, the evolving history of South Africa was never reducible to Boer versus Briton (or, for that matter, to white versus black). British settlers in the Eastern Cape resented John Philip and the work of the London Missionary

Society as much as their Boer counterparts did, and they were every bit as determined to conquer and subjugate the black Africans who contested their control of land and other valuable resources. Although British authorities often spoke of the need to safeguard the rights of the "Native" population, in the end they usually allowed the settlers to have their way. In fact, by launching brutal scorched-earth campaigns against a succession of African polities, the British army served as the ultimate guarantor of the settlers' agenda.[44]

The roots of the war of 1899–1902 can be traced most directly to the 1870s and the British government's effort to extend and rationalize its authority by creating a federal union of the four separate white regimes (the Cape Colony, Natal, the Orange Free State, and the Transvaal, formally known as the South African Republic). In pursuit of this objective, Britain annexed the independent Transvaal in 1877, thereby provoking a surge of grassroots resistance that culminated in an armed uprising and the defeat of British forces at Majuba Hill, on the Transvaal-Natal border, in February 1881. The South African Republic thus regained its independence, with the reluctant acquiescence of the British government. Soon thereafter, however, the discovery of huge gold deposits on the Witwatersrand transformed a "ramshackle" republic into a vital economic asset for Britain and a strategic beachhead for the entire empire. The gold rush on the Rand led to the influx of large numbers of foreigners, or *Uitlanders*, many of them British citizens. Soon a "deep cultural gulf" separated the rural, God-fearing, and insular Boers from the urban, secular, and aggressively self-serving *Uitlanders*. When the government of President Paul Kruger sought to limit the power of the newcomers and resisted demands to liberalize the franchise to accommodate them, a crisis ensued. Speaking the language of "justice, liberty, and humanity," leading British politicians and imperial administrators such as Joseph Chamberlain and Alfred Milner seized the opportunity to demonstrate that "we, not the Dutch, are Boss."[45]

The war began in October 1899.[46] In its early stages, the "plucky Boer farmers" caught the British off guard and won a succession of spectacular victories that made them folk heroes throughout much of the world.[47] But after sending massive reinforcements to South Africa, Britain regained the upper hand, and the conflict became a stalemate between two determined but unequal adversaries.[48] The Boers responded to Britain's numerical superiority with a brilliant campaign of guerrilla warfare in which "bands of Boers who seemed to spring from the earth" harassed and obstructed their ponderous adversaries with great skill.[49] The British in turn pursued a scorched-earth policy—reminiscent of Sherman's famous march through Georgia—that included the burning of Boer farms, the confiscation or killing of livestock, and, eventually, the imprisonment of Boer women and children in concentration camps, where nearly thirty thousand of them died of malnutrition and disease. "Any one knows that in war, cruelties more horrible than murder can take place," the Boer general

Christian de Wet acknowledged, but he professed amazement, even disbelief, that such atrocities had been "committed against defenseless women and children . . . by the civilized English nation."[50]

In 1899 Michael Davitt joined with an emerging cohort of radical nationalists—notably, James Connolly, Maud Gonne, and Arthur Griffith—to build a mass movement in support of the Boers. Connolly was sui generis, certainly in the Irish context. Compelled by grinding poverty to leave school at an early age and to join the British army soon thereafter, he became a brilliant Marxist theoretician who played a pioneering role in the quest to reconcile nationalism with revolutionary socialism. He was contemptuous of home rule, which he regarded as a "sham and a fraud, supported and advocated by timeservers and tricksters."[51] But he was sympathetic to cultural nationalism. Indeed, in recent years scholars have recognized his *Labour in Irish History* (1910) as an important contribution to the Irish Literary Revival, and after his execution, one of his most thoughtful contemporaries acknowledged that "his was the most vital democratic mind in the Ireland of his day." Connolly differed from most home-grown socialists in his belief that Irish republicans could be won over to the goal of creating a "workers' republic," and he worked hard to develop ties with Gonne and Griffith. Above all, he sought to use every crisis, international and domestic, to advance his goal of the revolutionary overthrow of British—and capitalist—rule in Ireland. Thus he welcomed the coming of the South African War as the "beginning of the end" for the "great, blustering British Empire" and threw himself into the task of hastening the empire's demise.[52]

Gonne was a compelling figure in her own right—a "goddess," one of her many admirers called her, and a "creature from another planet." The daughter of a British army officer, she was nonetheless a zealous Irish nationalist. The lover of a reactionary French Royalist who believed that "too much democracy was weakening France," she was nonetheless willing to join with James Connolly, Ireland's leading advocate of socialist revolution, in supporting the Boers. A woman who was drawn to the stage and to street protests like the proverbial moth to a flame, she engaged in a flamboyant campaign to undermine British army recruiting in Dublin. Like Connolly, she dared to hope that war against England was on Ireland's horizon and that "through the smoke, and the fire, and the darkness, life, light, and regeneration will come."[53]

Unlike Connolly and Gonne, Griffith had close and direct ties to Afrikaner nationalism, for he had lived and worked in the Transvaal for more than eighteen months in 1897 and 1898.[54] He came home to edit the *United Irishman*, a separatist weekly that first appeared in March 1899, soon after his return. To counteract and undermine British rule, Griffith preached self-reliance and called for grass-roots initiative to build the infrastructure of a fully autonomous Irish nation within the shell of the decadent old order that Britain had imposed on Ireland.

But in the context of 1899, he looked outward as well as inward, and he turned the *United Irishman* into an aggressive purveyor of pro-Boer propaganda. Indeed, it was in part because of Griffith's unstinting effort that October 1, 1899, witnessed one of the largest political demonstrations in Dublin's history as a raucous crowd of twenty thousand gathered in the city center. (There was a similar, although much smaller, rally in Johannesburg's Von Brandis Square on the same day, organized by the militantly pro-Boer Irish community in the Transvaal.)[55] According to the *United Irishman*, "A vast impromptu procession swept through the streets [of Dublin], cheering for the Boers, the Irishmen of the Transvaal, and Majuba Hill."[56] The size of the demonstration surprised its organizers. It also stunned the authorities, as the event served to crystallize a euphoric belief that the resistance offered by the Boers would mean the "downfall of England." Irish Unionists and their Tory allies charged, with some basis, that there was more than a hint of sedition in the escalating pro-Boer movement. Irish Parliamentary Party MP Patrick O'Brien waved the *vierkleur*, the flag of the South African Republic, at the October 1 rally and expressed the hope that "instead of firing on the Boers[, Irish regiments in South Africa] would fire on Englishmen." In the same vein, Maud Gonne pleaded with Irish soldiers serving in the British army to "cast off the hideous English uniform and fight on the side of right and justice."[57] In this case the "side of right and justice" meant the Irish Transvaal Brigade, headed by Colonel John Blake, a West Point graduate and veteran of the U.S. Cavalry, and Major John MacBride, an Irishman from County Mayo who would later fight and die in the Easter Rising of 1916. Eventually, two Irish brigades fought with the Boers, but they enrolled no more than several hundred men, whereas more than thirty thousand Irishmen served in the British army in South Africa.[58] Undaunted by this disparity, Gonne and other women took the lead in confronting British soldiers and their Irish girlfriends on the streets of Dublin. She bragged that "almost every night there were fights in O'Connell Street," and Unionists were soon complaining that "at the present moment Her Majesty's soldiers are forbidden to walk through the streets for fear of offending the tender susceptibilities of Boer sympathisers."[59]

There were Dublin neighborhoods where family members and friends rallied around the men who had "taken the shilling," and even many nationalists could not help but feel proud of the "gallantry" of the Irish regiments serving in South Africa. But the predominant sentiment—in Dublin and throughout much of the nation—was decidedly pro-Boer. William O'Brien, one of the few leaders of the Irish Party who did not support the Transvaal's war of independence, readily acknowledged that "an all but delirious enthusiasm for the Boer cause . . . is convulsing Ireland." And the French sociologist Louis Paul-Dubois recalled that "in the early days of the South African war, I used to watch the effect of the announcement of British defeats on the people of Dublin. The crowds would thrill with excitement, and men, radiant with delight, would stop in the streets to express to utter strangers the pleasure that the news gave them."[60]

Davitt resigned his seat in Parliament in October 1899 to protest Britain's war against the South African republics. In late March 1900 he arrived in Pretoria and served for nearly three months as a correspondent for William Randolph Hearst's *New York Journal American* and the Dublin *Freeman's Journal*. He visited the sites of major battles, interviewed a number of leading Boer generals and politicians, and was present at the last meeting of the legislature of the South African Republic before the British forces entered Pretoria.[61] In his articles, he not only exalted the "superior" physical and moral qualities of the Boers but also allowed himself to become their mouthpiece to the wider world on the "native question." From a physical standpoint, he wrote, he had never seen "a finer type of manhood" anywhere. The Boer combatants were "strong, healthy, sinewy men, with bodies that seemed built to defy fatigue, and with faces which you would never associate with fear." He found their character and moral qualities even more impressive. He described them as "quiet, sober-looking, and earnest men" among whom "there was no rowdyism of any kind, no disorder, no intoxication." Most of them were "sons of the soil," and, he told his Irish audience, they owned the land they worked. There was "no landlordism" in the Boer republics, he reported, and there were "no evictions." In fact, there had been significant levels of social and economic inequality among Dutch South Africans since the emergence of a rural elite in the eighteenth century, and this inequality was magnified by the impact of the mineral revolution. Many white farmers *were* landless and thus conspicuously lacking a "status commensurate with their colour." Some were forced into unskilled labor and were observed working "side by side with Zulus and Fingoes." Significant numbers of *bywoners*, as landless farmers and laborers were known in Afrikaans, refused to fight to defend the Transvaal, and they were prominent among the Boer soldiers who surrendered to the British and even joined the ranks of the imperial armed forces.[62] Nonetheless, Davitt insisted on seeing the Boers as a unified race and making sweeping generalizations about their character. "Taking the Boer nation as I have found them," he concluded, "I would unhesitatingly say that they are a braver, a better, and a more civilised people than the British."[63]

His experience in South Africa led Davitt to write *The Boer Fight for Freedom*, a massive tome—with 589 pages of text and numerous photographs—that was published in 1902.[64] In it he fell prey to a kind of settler Zionism, premised on the exaltation of heroic white races that brought democracy (for themselves) and a "civilizing" mission to lands that appeared to have no history, no culture, no purpose, other than to be transformed into appendages of European civilization. In the Zionist narrative, the people who inhabited these lands were either rendered invisible or demonized as "savages."[65] To a remarkable degree, Davitt swallowed the Boer narrative of history whole. He not only believed the Boers were "making the noblest stand ever made in human history for their independence" but also wholeheartedly embraced Afrikaner nationalism's creation myth, rooted in the Great Trek of the 1830s in which thousands of *Voortrekkers*

5.2. Boer soldiers, ca. 1900 (Popperfoto/Getty Images)

"ventured forth, trusting in God, to rid themselves of all human despotism, in search of a free land for their children and their children's children."[66]

When the Voortrekkers arrived at the Vaal River, Davitt wrote, they "regarded the new country as their El Dorado." In fact, this "new country" had long been inhabited by various African peoples who had often been as hostile to each other as they were to the European intruders. In a succession of battles that, in the early stages, claimed the lives of hundreds of Boer men, women, and children, the Voortrekkers won a decisive victory over the "cruel and barbarous" Zulu king Dingane at the Battle of Blood River on December 16, 1838, a day the Boers continued to celebrate every year thereafter as Dingane's Day. Davitt joined them in honoring their stunning triumph and in attributing it not to the obvious superiority of the Voortrekkers' rifles and cannons over their adversaries' spears but to the "protecting care of the Almighty." Acknowledging that the Boers had succeeded in creating a "country . . . for white men," he criticized the British for "subjugat[ing]" these heroic "Dutch farmers" and allowing them "few rights or privileges . . . beyond those enjoyed by the Kaffirs around them."[67]

In calling Africans Kaffirs, Davitt dismissed them as "pagans" or "infidels" who were beyond the pale of civilization and Christianity.[68] (In fact, many blacks were Christians, and some of the converts who lived on Protestant

the color question again?

mission stations were quasi-independent landed proprietors whose standard of living was higher than that of many *bywoners*.) In charging that blacks were hanging around "the borders of European possessions" and threatening white settlers with bloodshed, he ignored the fact that it was the "Kaffirs" who had been robbed of their land at a staggeringly asymmetrical cost in human life.[69] (The Boers suffered no fatalities in their victory over Dingane and his warriors in 1838, whereas the Zulu lost more than three thousand lives. The bones of the dead littered the veld for years thereafter.) For black Africans the loss of their land, and their independence, was followed by entrapment in various forms of indentured labor—first in agriculture and then, after the discovery of gold, in the mines of the Rand. As a long-time partisan of the British labor movement, Davitt naturally took the side of the white miners in their class struggle against the mine owners (the "Randlords"). However, his class perspective excluded black mine workers, whose numbers had reached a hundred thousand by 1899. They were relegated to a caste status well below that of the whites and were subjected to a regime of superexploitation that took a horrendous toll in lives, not only from silicosis (the miners' disease) but also from pneumonia and tuberculosis as well. But Davitt refused to treat the massive black presence in the mines as anything but an issue of social control. In *The Boer Fight for Freedom*, he never referred to black miners as workers; rather, they remained "Kaffirs," even "savages," and he congratulated the Boer police and magistrates who "kept [them] under orderly control without undue severity."[70]

The pro-Boers also failed to comprehend another development of major importance that was taking place in the relations between blacks and whites. In many rural areas, African peoples took advantage of the war to pursue an agenda that came to include the restoration of land and livestock the Boers had stolen from them. The key to this development was the arming of black Africans, which went very much against the grain of whites' understanding of the norm in race relations and of the nature of the war. Few whites believed that the indigenous peoples of South Africa had any legitimate aspirations beyond the hope of a modicum of liberty, to be granted at whites' discretion over a period of decades. Given the "savage" reputation of the "Kaffirs" and the fact that they constituted the vast majority of South Africa's population, most whites emphatically believed that participation in the war must be limited to white men. Once the war began, one of the most persistent charges against the British was that they had provided weapons to "all the Native tribes in and around the South African Republic" and that these armed partisans had then committed "horrible atrocities."[71] This was common knowledge, the Boer political and military leader Jan Christian Smuts charged, and in fact historians have estimated that more than one hundred thousand black Africans served with the British forces, and that perhaps as many as thirty thousand of them were armed. In arming "the Natives," Boer general Piet Cronje admonished his British counterpart during the siege of Mafeking, "You have committed an enormous act of wickedness." "Disarm your blacks," Cronje pleaded, "and thereby act the part of a white man in a white man's war."[72]

The arming of blacks and their participation in British military campaigns set the stage for an extraordinary "rebellion from below." Throughout much of the war zone, blacks were active and aggressive participants in the looting of Boer farmhouses, the confiscation of Boer livestock, and even the occupation of Boer farms on a massive scale. In the northern Cape and the western Transvaal, large areas of land were coming under black control. The Kgatla, in particular, "retook land that had been taken from them in the previous forty years" and, according to Shula Marks, "came to control the entire western Transvaal."[73] When Louis Botha, the commandant general of the armed forces of the South African Republic, returned to his farm after the war, he reported, "My Kaffirs told me I had no business there, and I had better leave."[74]

The war created many and diverse opportunities for black insurgency and thereby played a major role in turning the Boers' already precarious world upside down. In a letter to the pro-Boer journalist W. T. Stead, Jan Smuts gave vivid testimony to the reality of this "overturning," as well as to the lurid fantasies it engendered.

> When armed Natives and Coloured boys, trained and commanded by English officers, tread the soil of the Republics in pursuit of the fugitive Boer and try to pay off old scores by insulting his wife and children on their farms; when the Boer women in the Cape Colony have to cook for and serve the brutal Coloured scouts, who roam about the lonely farms of the veld, and are forced to listen to their filthy talk; when they hear these Coloured soldiers of the King boast that after the war the latter will be the owners of the farms of the rebellious Boers and will marry the widows of the heroes who have gone to rest[,] . . . a wound is given to South Africa which Time itself will not heal.[75]

This kind of testimony was common on the Boer side of the conflict. Thus women in the district of Potchefstroom in the Transvaal complained that they were compelled to undertake a forced march, during which their "Kaffir" guards tore the clothes from their bodies and took their children away from them. In despair, "the women knelt before these Kaffirs and begged for mercy," but in return they "had to endure even more impudent language and rude behaviour," including the boast, aimed at hapless Boer men, that "we will make your women our wives."[76]

Like most of his contemporaries, Davitt could not have comprehended the scale and character of the black rebellion from below, and he would not have welcomed it if he did. Instead, he dismissed the Kgatla and other African combatants as mere pawns of the British and routinely denounced them as "cowardly savages."[77] But it had not always been so. In 1879 he had seen the interests of Irish tenant farmers and black Africans as identical, and he had joined his countrymen in arguing that the cause was the same "from the cabins of Connemara to the kraals of Kaffirland, from the wattled homes of the isles of Polynesia to the wigwams of North America." Mass meetings at Westport, County Mayo, and Milltown, County Galway, in June of that year had featured green banners proclaiming "The Land for the People!" and cheers for the French Revolution, the Irish Republic, and the embattled Zulus. (According to historian Paul Townend, "Pro-Zulu cheering became a trademark of Land League meetings.") During his visit to Australasia in 1895, moreover, Davitt was scathingly critical of white settlers' abuse of the Aborigines of Western Australia. "With the game they lived upon gone and their hunting grounds fenced in [by white farmers and ranchers]," he wrote, "[the native people] are forbidden to look for food where it was once found in freedom and abundance." When, in desperation, one of them stole a sheep from a settler, he was likely to be shot. "The white man's law justifies him in stealing the black man's country, his wife and daughters whenever he wants them," Davitt concluded in his *Life and Progress in Australasia*; "but to take a sheep from this moral professor of the ten commandments is to earn the penalty of a bullet!"[78]

Those Aborigines who persisted in trespassing on their own land and survived the experience were punished with sentences of hard labor, during which they were not only "chained to their barrows" but also were compelled to wear iron collars that left terrible burns on their necks when the collar was heated to unbearable temperatures by the "broiling tropical sun." Clearly, in this instance, Davitt's sympathies were entirely with the "black man," but he was nonetheless convinced that the Aborigines were doomed to extinction. "The white man's presence means death to the black man of Australia," he concluded, "and nothing will avert his doom."[79]

Davitt's observations on the appalling condition of the "black man" in Australia were published only two years before his journalistic dispatches from South Africa appeared in American and Irish newspapers. And yet the difference in tone could hardly have been greater. In Australia he saw the Aborigines as victims of aggression and theft on the part of white settlers; this applied not only to their land but also to their wives and daughters, who were defiled, even "stolen," by white men. In South Africa, however, Davitt condemned the native people as "hordes of Kaffirs" who were seeking to dispossess the white settlers! And the "Kaffir" women were also a threat; he reported that their very presence at the edge of Boer military encampments confronted white men with the prospect of "disgrace."[80]

How does one explain the dramatic change in tone in only two years? In the case of the Aborigines of Western Australia, they were doomed to "extermination" and hence were the objects of pity. In this case, moreover, most "white settlers" were British or of British descent (although Davitt was keenly aware that there were large numbers of Irish settlers in Australia as well). But in the Transvaal and the Orange Free State, the "white settlers" were Boers, whose *enemies* were British. Moreover, the "Kaffirs" were not a doomed race; on the contrary, they constituted more than two-thirds of South Africa's population, and their numbers were growing rapidly.[81] Could it be that for Michael Davitt, and for other pioneers of the emerging movement that prefigured the major human rights campaigns of the twentieth century, indigenous peoples were worthy of sympathy only when they appeared as helpless, childlike victims of brutal exploitation by European imperialists?[82]

Alice Stopford Green also played a major role in propagating the myth of the heroic Boers. Born Alice Sophia Amelia Stopford, she was the descendant of a Cromwellian settler who became the owner of large tracts of land in County Meath. Her paternal grandfather was the Anglican bishop of Meath; her father, Edward Adderly Stopford, was also a leading Anglican churchman. One of her five brothers became a colonel in the British army, another served in the British navy, and a third was involved in the construction of railroads in Africa. All in all, hers was a reflexively Unionist family whose members were intensely committed to the British connection and the defense of the empire.[83]

How, then, did she become an Irish nationalist? Perhaps, in part, by marrying John Richard Green, a former Church of England clergyman turned historian who, according to the *Freeman's Journal*, "almost alone among Englishmen . . . looked upon liberty as the right of all and not as the special property of the Briton."[84] With its focus on the social and cultural life of ordinary Englishmen and -women, his *Short History of the English People* quickly became a classic, if controversial, work of social history. Alice Green assisted her husband in the research and writing of his books, and when he died in 1883, after less than six full years of marriage, she took up his legacy and became a historian in her own right. Rejecting the work of the leading Anglo-Irish historians as self-serving apologias for "aggression and confiscation," she wrote several popular histories of Ireland, beginning with *The Making of Ireland and Its Undoing* in 1908.[85]

A gracious hostess and keen conversationalist, Green turned her London home into a salon for leading Liberals, Fabian socialists, Boer generals, African reformers, and Irish nationalists ranging from the youthful Irish Party activist Thomas Kettle to the born-again Fenian Roger Casement. Her connections in society and government enabled her to arrange a visit to the Boer prisoner-of-war camp on the desolate island of Saint Helena in the fall of 1900. (She later claimed that she was the "only civilian who was ever allowed to land there during the war.") Thereafter, in two articles published in the journal *Nineteenth Century*, she offered an allegedly neutral but intensely partisan portrayal of the Boers. They were, she reported, a "towering crowd" of "peasant warriors" who demonstrated all the roughness and insularity of their rural, frontier environment. At the same time, she found them the soul of "courtesy and consideration"; indeed, by her lights they were men of the "utmost politeness and good breeding." She feared that Britain's intent was to break their spirit through the imposition of a "system of military discipline." But, she warned, it would fail.

"It would fail with Europeans—how much more with this people," the hardy frontiersmen who were "accustomed to track their way over the veldt by the stars, riding as owners over those wide solitudes, the priests and patriarchs of their homes, with the stubbornness of free men, and the pride of a dominant race!"[86] (All of this from an author who had promised to convey the situation on Saint Helena "in the Boers' own words, without any comment whatever on my part"! No wonder Jan Smuts would one day say to her, "I look on you as a Boer. I talk to you as a sister.")[87]

At times Green was far more willing than Davitt to recognize the complexity of South African society and even to acknowledge some diversity of opinion among the prisoners of war she encountered. In the articles she wrote after her visit to Saint Helena, she reported meeting with "traders, schoolmasters, labouring men, [and] big farmers" and described one Boer prisoner as an "extremely poor man."[88] However, in the privacy of her diary, Green gave voice to views that implied racial superiority on one side and inferiority on the other. Inevitably, most of the Boers Green encountered were farmers, "huge, powerful men" who were, at the same time, "sober, moderate, reasonable." Their antithesis was the English prison guard whose nickname was Alexander the Rat. According to Green, he had a "narrow mean forehead, small nose, [and] red blotched face with coarse scanty whiskers." Like him, other British soldiers in the camp were "vastly inferior to the Boers in physique and manner—much smaller and curiously *meaner*—lying about and standing around in an ill-governed vulgar way."[89]

In her idealization of the Boers, Green focused overwhelmingly on the men, whom she clearly found magnetically attractive. But for many observers all over the world, the horrific conditions Boer women faced became one of the major motifs of the war, especially when the British insisted on herding them and their children into disease-ridden concentration camps. Maud Gonne took up the task of acquainting Irish nationalists with the Boer women's plight and with their exemplary heroism. A rebel who took the lead in founding *Inghinidhe na hÉireann* (Daughters of Erin) because she resented the virtual exclusion of women from male-dominated nationalist organizations in Ireland, Gonne nonetheless insisted that the Boer women were upholding the ideal of domesticity even as they actively joined the fight against the hated British. "The Boer women go to battle with husbands and fathers," she wrote in the *United Irishman*. They used rifles and pistols "with the skill of a sharpshooter" and had "muscles like iron." And yet even in a war that obliterated the boundary between the private and public spheres, she assured Irish readers that "the Boer woman . . . is strictly a domestic woman. She is satisfied by her own fireside. Her whole heart is centered in the little world that she calls by the sacred name of home."[90]

Like Davitt, Gonne easily fell into a pattern of demonizing not only the British but also the indigenous peoples whom she linked with the British as the

Boers' enemies. Thinking, no doubt, of the legend of the Great Trek, she asked her Irish readers to remember that "the Boers have been driven like cattle before the encroachments of the English. They have to deal with the persecutions of the white man and the fiendish treachery of the native tribes." Shifting her frame of reference to North America, she asked her readers to "look back to the Puritan maidens" and to the "women of the frontier." "In their constant fear of the Indians[, American women] were ever ready to protect their homes." In this they were very much like the women of the Transvaal, who also faced "savage enemies . . . ever on the watch to despoil their homes."[91] Once again, it was a case of creating a Manichaean contrast between "civilization" and "savagery" and of siding with white settlers against dark-skinned indigenous peoples.

Inevitably, some critics of the pro-Boers pointed out that they ignored "the great[est] question of all, the relation of the Boers to the dark people they dwell among. [Alice Stopford Green] writes always as if the Dutch were the natural rulers of the country," an article in the *Spectator* charged, "not invaders who a few years ago . . . had taken it by force from its owners. God is always with them, she thinks, never with the English, or with the blacks, who have so much to avenge."[92] One must ask, too, about Green's frame of reference when she called the Boers a "superior and dominant race." She seemed to harbor a Darwinian belief that the combination of their frontier environment and their struggles against "savages and wild beasts" had made the Boers superior. But by the time she offered up her public commentary, the Boers were suffering one setback after another on the battlefield, and Green must have recognized that they would be defeated by the British. She may, nonetheless, have preferred the Boers' racial traits to the Britons', but insofar as they were "dominant," it can have been only over the indigenous peoples they had so ruthlessly suppressed. From their vantage point, Green's portrayal of the Boers as "kind" and "peace-loving" was surely a cruel hoax; her recommendation that Britain should learn something positive from the Boers' view of the "native problem," a chilling prospect.[93]

As for Davitt, his Manichaean propensities led him to claim that the Boers "governed their black subjects with more justice and humanity than any English colony in South Africa or elsewhere has ever done."[94] Here, alas, was the kind of (unconscious) falsehood that had undergirded the nineteenth-century argument that the condition of the black chattel was superior to that of the white "wage slave." Not that the British had governed black Africans with justice and humanity. In spite of some rhetorical, and even legal, gestures in that direction, Britain had willingly used "violence and terror" on a massive scale to conquer independent African peoples, and thereafter they had consistently subordinated their needs and aspirations to considerations of commercial interest and imperial strategy. However, although most British policymakers were imbued with an outlook that Philip Curtin has called "evolutionary racism," the Boers' racism was even deeper and more fundamental.[95] They believed that blacks had been created to serve their white masters as "hewers of wood and drawers of water." Indeed, theirs was a worldview that rationalized the permanent subordination, and even annihilation, of the "heathen," who could "be brought to do good and shun evil" only by violent means.[96] In swallowing the narrative of Boer Zionism whole, Davitt averted his gaze from a central element of Boer identity and practice. It was a sorry performance on the part of a man who had earned an international reputation for humanitarianism, but it expressed a viewpoint shared by most of the Irish nationalist community, in Ireland and the diaspora, and by pro-Boers throughout the world.

In idealizing the "Dutch race" of their imagination and demonizing the British, Irish nationalists were, in effect, creating and re-creating themselves. Their monolithic portrait of the Boers as a rural, agricultural, and deeply religious people was a carbon copy of their equally one-dimensional portrayal of their own society. This pastoralism became a major motif of Irish cultural nationalism at the end of the nineteenth century and the beginning of the twentieth. Declan Kiberd argues that it was a "wholly urban creation," by means of which the "urbanized descendants of country people"—many of whom had close ties with London and Paris as well as Dublin—"helped to create the myth of a rural nation."[97] This was as true in South Africa as it was in Ireland. The creators of the mythology of the Great Trek and inventors of the Boer as quintessentially rural and pastoral were disproportionately drawn from the more urban and cosmopolitan areas of the Cape Colony. Indeed, some of the most influential of these Afrikaner nationalists were European immigrants who had been trained in the universities and theological seminaries of Holland and Germany. The very fact that both Ireland and the Transvaal were rapidly becoming integrated into a modern capitalist economy, and that even the most remote communities in these two nations were by now enmeshed in a social order defined by commerce and consumption, made it all the more important to imagine the Boer and the Irish peasant as chaste, undefiled, spiritual—as living beyond the pale of modernity and its corrosive influences.[98]

In this regard, both the Irish and the Afrikaners defined themselves over against the English, who had forsaken spiritual pursuits for the allure of material gain and imperial conquest. Maud Gonne portrayed the differences vividly in her famously controversial article "The Famine Queen." "England is in decadence," she exclaimed in April 1900. "She has sacrificed all to getting money. . . . The men who formerly made her greatness, the men from the country districts[,] have disappeared; they have been swallowed up by the great black manufacturing cities; they have been flung into the crucible where gold is made" and reduced there to a "struggling mass of pale, exhausted slaves."[99]

Alice Stopford Green's romantic portrayal of the Boers reflected the same tendency to idealize the rural, agrarian social order of her imagination and to portray it as a necessary antidote to the new urban world of manufacturing and unfettered commerce.[100] "It is enough to see the Boer as he passes," she exulted about something she had in fact never seen, "and watch his free independent bearing to recognise in him a sort of country aristocrat. Those vast stretches of veldt over which he rides as owner, the wide freedom of the farmer's life, the big solitudes, . . . the patriarchal home, the fact of belonging to the superior and dominant race, these things give the Boer something of self-reliance and native dignity which in these crowded lands we have nearly lost."[101]

Green was creating identities that, for the most part, meshed neatly within a set of binary opposites. The Boers' dignity and resolve derived from their roots in agriculture. "Independence is [the farmer's] very existence," she was told, and it was the farmer's independence that made the Boer such a formidable adversary. Meanwhile, Irish nationalists argued, English soldiers had "no blood in their veins, no strength in their arms." Like Green, some nationalists went even further and claimed that the rank-and-file soldier the British celebrated as "Tommy Atkins" was actually the wretched refuse of urban society—a stunted, mean creature who was physically and morally unfit for the demands of warfare. Thus it was the robust and courageous Irishmen—"our misguided countrymen"—who were sent to the frontlines and sacrificed there so that "the scum of England's cities may live."[102]

The danger that Britain represented came not just from the corrosive effects of urbanization and industrialization but also from the pervasive influence of English culture. In the first issue of the *United Irishman*, Arthur Griffith exhorted the "mothers of the nation to see that their homes shall be kept sacred from the contaminations of the British Press and the gag of the music hall." Above all, "They should look to the preservation of their children's national faith" lest they become "mere mongrels." *Inghinidhe na hÉireann* declared that one of its main goals was "to discourage the reading and circulation of low English literature, the singing of English songs, [and] the attending of vulgar English entertainments at the theatres and music halls." Remarkably, James Connolly, the revolutionary socialist, placed an even more explicit emphasis on the theme of Anglicization as a fount of immorality. Keenly aware of the British military presence in Ireland, he charged that the army was "a veritable moral cesspool, corrupting all within its bounds, and exuding . . . a miasma of pestilence." Its presence—anywhere—was so devastating, he argued, that the "desolation of war would inflict . . . less injury than a peaceful occupation by the 'Soldiers of the Queen.'"[103]

In South Africa there were similar complaints. Facing the increasingly painful consequences of industrialization, the Boers and their allies lashed out at the city, above all at Johannesburg, as the antithesis of everything they valued.[104] "This great fiendish hell of a city," Olive Schreiner called it, "a city which for glitter and gold, and wickedness . . . beats creation." Gone were the social cohesion and sense of common purpose that had characterized the Boer republics as she remembered them. Instead, there were "carriages, and palaces and brothels, and gambling halls," and "every man living for himself, every man fighting for gold, gold, gold, and tramping down everything that stands in his way."[105] But it was not just a matter of precious metal on the Witwatersrand or brothels in Johannesburg. As in Ireland, the reach of "English culture" was even more pervasive and insidious. According to an Afrikaner newspaper, "Our biggest daily papers, the cinemas, the school system, the language of our courts, the shops with their fashions and merchandise, the furniture in our houses are all bastions and agents of a foreign culture which claims for itself the right to overrun and conquer the world."[106]

Ireland's task, then, many cultural nationalists argued, was to be faithful to her own past in constructing her future. Ireland's goal was to build a civilization that was Gaelic, Catholic, rural, and agricultural. Ireland's hope lay in the undeniable fact that in spite of conquest and the cultural genocide that Anglicization portended, the Irish people had always maintained "an enthusiastic fidelity to their National Faith and passionate attachment to the soil."[107]

Here, again, comparisons to the "Dutch race" were irresistible. Michael Davitt, who was repelled by prostitution among the lower orders of British society and sexual infidelity among the fashionable "upper tenth," was deeply moved by the religious faith and morality—above all, the sexual morality—of the Boers.[108] He was equally impressed by their simplicity and complete lack of pretense, and yet this advocate of radically egalitarian land reform in Ireland praised the Boers as noble and chivalrous, a natural aristocracy. General Louis Botha was a farmer but also a "gentleman in manner, and a born soldier." (His wife was an "enthusiastic 'Irish Boer,'" the daughter of an Irish immigrant to South Africa, who "boasts, with much pride, that the blood of Robert Emmet runs in her veins.") General Koos de la Rey "dressed like an artisan"; his Bible was his "inseparable companion." De la Rey thrilled Davitt with his declaration that "England . . . may, for a time, appear to subdue us by her overwhelming strength; but God Almighty is on our side, and in the end we must win." Davitt seemed to suggest that if only the Irish could emulate the absolute certainty and quiet heroism of the Boers, they too could achieve their liberation.[109]

There was, however, one important factor that might have driven a wedge between the two peoples. The Irish honored the religious commitment and spiritual intensity of the Boers, in which they saw a mirror image of their own national character. But the Boers were Calvinists—extreme Protestants—by reputation, and Irish Catholics had been victimized for centuries by Protestant settlers, Protestant landlords, and the lingering weight of an oppressive Protestant Ascendancy. In South Africa the Boer republics had their own penal laws that prohibited Catholic worship—actually, any form of worship except that of the Dutch Reformed Church—and some Catholics regarded the Boers as a "bigoted and proselytizing group of Protestants." How, then, could the Irish and the Dutch come together across this familiar sectarian barrier? In practice, it proved to be relatively easy, for several reasons. First, for the most part the Boers were *not* proselytizers in the sense in which the Irish Catholic community had experienced this phenomenon. Unlike Irish (and British) Protestants, the Boers did not seek to convert Catholics to the "true" religion; instead, they were famous for their desire to turn inward rather than outward, to be left alone. Second, as early as the 1850s, the struggling Roman Catholic Church in South Africa joined Dutch and British settlers in opposing the policies and outlook of John Philip and the London Missionary Society and in advocating racial segregation and subordination as the only solution to the deadly antagonism that characterized the relations between European settlers and Africans. Ultimately, it appears, race trumped religion: the penal laws of the Boer republics were loosely enforced, if at all, and the need for white solidarity took precedence over doctrinal and ecclesiastical disagreement. After all, South Africa was a place where blacks outnumbered whites by a substantial—often overwhelming—margin. Many Boers lived in isolated rural communities, surrounded by black servants, tenant farmers, and agricultural laborers. In these circumstances, they were more than willing to offer hospitality to other white men and women, whatever their religious persuasion, so long as their guests did not pass judgment on the Boers' way of life—above all, on their relations with the indigenous peoples who served as their subalterns. Thus Father James O'Haire, an Irish Catholic priest and outspoken pro-Boer who lived in the Transvaal for twelve years, reported: "I spent half my time traveling about, ministering to my scattered flock, and had to depend upon the hospitality of the Boers—who were all Protestants. That hospitality was never denied me. I found the Boers simple, honest, moral, religious and kind people."[110]

In the final analysis, David did not triumph over Goliath in the South African War. The leaders of the Orange Free State and the Transvaal surrendered to their British adversaries in May 1902. However, although the Boers lost the war, they won the peace. The Union of South Africa became a bastion of Afrikaner power and a major stepping-stone on the long road to complete independence. Even in defeat, the Boers continued to offer inspiration and instruction to their Irish counterparts. "Whenever England goes on her mission of empire, we meet and we strike at her," declared Patrick Pearse in 1914. "Yesterday it was on the South African veldt, tomorrow it may be on the streets of Dublin." During the Easter Rising, the paramilitary forces that Pearse led wore "Boer-style hats known as 'de Wet caps,'" named after the legendary general Christian de Wet. In 1921 Michael Collins, the "Irish de Wet," told his Boer counterpart, "Your great fight against the same foe was the earliest inspiration of the men who have been fighting here for the past two years against foreign aggression. Everyone—man and woman—in Ireland will be delighted to know you are on our side." When Collins was martyred during the Irish Civil War, one of his admirers lamented, "We have lost our young Louis Botha." But it was not just a matter of a single Irish counterpart of de Wet or Botha. The Dublin-based journalist, poet, mystic, and practical philosopher George Russell referred to the entire cohort of "Sinn Féiners" who laid claim to the legacy of Easter 1916 as "our Irish Boers."[111]

Clearly, then, the South African War played a major role in regenerating Irish nationalism as a genuine mass movement, in centering that movement, once again, on questions of sovereignty, and in creating a long-term sense of affinity between Afrikaner and Irish nationalists. P. J. Mathews points out that the war "served to bring forth a new type of separatist nationalism, not secretive like the Fenian movement, but overt in its articulation of an independent foreign policy for the Irish nation." But the agitation that flowed from the South African crucible channeled the discourse of race and nation toward the theme of white entitlement and thus narrowed the parameters of anticolonial solidarity. Indeed, Michael Davitt's refusal to see black Africans as fully formed human beings with their own legitimate grievances and aspirations made them a "people without history" who could have no "agency," no right to act on behalf of their own interests, a people whose choice, as Davitt conceived it, was to serve either as obedient subalterns of the Boers or as malevolent instruments of British imperialism. Davitt, no less than Arthur Griffith, argued that the "Boer fight for freedom" was a "white man's war" about white men's rights—or, as the British labor leader and parliamentary firebrand John Burns put it, about "equal rights for all white men the world over."[112]

CHAPTER SIX

"Because we are white men"

ERSKINE CHILDERS, JAN CHRISTIAN SMUTS, AND THE IRISH QUEST FOR SELF-GOVERNMENT, 1899–1922

> The war between the white races will run its course and pass away. . . . But the Native question will never pass away; it will become more difficult as time goes on.
>
> —Jan Christian Smuts, January 1902

> Ireland is now the only white nationality in the world . . . where the principle of self-determination is not, at least in theory, conceded.
>
> — Erskine Childers, May 1919

THE THEME OF "equal rights for all white men the world over" reemerged as a major motif of the campaign for self-determination that accompanied and followed the Great War.[1] At a moment when newly independent states were arising out of the collapse and military defeat of historic empires, some Irish nationalists were eager to place themselves and their aspirations within a "white" and European framework. Perhaps the most vivid representative of this trend is Erskine Childers, the English-born veteran of the South African War and the Great War and the principal architect and hero of the dramatic Howth gun-running of 1914, which provided rifles and ammunition for the Irish Volunteers. "Without the guns landed at Howth," Martin Mansergh has asserted, "the 1916 Rising would not have been possible."[2] Childers went on to become one of the leading propagandists for the Irish Republic. In June 1919 he characterized Ireland as "a lonely, symbolic figure" that was "tragically isolated" from other European nations. Why? Although "the future of some Asiatic races is still undecided," he wrote, "Europe . . . now consists of free peoples, with the one solitary exception of Ireland." "But that is not the full extent of the anomaly," he continued. "White peoples in the rest of the world, all of them offshoots of Great Britain, ha[ve] already made good their right to self-determination, so that Ireland survives as the only white community on the face of the globe where . . . 'government by consent' . . . is not established."[3]

Childers becomes important for our purposes precisely because he spent much of his adult life coming to terms with thorny, and bitterly contested, questions of self-government in a British imperial context and because—more than any other partisan of Ireland's cause—he linked the right of self-government to whiteness. In this regard he had much in common with the South African leader Jan Christian Smuts.[4] Both men were born in 1870; both attended Cambridge University, the one as a member of the British establishment, the other as a self-described "barbarian from the outer marches of the Empire." Both fought in the South African War, but on different sides, and both saw South Africa and its battle for self-government as vital to the future of Britain's evolving empire-commonwealth. But their paths also diverged, in important ways. Smuts first earned fame as a "Bitter Ender" who swore to fight against British imperialism until "Right" finally triumphed over "Might," no matter how great the odds and the attendant suffering.[5] Then, sensing the inevitability of defeat, he abruptly changed course and became a lifelong advocate of conciliation, "fusion," and the knitting together of Britain's Dominions into a powerful force for good on the world stage. Childers also came away from the South African War as an advocate of conciliation and "fusion" but evolved, gradually, into an unrepentant Irish Republican, a Hibernian variant of the Boer "Bitter Ender." Ironically, though they had many friends in common, the two men met directly only once, in the summer of 1921, and by that time they had become adversaries of sorts.

In the end their lives turned out to be dramatically asymmetrical. Smuts continued to play a major role in South African politics until he was defeated, finally, by the National Party in 1948. Throughout, he had remained a South African patriot who was also an internationalist and a cosmopolitan. He could take comfort from the fact that Cambridge University named him its chancellor, and reinforced his international stature, at virtually the same time the Nationalists displaced him in domestic politics. Two years later, in September 1950, he died, surrounded by family and honored throughout much of the world. For Childers, it could not have been more different. By the end of 1919, he had opted for the Irish side of his conflicted self, and he became an increasingly active partisan of the Irish Republic. When the Free State was created and the independence movement divided into warring camps, his Republican allegiance became more controversial than ever. His Irish adversaries denounced him as a "damned Englishman"; his English detractors—notably, Winston Churchill—vilified him as a "murderous renegade . . . actuated by a deadly and malignant hatred for the land of his birth." Finally, in November 1922, he was captured and executed by Free State forces. He faced the firing squad alone but with remarkable equanimity, secure in his commitment to the course he had chosen.[6]

In spite of the stark differences in the outcome of their lives, the ideas and careers of these two men intersected and overlapped for nearly two decades, from the end of the South African War to the negotiations that preceded the signing of the Anglo-Irish Treaty. Separately, but in remarkably similar language, they developed parallel arguments that focused on the virtues of self-government and the vision of an empire-commonwealth founded on "the true principles of national freedom and political decentralization." Above all, they insisted on the need for racial equality among "white peoples."[7]

In the summer of 1919 Childers was recruited by Sinn Féin to publicize Ireland's case at the peace conference in Paris. He brought a number of formidable gifts to the task. In addition to his distinguished record of service in the British armed forces during the Great War, he was the author of a widely read novel, *The Riddle of the Sands*, which as early as 1903 had predicted the coming conflict between England and Germany. He was also, in the words of Frank Pakenham, "a specialist of world renown on matters military and naval" and a student of the constitutional foundations of the empire and its Dominions whose knowledge and analytical skill rivaled that of his most formidable British adversaries.[8]

Nonetheless, to many observers, Childers must have appeared an odd choice to represent the Irish Republic, for he had lived much of his life within the confines of the British upper classes and their worldview. His father, Robert Caesar Childers, had served the empire in Ceylon before becoming a pioneer Orientalist at University College London. His mother, Anna Barton, came from a prosperous Anglo-Irish family in County Wicklow. Tragically, Robert Childers died of tuberculosis when Erskine was only six, and Anna Barton Childers was then consigned to a "home for incurables." (She died there eight years later without seeing her children again.) Erskine and his four siblings were taken to Glendalough House, the Barton family home in Wicklow, where they were raised by Anna's brother Charles Barton and his wife, Agnes, who was Robert Childers's sister. Proudly conservative and reflexively Unionist, the Barton and Childers families were deeply embedded in the mental world of England's— and Ireland's—*ancien régime*. Erskine's accommodation to this worldview was reinforced by secondary education at Haileybury, an English public school of "the middling sort" that sent many of its graduates to the army and the Colonial Service, and then by matriculation at Trinity College, Cambridge, and a clerkship in the House of Commons.[9]

At the end of 1899, Childers volunteered for service in the Honourable Artillery Company and was sent to South Africa for eight months. The artillery company was affiliated with the famed City Imperial Volunteers, whose members—many of them employees of London's most prestigious financial institutions—were recruited with great fanfare during the wave of patriotic fervor that swept across Britain and its imperial metropolis during the early stages of the South African War. During his sojourn in South Africa, he mingled with soldiers from all of Britain's far-flung Dominions and came to see them as "a microcosm of the empire, recruited by voluntary enlistment . . . from every member of a family of states the most intelligent and virile the world has ever seen." Among them were Irishmen, fighting under the Union Jack, whom he remembered as "loyal, keen, and simple soldiers, as proud of the flag

6.1. Erskine Childers as a Cambridge undergraduate (courtesy of the Board of Trinity College Library Dublin)

as any Britisher." Much less memorable, apparently, were the many Africans he encountered—"Kaffirs," "niggers," and "boys," he called them—even though they were an indispensable part of Britain's military machinery in South Africa. For him, the "Kaffir drivers" seemed to have more in common with their mule teams than with the white men who served as his comrades in arms.[10]

Above all, as a rank-and-file soldier, he welcomed the enforced separation from the "complex civilization" he had left behind and cherished the subordination of self to the grandeur of a great cause. "It is something," he re-flected, "to have reduced living to its simplest terms, and to have realized how little one really wants. It is much to have learnt the discipline, self-restraint, endurance and patience which soldiering demands. . . . Perhaps the best of all is to have given up newspaper reading for a time and [to] have stepped . . . into the region of open-air facts where history is made and the empire is moulded." To a remarkable degree, he was comfortable with the fact that "all classes are fused" in this world; indeed, he relished the opportunity to live and fight side by side with the men of the regular army, symbolized by the mythical "Tommy Atkins."[11]

After returning to civilian life, Childers edited and wrote most of volume 5 of *The Times History of the War in South Africa*, which was published in 1907. This period of reflection accelerated his development away from Toryism and toward a more nuanced view of Britain's role in the world and responsibility to-ward its colonies. In the short term, he adopted the outlook of Lord Kitchener, who had served as the British commander in chief during the "guerrilla" stage of the war, over that of Lord Milner, Britain's high commissioner in South Af-rica. Alfred Milner was an unabashed British chauvinist and advocate of "racial supremacy." "I am a Nationalist and not a cosmopolitan," he would declare in his famous "Credo" late in his life. "I am a British (indeed primarily an En-glish) Nationalist. If I am an Imperialist, it is because the destiny of the English race . . . has been to strike roots in different parts of the world."[12] To Milner, this meant that British institutions, values, and—insofar as possible—settlers had to predominate in all of South Africa. Kitchener, meanwhile, had adopted a scorched-earth policy to bring the Boers to heel. But ultimately, Childers be-lieved, he proved to be "a truer judge of human nature and a better Imperialist at heart" than Milner. Why? Because Kitchener realized that in the resolution of the conflict, "the self-respect of the Boers was a precious asset, not a dangerous menace, to the Empire, and that the whole fate of South Africa depended on a racial reconciliation on the basis of equal political rights." When Boer delegates finally surrendered to their British adversaries on May 31, 1902, it was Kitchener who shook their hands and assured them, "We are good friends now."[13]

For years Childers continued to believe that Britain's basic purpose in wag-ing the war—namely, "the unification of South Africa under the British flag"—had been just and necessary, and he continued to advocate the "closer incor-poration [of South Africa] in the Empire."[14] He did offer a mild criticism of the Boers' treatment of black Africans, but he sympathized wholeheartedly with their determination to maintain "white prestige." They were not, after all, "coloured barbarians like the races we had been accustomed to deal with, but white men accustomed to free institutions." For Childers, the key fact was that Boer and Briton constituted "two white races . . . destined . . . to live side by side in the midst of a vast coloured population," and they were entitled to take whatever steps were necessary to maintain their "prestige."[15]

By 1907 Childers was sounding more and more like Britain's much-maligned pro-Boers, for whom a commitment to "race fusion" and "equal rights for white men" had been the basis of their bitter opposition to the policies of Milner, Joseph Chamberlain, and other architects of the conflict.[16] Already in 1900 he had expressed cautious admiration for the Boers' military skill, their generosity toward British prisoners (some of whom he interviewed after their release), and their religious faith, which sustained them in the face of insuperable odds. Later, he expressed the opinion that "man for man the average Boer was more than a match for the average Briton." In the crucible of war, especially a war of attrition like that in South Africa, he came to believe, "It was the fittest of the Boers," "the toughest and most virile elements" who survived, "so that their standard of efficiency rose inversely to their numerical strength." In the Darwinian idiom that characterized so much of the racial discourse of the long nineteenth century, he seemed to be arguing that the Boers' toughness, virility, and high "standard of efficiency" made them superior candidates for citizenship in the new South Africa that he envisioned.[17]

He could take comfort from the fact that conciliatory voices were coming to the forefront on the "Dutch" side, most notably in the person of Jan Christian Smuts. On the eve of the war, Smuts and other defenders of the Transvaal had denounced the "hypocritical spirit of annexation and piracy which has always characterised . . . [the British government's] relations with our people." But in the face of inevitable defeat, he had embraced Kitchener's affirmation of friendship more than any other Boer leader and had become the leading Dutch advocate of "fusion." "The whole meaning of Union in South Africa is this," Smuts declared in 1910. "We are going to create a nation—a nation which will be of a composite character, including Dutch, German, English and Jew, and whatever white nationality seeks refuge in this land—all can combine. All will be welcome." In this context Childers not only advocated home rule for the Boers but also expressed confidence that "thinking men in South Africa are forgetting race and concentrating their minds on united national development."[18]

The outcome was far more complex than he had hoped. The Boers went beyond home rule to win dominion status, and even *de facto* independence, as part of the Union of South Africa. But most of them continued to maintain a separate racial identity—separate from the British settlers as well as from Africans—and over time they embraced a particularly virulent form of Afrikaner nationalism.[19] Nonetheless, in continuing to assert their right to self-government, the Boers taught Childers an important lesson. Self-determination was the birthright of white people. Justice, as well as prudence, required that the relations between "white nations" be based on equality rather than ascendancy.

With the completion of volume 5 of *The Times History of the War in South Africa*, Childers's thoughts turned increasingly toward Ireland and the contentious question of home rule there. According to Basil Williams, his close friend and fellow South African War combatant, he had something like a conversion experience during a "very quiet and happy holiday in Ireland" in 1908. He and his cousin Robert Barton had set out from Glendalough House to inspect a number of agricultural "co-operative societies," which were then very much in vogue in some quarters as the potential "salvation of Ireland." Childers informed his friend, "I have come back finally and immutably a convert to Home Rule, as is my cousin, though we both grew up steeped in the most irreconcilable sort of Unionism."[20]

The "co-operative societies" that interested Childers and Barton were components of the Irish Agricultural Organisation Society (IAOS), founded by Horace Plunkett in 1894 to help the emerging class of Irish landowning farmers compete more effectively in an increasingly complex agricultural marketplace, using the weapons of modernization and cooperation. Although Plunkett tried to separate the IAOS from party politics, his innovation seemed frighteningly radical to conservative Unionists and insufficiently political to ultranationalists. Still, it grew dramatically (more than a thousand cooperative societies were founded over a twenty-year period), and it attracted a wide range of adherents, from the Jesuit economist Father Tom Finley to the eccentric Protestant philosopher George Russell (Æ).[21]

With its rural location and agricultural focus, the IAOS was, perhaps, the perfect environment for Robert Barton. Raised in upper-class comfort at Glendalough House and educated in economics at Christ Church, Oxford, he made the management and modernization of his family's extensive holdings in Wicklow the focus of his life. In this setting, he found himself particularly attracted to the work of the IAOS, which seems to have played a significant role in accelerating his identification as an Irish nationalist. In 1920 Childers would say of his cousin's evolution in the last decade: "To his own people he is known and loved as an Irish gentleman devoted to the service of his country and of singularly attractive and distinguished character; a considerable landowner in Wicklow, a keen and progressive farmer, chairman of his Local Council and a pioneer . . . of the Cooperative movement in agriculture."[22]

He was also, Childers maintained, "one of those Irishmen whom England has had golden opportunities of conciliating." He came, after all, from an Anglo-Irish and staunchly Unionist background, and he volunteered for military service in the Great War. But the war took a horrendous toll on his family. Of his two brothers, one was killed in battle, and the other was badly wounded. One of his sisters was hospitalized after suffering an accident while doing civilian war work; the other suffered a nervous breakdown trying to manage the family's affairs while the world she had known was collapsing around her. But Barton's own wartime experience may have played the largest role in triggering his final break with Britain and with his own hyphenated identity. A lieutenant in the Royal Dublin Fusiliers, he was stationed in the Irish capital during the Rising of 1916. He thus saw—and, in a small way at least, was an unwilling party to—Britain's ruthless suppression of the rebellion, execution of the Rising's leaders, and imprisonment of thousands of Irishmen and -women for their alleged complicity in the plot. As a result, he became a "very keen Sinn Féiner," was elected to Parliament on the Sinn Féin ticket in the 1918 general election, and in January 1919 took his seat—not at Westminster but in Dáil Éireann, the parliament of the Irish Republic. At a time when his esteemed cousin was still serving in the British armed forces, Barton was appointed minister for agriculture in the new Irish government. He was arrested in February and incarcerated in Dublin's Mountjoy Prison, from which he soon escaped and went "on the run." Ten months later he was arrested again and locked up in Portland Prison until the military truce of July 1921.[23]

Erskine Childers was eleven years older than Robert Barton. As clerk in the House of Commons, member of the Honourable Artillery Company in South Africa, and prolific and increasingly distinguished author, he was, no doubt, a daunting role model for his cousin. But in this case it was the young "country gentleman" who made the most direct and rapid transition to republicanism and participation in the struggle for Irish independence. Erskine's embrace of the Irish Republic would come later and by a far more complex route. It began with the election of a Liberal government in 1910, a victory achieved with decisive support from the Irish Parliamentary Party, which meant that home rule for Ireland came to the forefront again, for the first time since 1893. Feeling a new sense of urgency, Childers resigned his clerkship in the House of Commons and dedicated himself unreservedly to the cause. In the process, he became one of the leading voices speaking on behalf of Ireland's right to self-government. In 1911 he published *The Framework of Home Rule*, a 354-page apologia that dramatically enhanced his reputation among English Liberals and moderate Irish nationalists. It is a remarkable work, not only for the breadth and force of its argument but also for what it reveals about a man who would become one of the most uncompromising of Irish Republicans. At this stage of his life, he clearly remained devoted to the empire, claiming in *The Framework of Home Rule* that because "Ireland has taken her full share in winning and populating the Empire, the result is hers as much as Britain's." A year later, while agreeing with Parnell's affirmation that "no man has the right to fix the boundary to the march of a nation," he nonetheless expressed the belief that

> without sacrificing a particle of her national pride, Ireland may and should . . . set before herself the conscious purpose of identifying her own destiny now and forever with that of the British Empire. She has helped to build that Empire; it is bone of her bone and flesh of her flesh. Far and wide throughout its scattered dominions her sons are joining in the appeal to justice for the country which is the home of their race, and longing to see Ireland take her place as a contented and above all a responsible member of the Imperial family.[24]

In his portrait of Ireland in 1911, Childers saw many hopeful signs. He believed that incremental changes over several generations had "laid the foundations of a new social order. Agrarian crime has disappeared and material prosperity has greatly increased." Moreover, "Government in the interest of a small favoured class [of Protestant landlords] has almost vanished." In numerous fields of endeavor, he perceived a spirit of reform and innovation that was pushing aside old sectarian hatreds and nurturing a new spirit of cooperation. The jewel in the crown of his new Ireland was the Irish Agricultural Organisation Society, which united southerner and northerner, Unionist and home ruler, in an organization where "liberality, open-mindedness, brotherhood, and keen, intelligent patriotism" were the norm. "The atmosphere is not political," he said. But after a visit to Plunkett House, "You will come away with a sense of the absurdity . . . of saying that a country which can produce and conduct fine movements like this is *unfit* for self-government."[25]

Not surprisingly, there was no room for "physical force" in the Ireland Childers imagined. His was the nationalism of John Redmond, not John Mitchel or John Devoy. "Fenianism is altogether extinct," he assured his readers. "The extreme claim for the total separation of Ireland from Great Britain" lived on only among "a handful of the older men," reflecting "the fierce hatreds provoked by the miseries and horrors of an era which has passed away." Thus, he argued, the long-standing demand for home rule could be all the more safely accommodated. Indeed, for Ireland to function as a "normal" country, for it to reap the benefits of self-government that had already accrued to South Africa and the other Dominions, home rule was an absolute necessity.[26]

The Framework of Home Rule was reviewed widely in Britain and Ireland. Significantly, many of the reviews identified Childers as an Englishman. This was especially true of Irish newspapers. Writing in the *Irish Independent*, "Hibernicus" called *Framework* a "remarkable book" and declared it "quite a marvel [that] an Englishman could have written it." Another writer in the *Irish Independent* found it paradoxical that "the most exhaustive, thorough, and lucid presentation of the Irish case has been made by an Englishman." The *Dublin Review* also praised the book and identified its author as "an Englishman, a well-known writer on military subjects, and an ardent Imperialist." Writing in an English newspaper, the Belfast Presbyterian Robert Lynd called *The Framework of Home Rule* "the ablest and most clear-sighted book that has ever come from any English writer on the subject." But most reviews published in England and Scotland made no reference to Childers's nationality. They apparently took it for granted that he was English, part of the coterie of Liberal Party leaders and their intellectual allies that was gearing up to introduce home rule legislation in the British Parliament.[27]

It is striking that none of the Irish reviewers qualified their identification of Childers as an Englishman by pointing to the fact that his mother was Irish, and that after his father's death and her virtual imprisonment in a home for "incurables," he and his siblings had come to live with their aunt and uncle at Glendalough House in County Wicklow. After his conversion from Unionism to home rule in 1908, he remained—until his death in 1922—an increasingly active and outspoken advocate of Ireland's cause as he understood it. And yet there was always something ineradicably "English" about Erskine Childers. England was his birthplace and the site of his education at Haileybury and Cambridge. There, and in London society, the British military, and the House of Commons, he internalized a culture and a mode of self-presentation that, quite apart from his political commitments and ideals at a given moment, marked him for the rest of his life. Eventually, his political adversaries in Ireland would use this "Englishness" against him with deadly effect, but even many of his Irish friends continued to regard him as "essentially English in spirit, training and outlook." While acknowledging Childers's vital role in the Howth gunrunning of 1914, the Dublin Protestant Darrell Figgis remembered thinking it "strange . . . that an Englishman should desire to bear these risks in our service." Childers would one day "maintain his rights as an Irishman," Figgis conceded, but he emphasized that in the summer of 1914 "none of us thought of him as other than a well-known English publicist who had eloquently and learnedly espoused our cause." Edward MacLysaght, a Sinn Féin sympathizer who worked closely with Childers in 1917, called him "an Englishman who showed an intelligent and sympathetic interest in Ireland." Even Frank O'Connor, who worked under Childers's direction to disseminate Republican propaganda during the Irish Civil War and regarded him as a person of "extraordinary nobility and purity," maintained in retrospect that "there was something peculiarly English about him; something that nowadays reminds me of some old parson or public-school teacher I have known, conscientious to a fault and overburdened with minor cares."[28]

Who, then, *was* Erskine Childers? Above all, how did he view himself in relation to questions of citizenship, allegiance, and identity? Apparently, from an early age, his experience of Glendalough House and its bucolic setting provided him with an enduring sense of identification with Ireland. But from the standpoint of citizenship, his principal allegiance was to England, and beyond it to the empire, for much of his life. When he served with the Honourable Artillery Company in the South African War, he referred to the Irish troops he encountered there as "Paddies." He took delight in hearing their "rich Cork brogues" and took comfort from the fact that they appeared to be "as proud of the flag as any Britisher." Still, they were "Paddies," "them," not "us." Similarly, in emerging as a leading public advocate on Ireland's behalf in *The Framework of Home Rule*, he routinely referred to Britain in the first person and to Ireland in the third. According to his later testimony, he did not definitively embrace the Irish side of his identity until much later. "With the formal establishment of the Republic in 1919," he told the military court that was to sentence him to death, "it became necessary for people like myself, of mixed birth, to choose our citizenship once and for all. I chose that of the Irish Republic."[29]

Apart from such a declaration, it is difficult to pinpoint Childers's identity at any given moment because, until the eve of his death, he did not dwell on it.

It was action, duty, fidelity to principle, and the pursuit of the ideal that ultimately mattered most to him. In spite of the fact that he was a member of the
British upper classes who graduated from the most prestigious English schools,
served in the administrative apparatus of the House of Commons, and won a
Distinguished Service Cross in the British military, he was, by temperament
and perhaps by choice, something of an outsider, and he was also, by tragic circumstance, an orphan. His parents' death was followed, only two years later, by
the death of the uncle who had adopted him. As a young man, he spent much of
his free time sailing—often alone—in the turbulent waters of the North Sea and
the Baltic. In South Africa he served as a stableman and spent as much time
with horses as with men. Indeed, he reveled in the lowly status—the turning
of his world upside down—that defined his South African experience. Characteristically, he never sought rank or fame, and yet he was driven by a strong
sense of duty to risk everything for the causes he believed in. Ironically, when
Childers finally sought to shed his outsider status by throwing himself unreservedly into the "domestic discords of Irish politics," the experience led to his
execution and the accusation—by those who should have known better—that
he was a diabolical "Englishman" whose one goal was to ensure that "this thing
that is trying so hard to be an Irish nation will go down in chaos, anarchy and
futility."[30]

Long before that awful event, however, there was the glory of Howth. By
1914 Childers had emerged as the intellectual leader of a remarkable coterie of
Anglo-Irish men and women who were becoming deeply committed Irish nationalists. Some of them were responsible for the formation of the Anglo-Irish
Committee, whose *raison d'être* was providing weapons for the Irish Volunteers.
But the informal ties that bound them together lasted much longer. Erskine and
his wife, Mary Alden "Molly" Childers, were at the heart of the group, along
with Robert Barton, Mary Spring-Rice, Alice Stopford Green, and through her,
briefly, Roger Casement, who provided a vital link to the Irish Volunteers.[31]

If Erskine was the intellectual leader of the group, Molly had no rival as its
spiritual leader. She was an American, raised in affluence on Boston's Beacon
Hill by a father who was a distinguished physician and a friend of Sigmund
Freud and a mother who claimed spiritual descent from William Blake and
believed deeply in "the sacredness of human life and the power of love to conquer all." Molly was physically frail and suffered from a "diseased hip" that had
robbed her of a normal childhood but not, it turned out, of an exceptionally
active adult life. She and her husband were famous for thinking as one, for loving each other deeply and unreservedly, and for exuding a kind of physical and
spiritual energy that proved to be contagious. The Episcopal bishop who married them observed that they were "not religious in the Christian sense but are
the most deeply spiritual people I can imagine." It was Molly who clearly stood
out in this regard. Although she was a newcomer to London society, her capacity for expressing sympathy, love, and affection, even under the most daunting
of circumstances, quickly became legendary.[32] Elizabeth Lazenby, an American

journalist who was a guest in the Childers home after the family moved to Dublin, found herself "drawn to [Molly Childers] as I have seldom at [first] sight been drawn to anyone." "How vividly I recall that first meeting," she wrote.

> Mrs. Childers lay on a couch in the sitting-room, which occupied half of the first floor of the small house. Books lined the walls on either side of her, and lay heaped on the tables. . . . The room, filled with spring-flowering things, glowed with and radiated sunlight; a perfect setting . . . for the woman who inhabited it.
>
> Except for her posture, there was nothing in Mrs. Childers' appearance to indicate the seriousness of the affliction from which she has suffered all her life. The blue silk shawl thrown over her, and the blue Chinese jacket she wore, set off the rich gold of her hair, and matched the vivid blue of her eyes. They were as nothing, however, to the charm of the woman herself, to which all who approached her fell victim.[33]

Molly's relationship with Robert Barton was so warm and passionate that it threatened to transgress the boundaries of Victorian propriety. He addressed her as "Darling," signed letters to her "Always I love you," and acknowledged, thirty years later, "What a revelation you were to me [when we first met]. . . . I have not got accustomed to it yet." During his incarceration in Portland Prison in 1920, she addressed him as "My precious Bob" and told him, "It is desperately hard to be unable to write all my heart holds. Yet you will know, will hear the unsaid words. Do you ever feel us in your cell with you? Close to you? . . . When Erskine visits you he will take me with him. You must think of me as there beside him, talking to you and loving you unendingly."[34]

Even Eamon de Valera, who—by reputation—was famously aloof and emotionally inaccessible, could lose his bearings when communicating with Molly Childers. "We have very few, if any at all, who are qualified to do the work you have been doing," he wrote to her in 1924, at a time when he and his allies were trying desperately to recover from military and political defeat. "I am afraid that you are burning yourself up and that we shall lose you." Then he concluded: "How I regret that I cannot say here [what] I want to write to you. At every word I feel myself crossing the boundary[,] so I conclude."[35]

Another pillar of the Anglo-Irish Committee was Alice Stopford Green.[36] Mrs. Green had been a strenuous partisan of the Boers, and thereafter she transferred much of that energy to Ireland, as a writer and active proselytizer. Erskine called her relationship with his wife "a union of two pure and beautiful minds." Molly regarded her not only as a close friend but also as a wise counselor and unceasing inspiration. "I have thought of you constantly," she wrote to Mrs. Green from aboard her husband's yacht as it carried its soon-to-be famous cargo toward Howth Harbor; "[of] your brave untiring spirit; of all the help and inspiration you have been and are to us. I have *felt* you with us, blessing us." As late as 1920, when Mrs. Green was seventy-two and both women had relocated from London to Dublin, Molly marveled that her friend was "like a young woman in her still-growing powers." "Her mind is like well tempered steel and shows no signs of decay."[37]

The third member of what became an extraordinary trio of female activists was Mary Spring-Rice. Of the three, she came from the most unlikely background, certainly the one that appeared to be least compatible with Irish nationalism. Her great-grandfather had served as chancellor of the exchequer in the 1830s. He was a staunch Unionist and opponent of O'Connell's Repeal campaign who went so far as to recommend, in a parliamentary speech in 1834, that Ireland be renamed West Britain. Her father, Lord Monteagle, was a peer of the realm and wealthy landowner in several counties—notably in Limerick, where Mount Trenchard, on the banks of the Shannon estuary, served as the family home. Her mother was the daughter of a Church of Ireland bishop; her cousin Cecil Spring-Rice served as British ambassador to the United States during the Great War. And yet Mary Spring-Rice became an Irish nationalist. Although her father would remain a Unionist for much of the pivotal decade from 1912 to 1922, he demonstrated an unusual willingness to seek out areas of agreement with the nationalist community, even with Sinn Féin, whose commitment to self-reliance he admired.[38] The first meeting of what became the Irish Agricultural Organisation Society took place at Mount Trenchard under his auspices. Over the years, he and his daughter and son continued to work closely with the cooperative movement in agriculture, using their estate as the base of numerous innovations—including a sawmill, a wheat-growing cooperative, a credit society, a workmen's club, and a branch of the United Irishwomen—all aimed at improving the lives of "their people." Mary was also an active Gaelic Leaguer, and it was she who suggested that private yachts be used to convey weapons to the Irish Volunteers in the summer of 1914. She recruited her cousin Conor O'Brien and his yacht, *Kelpie*, for that purpose and although she had no experience as a sailor, served as a crew member on Erskine Childers's yacht, *Asgard*, for the twenty-three days of its voyage.[39]

The voyage came about because the prospect of home rule had prompted northern Protestants to form the Ulster Volunteer Force (UVF) and land a substantial cache of weapons and ammunition at Larne, on the Antrim coast, in order to underline the seriousness of their promise to resist the imposition of "Rome Rule."[40] Leading members of the Conservative Party had strongly endorsed this threat of insurrection, and British army officers stationed in Ireland had declared publicly that they would not take part in suppressing their Ulster comrades.[41] These developments placed the Liberal Party and its plan for home rule on the defensive and led, eventually, to the formation of the Irish Volunteers in order to restore momentum to the nationalist side.

But the Irish Volunteers were virtually without weapons, and the members of the Anglo-Irish Committee determined that they must have sufficient arms—not only to defend themselves but also to strengthen the backbone of a wavering Liberal government. Funds were raised; an agreement with a Hamburg arms dealer was consummated; Mary Spring-Rice promoted her audacious plan to enlist her cousin and her friend as gunrunners; and *Asgard's* voyage commenced on July 3, 1914, with a crew that included Erskine and Molly Childers; Mary Spring-Rice; Charles Duggan and Patrick McGinley, who were fishermen—and Irish speakers—from Gola Island in County Donegal; and Erskine's friend Gordon Shephard, who was compelled to disguise his identity because he was on active duty in the Royal Flying Corps. An experienced sailor who the previous autumn had sailed *Asgard* more than a thousand miles, from Christiana, Norway, to Holyhead, Wales, even Shephard readily deferred to Erskine's superior skill and knowledge of the sea.[42]

There were two decisive moments in the voyage—the first, on July 12, when *Asgard* and its crew met with a German tugboat in the North Sea and the transfer of arms took place; the second, on July 26, when the guns and ammunition were landed at Howth in an audacious daylight rendezvous with uniformed members of the Irish Volunteers. A letter from Molly Childers to Mrs. Green captures some of the drama of the first of these moments. The tugboat pulled alongside *Asgard* at about 7 p.m. and towered above it.

> Our hearts . . . sank into despair when we saw the 90 huge bales awaiting us and looked at our small boat. [Our task was] to unpack every bale and unroll every gun out of its straw. The six of us and about six of the tug hands worked like galley slaves until about 2 a.m. at the job. I wish you could have seen the scene. Darkness, lamps, strange faces, the swell of the sea making the boat lurch, guns, straw, everywhere, unpack[ed] on deck and . . . handed down and stowed in an endless stream; no supper, chocolate thrust into mouths of the crew and a mug of water passed round when frail nature was nearly spent—the vaseline on the guns smeared over everything; . . . men sweating and panting under the weight of the 29 ammunition boxes—heavy and hard to handle. . . . I nearly slept as I stood and handed down guns. It was all like a mad dream, with a glow of joy and the feeling of accomplishing something great at the back of it to keep the brain steady and the heart unperturbed.[43]

Once the guns and ammunition boxes were stowed, there was virtually no room for the crew to maneuver for the next two weeks of the voyage. "We sleep [on], crawl over, sit on, eat on guns," Molly continued in her series of reports to Mrs. Green:

> One can't stand; one crawls on one's knees, or walks doubled up, very low down. Mary and I are covered with black bruises! [The guns] catch you anywhere and everywhere when the boat gives a great lurch and throws you over. . . . We lie, like the ancient Romans at our meals, only twisted Romans, for we are generally clinging to something to prevent tobogganing across the table. . . . Dressing is the hardest operation. It is agonizing. How you would laugh if you saw Mary and me in our cabin. All full of guns.[44]

On top of all this, they were often soaking wet and sometimes terribly sick from the tossing of the yacht in the stormy waters of the Irish Sea. But these two remarkable women, one of whom spent much of her life "sofa-bound," not only

6.2. Molly Childers and Mary Spring Rice, running guns, July 1914 (courtesy of the Board of Trinity College Library Dublin)

endured the experience but also reveled in the camaraderie and sense of partic-ipation in a great cause. "It is all gorgeous fun," Molly concluded, "and, joy of all joys," "Mary and I are up to it and are not in the way." Mary was more assertive about the *right* of women to participate in the endeavor and was particularly in-censed by a newspaper reference to "two men on board dressed as women." She was also more confident about what they had accomplished. "Molly," she wrote several days after the landing at Howth, "I believe we've been making history!"[45]

What is most remarkable in retrospect is that they suffered all the hardships and took all the risks for home rule! It was their counterparts in the Ulster Volunteer Force who were the self-declared insurrectionists. In contrast, the members of the Anglo-Irish Committee believed they were serving the cause of Ireland by creating facts on the ground that would strengthen the resolve of the Liberal government. Years later Molly could still report that after the landing of the guns at Howth, "we . . . hurried back to London. There Erskine received congratulations from members of the Cabinet. The gunrunning was regarded as most helpful to the Government in their difficulty with Ulster."[46]

For all of its aura of triumph, the landing at Howth was also marked by tragedy. After trying, and largely failing, to disarm the Irish Volunteers, British soldiers fired into a large crowd of civilians who had been harassing them, kill-ing three and wounding thirty-eight at Bachelor's Walk in Dublin. Only a few days later, the Great War erupted, overshadowing the heroics of *Asgard's* valiant crew for most Irishmen and -women—but not for the members of the Irish Re-publican Brotherhood (IRB).[47] In 1911 Erskine had casually dismissed the IRB as a "handful of . . . older men" who were trapped in the "fierce hatreds" of the past. Since then a younger generation of neo-Fenians had come to the fore. By the summer of 1914 they had penetrated the leadership of the Irish Volunteers. Now they believed that with the landing at Howth, a historic milestone had been achieved. "Let the 26th of July be noted in the calendar of the Irish Nation," *Irish Freedom* declared in its August issue,

> for on that day the Volunteer Movement was formally and effectively baptised . . . in the blood of the Volunteers. . . . It was no little thing to land arms within a few gunshots of Dublin Castle in open day: it was a fine thing to march, as the Dublin Volunteers marched, until their breasts were at the points of the bayonets of the en-emy. . . . it was a great thing[,] and a heartening thing, to bring the arms safe into Dublin City. That is the gain to Ireland, . . . the most vital, actual and moral victory she has had for centuries.[48]

In spite of their own heroism on Ireland's behalf, Erskine and Mary Childers could not have agreed with the thrust and tone of this declaration. Indeed, they were still very much a part of the British establishment and were having tea at Westminster when Parliament declared war on Germany. Soon thereafter, Er-skine volunteered for service in the British armed forces again and went on to engage in high-risk intelligence work for the navy and the Royal Flying Corps, work that earned him a Distinguished Service Cross. When the Irish Volunteers split over Irish Parliamentary Party leader John Redmond's attempt to commit them to participation in the war and defense of the empire, Childers sided not with the neo-Fenians of the IRB but with the man who—to them—represented the quintessence of cowardice and betrayal. "There seems to me not a shadow of a doubt as to which party to support," he wrote to Mrs. Green in November 1914, "namely Redmond."[49]

Childers offered himself to his country at the age of forty-four because he believed that the war would be fought to defend the rights of small nations, including Ireland. Moreover, Naval Intelligence wanted him desperately. As a yachtsman and as the author of *The Riddle of the Sands*, he had demonstrated knowledge of the coast of northern Europe—above all, the coast of Germany—that few people could match. But Ireland was seldom far from his thoughts, and he became increasingly disenchanted with Britain's performance there. He was dismayed by the Rising of 1916. He found it "pitiful, in some respects hateful," because the rebels had sought German aid to accomplish their ends, and he characterized the "typical rebel" as "half-crazy and half-starved, a neurotic nourished on dreams." But ultimately he placed the blame squarely on Britain. "My opinion about Ireland is a very simple one," he wrote to a cousin in May 1916, "based on cause and effect as observed among all white races and many coloured ones, ... namely, that peoples denied freedom will rebel, the responsibility for the tragic results resting on those who deny the freedom." He believed there was "no moment in history ... when it would not have been best both for England and Ireland that Ireland should govern itself." He believed, also, that the granting of home rule would have led to Ireland's enthusiastic participation in the war. "There might ... still have been trouble from hot-headed separatists (as in South Africa)," he acknowledged, "but with the government in Irish hands it would have been negligible." Instead, "we have the disgrace of a rebellion in our own islands—we who were for the freedom of Serbia, Belgium and Poland."[50]

Recognizing his extraordinary record as an advocate of home rule for Ireland, the government granted Childers a leave of absence from his military duties in 1917 so that he could serve as assistant secretary of a convention that was seeking, once again, to find an acceptable solution to the Irish Question. The Irish Convention met at Trinity College Dublin from July 25, 1917 to April 5, 1918. For much of that time Childers continued to hope that effective advocacy of "Dominion Home Rule" would, as he put it in a letter to a friend, "carry the day and detach all but a fringe of irreconcilables from the Republican idea." Ultimately, however, the convention went nowhere—for many reasons; first and foremost, perhaps, the intransigence of the "arrogant Ulstermen."[51] By the time the convention ended, the threat of conscription was looming, much of Ireland was preparing to resist, and Childers had concluded that Britain was "pursuing an insane and criminal course." "Alas," he wrote in his diary, "a large part of Ireland is in a grave condition, under military law, with opinion stifled; the young men almost hopelessly estranged from Britain and not merely willing but anxious to die—not on French battlefields but in Ireland for Irish Liberty."[52]

So the break had come or, at least, was tantalizingly near. In 1922 he reflected upon the moment and his trajectory thereafter. He had finally become convinced that "Home Rule was dead, and that a revolution, founded on the rising of 1916, was inevitable and necessary." But ever the gentleman, he waited until the end of the war, "when I had faithfully fulfilled my contract with the British," to join the struggle to overthrow British rule in Ireland. And yet Molly Childers, who had become a deeply committed Anglophile during her years in London, had a different recollection. Reflecting on the "period of tremendous mental and spiritual development for us both" in the war's aftermath, she would write that "we both still [thought] of ourselves as British or English" at that time.[53]

Erskine moved from London to Dublin in the spring of 1919. After offering spirited resistance to the idea, Molly finally followed him in December. Meanwhile, in July the *Irish Independent* noted the arrival of "Major Erskine Childers" in Paris and reported that his presence "aroused more than ordinary interest." In a letter to the *Times* of London, he had already characterized Ireland as "the last unliberated white community on the face of the globe." Now he told the *Irish Independent* that "Ireland must be free" and must "secure freedom . . . by pressure under a common flag for an aim universally understood and already achieved by every white nation in the world but Ireland."[54]

Beginning with his experience in the South African War, the theme of white entitlement had formed a more or less continuous thread in Childers's thinking about Ireland's relationship to Britain and to the rest of the world—above all, about Ireland's right to self-government. *The Framework of Home Rule*, published in 1911, is full of references to the rights of "white men" and the relations between "white nations." "Home Rule [for Ireland] will eventually come," he announced confidently that year, because government by consent was the prerogative of "white men." In December 1912 he declared in the *Irish Times*, "Not a single solitary instance exists of anything but good resulting from a gift of autonomy to a white democracy, however deeply divided by religion or race."[55]

Britain's Dominions—Canada, Australia, New Zealand, and South Africa—and their evolution as "white peoples . . . [who have] already made good their right to self-determination" had long fascinated Childers. He was keenly aware that they had all become self-governing entities by forcibly suppressing indigenous "coloured" peoples and building "white nations" in the process. In 1919 he was also well aware that Australia's W. M. ("Billy") Hughes, Canada's Sir Robert Borden, and South Africa's Jan Christian Smuts were all playing important roles as members of the British Empire delegation at the peace negotiations in Paris. Hughes, the Australian prime minister, had come to power as an outspoken defender of the "White Australia" policy that had stanched the flow of the Japanese and other colored races to his emerging nation.[56] A veteran of union-organizing campaigns on the Sydney waterfront, he was not bashful about making white supremacy the centerpiece of his diplomacy in Paris.[57] Smuts, by comparison, was much more gentlemanly, but he too was there to defend white supremacy. In an influential memorandum on the League of Nations, he argued that whereas Finns and Poles would be capable of self-government almost immediately, the people of Germany's former colonies in Asia and Africa were barbarians "to whom it would be impracticable to apply any ideas of political self-determination in the European sense."[58]

When he wrote *The Framework of Home Rule* in 1911, Childers had believed that "the whole history of South Africa bears a close resemblance to the history of Ireland."[59] South African leader Jan Smuts was perhaps his most important intellectual ally in this regard. Smuts was the son of devout Afrikaner farmers from the western Cape. Although his parents had hoped he would become a clergyman in the Dutch Reformed Church, he chose the law instead. After demonstrating exceptional brilliance during his student days at Christ's College, Cambridge, he returned to South Africa and commenced a distinguished career as a lawyer, public servant, and military commander. Even an abbreviated version of his *vita* reveals a remarkable record of leadership. He served as attorney general of the South African Republic under the legendary President Kruger; as assistant commandant general of the republic's military forces during the war between Boer and Briton; as principal architect of the Union of South Africa; as his comrade, friend, and mentor Louis Botha's indispensable right hand in the government of the fledgling Union; as general in the South African defense forces during the Great War; and as a statesman of world renown in the British War Cabinet and the empire delegation at the Paris peace conference. When Botha died in 1919, Smuts succeeded him as prime minister of the increasingly fractious Union. John X. Merriman, a leading liberal in the Cape Colony who worked closely with Smuts over the years, characterized him as an "exceedingly able" man with "great intellectual gifts" and also observed, "He has a reputation for shiftiness, which is, I think, in some measure undeserved." His fellow Afrikaners called him Slim Jannie, a nickname that suggested cleverness mixed with cunning, intelligence with deviousness.[60]

In the years leading up to the South African War, Smuts had worked closely with the flamboyant British capitalist and imperial visionary Cecil Rhodes and then with his polar opposite, Paul Kruger, the president of the South African Republic, who had become the preeminent symbol of the Boers' rural simplicity, religious fervor, and republican intransigence. When war erupted in October 1899, Smuts not only advocated a quick Boer victory by means of an aggressive and unconventional military campaign but also dared to believe that there could be, "perhaps within a year, an Afrikaner republic in South Africa," stretching from Cape Town in the southwest to the Zambezi River in the north.[61] After a promising start, however, the war went badly. Kruger retreated into exile, and Britain appeared to be on the verge of a decisive military victory, until Smuts and a younger generation of political and military leaders emerged as "Bitter Enders" who declared they would never surrender, no matter what the cost. As the Boers resorted to guerrilla warfare, the British responded by intensifying and widening the scope of a scorched-earth policy that Smuts characterized as "a crime . . . which probably has no parallel in the history of the world." "Not William the Conqueror himself created a more complete desert between the Tyne and the Humber in the eleventh century than Lord Kitchener has created in South Africa in the twentieth," he charged in January 1902. Throughout the Transvaal and the Orange Free State, "all farms and the buildings thereon have been burnt down—all food-stuffs . . . [and] farming implements . . . have been ruthlessly destroyed; the towns not occupied by the British have been burnt down, the very churches not having escaped this sacrilege." Britain's cowardly acts of "racial revenge" only reinforced the Boers' sense that theirs was a divinely ordained mission of suffering and sacrifice that would be followed, somehow, by redemption. "God is the King of the Boer race," an Afrikaner woman proclaimed to Smuts; and he could only add, "The Boer cause has become a Boer religion. . . . The Boers fight now in a spirit akin to that of the early Christian martyrs."[62]

Having stated that the Afrikaner people were "absolutely and irrevocably resolved to proceed with this war to the bitter end," Slim Jannie suddenly changed course and extended the olive branch of peace to his adversaries. "In a generous spirit of forgive and forget," he declared, "let us try to found a stable commonwealth in South Africa, in which Boer and Briton will both be proud to be partners."[63] Symbolically at least, his statement of January 1902 marked the beginning of the war's end. Four months later sixty Boer leaders came together at Vereeniging in the southern Transvaal and decided, finally, to surrender. Smuts, who had presented the quest for independence as the mission of a "race . . . belonging to the moral aristocracy of humanity," now declared that "[we] must not sacrifice the [Afrikaner people] on the altar of independence. . . . We must not run the risk of sacrificing our nation and its future to a mere idea which can no longer be realized."[64] The seeds of his cautionary message to a later generation of Irish republicans were sewn at this moment.

Brilliant negotiator that he was, Smuts emerged as a major architect of the partial reconciliation between Boer and Briton that was consummated with the formation of the Union of South Africa in 1910. His goal, as articulated by his coworker Louis Botha, was "to bring about in this country a single nation of whites." The "coloured races," above all the black Africans who made up two-thirds of South Africa's population, were not a part of this nation. Rather, they were to remain a subordinate people—at the whites' disposal when needed for menial labor, but otherwise as far removed from the purview of the "white races" as possible. By Smuts's lights, this outcome was not only desirable but also a fundamental necessity. In his famous letter to W. T. Stead in January 1902, where he had spoken as both Bitter Ender and conciliator, he warned that "the war between the white races will run its course and pass away.... But the Native question will never pass away; it will become more difficult as time goes on." On occasion, to be sure, he struck a more humane note, telling his friend John Merriman, "I sympathize profoundly with the native races of South Africa whose land it was long before we came here to force a policy of dispossession on them. And it ought to be the policy of all parties to do justice to the natives and to take all wise and prudent measures for their civilisation and improvement." But he readily acknowledged that "I would . . . not give them the franchise," and in negotiating the treaty that ended the South African War, he played a key role in the decision to defer "the question of granting the Franchise to Natives" indefinitely.[65]

For Smuts, it was axiomatic that "racialism" was a necessity in the relations between whites and blacks in South Africa but a hindrance, even a "deadly peril," in the relations between "white peoples." The overwhelming majority of whites agreed with him on the first part of this axiom; the challenge was to get them to agree on the second part as well. Ironically, their shared goal of developing a nation founded on an emerging South African white identity made Botha and Smuts increasingly dependent on the support of British settlers and increasingly suspect to their fellow Afrikaners, many of whom resented the Union Jack and feared the ever-expanding tentacles of Anglicization. The answer, for many, lay in separation from the British interlopers. "In isolation lies our strength" became the slogan of a group of Dutch Reformed ministers and teachers who preached the sanctity of "our" religion, "our" language, "our" culture. Some were prepared to go further. When Smuts and Botha pledged their support for Britain's war against Germany in 1914, they were confronted with a rebellion among elements of the Afrikaner community, led by generals—heroes of the Boer people—who had been their comrades in arms during the South African War.[66]

From Smuts's perspective, the Afrikaner separatists had it all wrong. They preached "isolation"; he advocated "race fusion," the merging of Boer and Briton into one people. They aspired to build a great nation. He was sure it would happen, but only through the maintenance of the "British Connection" and the cultivation of South Africa's leadership within the empire. He achieved distinction for himself—and, he believed, for his nation and its people—in that very arena. At a banquet in his honor given by both houses of the British Parliament in May 1917, he softened up his audience by calling himself a "barbarian from the outer marches of the Empire" who had "survived to be your guest tonight." Conveniently forgetting that he had once called Britain's scorched-earth policy in South Africa "a crime . . . which probably has no parallel in the history of the world," he now informed his audience that the South African War had been "carried on by both sides in a sportsmanlike spirit, and in a clean, chivalrous

6.3. Jan Christian Smuts, ca. 1910 (Hulton Archive/Getty Images)

way." But at the same time he dared to insist that "we are not an Empire. . . . We are a community of States and of nations, far greater than any empire which has ever existed. . . . We are a whole world by ourselves." The "fundamental fact" of the "Commonwealth of nations" he envisioned was that it did not stand for "standardization," "assimilation," or "denationalization." Rather, it stood for "a fuller, richer, and more various life among all the nations that compose it."[67]

Smuts fervently wanted Ireland to be incorporated into the empire-commonwealth on precisely this basis. He was dismayed by Irish opposition to conscription, as well as by the great upsurge of republican sentiment that came to the forefront among Irish nationalists in the aftermath of the Easter Rising. But he was also dismayed by the recalcitrance he encountered among many members of Britain's elites when it came to Ireland. The Irish Question, he told a British audience in 1919, "has become a chronic wound, the septic effects of which are spreading to our whole system. . . . Unless the Irish question is settled on the great principles which form the basis of this Empire, this Empire must cease to exist."[68]

For the peoples of Europe, as for the (white) people of South Africa, he counseled a new spirit of "forgiving and forgetting." For Ireland, he sought not only that but also full dominion status. Buoyed by his reputation as "the most influential statesman in the Empire," he was now ready to "influence [Childers] and his colleagues on the side of moderation and what is practical." He arrived in England in June 1921 and conferred at length with King George V, who was about to leave for Belfast to address Ulster's new home-rule parliament. According to W. K. Hancock, Smuts's principal biographer, the speech the king delivered on this historic occasion "embodied the thought of Smuts and bore the imprint of his style. Words that Smuts had written and spoken at Vereeniging [in May 1902] were heard again at Belfast on 22 June 1921."[69] "I pray that my coming to Ireland to-day may be the first step towards an end of strife amongst her peoples, whatever their race or creed," said George V. "I appeal to all Irishmen to pause, to stretch out the hand of forbearance and conciliation, to forgive and forget, and to join in making for the land they love a new era of peace, contentment and good will." Almost immediately thereafter, the British government decided to invite Eamon de Valera to London for preliminary negotiations on a peace settlement. "If de Valera won't come over," the king said privately, "I hope Smuts will go over to him and make him come."[70]

In early July Smuts did indeed "go over" and confer with de Valera and other leaders of the republican movement at Dublin's Mansion House. (According to Smuts, Childers was present at the meeting only for "a short time," and he appeared "highly wrought and somewhat neurotic.")[71] In framing his remarks and recommendations, Smuts could not help but offer South Africa as precedent and model. Thinking back on his own transformation from Bitter Ender to conciliator in 1902, he observed that "the wise man, while fighting for his ideal to the uttermost, learns also to bow to the inevitable." Thus, in South Africa, he told de Valera, "the republican ideal for which we had made unheard of sacrifices had ultimately to give way to another form of freedom." In the aftermath of the South African War, the defeated Boer republics had accepted a "far less generous offer" than he believed Britain was now prepared to make to the Irish. But from that foothold, and with the benefit of Britain's subsequent "political magnanimity," the Boers had become a vital component of a "completely free country." He believed Ireland could achieve exactly the same status. But, he warned, "as a friend, I cannot advise you too strongly against a republic. Ask what you want, but not a republic."[72]

Smuts's written recollections were not always kind to the Irish leaders with whom he conferred. In reporting back to the British government, he referred to them as "small men" (a comment that deeply embarrassed him and alienated them when it was made public without his approval). "We argued most fiercely all morning, all afternoon, till late at night," he recorded. "And I found the men most difficult to convince were de Valera and Childers." De Valera's recollections were more generous. He later acknowledged that Smuts was "the cleverest of all the leaders he met in that period." He even stated that if anyone could have persuaded him to accept dominion status for Ireland, it was Smuts. But it's clear that in the final analysis the general's words had no more impact on Ireland's Bitter Enders than on the separatists in his own country. "The bulk of my own Dutch people are republicans," he was compelled to acknowledge; "[they] wish to secede from the British Empire."[73]

In 1911 and 1914, Childers would have welcomed the promise of dominion status and a "position of absolute equality and freedom" within the empire. This was the basis on which he had called upon Ireland to embrace the empire as "bone of her bone and flesh of her flesh." On the eve of his arrival in Paris in 1919, he continued to take the Dominions as his point of departure in articulating Ireland's objectives and her unfulfilled rights. It may well be that in spite of his association with Sinn Féin and its determination to achieve an independent Irish Republic, Childers still believed that the goal of dominion status was more realistic. "As to compromise," he wrote to Molly from Paris in late July, "I foresee no vital difficulty. To *advance* it, to *propose* it would be fatal"; it would undermine the "vital force" that Sinn Féin represented and seriously weaken Ireland's bargaining power. But "to *accept* [a compromise], under compulsion, is another matter," he wrote; and he went on to imply that even a modified form of dominion home rule would be an acceptable outcome of the negotiations that Sinn Féin sought.[74]

However, the attitude of Britain's envoys in Paris deepened Childers's alienation from the country he had served so devotedly and pulled him closer to the uncompromising republicans in the movement for Irish independence. "I have rarely seen [England's] . . . impenetrable egotism in such an insolent, anti-Irish form," he wrote to Molly in September, after an encounter with his old schoolmate Lionel Curtis and other members of the British delegation in Paris. "One speaks on behalf of a helpless country."[75]

Childers returned to Dublin eager to continue his work for Sinn Féin. He eventually served as Dáil Éireann's director of publicity, and in that capacity he played a crucial role in mobilizing British and American opinion in support of Ireland's struggle for independence. Whereas the British government insisted that its military forces were attempting to subdue a Sinn Féin–led "murder gang," Childers portrayed a Manichaean struggle between imperial arrogance and the unrelenting quest of a small nation for self-determination. Comparing Britain's shameful record of atrocities in Ireland with her scorched-earth policy in South Africa two decades earlier, he reminded his British audience that their country's war against the Boers,

> reinforced by the destruction of farms, the devastation of crops, and the formation of vast concentration camps . . . apparently succeeded, [but] actually failed. For South Africa, now publicly acknowledged by the British Government to have "absolute freedom to secede from the Empire[,]" is, in all but abstract theory, as free as air. To learn wisdom from these military failures is my last word to my English readers. You cannot govern Ireland. The Irish people can, and the island, I beg you to remember[,] is theirs not yours.[76]

Some Irish nationalists—notably, Arthur Griffith—were uncomfortable that an "Englishman" had become so central a spokesman for the Irish Republic. But others, including Michael Collins and Eamon de Valera, respected Childers's skills and admired his effectiveness. In May 1921 his credentials as an Irishman received a major boost when he was elected to the Dáil by the same West Wicklow constituents who earlier had chosen the imprisoned Robert Barton to represent them.[77]

In July 1921, soon after the beginning of the military truce that Smuts had helped to broker, British prime minister David Lloyd George offered Ireland dominion status as an integral part of a proposed peace settlement. The offer came with an insistence on the indefinite partition of Ireland; and even apart from partition, it was so hedged with qualifications, so obviously structured to safeguard Britain's geopolitical interests, that de Valera declared it driven by a "principle of sheer militarism" that could portend only an "end to liberty." Under such conditions, he asked, "can any small nation claim a right to a separate sovereign existence"?[78]

Nonetheless, face-to-face negotiations were a necessity, and at de Valera's insistence, Childers was named chief secretary of the Irish delegation that included Collins, Griffith, his cousin Robert Barton, E. J. Duggan, and George Gavan Duffy. During this time he drew even closer to "The President" and played an important role in shaping his alternative perspective on Ireland's constitutional relationship to the British Empire, known then, and since, as External Association. In parrying Lloyd George's offer of dominion status, de Valera and the Irish delegates proposed that Great Britain and the Dominions recognize Ireland as a "sovereign independent state." In return, Ireland would become an "External Associate" of the British Empire-Commonwealth. In that case, Ireland would not have been a Dominion; it would not have been "within the Empire"; and "there would have been no allegiance to the Crown." In the face of British refusal to countenance this proposal, the Irish delegation softened its position, allowing that Ireland would agree "to be associated with the British Commonwealth on all matters of common concern" and would agree also "to recognise the Crown as head of that association." But the British stood firm, insisting on dominion status and a modified oath of allegiance to the Crown; the Irish delegates became increasingly divided, with Collins and

Griffith advocating compromise and Childers taking the lead in resisting Britain's demands. In the process, Lloyd George came to the conclusion that even as a nonvoting member of the Irish negotiating team, Childers was its most obstinate, and "sinister," force, "a man who had used all the resources of an ingenious and well-trained mind, backed by a tenacious will, to wreck every endeavour to reach agreement."[79]

But the two delegations did reach agreement. On December 6, 1921, the Anglo-Irish Treaty received the assent of the five Irish delegates, causing a bitter split in nationalist ranks and leading, finally, to the outbreak of civil war in June 1922. The independence movement was now divided between treatyites and antitreatyites, or Free Staters and Republicans. Collins and Griffith led the Free State forces. Along with de Valera, Childers became one of the most committed Republicans. With his genius for publicity, he was named editor of the *Republican War News*, and also a staff captain in the Southern Brigade of the Irish Republican Army. Even more than de Valera, who was the lone surviving commandant of the Easter Rising and the former president of Dáil Éireann and the Irish Volunteers, Childers was relentlessly attacked as the prime mover and evil genius of the antitreatyite cause. Already, in the debate over the treaty, he had clashed with Arthur Griffith, who had been driven to near paranoia by the presence of this "damned Englishman" in the inner circle of Ireland's leadership. Griffith's ally Piaras Béaslaí typified the Free Staters' growing animus toward Childers in his recollection that "there was something particularly irritating in the spectacle of this English ex-officer, who had spent his life in the service of England and English Imperialism, heckling and baiting the devoted Griffith." By April 1922 Griffith was charging that Childers was an instrument of "England's secret service." Targeted as an enemy agent who sought to reduce Ireland to a "mangled, bankrupt wreck," he became—in Frank O'Connor's words—"the one man the Provisional Government was bent on killing."[80]

The Free State army arrested him on November 10, at his beloved Glendalough House, where he had taken refuge. He had a small, pearl-handled revolver in his possession at the time—ironically, it was a gift from Michael Collins—and, in the climate of tit-for-tat killings on both sides, the Free State authorities had declared that unlawful possession of such a weapon was punishable by death. Taken to Dublin, he was found guilty by a military tribunal. He informed Molly that he was "fully prepared" for what was to come. After all, a "soldier's death" was "such a simple thing," something that "millions risk and incur," something that "so many in our cause face and suffer daily." He made the older of his two sons promise to shake hands with every individual who had figured in his father's death, and on that last morning *he* shook the hand of each member of the firing squad. But in the end, as always, his tenderest thoughts were reserved for Molly. "I don't know where I end and you begin," he had told her on one occasion. Now he was sure there was no such place. "I am going, coming to you, heart's beloved," he wrote just before the final reckoning. "I shall fall asleep in your arms, God above blessing us."[81]

6.4. Erskine Childers shortly before his execution, 1922 (Hulton Archive/Topical Press Agency/Getty Images)

At sunrise on November 24, it was over. "Take a step or two forward, lads," he counseled the youthful soldiers of the firing squad. "It will be easier that way."[82]

Erskine Childers was a man of uncommon courage and commitment who gave of himself unstintingly for a nation that he loved but that never fully embraced him. Unlike many Irish nationalists, he did not regard the preservation and recovery of the Irish language and Gaelic culture as central to Ireland's quest for nationhood. Nor was he, until 1919, a direct participant in the institutional politics of republicanism. True, he had played a heroic role in promoting the home rule cause in 1914, but he was then pulled away from further involvement in Ireland's affairs by his commitment to Britain and its war against Germany. Over two decades, it was mainly the question of sovereignty that moved him— ultimately, the question of Ireland's right to freedom and independence "unfettered by any obligation or restriction whatever." He claimed on occasion that this right was rooted in Ireland's history as an "ancient and spirited nation." But for the most part, his frame of reference was the British Empire and its Dominions, and the right of "white nations" to "racial equality" and self-government.[83]

His claim to white entitlement hardly made Childers unique among Irish nationalists, but his near obsession with whiteness made him unusual. The difficult question is why he was so focused on race as color. He was, to be sure, a son of the British Empire, educated in some of its most prestigious institutions, and a veteran of the South African War who had sharpened his understanding of global politics and the rights of (white) nations in that crucible. But he did not *live* the color line on a day-to-day basis in the way that Jan Smuts did. Indeed, the contrast between the two men in this regard makes Childers's stance all the more remarkable. As an Afrikaner and a white South African, Smuts lived in the shadow of a smoldering racial volcano. Even as a secondary-school student, he had predicted that "the race struggle is destined to assume a magnitude on the African continent such as the world has never seen and the imagination shrinks from contemplating." Beyond his day-to-day experience in "normal" times, the South African War no doubt played a decisive role in shaping his conviction that the fusion of Boer and Briton into a unified white race and nation was central to the survival of "civilization" in southern Africa.[84]

Childers did not experience race as color in this way. Rather, a reflexive belief in white superiority and entitlement was in the air he breathed, the culture he inherited, and the Irish nation he envisioned and sought to build. For nearly two decades, beginning with his sojourn in South Africa, he claimed that whiteness was the essential foundation of the right to self-government. His model was the Dominions, England's settler colonies that had conquered indigenous colored peoples and created free nations that voluntarily continued their allegiance to the British Empire-Commonwealth. He and Smuts were very much in agreement on this basic point, until Childers came up against two major stumbling blocks. First, in 1919, when he cast his lot with Sinn Féin, he was compelled to acknowledge that the principal leaders of the struggle for Irish independence expressed no interest in dominion status within the empire. Their objective was a complete severing of the "British Connection." Second, with the military truce and Anglo-Irish negotiations that began in July 1921, it quickly became apparent that the British would not grant Ireland the full and unfettered freedom that Irish negotiators demanded; indeed, they were not even prepared to concede all the freedoms they had granted to the Dominions. Once again, Ireland was to be humiliated; once again, its geographic proximity to Britain circumscribed the rights of the Irish people. Smuts's argument at this moment must have been especially disconcerting. The man who had become the leading voice of the Dominions within the empire-commonwealth now insisted on telling the Irish negotiators what they could *not* aspire to and offered the example of South Africa as proof.

Where, then, was Childers to turn? The Dominions, which he had imagined as the exemplars of the right of white nations and peoples to self-government, remained hostile to republicanism and ostentatiously loyal to the empire from which Ireland's leaders were determined to escape. Among the more radical elements in the republican movement, some were prepared to link Ireland's struggle with that of India and Egypt. The Amritsar Massacre of 1919, where troops under the command of General Reginald Dyer killed 379 unarmed protesters and wounded more than 1,200 in the Punjab's second largest city, helped transform India into a powerful symbol of the global struggle for self-determination. Egypt was also "aflame," and it appeared to servants of the empire that radical nationalists there were about to "go Sinn Féin . . . and to create a Pan-Islamic-Sinn Féin machine making mischief everywhere." Suddenly, Ireland, India, and Egypt had become linked as symbols of the cause of freedom and of the empire's vulnerability.[85]

There were tantalizing moments when Childers gravitated toward a broader sense of solidarity. In 1916 he told a cousin that the history of "all white races and many coloured ones" clearly demonstrated that "peoples denied freedom will rebel," and that the blame for any tragic consequences that followed rested with "those who deny the freedom." Three years later he approvingly quoted Woodrow Wilson's "message . . . to all imperialists" that "we are fighting for the liberty, the self-government, and undictated development of all peoples." This, Childers emphasized, applied to "all subject nationalities, without distinction of race, colour, religion, or strategical situation"—a far cry from his reflexive dismissal of "coloured barbarians" in the aftermath of the South African War.[86]

Finally, there was a brief moment, in the summer of 1921, when he appeared ready to place Ireland's fight for freedom in the context of a worldwide struggle for self-determination that, increasingly, involved "coloured" peoples fighting to emancipate themselves from the oppressive weight of European colonialism. In his diary he was careful to record, with apparent approval, the evidence of a world in turmoil: July 5: "Labour troubles in Mexico"; July 23 and 24: "Fighting in Morocco"; July 27: "Italy—civil war continues"; July 28: "Revolution in Persia"; August 1: "India . . . Mr. Gandhi's bonfire of foreign cloth"; August 2: "Egypt and India—cable to Mr. De Valera promising assistance"; and on the same day, perhaps the most remarkable entry: "N[ew] York—Negro Race Convention [asks] King George [to] use influence for freedom of Ireland." The diary entries are terse; there is no additional commentary. But what stands out is not only an awareness of but also an apparent identification with colored nationalities and races whose struggle for liberation paralleled that of Ireland and who were, in some cases, demonstrating their solidarity with the Irish Revolution.[87]

Ultimately, however, Childers did not embark on that path. Rather, after abandoning his long-standing dominion frame of reference, he took refuge in the distinctive history of the Irish race and Ireland's status as an "ancient and spirited nation with an inherent claim to independence." In doing so he seemed to be following a course already charted by generations of cultural nationalists, although unlike many of them he refrained from Gaelicizing and Christianizing the Ireland of his imagination. For him, rather, his unwavering commitment to the Irish Republic was sufficient to propel him toward his rendezvous with a Free State firing squad. "It is as if a light ha[s] gone out in the world to think he is not there," Mary Spring-Rice wrote to Molly Childers the next day. "Somehow at the back of all this present misery I had a vision of peace and a happy Ireland in which Erskine's great brains were being used for the building up of the country."[88]

PART 4

Ireland and Revolution

CHAPTER SEVEN

Negro Sinn Féiners and Black Fenians

"HEROIC IRELAND" AND THE BLACK NATIONALIST IMAGINATION

> I suffer with the Irish. I think I understand the Irish. My belonging to
> a subject race entitles me to some understanding of them.
> —Claude McKay, 1921

> The New Manhood Movement . . . is nothing more nor less than a
> Sinn Féin movement among Negroes.
> —Anselmo Jackson, 1921

IN JANUARY 1919 THE NEWLY ELECTED representatives of Dáil Éireann (the Parliament of Ireland) issued their "Message to the Free Nations of the World," in which they called for full recognition of the Irish Republic and warned that "the permanent peace of Europe can . . . be secured . . . only by establishing . . . government in every land upon the basis of the free will of a free people." Meeting in Dublin's Mansion House, they also called on the "civilised world" to serve as the guarantor of Ireland's claim to national independence.[1] Practically speaking, these terms were meant to apply mainly to the nations of Europe and to the United States. But in the context of 1919, they were fraught with ambiguity. Did the "free nations" include revolutionary Russia? Did the "civilised world" include the nationalist movements in Asia, Africa, and Latin America whose leaders took the language of democracy and self-determination every bit as seriously as their white, European counterparts? Russia stood athwart the postwar world as an emerging colossus that was at once a beacon of hope and a portent of great danger. In their quest for allies, many Irish republicans were open to an alliance with Russia, especially since the Bolsheviks were even more aggressive than Woodrow Wilson in promoting the principle of self-determination and far more sweeping than the American president in their understanding of its meaning. Lenin and Trotsky argued that *all* peoples who were unwillingly subjected to foreign rule should be liberated. This led the *Irish World* to proclaim that "the Russian people stand today as the foremost champions of liberty, social justice and peace." In its editorial "All Hail Russia!" the venerable Irish American weekly predicted that "the Irish [will] become fit partners of the Russians in the regeneration of the world."[2]

Beyond the confines of Europe, there was a stirring among colonized peoples that one influential author characterized as "the rising tide of color against white world supremacy."[3] To some observers, this appeared to be the most dangerous development of all; to others, it signified the impending liberation of the majority of the world's people from the shackles of colonialism. But what was Ireland's relationship to this upsurge of national consciousness and racial pride? Could the people of a small island nation on the western edge of Europe see something of their own struggle in the rising tide of color? And could the newly assertive intellectuals and activists who stood at the forefront of this anti-colonial insurgency see Ireland as an ally in their quest for emancipation? How could the Irish Revolution serve as a beacon of hope for them?

In the context of the early twentieth century, Ireland's stance as a nation that was taking concrete steps to throw off the yoke of colonial oppression goes a long way toward explaining the sense of affinity that insurgent nationalists from India to Egypt to the Anglophone Caribbean felt with "Heroic Ireland." To those who were beginning to forge a path toward greater freedom and were seeking useful precedents from the struggles of other nations, Ireland's rich heritage of protest was vividly evident—in the constitutional tradition of the home rule elite and the electoral successes of the Irish Parliamentary Party; in the emphasis on self-reliance that was at the heart of the "Sinn Féin idea"; and in the proud record of clandestine preparation for armed struggle that was at the core of Fenianism. From the uprising of 1798 to the Rising of 1916, from the soaring rhetoric of O'Connell to the larger-than-life presence of Parnell, from the heroic sacrifice of Robert Emmet to the epic hunger strike of Terence MacSwiney, Ireland's record of resistance to colonial rule offered not a single blueprint but multiple paths to a brighter future. As early as 1906, a nationalist newspaper in Calcutta affirmed that "[we must] keep [Sinn Féin] before us as our model," and a year later, another paper from the same city pointed to the remarkable parallels between Sinn Féin and India's Swadeshi movement, declaring that "Swadeshi" (Our Country) was an "exact translation" of "Sinn Féin." Jawarharlal Nehru, who would become Gandhi's principal ally in the leadership of India's struggle for independence, visited Ireland in 1907 and 1910 and reported that Sinn Féin's "policy is not to beg for favours but to wrest them. They do not want to fight England by arms, but 'to ignore her, boycott her, and quietly assume the administration of Irish affairs.'"[4]

Meanwhile, far from the vast Indian subcontinent, a colored Jamaican named Solomon Alexander Gilbert Cox, who had studied law at the Middle Temple in London, began publishing a bimonthly journal in Kingston in 1910. He named it *Our Own*, apparently in conscious imitation of Sinn Féin and its argument that the cultivation of national distinctiveness and a strategy of self-reliance were the proper path to Irish independence. Cox also formed the National Club, an organization that, according to one of his associates, "incurred the wrath and antagonism of . . . British officials . . . by advocating Jamaica for the Jamaicans."[5]

Arthur Griffith had founded Sinn Féin in 1905. The organization came to include a wide array of nationalists, socialists, feminists, and republicans whose views were often at odds with Griffith's but who were united in their alienation from the Irish Parliamentary Party and its insistence on cooperation with the British state. Griffith wanted Irish representatives to withdraw from Parliament and to join him in creating alternative structures of government in Ireland that would render Britain and its administrative apparatus irrelevant. Nehru was informed by "people who ought to know" that "if [the Sinn Féin] policy is adopted by the bulk of the country, English rule will be a thing of the past."[6]

Although Griffith was not a pacifist, and Sinn Féin included "physical force" nationalists, the organization quickly evolved toward a reliance on "passive resistance" and became, for many observers, a middle way between the cravenness of the Irish Party and the Fenians' insistence on the necessity of violence. But for Griffith, the issue was not essentially one of tactics and strategy. For him, rather, the fundamental issue was the character of the Irish people, the recovery of their self-respect, and the building up of their capacity for self-reliance. Robert Lynd, an early member of Sinn Féin, put the matter eloquently. "Sinn Féin in the noblest of its aspects is but a Nationalist adaptation of the saying: 'The kingdom of heaven is within you,' " he wrote. "It is founded on a belief that each nation has a sort of 'inner light,' " and fidelity to that inner light was the key to its existence. "The Sinn Féiner . . . believes that the genius, culture and speech of every nation is worth preserving, and that to consent to servitude to a foreign kultur is a sin against the light."[7]

For most of its first decade Sinn Féin remained a relatively small group of intellectuals and activists whose agenda was eclipsed by that of the Irish Party and, increasingly, by the dynamic presence of the Irish Volunteers, the paramilitary organization founded in 1913 whose leaders were committed to the use of arms as a means of restoring Irish manhood. Within the Irish Volunteers, a handful of conspirators from the Irish Republican Brotherhood were determined to seize upon the opportunities that England's wartime difficulty afforded, and in April 1916 they launched the famed Easter Rising. The rising was quickly crushed by superior British arms, and initially it engendered more hostility than support even among Irish nationalists. But Britain's decision to execute fifteen of the rising's leaders turned them into heroes and martyrs.[8] "The greatest result of the Rising is the complete and amazing revival of Irish nationality," a young Irishwoman named Moira Regan told the *New York Times* several months later. "We have been asleep. . . . now we are awakened to the knowledge that we really are a separate nation."[9]

Ironically, even though Sinn Féin played virtually no role in the rising, the British government and much of the press, in Britain and Ireland, portrayed it as the "Sinn Féin Rebellion," thus adding—immensely—to the organization's prestige. Soon large numbers of republican militarists rushed to join Sinn Féin and to remake it in their own image. But the organization also evolved into a mass political party that used the electoral arena with stunning success to advance the cause of Irish independence. The very fluidity of this new embodiment of Sinn Féin—the fact that it combined an active commitment to physical force with mass, peaceful nation-building initiatives—added greatly to its appeal. Suddenly, in the eyes of besieged governing elites, "Sinn Féiners" rivaled "Bolsheviks" as the source of the instability that appeared to be sweeping the globe. Suddenly (or so it seemed), Irish nationalism, in its many manifestations, developed a magnetic attraction for men and women of color throughout the British Empire and beyond it.

This became especially true for a small but extraordinarily talented cohort of black nationalists from the Anglophone Caribbean who emigrated from their home islands to New York City and became major contributors to the "New Negro Manhood movement" that was emerging out of the crucible of the Great War and its volatile aftermath. Their ranks included Hubert Henry Harrison, Marcus Mosiah Garvey, Claude McKay, and Cyril Valentine Briggs.[10] Harrison, who was born on the island of Saint Croix and came to the United States at the age of seventeen, was widely regarded as the "Father of Harlem Radicalism." Garvey, an immigrant from Saint Ann's Bay, Jamaica, founded and led the Universal Negro Improvement Association and African Communities League (UNIA), the "largest black organization the world had ever known."[11] McKay, another Jamaican émigré, was a poet, novelist, and political activist whose *Home to Harlem* became emblematic of New Negro artistic expression. Briggs, who was born on Nevis, educated on Saint Kitts, and ultimately trained in journalism and politics on the island of Manhattan, was the founder of the African Blood Brotherhood, a vanguard organization that became a transmission belt between black nationalism and communism. (The leaders of the brotherhood, Winston James writes, "almost to a person," were Afro-Caribbean immigrants.)[12] Each of these men found the example of Ireland compelling, and each took particular lessons and inspiration from its struggle for independence. For Garvey, it was Ireland's long succession of patriotic martyrs, culminating in Terence MacSwiney's hunger strike in 1920. For Briggs, it was the Irish Republican Brotherhood and its commitment to—and clandestine preparation for—armed struggle. For McKay, it was the Irish people themselves, their "primitive . . . loves and hates" and their deep devotion to the land. For Harrison, it was, first, the Irish Parliamentary Party and then Sinn Féin's ideal of self-reliance. By 1917 Harrison was asserting that African Americans should "follow the path of the Swadesh[i] movement of India and the Sinn Féin movement of Ireland" and recognize that "our first duty is to ourselves."[13]

Soon enough, the symbolic links between the emerging New Negro movement and Ireland were becoming clear, to its adversaries as well as its friends. In 1919 the Military Intelligence Division of the U.S. Justice Department reported that "all the Colored speakers in Harlem [are] using the Irish question in their discussions"; another government agency warned that "all these negro associations are joining hands with Irish Sinn Feiners," and with "Hindu, Egyptians,

Japanese, and Mexicans."[14] Not that black nationalists regarded the Irish as "colored." But among some of them, as well as among Ireland's detractors, there was a persistent tendency to see the Irish as an "in-between" people who had more in common with the "darker races" than they did with the full-fledged whites of Europe. Thus, in *The Clash of Colour*, Basil Mathews observed that in articulating their "central war aim," "the Allies . . . had in mind the self-determination of Belgium, of Serbia, of Poland, and so on." Mathews then went on to note how other peoples such as "the Irishman," "the Indian," "the Arab," "the Negroes in America and in Africa," and the Japanese had taken up the cry.[15] On the other side of the racial divide, black nationalist intellectuals routinely accorded Ireland primacy "among the trio of Egypt, India, and Ireland" and linked the Negro's cause with the Irish struggle for independence. "Let the Irish cause be heard," declared the *Messenger*. "Let the Negro's cause be heard. Let the cause of all oppressed peoples be heard."[16]

This sense of affinity across the color line was facilitated by the long-standing discourse of race as national (and multinational) character. It was not only the common experience of colonial exploitation that created space for an alliance between the Black and the Green; it was also shared racial characteristics. Claude McKay was convinced that in their intense, and "primitive," emotions and their "peasant's passion for the soil," white Irishmen and black Jamaicans had important traits in common.[17] Anglo-Saxonists were even more eager to link the Irish and the Negro—but in this case as lazy, irrational, and unstable—and to see their own virtues in the vices of these two subject peoples. As the twentieth century dawned, however, there were intimations from many quarters that its defining feature would be the problem of the color line. Insofar as race as color was destined to prevail, the space for a shared sense of anticolonial affinity would contract dramatically. Insofar as whiteness became the only sure basis for claiming the right to self-determination, the Green and the Black seemed fated to occupy different, perhaps even adversarial, points on the compass of global politics.

Urgent questions about the meaning of race played out in an environment that was hardly conducive to dispassionate reflection, for during the Great War and its aftermath the United States experienced one of the most volatile and dangerous moments in its long history of racial oppression. The northward surge of black migration, the competition for jobs in an unstable labor market, the impact of black men wearing the uniform of the U.S. military and imbibing the rhetoric of democracy and self-determination, the virulent, often deadly, white backlash, north as well as south—all of this defined the moment and made it a particularly dangerous one. America's wartime season of bloodletting began in the spring and early summer of 1917, with intermittent rioting and then a sustained racist pogrom in the industrial town of East Saint Louis, Illinois. There, familiar grievances and resentments, sparked in significant measure by intense

7.1. Black soldiers, U.S. Army (W.E.B. Du Bois Papers, Department of Special Collections and University Archives, W.E.B. Du Bois Library, University of Massachusetts Amherst)

competition for employment, led to an outpouring of rage and destruction that left at least thirty-nine blacks and eight whites dead. One witness to the events, a Lieutenant Arbuckle of the U.S. Army Reserves, reported that he "saw members of the militia of Illinois shoot Negroes. He saw policemen of the city of East St. Louis shoot Negroes. He saw [the] mob go to the homes of . . . Negroes and nail boards up over the doors and windows and then set fire and burn them up. He saw them take little children out of the arms of their mothers and throw them into the fires." And this was just the beginning.[18]

Race riots again swept across the nation in the "Red Summer" of 1919, a period spanning the months from April to October and resulting in bloodshed in twenty-five cities and towns. A conservative estimate suggests more than 120 deaths. But it's possible that at a single site—Elaine, Arkansas—the "count of the dead approached two hundred."[19] Not all of those who died were black. Indeed, in perhaps the most famous testament to the new spirit of revolt welling up in Black America, Claude McKay greeted the horrors of the Red Summer with his sonnet "If We Must Die." McKay promised that

> Like men we'll face the murderous, cowardly pack,
> Pressed to the wall, dying, but fighting back![20]

Blacks did fight back, but they also did most of the dying. Overall, they found that on the home front as well as "over there," the contrast between the Wilsonian rhetoric of self-determination and the denial of the elementary rights of citizenship to African Americans could hardly have been more stark.

When black and other "coloured" soldiers from the empire were demobilized in British port cities at the war's end, they too encountered not a grateful public but an escalating sense of resentment at their very presence, a resentment that exploded in Britain's own season of bloodletting in the spring of 1919.[21] Ironically, some of the worst fears of "race mixing" were generated by the Labour Left—especially by the socialist *Daily Herald* and the human rights pioneer E. D. Morel, who criticized France for imposing a harsh military occupation force on Germany and for using black troops from its African colonies as part of that force. In April 1920 a banner headline in the *Daily Herald* read:

BLACK SCOURGE IN EUROPE
SEXUAL HORROR LET LOOSE BY FRANCE ON RHINE
DISAPPEARANCE OF YOUNG GERMAN GIRLS

Morel was a crusading journalist who had played a leading role in exposing the genocidal regime in the Congo under the rule of Belgium's King Leopold. He had also served six months at hard labor in London's Pentonville Prison for his opposition to the Great War. Now he accused France of "thrusting her black savages . . . into the heart of Germany" and charged that "primitive African barbarians" had become a "terror and a horror" there. "It is no use mincing words," he told a protest meeting in London organized by the Women's International League for Peace and Freedom. "You cannot quarter tens of thousands of Africans, big, powerful, muscular men with fierce, strong, natural passions—you cannot quarter these men upon a European countryside . . . without subjecting thousands of European women to willing, or unwilling, sexual intercourse with them." His pamphlet, *The Horror on the Rhine*, was far more inflammatory. "Woe to the girl returning to her village home, or on the way to town with market produce, or at work alone hoeing in the fields," he warned. "Dark forms come leaping out from the shadows of the trees, appear unexpectedly among the vines and grasses, rise from the corn where they have lain concealed."[22]

These lurid fantasies of black men raping white women fed into a much wider apprehension that threatened to overwhelm the Wilsonian language of self-determination and to make the "clash of colour" a greater preoccupation than the rights of "small [white] nations."[23] In the United States, scientists and pseudoscientists joined journalists and politicians in issuing stern warnings about the impact of the rising tide of color on American society and the entire world. At the same time, a renewed surge of nativism propelled Congress toward the passage of immigration-restriction legislation that applied the discourse of race, and "race suicide," to the "hordes" of European immigrants who were, once again, "inundating" American society. In this context, Madison Grant's *Passing of the Great Race*, published in 1916, became the sacred text of American nativists for the next decade and more. Grant, a Park Avenue

patrician with degrees from Yale and Columbia Law School, applied the pseu-
doscience of eugenics to problems of race and immigration, with devastating effect.[24] Having served as a vice president of the Immigration Restriction
League for twenty-five years, he now played an important role in persuading
members of Congress that "the blood of the nation" and its purity must be their
first concern. The result was a series of legislative enactments that reduced the
overall flow of immigrants by about 85 percent, prohibited Asian immigration
altogether, and, by stigmatizing the peoples of southern and eastern Europe as
racially inferior, nearly stemmed the once mighty tide that had brought millions of them to the United States.[25]

One source of Grant's popularity may have been his simplification of the
complex and convoluted definitions and classifications that characterized the
discourse of race in the early twentieth century. Some scholars recognized "45
races or peoples among immigrants to the United States," and others spoke of
"the fifty races of the world."[26] But in confronting the massive "new immigration" from southern and eastern Europe, Grant whittled the seemingly endless
number of alien nationalities down to three basic European races—the "Nordic," the "Alpine," and the "Mediterranean"—and argued that "the amount of
Nordic blood in each nation is a very fair measure of its strength in war and
standing in civilization."[27] The problem, by his lights, was not only that "aristo-
cratic" Nordics were being overwhelmed by "peasant and democratic" Alpines
and Mediterraneans but also that the inevitable result of "race mixing" would
be the creation of a "lower type" of humanity. Grant argued that "the cross between a white man and an Indian is an Indian; the cross between a white man
and a negro is a negro[;] . . . and the cross between any of the three European
races and a Jew is a Jew." What was the inevitable corollary of this kind of pseu-
doscience? The *Boston Herald* summed it up, simply, as the requirement that
"men must be selected and bred as sacredly as cows and pigs and sheep." Grant
himself warned that liberal immigration policies "and the maudlin sentimen-
talism that has made America 'an asylum for the oppressed' " were "sweeping
the nation toward a racial abyss."[28]

Although he characterized the Nordic as "*Homo albus*," or "the white man
par excellence," Grant actually worried much less about blacks and other "colored" peoples than he did about the danger that immigrants from southern
and eastern Europe posed. But as the Great Migration of African Americans
continued to accelerate and northern cities such as Chicago became cauldrons
of bloody conflict between blacks and whites, others saw the threat of a different kind of racial abyss. In these circumstances, it was perhaps inevitable that
the complex discourse of race as national (and multinational) character would
be superseded by the simpler, and ultimately more familiar, discourse of race as
color.[29] One of the leaders in this transition was Lothrop Stoddard, whose book
The Rising Tide of Color against White World Supremacy caused far more stir in
1920 than Grant's *Passing of the Great Race* had in 1916. Stoddard had earned

three degrees from Harvard, including a PhD. But his fame derived less from his Harvard pedigree than from his timely observation that "the world-wide struggle between the primary races of mankind—the 'conflict of color' as it has been happily termed—bids fair to be the fundamental problem of the twentieth century, and great communities like the United States of America, the South African Confederation, and Australasia regard the 'color question' as perhaps the gravest problem of the future."[30]

Already, with Japan's triumph over Russia in the Russo-Japanese War, Stoddard noted, "the legend of white invincibility" had been rendered "a fallen idol, in the dust." Then came the Great War and the apparent "suicide" of *Homo albus*, for the conflagration that pitted Britain against Germany was clearly a case of "Nordics . . . killing Nordics." "If the present drift be not changed," he warned, "we whites are ultimately doomed. Unless we set our house in order the doom will sooner or later overtake us all."[31]

Stoddard was a man of the political Right, but as we have seen in the case of E. D. Morel, there were similar fears on the left side of the political spectrum. Stoddard and Morel had many differences, but both saw the Great War through racialized lenses, and both feared the coming of what Morel called "wars of extermination." The problem, he believed, was rooted in the decision of the European belligerents to arm black Africans and introduce them into the war on the European continent, with the result that "the militarised African . . . has shot and bayoneted white men in Europe, [and] has had sexual intercourse with white women in Europe." In allowing this to happen, the European colonizer had destroyed the "legend of superiority" that had allowed a white minority to control the black majority for generations, even centuries. Africans, in turn, were responding with "contempt, loss of respect, . . . [and] the dawning of the question: Why, after all, do we tolerate these people?" "I will tell you what lies at the end of that road," Morel told his London pacifist friends; "wars of extermination between the two races, from one end of the African continent to the other."[32]

Black nationalist intellectuals were also keenly aware of the rising tide of color, and like Madison Grant, they had come to regard the Great War as a "civil war of the white world." For them, however, the carnage in Europe served to deconstruct the rhetoric of civilization and to demonstrate conclusively that "Europeans could be every bit as 'barbarous' as the so-called primitive races of Africa." For some blacks (and many whites), the unprecedented bloodletting they had witnessed became evidence of the "madness of civilization, itself."[33]

This skepticism about the merits of European civilization represented a dramatic, if not fundamental, change in perception—for a belief in the necessity of "civilizing" and "Christianizing" Africa had long been a major pillar of black nationalism. In 1861 the pioneer black nationalist Alexander Crummell began an address titled "The Progress of Civilization along the West Coast of Africa" with the acknowledgment that "mental and moral benightedness has enshrouded the whole of the vast continent of Africa, through all the periods of time, far back to the earliest records of history."[34] In this narrative, even slavery itself could be—and often was—perceived as a kind of divinely inspired trial by fire and ultimately as a divinely ordained gift, for enslavement in America had brought Africans to the blessings of Christianity. "I considered that trials and disappointments are sometimes for our good," the emancipated slave and Atlantic World itinerant Olaudah Equiano wrote in his famous autobiography, "and I thought God might perhaps have permitted this, in order to teach me wisdom and resignation."[35]

Crummell, an American-born clergyman and graduate of Queen's College, Cambridge, served for twenty years as an Episcopal missionary in Liberia, beginning in 1853. He welcomed "the influence of Anglo-Saxon life and civilization" there and affirmed that "God has thrown the responsibility of evangelizing this people upon the Anglo-Saxon race."[36] Upon returning to the United States in 1873, he became the pastor of Saint Luke's Episcopal Church in Washington, DC, a bastion of the black bourgeoisie at its most refined. There he became more convinced than ever that Negroes were "a nation set apart in this country." Employing the social Darwinist idiom of the times, he argued that "the Almighty seizes upon superior nations and, by mingled chastisement and blessings, gradually leads them to greatness"; and he made it clear that in his view Negroes were destined for greatness. To achieve that status, they had to imitate, and internalize, the values of Anglo-Saxon civilization, and the leaders of the race—the men whom W.E.B. Du Bois would immortalize as the Talented Tenth—had the twin tasks of nurturing color consciousness by building separate institutions and leading the rank and file to ever-higher levels of attainment. All of this was tailor-made for Du Bois—his temperament, his romantic racialism, his vision of the Negro's, and his own, destiny. "Instinctively," he wrote in *The Souls of Black Folk*, "I bowed before this man, as one bows before the prophets of the world." Together, in 1897 the aging patriarch and his eager and multitalented disciple formed the American Negro Academy as a step toward the achievement of their common purpose.[37]

Crummell died a year later. When his successors gathered at the first Pan-African Conference, which met in London in 1900, they prophesied that "the problem of the twentieth century" would be the problem of the color line. And yet, according to the historian Jonathan Schneer, "Most of the men and women who attended the . . . [conference] believed in the redemptive possibilities of imperialism," and most were also keen to affirm their loyalty to their respective "mother" countries.[38] In Britain's colonies there was a strong tendency to believe—often in the face of considerable evidence to the contrary—that the Crown and the government at Westminster had been the friend and ally of colored peoples in their battles against local settler elites and commercial exploiters. Thus, in Jamaica, a leader of the local black bourgeoisie proudly declared in 1913 that "with the Union Jack floating over his head, the Negro is a unit in the greatest Empire." A year earlier Claude McKay had penned a poem entitled "Old England," in which he expressed his desire to visit "de homeland" and to pay his respects at the grave of Queen Victoria, whom black Jamaicans often credited with having been responsible for the abolition of slavery in the Anglophone Caribbean. McKay, who as a teenager had declared himself a freethinker, a Fabian socialist, and a friend of "wrongdoers," could nonetheless imagine as a young man that

> I'd go to view the lone spot where in peaceful solitude
> Rests de body of our Missis Queen, Victoria de Good.[39]

But for many people of African descent, including a significant number among the four hundred thousand black men and women who served in the armed forces of the United States, the war ultimately engendered a deep sense of disillusionment and betrayal. Most black American troops were denied the right to engage in combat; instead they became "laborers in uniform" who performed menial tasks behind the lines. Lieutenant Charles Hamilton Houston recalled that "the hate and scorn heaped upon us . . . by [white] Americans . . . in France convinced me that there was no sense of dying in a world ruled by them." Like their North American counterparts, members of the British West Indies Regiment encountered a near-pervasive pattern of segregation and discrimination. Most were consigned to hard and demeaning labor under conditions that killed more than a thousand of them. (In comparison, only 185 died in combat or from combat-related wounds.) Ultimately, they were compelled to conclude, "We [were] treated neither as Christians nor as British citizens but as West Indian 'niggers.' "[40]

Disillusionment was a spur to radicalization and the creation of a "New Negro." By 1919 intelligence agencies of the U.S. government were acknowledging the rise of "Radicalism and Sedition" among African Americans and concluding that "beyond a doubt, there is a new negro to be reckoned with in our political and social life."[41] The New Negro movement was a nationwide, indeed an international, phenomenon, but its headquarters was Harlem, the section of upper Manhattan that was rapidly becoming not only a badly overcrowded Negro ghetto but also the proud capital of Black America. Within Harlem, moreover, there was a remarkable diasporic phenomenon—the growing presence of migrants from the Black Belt of Alabama and Mississippi, but also from the islands of the Caribbean, who were, in the words of W. A. Domingo, "a sort of leaven in the American loaf."[42] Domingo was an immigrant from Jamaica. He had departed for the United States in 1910 and settled first in Boston and then in New York, where, according to Winston James, he became "one of the most influential theoreticians of the New Negro movement." In Jamaica he and Marcus Garvey had joined Sandy Cox's National Club, and he served as one of Garvey's first contacts and allies when the UNIA leader arrived in New York in 1916. He even edited the *Negro World*, the newspaper of the UNIA, in its early stages. But his growing commitment to socialism complicated and soon undermined his relationship with Garvey. When he published an article entitled "Socialism the Negroes' Hope" in the avowedly socialist journal the *Messenger* and identified himself therein as the "Editor of the *Negro World*," Garvey forced him to resign.[43]

In 1920 foreign-born Negroes—the majority of whom came from the Anglophone Caribbean—made up nearly 20 percent of the total Negro population of New York City. Over time they became a significant minority within the larger black minority. Although their natural tendency was to affiliate with other emigrants from their home islands, the hostility of "outsiders"—black as well as white—caused them to come together as West Indians. As a group, Domingo argued, they were "independent to the point of being radical" and "possessed of great proselytizing zeal for any cause they espouse." He went so far as to claim that they constituted the essential backbone of the New Negro movement. "The outstanding contribution of West Indians to American Negro life," he argued, was "the insistent assertion of their manhood in an environment that demands too much servility . . . from men of African blood."[44]

Domingo's claim may have been an Afro-Caribbean conceit, but he was not altogether wrong. Although one can hardly discount the leadership of W.E.B. Du Bois, James Weldon Johnson, A. Philip Randolph, Chandler Owen, Jessie Fauset, Langston Hughes, and other native-born African Americans in the New Negro movement, it is undeniable that Afro-Caribbean immigrants contributed far more to the movement's political and cultural dynamics than their percentage of the population seemed to warrant. These men and women came from societies in which they constituted a majority, often the overwhelming majority, of the population. Thus they were unaccustomed to the etiquette of life "behind the veil," and their tendency toward forthright and unapologetic expression of even the most extreme views marked them as singular, if not unique, in the realm of American Negro life. Relative to their African American counterparts, moreover, many of them were well educated. More than a few of Harlem's Afro-Caribbean immigrants had attended outstanding secondary schools in the Caribbean. Cyril Briggs was a brilliant student on Saint Kitts; Hubert Harrison, on Saint Croix. Harrison later earned accolades as a "genius" in the night schools of the New York City educational system.[45]

But quite apart from formal schooling, these men and women were autodidacts, self-trained intellectuals who continued to demonstrate a remarkable appetite for learning—from books, from street-corner disputation, and, in some cases, from their travels far beyond the small islands on which they were born. Claude McKay, who emigrated from Jamaica in 1912, lived the rest of his life "a long way from home," in the United States, Britain, France, and North Africa.[46] Marcus Garvey left Jamaica in 1910 and traveled to Central America, where he edited short-lived newspapers in Puerto Limón, Costa Rica; and Colón, Panama. In 1912 he sailed to England and from there traveled to the continent, visiting Paris, Madrid, and other European cities. "I have seen wonders, I have learnt wonders and I hope to teach wonders," he wrote to a friend in Kingston.[47]

Although he was by no means the most radical voice in the New Negro pantheon, Garvey became the principal beneficiary of the extraordinary energies that the "Manhood Movement" unleashed. He was born in rural Jamaica in 1887. His parents, he said, were "black negroes." His father was an "artisan of some repute," but he died poor. His mother, a domestic servant, came from a family of small farmers. From these roots, Garvey evolved into a person of unusual pride and ambition. Life for him became "an everlasting struggle to reach the top." But especially after his travels in Europe, he linked his personal goals to a far broader sense of mission. He recalled that in London he had had a vision of "a new world of black men, not peons, serfs, dogs, and slaves, but a nation of sturdy men making their impress upon civilization and causing a new light to dawn upon the human race." Returning to Jamaica, he articulated a conservative ideology of racial uplift—reminiscent of Booker T. Washington's—that relied heavily on white patronage.[48] But in the context of the Great War and its aftermath, he changed course and boldly challenged the white world from his headquarters in the newly assertive Harlem community. "There are no more timid, cringing Negroes," he exulted in November 1918; "the new Negro is on the stage and he is going to play his part good and well." Seeking to shift the focus of debate from the quest for full citizenship in London, Kingston, and New York to the necessity of transforming Africa into "one mighty nation, one great empire," he declared that "the life I could give in France and Flanders and Mesopotamia I can give on the battle plains of Africa to raise the colors of the red, the black and the green forevermore." "You [will] have to spill blood in Africa," he warned his compatriots, "before you get what is belonging to you."[49]

Given the growing tendency of racial discourse to focus on the conflict between the colored and white races and the long history of antagonism between African Americans and Irish immigrants in the United States, it is all the more remarkable that in the aftermath of the Great War many black nationalists turned to Ireland for inspiration. No major figure within the ranks of African diaspora nationalism appropriated more lessons from Irish nationalism than Marcus Garvey. By 1919 his UNIA was growing at an astonishing rate and offering a formidable challenge to the leadership of more mainstream race organizations, above all to W.E.B. Du Bois and the NAACP. According to Winston James, the UNIA had "millions of followers" internationally and "hundreds of thousands of paid-up members" in the United States.[50] In August 1920 the UNIA convention, meeting in New York's Madison Square Garden, named Garvey provisional president of Africa. "After August," Garvey declared with the "amazing audacity" that was his trademark, "whenever any race or nation desires to treat with the Negro they will have to come to the accredited representatives of the Negro race"—namely, to Garvey himself and *his* "accredited representatives."[51]

The UNIA leader had lived in London during Ireland's home rule crisis of 1912–14, and his own program of "African Redemption" was profoundly influenced by Irish nationalism. His ringing slogan, "Africa for the Africans at home and abroad," echoed the oft-repeated Irish slogan "The Irish race at home and abroad." He named the UNIA's Harlem headquarters Liberty Hall in conscious imitation of Dublin's Liberty Hall, the headquarters of the Irish Transport and General Workers' Union and a symbol of the struggle for Irish independence.[52] He named his newspaper the *Negro World* after Patrick Ford's *Irish World*. He linked Ireland with "India, Egypt, Africa, the Negroes of the Western Hemisphere and the toiling masses everywhere [who] continued to groan under the yoke of oppression." With the signing of the Anglo-Irish Treaty in December 1921 and the emergence of the Irish Free State, he declared that "the Irish have succeeded, first among the trio of Egypt, India and Ireland, in winning a place of mastery among the nations and races of the world."[53]

But why, in Robert A. Hill's words, did Garvey "consistently [accord] the Irish independence struggle primacy among all other national movements of the era"?[54] Perhaps because the Irish were a people who lived in "exile" but maintained strong bonds of affection and sympathy with their homeland. Irish nationalist organizations were every bit as active in New York, Chicago, Liverpool, and London as they were in Dublin and Cork, and generous financial contributions from the diaspora helped to sustain the movement at home. Moreover, the struggle for Irish independence could be portrayed as "purely national" in character, in welcome contrast to the Russian Revolution, with its celebration of "the class struggle" and its aggressive internationalism. And yet Garvey's vision was capacious enough to embrace a wide range of insurgent movements, especially during the combustible years from 1919 to 1921, when he regarded the UNIA as the ally and beneficiary of the manifold upheavals that appeared to foreshadow the arrival of the New Jerusalem. At times he identified his cause as that of "suffering humanity" and declared that "the aristocracy that once ruled the common people must be destroyed according to the will of the common people." In explaining the significance of the red, green, and black of the UNIA flag, he stated on one occasion that the red signified "the UNIA's sympathy with the 'Reds of the World,' the green expressed a similar sympathy for the Irish in their struggle against the British, and the black stood for people of the African race."[55]

Sometimes, to be sure, he defined this apocalyptic moment in color-coded terms, as a struggle between "the white man" and "the black man." He called the UNIA "the greatest movement among Negroes in the world today . . . because it is the only movement . . . that is causing the white man to tremble in his shoes." He warned Europeans that their "continuous exploitation of Africa . . . shall only end in bloody war which will mean the extermination in Africa of the one race or the other." At the same time, he praised the soviet form of government, because "the Soviets' desire . . . is to place property in the control of the State,

7.2. Marcus Garvey in Harlem, 1922 (New York Daily News / Getty Images)

and cause the State to administer property in the interest of all concerned." "That is a very good system," he concluded. "Why should one man have billions of dollars and the other man be hungry all the time?" Above all, he warned that imperialists, "political grafters," and "capitalist fiends" would have a difficult time "in this new age, when the eyes of all men are open, whether they be Irish, Egyptian, Hindu or Negro."[56]

As a British subject, Garvey's attitude toward the empire had undergone a dramatic transformation since the beginning of the Great War. At that time he had spoken with reverence of "the *great protecting and civilizing influence of the English nation and people,* . . . and their justice to all men, . . . especially to their Negro Subjects scattered all over the world."[57] But with Britain's failure to deliver home rule to Ireland prominently in mind, he declared after the war that "England never kept the promises she made, and will never keep her promise." In the context of a resurgent anticolonialism, he criticized Englishmen for "go[ing] throughout the world robbing and exploiting other peoples," and he warned British prime minister Lloyd George, "If you want peace, get out of Africa."[58]

It was natural that as a Jamaican Garvey would feel a keen sense of solidarity with Ireland, India, and Egypt in their confrontations with the British Empire. But Ireland merited special recognition because of its tradition of "patriotic martyrdom." Again and again, Garvey offered a litany of Irish martyrs as examples for the New Negro to follow. "For 700 years," he declared in December 1921, "the Irish race has been waging a relentless campaign for the purpose of freeing their country from the domination of an alien race." During that time, "hundreds of thousands of Irishmen have died as martyrs to the cause of Irish freedom." He lauded the courage and tenacity of Irish patriots such as Robert Emmet, Daniel O'Connell, Roger Casement, and Terence MacSwiney. "The world laughed at them," he reminded his audience, just as much of the world was laughing at Garvey and the UNIA at this very moment. "The world mocked them, the world jeered at them for their cause; nevertheless they continued their agitation until . . . they compelled the attention of the world."[59]

Garvey had special words of praise for MacSwiney, the republican lord mayor of Cork who responded to his arrest by British authorities in August 1920 by embarking on a hunger strike that finally claimed his life after seventy-four days of escalating drama. According to the Irish republican historian Dorothy Macardle, MacSwiney's hunger strike was "more potent than all else combined [in drawing] the world's attention and sympathy towards Ireland." After the signing of the Anglo-Irish Treaty, Garvey told a UNIA audience, "I believe the death of [MacSwiney] did more for the freedom of Ireland today than probably anything they did for 600 years prior to his death."[60]

The corollary was clear. Just as Emmet, Casement, and MacSwiney had died for the cause of Ireland, so too the New Negro must be "ready to give his life for the freedom of the [N]egro race." In January 1922 Garvey declared that the

UNIA's fight "is the fight that Ireland made for 750 years, for which Robert Emmet gave his head, for which Roger Casement gave his life; and Marcus Garvey, like all the martyrs of other races, will give his blood at any time for the freedom of Africa." A few weeks later, speaking to an audience in Baltimore, he "referred to the successful accomplishments of those who had struggled for freedom in Ireland," above all to the martyrs of Easter 1916, stating that "they had sacrificed their lives for Ireland, and . . . all true [N]egroes must be ready likewise to sacrifice their lives for the Negro Fatherland and for their people."[61]

As much as Garvey portrayed himself as the Negro counterpart of the heroic martyrs of the Irish race, the Irishman with whom he identified most closely was Eamon de Valera, the president of the Irish Republic, who was, after all, very much alive. Among the leaders of the Easter Rising of 1916, de Valera was the highest-ranking survivor, and the fact that all of his fellow commandants were executed by British firing squads served only to enhance the mystique that surrounded him. In 1919 he escaped from a British prison and journeyed to the United States, where for eighteen months he waged a vigorous—but ultimately unsuccessful—campaign to achieve formal recognition of the Irish Republic. In city after city, he addressed overflow crowds of men and women who lionized him and his cause. In some quarters, he was even treated like a visiting head of state—exactly the reception, and the status, Garvey coveted for himself.

At the UNIA's First International Convention of the Negro Peoples of the World, in August 1920, Garvey read a telegram addressed to "the Hon. Edmund De Valeria" informing him that "25,000 Negro delegates assembled in Madison Squar[e] Garden in mass convention . . . send you greetings as President of the Irish Republic. Please accept sympathy of Negroes of the world for your cause," the telegram continued. "We believe Ireland should be free even as Africa shall be free for the Negroes of the world. K[eep] up the fight for a free Ireland." Later, in December 1920, a UNIA leaflet confidently announced a Liberty Hall meeting featuring speeches by "His Excellency Hon. Marcus Garvey, Provisional President of Africa," and "His Excellency Hon. Eamon de Valera, Provisional President of Ireland." In fact, de Valera secretly departed from the United States and returned to Ireland in December 1920. There is no evidence that he had agreed to address such a meeting.[62]

Nonetheless, Garvey's special sense of affinity with "my friend De Valera" continued. As late as 1932 he praised him in print as "the Great de Valera" and wrote, "We understand him and the spirit of the people he represents."[63] After his own indictment for mail fraud in January 1922, Garvey told a UNIA meeting in New York that "two years ago the English people would not treat with Eamon de Valera. He was an outcast; he was a seditionist; he was unworthy of the consideration of Great Britain." But de Valera had finally succeeded "by holding on with bulldog tenacity of purpose and an abiding faith in the righteousness and ultimate success of [his] cause."[64] Once again, Garvey was asserting his own bona fides by comparing himself to a leading Irish nationalist. He assured his audience that he would be as tenacious and purposeful as de Valera and dared to promise that through his leadership the people of the African diaspora would achieve no less than the Irish had won for themselves. "Marcus Garvey has no fear about going to jail," he told a New York audience in 1923. "Like . . . those who have led the fight for Irish freedom, so Marcus Garvey shall lead the fight for African freedom."[65]

Garvey was, finally, an individual of enormous complexity whose ideas mirrored several of the major ideological trends of his lifetime, on the right as well as on the left.[66] He was capable of the rankest racial chauvinism, as when he responded to the "lie" that "God is white" with the declaration that "to my mind, everything that is wicked, everything that is devilish, is white." As the backlash against the insurgencies of the war and postwar era gained momentum in the early 1920s, he began to disavow the radicalism that had characterized his rhetoric and even to court white supremacists in the hope that their support would lend greater weight to his racial separatism and his "Back to Africa" enterprise. In September 1921 he argued not only that "every race should develop on its own social lines" but also that "any attempt to bring about the amalgamation of . . . two opposite races is a crime against nature."[67]

Throughout his career, whether he veered to the left or to the right, Garvey continued to speak the language of social Darwinism and to argue that, as among individuals, so among races, only the "fittest" would survive in the great struggle of life. His disciple William H. Ferris, sounding very much like a black Anglo-Saxonist, observed in 1920, "The Negro has recently learned what the Teutons learned in the forests of Germany two thousand years ago, namely that the prizes of life go to the man strong enough to take and hold them."[68] In 1922 Garvey himself warned Negro men and women, "It is a question of the 'survival of the fittest.' If you yield now, let me tell you that you are doomed; your death is sealed."[69]

Paradoxically, while he raged at the "white man" and denounced Europeans for their crimes in Africa, Garvey also believed that black people could survive only by emulating the "great white race" and the "civilization" it had constructed over the centuries. In America, he predicted, "even as there is a White Star Line owned by white men, there is going to be a Black Star Line owned by black men."[70] The purpose of the Black Star Line, and of all of Garvey's agitation and institution building, was to remake Africa not only as a "mighty nation" but also as a "great empire."[71] Led by himself and the UNIA, black people were "traveling toward the destiny of empire" in order to "command the respect of [all] nations and races." But how to get there? "Go out and do what the white man has done," he told his audience at Liberty Hall in July 1920. "Go out and make barren Africa a great nation, as great a country as America is through the sacrifice of the blood of the Pilgrim Fathers and the early settlers who came here."[72]

At times Garvey even spoke of Ireland, India, and Egypt in Darwinian terms. "The strong race, the strong nation[,] will continue to take advantage of the weak," he declared. "Ireland has clamored for seven hundred and fifty years for her freedom, because Ireland does not want to be caught napping as a weak nation, a weak race." "Now, what are you going to do?" he goaded his listeners. "Are you going to allow Egypt, India, Ireland to be among the strong, while you remain the only weak people in the world?" If so, he warned, the "Hindus," the Chinese, the Egyptians, and the Irish would "join in with the others who are oppressing Negroes."[73]

But far more often Ireland remained an inspiration for Garvey, a nation eminently—indeed, uniquely—worthy of emulation by the people of the African diaspora. Thus he told a Jamaican audience in 1932, "There is no other country (I can safely say) outside of Ireland where there has been such a continuous flow of depopulation as Jamaica." But there the comparison ended, for the Jamaican émigré was an "outcast." "He has lost hope, he has lost character, he has lost self-reliance, he has lost everything that would tend to make him a man." But in the case of the Irish,

> even though the Irish have left their homes in millions for foreign parts, wherever they settled they became examples for others to follow. In South America, [in] New Zealand, in Australia, wherever you find Irishmen, their deeds are worthy of emulation, so that Ireland has developed a character that is made up of Irish men becoming illustrious citizens of other countries[,] making Ireland a great country not so much at home as abroad.[74]

Cyril Briggs and Marcus Garvey became bitter rivals and, increasingly, sworn enemies, but Briggs, the founder of the African Blood Brotherhood, shared Garvey's admiration for Irish nationalism and for the Irish Revolution as a phenomenon the sons and daughters of the African diaspora should rush to emulate.[75] The son of a colored woman and a white Trinidadian who worked as an overseer on a Nevis sugar plantation, he was very light skinned, so much so that he could easily have passed for white. But he chose to be black, and he confronted the taunts of his adversaries in Black America with the declaration that he was "a Negro by birth *and by choice!*"[76] Briggs emigrated from the Leeward Islands in 1905, arrived in the United States on July 4, and settled in Harlem, where, eventually, he worked as a writer and editor at the *Amsterdam News*. In 1917 he was drawn to Woodrow Wilson's "crusade for democracy" and rhetoric of self-determination, and he supported U.S. participation in the Great War. But from the outset Briggs acknowledged that his goal was "to help make the world safe for the Negro." He became increasingly outraged at the situation African Americans faced, in the European theater and on the home front. The bitterness of his editorial commentary on the proposed League of Nations (which he called a League of Thieves) led to government-inspired censorship and thus to his resignation from the *Amsterdam News*. Thereafter, his own journal, the *Crusader*, became an important expression of the new black militancy, albeit with a "distinctively Ethiopianist flavor."[77] The lead editorial in the *Crusader*'s inaugural issue was entitled "Africa for the Africans." In it Briggs declared that "Ethiopia shall yet stretch forth her hand to freedom and to God. And not Ethiopia alone, but ALL the oppressed of the earth."[78]

In 1917 Briggs had sounded a distinctly separatist note, arguing that "for purposes of self-government and the pursuit of happiness," African Americans should take possession of "one-tenth of the territory of [the] continental United States." Under the influence of Garveyism, he soon shifted his principal focus away from the United States and toward the theme of returning to "the mother land to work out a proud and glorious future for the African race." He was to remain a strong supporter of the UNIA for several years. In December 1919 he called on readers of the *Crusader* to "join the UNIA."[79] As late as the spring of 1921, long after he had become a harsh critic of Garvey, he was still encouraging African Americans to affiliate with Garvey's organization.[80]

But by 1919 he was also describing himself as a "Bolshevist" and beginning to explore the possibility of forming alliances with the "Class-Conscious White Workers." The way forward for him, and for the like-minded cadres who gathered around him, was complex; it reflected what Mark Naison has called a "difficult, perhaps impossible theoretical problem"—namely, how to combine black nationalism with interracialism and how to manage the tensions between race and class. By early 1921 he would embrace both and recommend "salvation for all Negroes through the establishment of a strong, stable, independent Negro State . . . in Africa or elsewhere; *and* salvation for all Negroes (as well as other oppressed peoples) through the establishment of a Universal Socialist Co-operative Commonwealth." And yet even as he envisioned a universal socialist commonwealth and declared that "the Negro's place is with labor," he insisted upon pursuing a "distinct black agenda." He emphasized that because "the Negro has been treated so brutally in the past by the rest of humanity[,] . . . he may be pardoned for now looking at the matter from the viewpoint of the Negro [rather] than from that of a humanity that is not humane."[81]

At some point, probably in mid- to late 1921, Briggs joined the Communist Party. In the meantime, beginning in 1919, he had founded and devoted much of his energy to the African Blood Brotherhood (ABB) for African Liberation and Redemption. The brotherhood's goal, in essence, was the "immediate protection and ultimate liberation of Negroes everywhere." It had fewer than twenty members at its founding and, according to Briggs's recollection many years later, "less than three thousand" at its peak. Although much of its membership, which included W. A. Domingo and Claude McKay, was in New York, its largest single branch was in West Virginia, a state with a relatively small black population.[82] Historians disagree about when Briggs joined the Communist Party and about whether the African Blood Brotherhood's major purpose, from the outset, was to recruit African Americans into the communist movement.[83] They do agree, however, that Briggs continued to be a militant nationalist and that, in Robert A. Hill's words, "it was the national question, and not the class question, that provided the Communist party's original attraction for Briggs and other black radicals." In October 1919 he went so far as to declare that his allegiance was to the "NEGRO FIRST, LAST AND ALL THE TIME!" But he frequently applauded "Heroic Ireland" in the pages of the *Crusader*. As late as February 1921, he hailed "the Irish fight for liberty," not the Bolshevik Revolution, as "the greatest Epic of Modern History."[84]

Although the African Blood Brotherhood's initiation ritual featured a "Historic Ceremony" allegedly "performed by many tribes in Black Africa," in which a new member would mix his blood with that of a veteran of the organization, it appears that the inspiration for the ABB was not African at all.[85] Rather, it came from the Irish Republican Brotherhood (IRB), the secretive cadre organization committed to the violent overthrow of British rule in Ireland and the establishment of an independent Irish republic. Since its founding in 1858, the IRB had insisted on its rightful place at the head of Ireland's Fenian movement of "physical force" nationalists. Briggs deeply admired the insurrectionary heroism that the IRB had displayed in 1916, but he was also keenly aware of the emergence of Sinn Féin as the mass organization at the head of Ireland's escalating "fight for liberty." And beyond Ireland's shores, particularly in the United States, Irish emigrants were pressuring their governments to support Ireland's claim to self-determination. There were important lessons here for African people throughout the diaspora, he believed, for Ireland was indeed "a Sight to Inspire to Emulation All Oppressed Groups." Thus, through the African Blood Brotherhood, black insurrectionists were girding their loins for the coming battle and were—in Briggs's words—preparing to "organiz[e] secretly a great Pan-African army in the same way . . . Sinn Fein built up the Irish Republican Army under the very nose of England." And through mass organizations, a much wider public had to be mobilized, for "we can never liberate Africa," Briggs argued, "until the American Section of the Negro Race is made strong enough to play the part for a free Africa that the Irish in America now play for a free Ireland."[86]

Finally, though, for Briggs, as for Garvey, it was not mass organizations but Ireland's insurrectionists and martyrs who offered the most inspiring examples for other oppressed peoples, and for the Negro race in particular. When Terence MacSwiney died in British custody after seventy-four days on hunger strike, Briggs compared him to John Brown. Indeed, Briggs's intense admiration for Irish republicanism's tit-for-tat military campaign for freedom has led Robert A. Hill to suggest that he and the African Blood Brotherhood represented "a black Fenianism inside the New Negro movement." One of Briggs's contemporaries and close friends went a step further, arguing that the "New Manhood Movement" as a whole was "nothing more nor less than a Sinn Féin movement among Negroes."[87]

Surely, no matter when he joined the Communist Party, it was as an unrepentant nationalist that Briggs warmed to the Irish struggle and lauded the Irish example of armed insurrection.[88] More than that, perhaps, the Irish offered an example of the *racial* vindication of an oppressed people who were standing up to a self-proclaimed "superior race." Briggs called on African Americans to learn from the Irish that "he who would be free himself must strike the blow." "It should be easily possible for Negroes to sympathize with the Irish fight against tyranny and oppression, and vice versa," he concluded, "since both are in the same boat and both [are] . . . victims of the same Anglo-Saxon race."[89]

Claude McKay also claimed a special affinity with the Irish, for reasons that had much to do with his own life experience and racial sensibilities. The youngest son of a dark-skinned family of Jamaican peasants, McKay remembered his father as "a Presbyterian Calvinist. A real black Scotchman . . . [who] was so entirely different from all our coloured neighbours with their cockish-liquor drinking and rowdy singing." Thomas McKay was deeply imbued with the Protestant ethic and with a fierce desire for the economic independence that had eluded so many of his countrymen. He worked "grimly hard," his youngest son remembered, "buying a piece of land wherever it was for sale until he owned over a hundred acres."[90] Claude respected his father's achievements, but as he grew to maturity amid the lush and sensual beauty of rural Jamaica, he developed a deep aesthetic connection to the land and a "most improper" sense of solidarity with Jamaica's oppressed but resilient lower classes. Much of his early poetry focused on people on the margins of society—prostitutes, drifters, and other "wrongdoers"—and he made a conscious choice to write in Jamaican Creole, the "people's language," rather than in the "English English" that had long been the mode of respectable discourse among educated blacks as well as whites.[91] Characteristically, he justified this decision in terms that were racial as well as personal. "We blacks are all somewhat impatient of discipline," he asserted in 1912, "and to the natural impatience of my race there was added, in my particular case, [not only] a peculiar sensitiveness which made certain forms of discipline irksome, [but] a fierce hatred of injustice."[92]

McKay immigrated to the United States in 1912 and began a life of wandering that took him to college in Kansas, employment as a dining-car waiter on the Pennsylvania Railroad, intellectual stimulation in the salons of Greenwich Village, and a memorable sojourn of several years in Harlem.[93] His experience in Harlem and, even more so, his travels on the Pennsylvania Railroad in the ominous, and increasingly deadly, climate of 1919 led him to write his most famous poem, "If We Must Die," which became the unofficial manifesto of the New Negro movement.[94]

In the fall of 1919, he embarked on another journey—this time to England, to pursue his vocation as a writer and his avocation as a radical activist. Ultimately, he would characterize the English as "a strangely unsympathetic people" who, in sharp contrast to the Irish, were "as coldly chilling as their English fog."[95] For nearly eighteen months, he immersed himself in Britain's emerging communist movement and also found solace in the fleeting but indispensable community of black émigrés—merchant seamen, ex-soldiers, boxers, intellectuals, and protonationalists from many parts of the African diaspora—who shared with him the joys of brotherly communion as well as the bitter fruits of discrimination and humiliation. McKay moved back and forth between these worlds with relative ease, but most of his black friends were either indifferent to or distrustful of the new revolutionary movement, and many of his left-wing associates were blissfully unaware of their own racism.[96]

It was in London's separate worlds of Black and Red that McKay witnessed the growing prominence of the Irish Question. By this time his principal allegiance was to international communism, which was then in its most euphoric and hopeful stage of development. He joined the Workers' Socialist Federation (WSF), a small organization led by the militant suffragist Sylvia Pankhurst, and contributed many articles and poems to the group's newspaper, the *Workers' Dreadnought*. Although the WSF was sharply at odds with other avowedly revolutionary organizations, McKay attended the Communist Unity Conference in the summer of 1920, which led to the establishment of the Communist Party of Great Britain. In the winter of 1921, when he returned to the United States, he became a member of the underground Communist Party of America. Then, in the fall of 1922, he traveled to Moscow and addressed the Fourth Congress of the Communist International. Altogether, he spent more than six months in the Soviet Union, where, to his amazement, he was feted by Soviet leaders and, even more remarkably, welcomed with great enthusiasm by ordinary Russians in the streets of Moscow and Petrograd. "Never in my life did I feel prouder of being an African, a black," he recalled. "I was the first Negro to arrive in Russia since the revolution, and perhaps I was generally regarded as an omen of good luck," a "black icon in the flesh."[97]

During this period, McKay continued to grapple with the complex and multilayered relationship between race and class. "My race . . . is especially a race of toilers," he told the Fourth Congress of the Comintern, "that belongs to the most oppressed, exploited, and suppressed section of the working class of the world." Although this stance implied that the fate of the Negro was inseparable from the struggle of the working class of the world for emancipation, it led many white communists to downplay the importance of race in the revolution they envisaged, so much so that McKay felt compelled to exclaim, "The Communists of America . . . have got to emancipate themselves from the ideas they entertain toward Negroes before they can . . . reach [them] with any kind of radical propaganda."[98]

The "national question" proved to be equally contentious. McKay and other Marxist revolutionaries found it necessary to come to terms with the powerful surge of nationalism that swept across Europe in the aftermath of the Great War and to situate it in relation to the keenly anticipated upheaval of the international proletariat. But here, too, there was widespread reluctance among white

7.3. Claude McKay (right) and Otto Huiswood in Moscow, 1922 (Claude McKay Collection, Yale Collection of American Literature, Beinecke Rare Book and Manuscript Library)

radicals to see the two great struggles of this epic historical moment as complementary and mutually beneficial. "Some English Communists have remarked to me that they have no real sympathy for the Irish and Indian movement because it is nationalistic," McKay complained. Especially in relation to Ireland, "English revolutionists, anarchists, socialists, and communists" seemed to assume that "they must back the red flag against the green."[99]

McKay was determined to uphold the "red flag," but not "against the green." "I believe that for subject people at least, Nationalism is the open door to Communism," he wrote in January 1920, soon after his arrival in England.[100] Here communism remained the final goal, but the needs and aspirations of subject people were important to McKay. They were makers of history in their own right, not mere instruments in the service of a larger cause. This became evident in his article "How Black Sees Green and Red," in which he reported on his attendance at a "monster" Sinn Féin rally in London's Trafalgar Square in the summer of 1920. "All Ireland was there," it seemed, "all wearing the shamrock or some green symbol." McKay, who was there in part to promote the Workers' Socialist Federation and sell its newspaper, "wore a green necktie and was greeted from different quarters as 'Black Murphy' or 'Black Irish.'" "For that day at least," he wrote, "I was filled with the spirit of Irish nationalism." As an avowed communist, he felt compelled to reaffirm his belief that "the yearnings of the American Negro" could come to fruition only through "the class struggle." Nonetheless, McKay continued to feel a deep sense of connection to Ireland's fight for freedom. "American Negroes hold some sort of a grudge against the Irish," he acknowledged. "They have asserted that Irishmen have been their bitterest enemies." But, he wrote,

> I react more to the emotions of the Irish people than to those of any other whites; they are so passionately primitive in their loves and hates. They are quite free of the disease . . . [of] Anglo-Saxon hypocrisy. I suffer with the Irish. I think I understand the Irish. My belonging to a subject race entitles me to some understanding of them. And then I was born and reared a peasant; the peasant's passion for the soil possesses me, and it is one of the strongest passions in the Irish revolution.[101]

Like the Irish, McKay was a member of a subject race, and his peasant memories of the lush green hills of Jamaica, of his father's unending quest for independence on the land, of the displacement of so many members of his own generation and their migration to the slums of Kingston and New York, also shaped his understanding of the Irish and of communism. There, in London's Trafalgar Square, McKay forged a Red variant of the pastoral vision that animated so many Irish nationalists. "When one talks to . . . an Irish rebel," he wrote, "one hears the yearning hunger of the people for the land in his voice. One sees it in his eyes." And it was not just the Irish. "When one listens to an earnest Welsh miner, one gets the impression that he is sometimes seized with a desire to destroy the mine in which his life is buried." But the English worker was different. "In England the land issue . . . finds no response in the heart of the proletariat. That is a further reason why England cannot understand the Irish revolution. For my part I love to think of communism liberating millions of city folk to go back to the land."[102]

Ultimately, McKay proved to be too much of a heretic to remain within the confines of an increasingly centralized, hierarchical, and dogmatic communist movement, whether in Moscow, London, or New York. He was first and foremost an artist, a writer, and above all a poet, and as his principal biographer points out, his approach to knowledge remained "intuitive" and "highly romantic." As early as 1922 he argued that "in America, it is much less dangerous to be a Communist than to be a Negro," and to those who preached an abstract gospel of proletarian solidarity, he pointed out that, quite understandably, blacks regarded white workers as their "most bitter enemies."[103] In the context of the literary upheavals of the 1920s, he found meaning and integrity in the struggles of rank-and-file Negroes to survive and to achieve not political emancipation but sensual pleasure in a world that stubbornly refused to appreciate their distinctive gifts. These themes were developed at length in his novels *Home to Harlem* (1928) and *Banjo* (1929), where he indulged in lyrical bursts of racial essentialism and argued that people of African descent possessed a primitive vitality that was sadly lacking among overcivilized Anglo-Saxons.[104]

Although McKay increasingly tended to see the world in terms of black and white, he was keenly aware of the many divisions among people of African descent—rooted in class, color, and, to some extent, ethnicity and national-ity. This was especially evident in *Banjo*, which was situated in a diasporic context—the Vieux Port of Marseilles, where black seamen, dockworkers, and drifters from Madagascar, Martinique, Guadeloupe, French West Africa, and the United States alternated between the necessary but alienating demands of wage labor and the liberating pleasures of the flesh. In Marseilles McKay en-countered a hierarchy of black ethnicity, with the Martiniquans and Guadelou-pans making "a little aristocracy of themselves," the Madagascans and North African Negroes somewhere in the middle, and "the Senegalese," who were derided as "savages," at the bottom.[105] He was also prepared to acknowledge sig-nificant racial and cultural differences among whites. As late as 1929, he called the Irish "whites of a different type," and he counseled Negro intellectuals to break the chains of their enslavement to "Anglo-Saxon standards." "Study the Irish cultural and social movement," he recommended; "read about the Russian peasants"; "learn all you can about Gandhi and what he is doing for the com-mon hordes of India"; embrace "the native African dialects and . . . be humble before their simple beauty instead of despising them."[106] Here race as color was clearly less important than the common threads of a shared experience rooted in rural life, in indigenous cultures that were resisting the destructive impact of "superior" civilizations, in the integrity of a way of living that self-consciously stood over against the materialism and intellectual arrogance that predomi-nated in the centers of power in Europe and North America.

McKay could not help but be keenly aware of the tensions and contradic-tions that permeated his art and, more broadly, his life and the lives of his friends within the New Negro movement. At every juncture, he appeared to face a choice between race and class, art and politics, instinct and intellect, and, finally, between the vitality of black life and the soul-killing pressures to conform to the mores of (white) civilization. Winston James reminds us that McKay never abandoned politics altogether. But as an artist he appeared to opt for instinct over intellect and to be content to celebrate the "keen ecstatic joy a man feels in the romance of being black."[107] Significantly, his novels provided inspiration for a later generation of writers and activists such as Léopold Sen-ghor of Senegal and Aimé Césaire of Martinique, who saw in McKay's work the validation of a distinctively African culture and value system they called *Négritude*. Senghor, who served as the president of Senegal from 1960 to 1981, argued that "Claude McKay can rightfully be considered the true inventor of *Négritude*. . . . [In McKay,] far from seeing in one's blackness an inferiority, one accepts it, one lays claim to it with pride, one cultivates it lovingly."[108]

It may not be surprising that Afro-Caribbean intellectuals who were born and raised within the confines of the British Empire would feel a strong sense of affinity with Irish nationalism. But what about African American intellectu-als such as W.E.B. Du Bois and A. Philip Randolph? They had grown up on American soil and were obviously aware of the long history of antagonism that had marked the relationship between blacks and the Irish in the United States. In fact, neither Randolph nor Du Bois minced any words on this subject. In the pages of the *Messenger*, Randolph called the Irish "the race which Negroes . . . dislike most," and Du Bois reminded readers of the *Crisis* that "no people in the world have in the past gone with blither spirit to 'kill niggers' from Kingston to Delhi and from Kumasi to Fiji" than the Irish.[109]

As a young man, Asa Philip Randolph had the honor of being labeled the "most dangerous Negro in America." He was born in Crescent City, Florida, in 1889. His father was a tailor whose real calling in life was the ministry; he pastored several small African Methodist Episcopal churches in the Jacksonville area. Randolph described his father as "coal black" and his mother as "almost white." But both had an "unusual sense of racial pride." From them he imbibed the Victorian virtues of piety, hard work, and "purity of conduct," as well as the belief that "you must be ready to fight for your rights." After graduating from high school, he moved to New York City, where he found his calling in the socialist movement. In November 1917 he and his close friend and fellow socialist Chandler Owen produced the first issue of the *Messenger*. They called it "The Only Radical Negro Magazine in America."[110]

Although his politics moderated over the years, Randolph remained a committed socialist and an indefatigable trade union leader and civil rights activist.[111] But to a remarkable degree, during the formative years of the *Messenger*, he was willing to place Ireland and the oppression of its people on an equal plane with the struggles of the "colored races." Although he came to despise Marcus Garvey and eventually used the *Messenger* as the propaganda arm of a virulent "Garvey Must Go" campaign, he sounded very much like the charismatic Jamaican in his condemnation of England for grinding "under her imperial heel the bleeding body of Ireland, the suffering soul of India, and the dusky slaves of Egypt." On one occasion, he even argued that "Brown Hindu, Yellow Chinese, and White Irishmen are equally, and in some instances, more oppressed than Negroes." Like Garvey and Briggs, moreover, Randolph called upon blacks to emulate the Irish in their struggle for full emancipation. He welcomed the formation of the Friends of Irish Freedom and announced that the *Messenger* would seek to form a parallel organization, the Friends of Negro Freedom.[112]

If Randolph became one of the most famous and widely respected civil rights activists of the first half of the twentieth century, William Edward Burghardt Du Bois, the son of a dark-skinned domestic servant and an itinerant barber of "indeterminate color," emerged as the century's most important African American intellectual. "Willie" Du Bois, as he was known to family and friends during his childhood, was born in 1868. In racial and ethnic terms, he came from a remarkably hybrid lineage. On his father's side he was descended from Dr. James Du Bois, a wealthy Hudson Valley physician of French Huguenot origins who sided with the British during the American Revolution. For his loyalty, the Crown awarded him plantation land in the Bahamas, and from that base he became the owner of plantations in Haiti as well. He also fathered at least four children by various slave mistresses. One of them, Alexander Du Bois, was Willie's grandfather. Alexander's son Alfred Du Bois, who was born in Haiti, was Willie's father. It is not clear when Alfred came to the United States, but he served briefly in the Union Army during the Civil War and lived only briefly with Willie's mother, Mary Silvina Burghardt, and their newborn son in Great Barrington, Massachusetts.[113]

Tom Burghardt, the patriarch of Mary Silvina's family, was born in West Africa, transported to North America on a slave ship, and sold to a Dutch New Yorker, probably in the 1740s. The Burghardts, or at least some of them, were considerably darker than Alfred Du Bois; apparently they considered him "too white."[114] Through them, Willie Du Bois found his direct linkage to Africa, "a tie which I can feel better than I can explain," he was compelled to acknowledge. He claimed that his heritage included "a flood of Negro blood, a strain of French, a bit of Dutch, but, Thank God! No 'Anglo-Saxon.'" However, Great Barrington was a community in which there were probably no more than forty African Americans, but "Anglo-Saxons" were virtually everywhere. Du Bois recalled that during his childhood there was more prejudice against Irish Catholic immigrants than there was against the Negro residents of Great Barrington, who, no matter how light or dark their skin, were always resolutely Protestant. The Irish worked in the textile mills, whereas the Burghardts and other African Americans were employed in "gentler jobs" in the realm of "personal service." "As a boy," Du Bois wrote, "I was afraid of the Irish and kept away from their part of town as much as possible. Sometimes they called me 'nigger' or tried to attack me." From a distance, he "cordially despised" them in return. After all, "None of the colored folk I knew were so poor, drunk, and sloven." But in a society where color lines were hardening and European immigrants were laying claim to the jobs that even light-skinned, refined blacks had once owned, the Burghardts' trajectory was clearly downward. Only his undeniable intellectual gifts, and the encouragement and philanthropic assistance offered by teachers, clergymen, and other upstanding members of the local community, made it possible for Willie Du Bois to receive the education that would provide a way out, and up, for him.[115] The rest is the stuff of legend. He graduated from Nashville's Fisk University in 1888 and then earned a BA, an MA, and a PhD from Harvard, where he studied with distinguished scholars and teachers such as William James, Josiah Royce, and George Santayana. He also did graduate work at the University of Berlin and saw his dissertation, "The Suppression of the African Slave-Trade to the United States of America, 1638–1870," published in 1896 as the first volume in the Harvard Historical Studies series.

According to one admirer, Du Bois was "the master builder, whose work will speak to men as long as there is an oppressed race on the earth."[116] He was also a man of many unresolved contradictions, which were reflected in his writings throughout his life. But whatever the focus of the moment—Victorian

7.4. W.E.B. Du Bois, 1907 (W.E.B. Du Bois Papers, Department of Special Collections and University Archives, W.E.B. Du Bois Library, University of Massachusetts Amherst)

moralism, liberal integrationism, Pan-Africanism, democratic socialism, or Stalinist Marxism—Du Bois always wielded his powerful pen on behalf of the "darker races" and their emancipation. For twenty-four years he edited the NAACP journal, the *Crisis*, and most of what he wrote there, and elsewhere, appeared to leave few openings for the convergence of the struggles of the African diaspora with Ireland's fight for freedom. In "The African Roots of the War," which appeared in the *Atlantic Monthly* in 1915, he argued that the Great War was attributable first and foremost to economic competition among the nations of Europe, above all to the deadly imperial rivalries that their rush to devour the land and mineral riches of Africa had engendered. He argued, too, that these regimes of despoliation and aggression abroad had developed hand in hand with the broadening of the franchise and the development of a welfare state for the white masses at home. Offered the opportunity to share in the exploitation of "chinks and niggers," the white workingman accepted; and accepted, as well, the corollary that "color" signified "inferiority." Thus, instead of the class struggle that Marxists envisioned, Du Bois posited a kind of racial Darwinism on a global scale, a struggle for supremacy and survival culminating in a "War of the Color Line [that] will outdo in savage inhumanity any war this world has yet seen."[117]

A year later Du Bois veered in a quite different direction. Forgoing the anti-imperialist stance that had characterized "The African Roots of the War," he now called Britain "the best administrator of colored peoples" and declared that in comparison with Germany, England was an "Angel of light." "We of the colored race have no ordinary interest in the outcome" of the Great War, he would write in 1918. "That which German power represents today spells death to the aspirations of Negroes and all the darker races for equality, freedom and democracy."[118]

Du Bois's attitude toward Irish nationalism evolved over time, and his identification with Ireland's struggle for independence grew with the independence movement's ability to command the attention of the world. In the aftermath of the Easter Rising, he defended Roger Casement against the charge of treason, calling him a "Patriot" and "Martyr." But in characterizing the decision to execute Casement as a "blunder," Du Bois blurred the line between effective colonial administration and the right of an oppressed nation to full self-determination. Moreover, in an article published in May 1919, he referred dismissively to Ireland as one of the "little groups who want to be nations" and were clamoring for the world's attention at the Paris peace conference.[119]

Faced with the growing drama of the Irish War of Independence, however, he changed course again. Now it was the uncompromising, and insurrectionary, dimensions of the Irish Revolution that appealed to his romantic sensibilities. With the signing of the Anglo-Irish Treaty, he claimed that it "brings Irish Freedom nearer and increases the hope of freedom for all men." But when the divisions within the Irish republican movement became clearer and the drift toward civil war had begun, he asked the same question many people in Ireland were asking: "Is a half loaf better than war? Probably it is," he answered. And yet the refusal of the most zealous Irish republicans to accept anything less than complete independence won his begrudging admiration. "Those who stand on principle have a right to be heard," he wrote. "Civilization advances with half loaves usually, but the goal remains the whole loaf."[120]

When confronted with the Fenian enthusiasms of Garvey and Briggs, Du Bois felt compelled to remind them of the willingness of Irish soldiers to "kill niggers" across the arc of the British Empire. And yet for all of his ambivalence about the American Irish, going all the way back to his childhood in western Massachusetts, he had forged a racial consciousness that opened outward not only toward the African diaspora but also toward solidarity with other peoples—even the Irish—who were struggling to be free. "We must remember," he wrote in 1916, "that the white slums of Dublin represent more bitter depths of human degradation than the black slums of Charleston and New Orleans, and where human oppression exists there the sympathy of all black hearts must go."[121]

CHAPTER EIGHT

"The Irish are for freedom everywhere"

EAMON DE VALERA, THE IRISH PATRIOTIC STRIKE, AND THE "LAST
WHITE NATION . . . DEPRIVED OF ITS LIBERTY"

> We will be rebels [not only] to England [but] to any form of injustice
> in any country the world over
> —Liam Mellows, March 1918

> Ireland is now the last white nation that is deprived of its liberty.
> —Eamon de Valera, October 1920

THE IRISH LAID CLAIM to their birthright of freedom at an extraordinary moment in the world's history—one characterized by a devastating war that took the lives of nine and a half million combatants, a revolution in Russia that threatened to spread far beyond the borders of the Russian Soviet Republic, a wave of working-class insurgency that culminated in the great strike wave of 1919 and 1920, and a rising tide of nationalism that the victorious Allied powers helped to inspire but could not contain.[1] In this combustible environment, Irish nationalists not only fought with ballot and bullet but also sought to define the contours of the nation and illuminate the character of the race. Although they were, of necessity, turned inward and deeply preoccupied with the meaning of "Ourselves," they also reached out to a wider audience, in part to make their case and win support for it among the great powers, in part to link their own suffering and struggle with that of other nations and peoples around the world. Thus, at the end of December 1918, Patrick McCartan, a medical doctor from County Tyrone who served as the official envoy of the self-proclaimed Irish Republic in the United States, announced that "the free and independent people of Ireland hold out the hand of fellowship to all the free and subject peoples of the world." He issued this statement in the aftermath of Sinn Féin's stunning triumph in the general election of December 1918, which he chose to call "the final and complete vindication of Irish Nationhood by the Irish people." "We feel special kinship with the people of France and Belgium, so lately freed from the usurping power of military might," he declared. "The wrongs of the people of Russia, Poland and Palestine we feel as our wrongs; and we shall afford what aid we can to right them." But most of all, he looked to the United States for encouragement and assistance.[2]

A strong sense of kinship with America had long been a hallmark of Irish nationalism. Young Ireland had been repelled by O'Connell's scathing critique of the crimes of the White Republic and had defended the United States as a land of liberty and an indispensable haven for Irish exiles. A decade later, the Fenians constructed one of the twin pillars of physical force nationalism in New York, where for generations Clan na Gael served as a vital source of material and moral support for Irish republicans. And leaders of the Land League and the Irish Parliamentary Party such as Davitt and Parnell made the obligatory journey to the United States often. In Davitt's case, as in so many others, America meant family—the place where his parents were buried and where he met his wife. Now, in the context of war and revolution, it appeared that America had once again become the "champion of universal freedom," the "cradle of democracy," the "only hope of Ireland."[3]

It was natural, then, that in his capacity as leader of the Irish struggle for independence, Eamon de Valera would make the same journey and articulate a similar message. De Valera ("Dev" to his many admirers, "the Chief" to his closest associates) arrived in the United States as a stowaway on a British merchant vessel in June 1919 and departed in the same way in December 1920.[4] In his initial press statement, issued in New York City on June 23, 1919, he offered numerous comparisons between the American colonists' struggle for independence in the eighteenth century and Ireland's war for freedom in the twentieth, and then concluded, "The men who established your Republic sought the aid of France. We seek the aid of America. It is to seek that aid that I am here and I am confident that I shall not be disappointed."[5]

At some level, the logic of de Valera's appeal seemed to be unassailable. If, indeed, the Great War had been fought in the name of the right of all nations to self-determination, as President Woodrow Wilson insisted again and again, then Ireland—"one of the most ancient nations in Europe, . . . [which] has preserved her national integrity . . . through seven centuries of foreign oppression"—was entitled to be free.[6] But in the war's aftermath, even Wilson was no longer so sure. He acknowledged that he had not anticipated how many nations would emerge and lay claim to the rights he had enunciated and how much instability their demands would create. When a delegation of Irish American representatives approached him in Paris on Ireland's behalf, he responded, "You have touched on the great metaphysical tragedy of today." His secretary of state, Robert Lansing, ventured even further, complaining bitterly that

> the more I think of the President's declaration as to the right of "self-determination" the more convinced I am of the danger of putting such ideas into the minds of certain races. It is bound to be the basis of impossible demands on the Peace Congress and create trouble in many lands. What effect will it have on the Irish, the Indians,

the Egyptians, and the nationalists among the Boers? Will it not breed discontent, disorder, and rebellion? . . . The phrase is simply loaded with dynamite. It will raise hopes which can never be realised.[7]

Meanwhile, Britain was determined to keep Ireland within the confines of the empire, and French premier Georges Clemenceau, who presided over the peace conference, insisted that any intervention on Ireland's behalf would constitute interference in the internal affairs of an allied state, which could not be tolerated "under any circumstance whatever." From the standpoint of Irish republicans, then, it was becoming increasingly clear that this was a peace imposed by and for the victors. By April 1919, even before de Valera's departure for America, Wilson was criticized openly in the Dáil as "the Machiavelli of the new world, who use[s] guile and treachery to accomplish his ends."[8]

In coming to the United States, de Valera was, in a sense, coming home, for he was born in New York City in 1882. His mother, Catherine (Kate) Coll, was a domestic servant from Bruree, County Limerick, who left Ireland in 1879 and worked in the same occupation in New York. His father, Juan Vivion de Valera, was a Spanish sculptor, bookkeeper, and music teacher from an affluent family, who died of tuberculosis in 1884, soon after his son's second birthday. Apparently, there is no proof that Kate Coll and Vivion de Valera were married; one of Eamon de Valera's recent biographers argues that they were not. Thus, in a Catholic culture that placed a premium on sexual restraint and social conformity, the man whom many came to regard as *the* leader of the Irish nation had to fight the persistent rumor that he was "illegitimate," as well as the accusation that, as the son of a Spaniard, he had "not the instinct of the Irishman in his blood."[9]

Soon after her son's birth, Kate Coll turned him over to a Mrs. Doyle, also an immigrant from Bruree, and "went out to work again." At the age of two he was taken to Ireland by his eighteen-year-old uncle, Ned Coll, and placed in the care of his grandmother, a farm widow and native Irish speaker who raised him in a laborer's cottage on a half acre of land in Bruree. To those detractors who insisted that he lacked "the instinct of the Irishman in his blood," he later claimed, "The first fifteen years of my life that formed my character were lived amongst the Irish people down in Limerick." Somehow this experience meant that whenever he wanted to understand the aspirations of his countrymen and -women, "I had only to examine my own heart and it told me straight off what the Irish people wanted."[10]

De Valera proved to be an outstanding student wherever he matriculated, from Bruree National School and Charleville Christian Brothers School as a boy to the Royal University of Ireland, from which he graduated with a degree in mathematics as a young man. He went on to teach math, and his chosen discipline may help to explain his reputation as a hairsplitting logician of great skill and even greater tenacity. To his many admirers, he was a brilliant wordsmith and principled advocate of Irish freedom. But to his adversaries—and they too were numerous—he was "arrogant, prickly, and pig-headed"; at the very least, a "man whose tongue often outran his judgement."[11] Some critics went further, but surely no further than John Devoy, who, after butting heads with de Valera for nearly a year, denounced him as "the most malignant man in all Irish history."[12]

It may be fair to conclude that Dev combined within himself the dogmatic and practical dimensions of Irish republicanism to an unusual degree. When he confronted the pragmatists in the movement, he became—in their eyes—an unbending dogmatist; but when he was surrounded by uncompromising republicans, as he would be during the civil war, his penchant for compromise and rationality came to the forefront. In a letter to his ally and friend Mary Mac-Swiney, one of the genuine dogmatists in the republican camp, he described her as "one who keeps [on] the plane of Faith and Unreason," and then he declared:

> Unfortunately for me, Reason rather than Faith has been my master. . . . I have felt for some time that this doctrine of mine unfitted me to be leader of the Republican Party. I cannot think as you . . . [think]. Nature never fashioned me to be a partisan leader in any case. . . . I must be the heir to generations of conservatism. Every instinct of mine would indicate that I was meant to be a dyed-in-the-wool Tory or even a Bishop, rather than the leader of a Revolution.[13]

Nonetheless, he did become the leader of a revolution. From enthusiastic participant in the Gaelic League to enlistee in the Irish Volunteers to commandant (the only surviving commandant) in the Easter Rising in Dublin, he seemed destined to become the outstanding figure in the generation of 1916. The fact that so many other members of that extraordinary generation were killed in battle or executed by the state played a major role in clearing his path toward a singular leadership role in twentieth-century Ireland. Already, when he arrived in New York City in June 1919, he came as president of Dáil Éireann, president of Sinn Féin, and president of the Irish Volunteers. For good measure, soon after his arrival, he declared himself "President of the Irish Republic" as well.[14]

De Valera's critics complained that during his mission to the United States, he acted more like visiting royalty than like an IRA commandant who had—only recently—escaped from a British prison.[15] His headquarters was the Waldorf-Astoria, one of the nation's most lavish and prestigious hotels. From there he launched his "Grand Tour," in which (according to his associate Patrick McCartan) "receptions, greater than those ever accorded to any American President, were given to President de Valera in practically every State and every city of importance in the country." His first stop was Boston, where he spoke to a crowd of 70,000 at Fenway Park and then addressed both houses of the Massachusetts legislature. In Manchester, New Hampshire, a much smaller city than Boston, he attracted an audience of 30,000. In Chicago 50,000 people greeted him with "an ovation of nearly thirty minutes." And so it went: in San Francisco a gold plaque from the mayor and an honorary doctorate from Saint Ignatius University (now the University of San Francisco); in Montana, an address to a joint session of the state legislature; in Saint Louis a twenty-one-gun salute and triumphant parade through the city. Through it all, he enjoyed the finest accommodations and the company of the wealthy and powerful.[16]

In such company, and in his plush headquarters at the Waldorf-Astoria, de Valera could insulate himself from the clamor of the many insurgent movements that were so much a part of the American, and global, scene during the Great War's volcanic aftermath. But once he set foot on the streets of New York and other American cities, once he entered great meeting halls such as Madison Square Garden, or consulted newspaper headlines, it was a different story. It was of no small significance that he arrived in the United States in the summer of 1919, a time when racial violence was at a fever pitch. In July, Washington, DC, erupted in racial violence, much of it initiated by soldiers and sailors in uniform, leaving three dead and more than a hundred injured. Then, beginning on July 27, Chicago became the site of the most devastating of the 1919 riots, only two weeks after de Valera's triumphant visit to the city. In the course of twelve days of skirmishing in Chicago, 38 people died, more than 500 were wounded, and another 1,000 were rendered homeless.[17]

However ignorant de Valera may have been of the realities of racial oppression in the United States, surely he knew that something of major proportions was happening, and he had ready access to a wide range of individuals who had opinions on the subject. Many of them were no doubt steeped in the mores of white supremacy, but others—including some of the men and women closest to him—were racial egalitarians who insisted that the Irish Republic could triumph in its propaganda war with England only by appealing to "all people who desire the widest possible extension of liberty."[18]

It was equally significant that de Valera's sojourn in the United States coincided with an unprecedented wave of labor militancy, with millions of workers on strike, a breathtaking expansion of the ranks—and apparent power—of organized labor, and widespread demands for "industrial democracy," even a workers' republic. This virtually compelled a sympathetic response from Dev and his associates. When he addressed labor audiences in New York, San Francisco, and Butte, he not only agreed that "they should enjoy the fruits of what they produce" but also assured them that "the future of the world lies with the workers of the world."[19]

In this regard, there may have been a significant difference between the struggle for Irish independence in Dublin and in New York. In Dublin, and throughout Ireland, the leaders of Irish nationalism sought to build a wall between the national and social questions, and they insisted (in the words of Cathal Brugha) that "Labour people have . . . the intelligence and patriotism to let their class claim wait until we have cleared out the enemy."[20] But the exiles

8.1. Harry Boland, Liam Mellows, Eamon de Valera, John Devoy (*seated*), Patrick McCartan, and Diarmuid Lynch, New York City, June 1919 (Eamon de Valera Papers, P150/1079, University College Dublin Archives; courtesy of the UCD-OFM Partnership)

and emissaries who carried the torch for Irish freedom in New York were operating in a context where they were bound to encounter and interact with socialists, labor militants, suffragists, pacifists, and Indian and African diaspora nationalists, many of whom articulated a broad perspective that was the antithesis of a narrow preoccupation with "Ourselves." On this terrain carefully constructed walls between emancipatory movements proved to be porous, and the themes of class, race, and nation often converged. De Valera's sojourn in the United States offers the opportunity to examine the complex ways in which this convergence occurred not only for him but also for men and women such as Frank P. Walsh, Liam Mellows, Harry Boland, and Helen and Peter Golden.

De Valera was, of necessity, preoccupied with the fundamental goal of his mission—to win the support of the American government for the cause of Irish independence. This placed significant constraints on his freedom to speak and to act, for he could not hope to win over his hosts by challenging the conventions they lived by. But whether by accident or design, he surrounded himself with men and women who were much less inclined to honor those constraints. Although they shared many of his assumptions and accepted the strategic necessity of his chosen course, they were moving in a different direction politically, toward an alliance with the insurgent forces that were threatening to turn the prewar social order upside down. To be sure, their politics were hardly monolithic. Walsh was an American success story, but also a self-proclaimed "poet and . . . revolutionist." His goal was to "swing the Irish Movement in this country to the radical movement."[21] Boland, a skilled worker in the garment trades, had an "undoubted inclination towards elements of socialism," but, his biographer assures us, "his first commitment was to the [Irish] Republic." Liam Mellows and Peter Golden would ultimately move in quite different directions on the spectrum of Irish republicanism—one toward a merging of the social and national questions and the other toward the embrace of an ideology that was willfully class unconscious. Nonetheless, the course they followed together in the volatile crucible of wartime and postwar New York offers a portrait of a different kind of nationalism—one that was turned outward toward a wider world of struggle and possibility and that represented a sharp break with the hostility toward radicals and socialists that had become an article of faith in much of Irish America.[22]

Few, if any, Irish Americans were closer to de Valera than Frank P. Walsh, an attorney whose many accomplishments gave him access to the upper echelons of the legal profession, the Democratic Party, and the Catholic elite, lay and clerical. Walsh was born in 1863 to Irish immigrant parents in Saint Louis's Kerry Patch. When his father died, he was compelled to leave school and seek employment as a messenger, factory worker, and railway clerk. Eventually, he began studying law and, in 1888, was admitted to the Missouri bar. Two years later, in Kansas City, he married Katie O'Flaherty, the organist at Saint Aloysius Church. Together, they would have eight children, and Walsh would remain a devout Catholic all his life.[23]

Although Walsh became a successful corporate lawyer, his "lace curtain" achievements did not sit well with him. Thus, in 1900, he "resigned from every corporation with which I was connected" and became, in effect, a "people's lawyer." As the Progressive movement developed, his politics moved leftward, toward an active identification with the labor movement. He also became a racial liberal, a strong supporter of women's suffrage, and a friend of radical feminists and others whose lives and outlook were far removed from the ethos and institutional networks of Irish America. But as Joseph McCartin points out, Walsh "would never completely break his ties to the legal profession, the Democratic Party, or his Irish Catholic culture."[24]

Walsh's vision of a cooperative commonwealth and its ideal of "production for the good of all mankind" was grounded in an array of principles and practices that were distinctively (but by no means uniquely) American. His frequent denunciations of the "heart-destroying, soul-shriveling idea of production solely for . . . profits" reflected a socialist impulse, if not a full commitment to socialism as doctrine and political affiliation. More often, he focused on the goal of industrial democracy and the hope that a militant labor movement could achieve a "fundamental realignment of class power" in the United States.[25] His Irish American coworker Dudley Field Malone came to embody many of the same political tendencies. Malone had served in the Wilson administration and become "a member of the president's inner circle." But he was radicalized by the events that accompanied the Great War, and he became a strong supporter of the NAACP and the women's suffrage movement. In 1919 he formed the League of Oppressed Peoples, which, according to Robert A. Hill, was "primarily interested in promoting self-determination for China, India, Korea, and Ireland."[26]

In the crucible of 1919, the ideas and impulses that animated Walsh and Malone found institutional expression in the Irish Progressive League (IPL), which emerged in New York in October 1917 as a coalition of "revolutionary nationalists and left-of-center Irish Americans." For the next three years, the league's small but extraordinarily active core membership played a vital role in Irish America's agitation on behalf of Ireland's independence.[27] League members maintained close ties with a group of Carmelite Fathers, led by Peter Magennis, whose priory on East Twenty-ninth Street not only served as a welcome refuge for Irish exiles in New York but—Father Magennis proudly declared— also became a "hotbed of sedition [and] treason."[28] What made the league most distinctive, however, was its successful effort to involve socialists and other progressives in the struggle for Ireland's emancipation and its willingness to affirm that self-determination and freedom were universal doctrines that could not be applied to Ireland alone. Thus, although the league claimed to be a "purely Irish organization that would stand at all times for the independence of Ireland," its *Bulletin* also announced that one of the league's main goals was to "keep in touch as closely as possible with progressive movements everywhere that were for the betterment and uplift of the human race." The *Bulletin* went on to make a remarkable claim—that the league had "never refrained from voicing its sympathy with people of whatever race, color, or creed who were struggling to live their lives as they themselves desired and not as alien exploiters would have them [live]." One could argue that these were mere words. But even to voice sympathy and, by implication, solidarity with people of "color" in September 1919, in the waning but still volatile moments of one of the most deadly and sustained racial pogroms in American history, marked the league as extraordinary.[29]

In announcing its first public meeting, in October 1917, the league called on its constituents to "come in your thousands and prove that the Irish are for freedom everywhere." The main order of business was to endorse Morris Hillquit's candidacy for mayor of New York. Hillquit, a veteran Socialist Party leader, was running against not one but two Irish American candidates: the incumbent mayor John Purroy Mitchel—grandson of the legendary John Mitchel—and Brooklyn judge John F. Hylan. It is ironic that of the three, Hillquit was the only one who unequivocally supported Ireland's right to national independence. He also made opposition to America's participation in the Great War a major focus of his campaign. "We are for peace," he declared in accepting the Socialist Party's mayoral nomination. "Not warfare and terrorism, but Socialism and social justice will make the world safe for democracy." In the final analysis, much of the Irish community voted for Judge Hylan, who was, after all, the candidate of the Democratic Party and Tammany Hall; he won the election by a comfortable margin. Hillquit, the antiwar candidate, won more than 145,000 votes (22 percent of the total) and generated tremendous enthusiasm—most notably in the Jewish and working-class districts of Manhattan's Lower East Side. But his candidacy also generated hysterical opposition—from the business community and from prowar zealots such as former president Theodore Roosevelt, who, according to Hillquit, issued "thinly veiled" appeals to "mob law and to lynching." That in this volatile and dangerous climate the Irish Progressive League would steadfastly support a Jewish socialist against two Irish American Catholics for mayor of one of the world's most Irish cities speaks volumes about the forces that were coalescing on the left wing of the nationalist movement.[30]

Over time the league became the principal outlet for the political activity of Irish exiles of the 1916 generation—most notably, Liam Mellows. A member of the Irish Republican Brotherhood (IRB) and the Irish Volunteers, Mellows was born at a military barracks in England in 1892. His father, grandfather, and great-grandfather had all served far afield in the British army, but Liam was raised in Wexford, Cork, and Dublin, where he was educated by the Christian Brothers. Even as an adult, he stood no more than five feet, three inches and weighed 128 pounds. But his courage, integrity, and uncompromising republicanism more than made up for his small physical stature. In 1916 he was the leader of the rising in the west of Ireland. From there he escaped to Liverpool, where he secured forged seaman's papers and a berth on a merchant vessel that arrived in New York Harbor in December.[31]

In spite of—sometimes because of—the large and active Irish American community he encountered in New York and other American cities, Mellows never felt at home in the United States. His incarceration in Manhattan's infamous Tombs Prison for ten days in the autumn of 1917 no doubt contributed much to his sense of alienation. Even before his arrest, for "conspiracy to represent himself as an American citizen with a view to procuring a false seaman's certificate," he had witnessed a draconian crackdown on dissent—a crackdown that reached into the Irish community with the arrest of Elizabeth Gurley Flynn, the legendary "Rebel Girl," who was charged with conspiracy to violate the Espionage Act (in effect, with engaging in antiwar activities).[32] Jeremiah O'Leary, the irrepressible anti-British polemicist, was arrested on the same charge. O'Leary reported that "jail is a fine place when you are put there by tyrants . . . and I intend to stay here as long as possible." Mellows could feel no such equanimity. He soon concluded that "in the United States there is no such thing as law."[33]

In fact, his alienation had deeper, more existential roots. This becomes vividly evident in a letter he wrote about an obscure Irish immigrant he encountered in a New York City hospital. Catherine Davis, a "poor Galway woman," had been suffering from heart disease for years. She "had only one desire," he wrote, "to die in Ireland." When she heard of Mellows's leadership role in the Easter Rising in Galway, she asked to meet him. "Her delight was obvious when I answered her salutation in Irish and told her I knew her birthplace well." But then, during his coast-to-coast travels on behalf of the Irish Republic, he lost track of her. Finally, a priest in Pennsylvania informed him she was in Saint Mary's Hospital in Brooklyn.

> [I] called at the hospital when I returned to New York. . . . Poor soul! Her one earthly wish will never be gratified. Her days, nay, her very hours are numbered. She didn't recognize me at first, and then, when she did, was unable to speak: [she] simply held my two hands and repeated time after time, "don't go." I stayed with her for about an hour and had to tear myself away. She will never see Ireland again and her heart is broken.

Clearly anguished and embittered by her situation, Mellows claimed that countless others had shared the same fate: "To eat their hearts out in exile and to die in the land of the stranger with their thoughts on the land of their love."[34]

A devout Catholic himself, Mellows managed to find a supportive network of Irish priests—above all, the Carmelite Fathers in Manhattan—and several devoted nationalist families who took him in, offered him nourishment for body and soul, and helped nurse him through several illnesses, including a bout with the flu that almost took his life during the great influenza epidemic of 1918–19. Nationalist crowds revered him; they sometimes demanded that he address mass meetings even when he was not among the scheduled speakers. But Mellows came to regard Irish America, particularly its New York City headquarters, as a "maelstrom of bitterness and perversity," where "prejudice is rampant—fierce—unbelievable."[35] At first he had been welcomed, and warmly embraced, by John Devoy, Judge Daniel Cohalan, and the leadership of Clan na Gael. Devoy even offered him a staff position on his newspaper, the *Gaelic American*. But over time a definite rift developed in the relations between the self-appointed leaders of Irish America and the young exiles of the 1916 generation who were—critics charged—determined to claim "ownership" of the Irish struggle in the United States.[36] Even before Eamon de Valera arrived in New York and allegedly "split the Irish movement in America," Mellows and his allies were engaged in a bitter cold war with Devoy and company.[37] In August 1918 he admitted that "I looked on my sojourn in this place as a mild form of purgatory." By February 1920 the purgatory had become anything but mild. Mellows maintained then that until de Valera's arrival in the United States offered him a new assignment and sense of purpose, "my life was misery night and day."[38]

Part of the controversy derived from Mellows's willingness to speak plainly, and undiplomatically, about America's relationship to the struggle for Irish independence. With the U.S. declaration of war on Germany, Judge Cohalan, in particular, went out of his way to assert that throughout the nation "there would not be . . . a single man of Irish blood who would not now think of America first." But Mellows insisted on thinking of Ireland first and judging the United States accordingly. On the day after British authorities arrested many of the leaders of Sinn Féin on the pretext that they had participated in a "German plot" to foment rebellion in Ireland, Mellows rightly characterized the alleged conspiracy as a hoax and charged that "America, by its silence on the question of Irish independence, has been and still is . . . tacitly acquiescing in England's domination." "Let America speak now on behalf of Ireland," he told the Irish Race Convention of May 1918, "or let it stop talking about the freedom of small nations."[39]

Mellows's words were far too jarring and confrontational for Judge Cohalan and, increasingly, for John Devoy as well. They sought to rein him in, but it was no use. He resigned from the *Gaelic American* and told his close friend Nora Connolly, "I am beyond redemption. Am looked upon as wild, hot-headed, undisciplined—liable to get the movement into trouble—dubbed a Socialist and Anarchist." "Liam hates America and will go home," his friend and fellow worker Harry Boland reported. But Mellows was unable to escape from the "land of the stranger" until the autumn of 1920, when he again secured forged seaman's papers and sailed for Liverpool on a merchant ship.[40]

Mellows's politics had been conventionally republican when he arrived in the United States. But he was soon spending considerable time with Irish radicals in exile such as Frank Robbins, a socialist, member of the Irish Citizen Army, and participant in the 1916 Rising; and Nora Connolly, the daughter of the martyred James Connolly who was a committed socialist herself. With the formation of the Irish Progressive League, he found himself in the company of leading members of the Socialist Party of America such as Morris Hillquit and Norman Thomas. In the context of the wartime repression that had ensnared him and cowed much of Irish America into uneasy silence, he couldn't help but notice that it was the socialists, and the members of the Irish Progressive League, who continued to stand up for their beliefs. Many years later, Robbins recalled an encounter with Mellows in the spring of 1917, during which he emphasized his own identity as a socialist and Mellows responded that "he knew nothing about socialism but had read Connolly's book [*Labour in Irish History*] and agreed with it."[41] Over the next twelve months, Mellows's respect for Connolly, and his own commitment to socialism, apparently grew dramatically, for on Saint Patrick's Day 1918, at a meeting to form the James Connolly Socialist Club, he declared publicly, "We are not fighting to free Ireland from the foreign tyrant in order to place her under the thumb of domestic tyrants." Borrowing from Connolly's argument that Gaelic society had been founded upon the "communistic clan," he argued that "the present movement in Ireland . . . is not called socialism. It is called by many names. Some have called it Sinn Féin, but call it what you will, Ireland wants to continue her old civilisation along the lines of socialism, communism or cooperation."[42]

Peter Golden served as secretary of the Irish Progressive League from its inception in 1917 until its dissolution in 1920. An actor, poet, and singer, he was born in Macroom, County Cork. In 1901 he joined a brother and two sisters who were living in Saint Louis. He graduated from the Saint Louis School of Elocution and Dramatic Art, became a U.S. citizen, and, in addition to writing poetry, developed a successful career in the theater, where he met his wife, Helen Merriam, when both were performing in Shakespeare's *Comedy of Errors*. He was also a deeply committed political activist, with long-standing ties to Sinn Féin. The *San Francisco Leader* claimed that "from end to end of the [United] States, as well as in his beloved Ireland, he is known as a virile and successful poet-preacher of the fiery gospel of Irish nationality." Less charitably, the *Hartford Courant* conceded that he was "madly in earnest" but also called him "excessively Irish." Perhaps this was a reference to the passionate hatred of England that infused his speeches and poems. In 1914, in the face of Britain's conditional offer of home rule to Ireland, he wrote in the preface to his *Ballads of Rebellion*, "We must above all block England's policy, thwart her plans, and strike at her wherever, whenever, and however we can." Was this a "doctrine of hate," as some critics charged? "So it is meant to be," he answered. In a poem denouncing the Irish Parliamentary Party leader John Redmond for linking Ireland's destiny with England's during the Great War, he "pray[ed] God to wither and blight and annihilate and destroy England."[43]

For several years Golden worked closely with John Devoy and his circle. But he became increasingly dismayed by the timidity that afflicted Clan na Gael and other Irish American organizations during the Great War. "Our people lay down everywhere while the war was on," he would later recall. Even worse, many activists "scurried like rabbits to the warren, when they should have stood their ground." By 1918 he had become so alienated from Clan na Gael and Devoy's weekly newspaper, the *Gaelic American*, that he gave serious consideration to founding a rival publication, tentatively called the *Irish Standard*. It would, he told prospective readers, "be a loyal champion of the old cause." But it would also be much more than that, for, he announced, "the IRISH STANDARD will be in all things PROGRESSIVE[,] standing for the oppressed of the world and advocating the true principles which make for human well-being and the amelioration of the destiny of those who Labor."[44] These words are vague and imprecise, to be sure, but in "standing for the oppressed of the world" and placing "Labor" at the center of his vision of progressive change, Golden was clearly turning outward and seeking to build alliances with other grassroots social movements.

Moreover, at a time when Catholic publications, notably the Jesuit weekly *America*, were denouncing "the Socialist" as "ever the sower of discord and the arch-enemy of union and cooperation," Golden often shared the meeting hall and the rostrum with the growing number of socialists who were regularly featured at league meetings.[45] Like Liam Mellows, he remained first and foremost an uncompromising Irish republican. But unlike Mellows, he refused to become a socialist himself. In a letter to his friend Patrick McCartan, he warned of tensions within the league based on ideological and political differences. "Another group has become dissatisfied . . . with myself," he informed McCartan in March 1919. "Why I don't know. Probably because we don't become Socialists altogether. But I notice that Socialists and all others put their own business first and I don't see why we should not do likewise." Nonetheless, as the principal public voice of the league, Golden appeared to move comfortably within the orbit of the Left. In that capacity he explicitly linked the struggles of Russia and Ireland, calling for the withdrawal of "arm[ies] of occupation" from the two nations "so that the Irish and Russian peoples may be left to work out their own destiny" and hailing Russia as "the first government to recognize Ireland in her struggle for self-determination."[46]

In Peter Golden's case, the league benefited immeasurably from a kind of "two for the price of one" arrangement, because his work was often complemented by that of his wife. Helen Merriam Golden was not Irish; she came from a wealthy Anglo-American Protestant family that included two ancestors who had fought in the American Revolution and a great-uncle who had served two terms in the U.S. House of Representatives. But she fully shared her husband's passionate commitment to the cause of Irish independence. During a critical moment in the struggle, in the summer of 1920, it was Helen Golden who came to the forefront in remarkable ways—organizing a boycott of British shipping on the New York waterfront and negotiating sensitive issues of racial turf and biracial alliance with representatives of the Universal Negro Improvement Association. Her activity, through the Irish Progressive League and another militant organization known as the American Women Pickets for the Enforcement of America's War Aims, is symbolic of the extraordinary degree to which the forces that coalesced around the IPL were open not only to women's activism but also to female leadership in the movement. According to historian Francis M. Carroll, the league was "dominated" by four individuals. One of them was Peter Golden; the other three were women: Hanna Sheehy Skeffington; Margaret Hickey, the league treasurer; and Dr. Gertrude Kelly, a veteran activist who, by the time of the league's founding, had already had a long career in the fight for Irish freedom and in many other progressive causes. "For years I have been running across her name, spirit and reputation," Frank Walsh acknowledged, "and always in the case of some apparently 'down and out' individual or cause."[47]

Born in County Waterford in 1862, Gertrude Kelly immigrated to the United States in 1873, became a medical doctor, and operated a surgical clinic at the New York Infirmary for Women and Children for thirty years. Many of her patients were poor, and she became famous not only for visiting them in their homes but also for "slipping $5 under the plate instead of taking a fee" when she bade them farewell. She had maintained close ties with Henry George and his clerical ally, Father Edward McGlynn, in the 1880s and had called herself a philosophical anarchist at that time. But in later years she became a socialist. She was also unusual in at least two other respects. First, she was openly irreligious; in a room full of priests, she once referred to herself proudly as "one of the unredeemed pagan Irish." Second, she never married but lived openly for much of her adult life with her "companion," Mary Walsh.[48] One could reasonably conclude, then, that Kelly embodied one of the most remarkable characteristics of the Irish Progressive League—namely, the ways in which it was rooted in the Irish American community but also challenged some of its most "essential" orthodoxies. For here was an individual whose "racial" and familial bloodlines were impeccably Irish and who claimed to have been a member of "every Irish society on record" over the years, but who was also a socialist, a self-proclaimed "pagan," and a woman who lived for many years in a "Boston marriage" that, to a relentlessly patriarchal and reflexively heterosexual subculture, must have suggested overtones of homoerotic affection and behavior.[49]

As extraordinary as Kelly's career and beliefs were, even she was overshadowed by Hanna Sheehy Skeffington, whose politics and choice of political allies also demonstrate how far the league's leading members were prepared to move beyond the traditional parameters of Irish America. Hanna was the widow of Francis Sheehy Skeffington, a well-known Dublin activist who was murdered by a deranged British officer during the Easter Rising. Throughout his adult life, Francis had been a "pacifist and socialist, feminist and vegetarian, teetotaler and nonsmoker," and Hanna was committed to many of the same causes. Beginning in December 1916, she spent eighteen months in the United States, crisscrossing the country to speak on behalf of Irish independence. Federal agents routinely monitored the content of her speeches, she charged, and sometimes "tampered" with her luggage and "ransacked" her desk. In response, she dared them to arrest her and declared that she would go on hunger strike if they did.[50]

Publicly, Sheehy Skeffington claimed that "the Irish in America . . . cling to . . . thoughts of Ireland . . . with a tenacity that is shown by the descendants of no other country." But privately, she became increasingly determined to move beyond what her biographer has called "the tired old circuit of Irish-American males." By March 1918 she was reporting that "most of my support has been from suff[ragist]s, radicals and progressives—and very little from the Irish." In part, this reflected her choice of audience and the network of relationships that she found most congenial. In Butte, Montana, she got caught up in the Left-Right quarrels that were convulsing the city's labor movement and was accused of being a "labor agitator" and even a "traitor." In Portland, Oregon, she developed a friendship with Marie Equi, a well-to-do physician, birth-control advocate, and open lesbian who was soon to be arrested and sentenced to three years in prison for violating the Espionage Act. In Washington, DC, she joined hands with Alice Paul and other radical feminists who were coalescing around the National Women's Party.[51]

Sheehy Skeffington returned to Ireland in June 1918, but the substance—and the militant style—of her politics lived on in the women of the Irish Progressive League and among the members of the American Women Pickets for the Realization of America's War Aims. In spite of the name of their organization, most members of the American Women Pickets were militant Irish nationalists and suffragists who were influenced by the confrontational politics of the suffrage movement. In their campaign for Irish freedom, they adopted a strategy of "deliberate provocation"—burning British flags on the steps of the Treasury Department in Washington, DC, "bombing" the British Embassy from the air with leaflets denouncing Britain's military aggression in Ireland, engaging in acts of civil disobedience, and then refusing bail when they were arrested. In the final analysis, most of them were loyal to de Valera and his vision of the Irish Republic, and it was natural that they would work in close tandem with the Irish Progressive League.[52] Although by the summer of 1920 Helen Golden was the mother of three children, including one-year-old twins, she found far more personal fulfillment in street agitation and strike activity than she did in her role as wife and mother. On at least one occasion, she suggested to her husband that "perhaps we should exchange places," and she eventually succeeded him as league secretary.[53]

Harry Boland—who became, in effect, Dev's "personal servant" as the two men crisscrossed the United States together—was also pulled leftward at this time, toward visions of a global struggle against the British Empire. A leading member of the Irish Republican Brotherhood and a veteran of the 1916 Rising, Boland was a Dubliner, from a family that was "rich in rebel associations." He was effervescent, unfailingly good-natured, and eminently likable—so much so that de Valera once admitted, "I have got a bad reputation here as 'a very stubborn man,'" but "Harry is liked by everybody."[54] When it became clear that Dev's mission would not yield the recognition he sought from the American government, Boland turned toward insurgent labor as the key American ally in Ireland's fight for freedom. In July 1920 he wrote, "[We must] bend all our efforts to build an alliance with Labor, so that in the event of England's attempting war on our people we can rely on direct action here against her."[55] This alliance came to fruition, in a limited but significant way, in a strike on the New York waterfront—more specifically, on the Chelsea piers on Manhattan's West Side, where most of the dockworkers were Irish immigrants. These men were members of a conservative union, the International Longshoremen's Association (ILA), which was far more interested in collecting dues and upholding contracts than it was in engaging in strikes of any kind. And yet on August 27, members of the American Women Pickets—variously described in the press as "Irish women," "Irish girls," a "little group of plainly clad women," and "comely

Irish American[s]"—marched to the Chelsea piers and triggered what became known as the Irish Patriotic Strike.[56]

The strike, which tied up shipping in New York Harbor for three and a half weeks, was actually a boycott of British shipping waged by rank-and-file long-shoremen and their allies with no support from their union. From the West Side of Manhattan, the boycott spread to Brooklyn, and then to Boston, where it included freight handlers and grain elevator operatives as well as longshoremen. There were letters of support—and, sometimes, promises of strike action—in port cities stretching from Halifax, Nova Scotia, to Galveston, Texas. At the boycott's epicenter, strikers at a "huge meeting" near the Chelsea piers vowed they would "stand by Ireland forever, [and] . . . humble the British Empire." A resolution prepared by a rank-and-file committee of boycotters declared, "We hereby pledge our undying adherence to cease work on British ships throughout the world until England recognizes the 'Irish Republic,' bows her head on the altar of labor and takes the terms handed down by American labor, whose voice we here [represent]."[57]

The immediate cause of the boycott was the fate of two Irish patriots who were very much in the headlines at that moment. The first was Daniel Mannix, the Roman Catholic archbishop of Melbourne, Australia; the second was Terence MacSwiney, the republican lord mayor of Cork, who two weeks earlier had begun a hunger strike to protest his arrest by British authorities. Although the drama of MacSwiney's hunger strike was unsurpassed, Mannix played an even more direct role in triggering the Irish Patriotic Strike. A former president of Ireland's National Seminary at Maynooth, he had emigrated to Australia in 1913 and almost immediately had become a towering, and fiercely controversial, figure. He supported the Australian Labor Party and helped to make Irish Catholic workers its chief constituency. He denounced World War I as a capitalist war and, in 1916, helped spearhead a successful anticonscription campaign in Australia. By 1920 he was, by reputation, a "rabid Sinn Féiner," and he attempted to return to Ireland, allegedly to visit his mother. On July 31, amid great fanfare, he sailed from New York's Pier 60 on the White Star liner *Baltic*. British prime minister David Lloyd George had already stated publicly that Mannix would not be allowed to travel to Ireland, and four Royal Navy destroyers intercepted the *Baltic* as it prepared to make a regularly scheduled call at Queenstown, County Cork. Eventually, a naval officer and two Scotland Yard detectives removed Mannix from the ship and brought him ashore at Penzance, on England's southwest coast. It was, of course, a clumsy act of repression that only fed the fires of Irish nationalism. "Up Mannix," declared the protest placards. "Down with the Pirates of Penzance." When the *Baltic* returned to New York and docked at Pier 59 on August 27, the American Women Pickets called on members of the engine-room crew, or "black gang," to walk off the ship to protest British policy in Ireland. According to the *New York Tribune*, about 150 of them answered the women's call, and the strike was on. They were joined, immediately, by longshoremen working on Pier 59 and others nearby.[58]

"The Mannix incident gave us an opportunity to test the spirit of the men along the New York docks," Harry Boland exclaimed, "and their response was magnificent." Even though he was neither a maritime worker nor an active trade unionist, Boland played a vital role in setting this chain of events in motion. On July 28, acting in his capacity as leader of the Irish Republican Brotherhood in the United States, he met with several key members of the *Baltic*'s "black gang"—men who no doubt were committed Irish republicans themselves—and they in turn arranged a meeting of engine-room workers that led to their mobilization in support of Archbishop Mannix and, eventually, to their participation in the Irish Patriotic Strike. Laconically, but with obvious delight, Boland recorded the meeting in his diary: "Look[ed] up good friends and arrange[d] to fix the Mannix journey so that, if he should be prevented from travelling, we can hold up all the vessels in the port."[59]

The strike that Boland envisioned occurred exactly one month later. One can argue that his quest for an alliance with labor was purely instrumental. It had little to do with workers' demands for better wages and conditions and for greater power at the point of production, even though it came during a period of tremendous ferment in the ranks of labor and in the aftermath of the greatest strike wave in American history. However, one must also acknowledge that freedom for Ireland and for other oppressed nations had become a demand that workers embraced as their own. What Boland wanted, most of all, was to harness labor insurgency to make it serve the immediate objectives of Ireland's military struggle for independence. Already the IRB had succeeded in building an effective network of maritime communication—centered in Liverpool—that ran guns across the Irish Sea and shuttled men and messages between Liverpool and New York. At the hub of this network was Neil Kerr, a member of the IRB and friend of Michael Collins who was employed by the Cunard Line in Liverpool. He recruited Irish seamen to serve as his couriers. (Patrick McCartan remembered one of them as a "man who would steal a bridle off a nightmare, but he could be absolutely relied upon in Irish matters.") He also helped arrange for republican emissaries such as Boland, Mellows, and de Valera to make the journey across the Atlantic, either as "coal stokers" working with forged seaman's papers or as stowaways. In November 1920 he and several of his accomplices were arrested for their alleged role in a well-coordinated assault on Liverpool's docklands that involved "well over a hundred men" and the burning of nineteen buildings in a single night. Kerr ended up serving a prison term in England.[60]

Extending Neil Kerr's network may have been an important part of Boland's objective in making connections with longshoremen and other workers on the New York waterfront. The reprisal burnings in Liverpool and other British cities were looming on the near horizon, and Boland may have regarded British

installations in New York as legitimate and necessary targets in Irish republicanism's incendiary war with enemy military forces. According to a "confi-
dential source" associated with the U.S. Bureau of Investigation, Boland met
with a group of friends at Helen and Peter Golden's apartment just as the Irish
Patriotic Strike was ending, and the subject of the evening was "plans for the future, such as the [disruption] of all British shipping, a suggestion that all British
[consulates] in this country be destroyed at a certain time, and plans to cause
a general disturbance," presumably one aimed at crippling the empire. And yet
in the excitement of this extraordinary moment, Boland also hoped to link up
with insurgency anywhere and everywhere. "Our dream is a world-wide organisation," he wrote to his fellow conspirator Joe McGarrity in August 1920,
"with a plan of campaign whereby we can meet the enemy not alone in Ireland
but all over the globe. . . . To Australia, Canada, South Africa, India, Egypt, and
Moscow our men must go to make common cause against our common foe."[61]

Walsh, Mellows, Boland, and Peter Golden all became de Valera's indispensable allies not only in reaching out to American audiences but also in waging
the factional quarrels that increasingly characterized his relationship with the
recognized leaders of Irish America. Generally, he maintained more decorum
than they did and was more cautious about what he said and where he said it.
But there were times when he followed them into the realm of labor and radical
politics, and he gave some of his most inflammatory speeches on those occasions. An outstanding example is the address he delivered at New York's Labor
Day celebration on September 1, 1920. Here, too, as in Butte and San Francisco,
he spoke the language of class, declaring that "if the plain people of the world
are ever to free themselves from their present economic subjection, it can only
be by the closest cooperation between the working classes of the different nations." He also invoked the name of James Connolly, Ireland's most brilliant
and visionary socialist and a prominent leader and martyr of the 1916 Rising.
Connolly had lived in the United States for nearly seven years, beginning in the
autumn of 1903, and had been, at best, on the margins of the mainstream labor movement then. But de Valera introduced him to a convocation organized
by the relatively conservative American Federation of Labor as a man "whom
many of you knew personally." He argued, moreover, that Connolly's socialism was entirely compatible with the historic values and current objectives of
Irish republicanism. "Much of what the modern socialist is groping after was
already a fact in the social system of ancient Ireland," he claimed. Thus "the
establishment of social justice, which the working people throughout the world
are striving for, would be nothing in Ireland but a re-establishment."[62]

De Valera went on to invoke the Democratic Programme, which Dáil Éireann had adopted as the social and economic policy of the Irish Republic at its
first meeting in January 1919. The Democratic Programme was a concession
to the Irish labor movement for agreeing to defer to Sinn Féin and not run

candidates in the general election of December 1918. Its initial language had been carefully modified by leading republicans (including Boland), and Kevin O'Higgins, one of the founding fathers of the Irish Free State, would later dismiss the document as "largely poetry." And yet here was de Valera, choosing to quote the most controversial section of the Democratic Programme. The Irish Republic's sovereignty, he declared, extended "not only to the men and women of the Nation, but to all its material possessions, . . . subordinating the right to private property to the public right and welfare, promising to every citizen in return for service to the Nation a right to an adequate share of the produce of the Nation's labor."[63] There was, to be sure, considerable ambiguity in this language. Surely it was not "communistic doctrine," as O'Higgins would later charge.[64] In fact, it owed more to Patrick Pearse than it did to Karl Marx. But it invoked a far more radical vision of democracy than the one that prevailed in the United States, a vision that had much in common with the proposals emanating from American proponents of industrial democracy and a workers' republic.

But de Valera the incendiary speech maker was also de Valera the diplomat, for in spite of his highly charged rhetoric, he was careful not to advocate any course of action that would offend the leadership of the American Federation of Labor in New York. He addressed the city's "great Labor Day celebration" on the sixth day of the Irish Patriotic Strike. Surely this boycott of British shipping was a step toward the "closest cooperation between the working people of all nations" that he endorsed, and it exemplified the kind of alliance between Irish nationalism and insurgent labor that his aide Harry Boland was determined to create. But the International Longshoremen's Association was an affiliated union of the American Federation of Labor. The union's leadership had opposed the Irish Patriotic Strike from the beginning and would soon denounce it publicly as "illegal, unauthorized and foolish."[65] It appears, then, that in effect de Valera addressed two separate audiences on Labor Day. To the rank-and-file workers who made up the majority of his listeners, he articulated a vision of international working-class solidarity, as well as an apparent endorsement of socialism in the Irish context. But in deference to the leaders of labor who surrounded him on the platform from which he spoke, he made no mention of the concrete expression of international working-class solidarity that was unfolding on the New York waterfront.

During his American sojourn Dev also addressed the Friends of Freedom for India, an organization that was founded in early 1919 to aid the struggle for Indian independence and to defend Indians in the United States who were being harassed and in some cases deported for their political activities. It took much of its inspiration from the Friends of Irish Freedom, and its leaders looked to Irish Americans such as Frank Walsh and Dudley Field Malone as indispensable allies of India's cause.[66] In February 1920, in New York City, the Friends of Freedom for India gave a dinner in de Valera's honor, attended by more than five hundred people. Hundreds more joined the proceedings to hear his speech, in which he declared, "Patriots of India, your cause is identical with ours." Keenly aware of Gandhi's growing influence in the Indian independence movement and of his commitment to nonviolent struggle, Dev warned that "while moral force was powerful, no nation could afford to fling away any weapons by which nations in the past have achieved their freedom." Calling the British Empire "a vampire that is fattening on our blood," he declared, "We of Ireland and you of India must each of us endeavor, both as separate peoples and in combination, to rid ourselves of the vampire."[67]

The speech was subsequently translated into several of India's vernacular languages and circulated there; in it de Valera pledged that Ireland would make common cause not only with India but also with other colored peoples fighting to emancipate themselves from Britain's suffocating embrace—notably, "our brothers in Egypt and in Persia." "Tell them also," he concluded, "that their cause is our cause." His words signified a moment of convergence when leading elements in the Irish and Indian independence movements actively sought to forge a united front. Declaring that "the mighty people of India are rising in open revolt to kick England out of their country," the *Irish World* reminded its readers that "their fight is our fight, and our fight is their fight. . . . we must win the victory together." This aspiration toward unity became vividly evident in New York's Saint Patrick's Day Parade in March 1920, when a contingent of Indian nationalists and their American allies joined the line of march, and Salindra Ghose, cofounder of the Friends of Freedom for India, paraded on horseback "wearing a green turban and sashes of red, gold, and green."[68]

For the most part, however, de Valera was far more cautious when appealing to the American people and their government. Given the rising tide of reaction that gripped the nation—the Red Scare, the racist pogroms, the nativist clamor for immigration-restriction legislation—he knew that he had to tread carefully. Since his arrival in the United States, powerful forces, including the American Legion and influential Protestant churchmen, had mobilized to defend the Anglo-American alliance and to ward off what many perceived as a papist threat to Protestant interests. In these circumstances, Dev continued to flatter his hosts and to reiterate the theme of America's long-standing role as a beacon of freedom.[69]

But as the struggle in Ireland grew more bloody by the day, de Valera also resorted to a quite different discourse—of the Irish as a unique people, "like no other race on earth," and of Ireland as a singular beacon in its own right on behalf of civilization and Christianity. Thus, on Saint Patrick's Day 1920, he reminded Americans that "once before our people gave their soul to a barbaric continent and led brute materialism to an understanding of higher things. It is still our mission 'to show the world the might of moral beauty,' to teach mankind peace and happiness in keeping the law of love, doing to our neighbour what we would have our neighbour do to us." The contrast with his speech to the Friends of Freedom for India, only two and a half weeks earlier, is remarkable. There he had emphasized the necessity for armed struggle against the British "vampire." Here, in invoking the themes of moral beauty, peace, and the golden rule ("doing to our neighbour what we would have our neighbour do to us"), he sounded like a Christian pacifist. Not only that, but he claimed that Ireland, rather than the United States, was the world's reincarnated exemplar of freedom. "*We* are the spear-points of the hosts in political slavery," he declared on Saint Patrick's Day; "we can be the shafts of dawn for the despairing and the wretched everywhere."[70]

This emphasis—on Ireland as a uniquely spiritual nation whose mission was to teach a benighted world to live by the true tenets of Christianity—came to the forefront again in a sustained way during the ordeal and eventual martyrdom of Terence MacSwiney. An IRA commandant and elected member of Dáil Éireann, MacSwiney had become lord mayor of Cork in March 1920, following the assassination of his predecessor and close friend Tomás MacCurtain by members of the Royal Irish Constabulary. He was arrested by the British military on August 12. On that day he began a hunger strike that lasted seventy-four days, ending with his death on October 25.[71] Through the extraordinary drama that accompanied his supreme act of self-sacrifice, MacSwiney came to embody a mystical republican faith that was steeped in the language of redemptive suffering and appeared to be entirely oblivious to the commitment to social transformation that animated Liam Mellows and other activists in the Irish Progressive League. Upon becoming lord mayor of Cork, MacSwiney had declared, "It is not they who can inflict most but they who can suffer most will conquer." Rooting his actions in the "spiritual liberty which comes to us dripping in the Blood of Christ Crucified," he continued, "the liberty for which we today strive is a sacred thing," and "because it is sacred, death for it is akin to the Sacrifice of Calvary."[72]

Long before MacSwiney's death, de Valera seized on his example as emblematic not only of Ireland's struggle for freedom but also of the Irish nation's essential character. On the fifteenth day of the lord mayor's hunger strike, he told an audience in New York City that MacSwiney's "dying in a British dungeon is typical of the country and the cause for which he is heroically offering up his life." The implication was that the country and the cause were uniquely spiritual and uniquely willing to sacrifice life and limb on behalf of the Irish Republic. (Patrick McCartan later reflected that "all the world came to respect the race that could produce a MacSwiney"; indeed, he maintained that "only the nation of Ireland could give the world a MacSwiney.") When MacSwiney finally died, along with two of the eleven republican prisoners in Cork whose hunger strike took inspiration from his, de Valera told a massive gathering at New York's Polo Grounds, "If God wills that the freedom of our country should . . . come in our own rather than in [the] blood of our enemies, we too shall not hesitate at the price or shrink from the sacrifice."[73]

8.2. Terence MacSwiney (courtesy of the National Library of Ireland)

Shortly before his death, MacSwiney addressed a letter to his fellow hunger strikers exhorting them to keep the faith and declaring that their sacrifice was of great significance not only for Ireland but also for oppressed people everywhere. "Comrades," he wrote, "if we twelve go in glorious succession to the grave, the name of Ireland will flash in a tongue of flame through the world, and be a sign of hope for all time to every people, struggling to be free."[74] Because of MacSwiney's highly publicized suffering and death, the name of Ireland did indeed "flash in a tongue of flame through the world," and revolutionaries whose outlook differed dramatically from his were nonetheless drawn to Mac-Swiney's example. Thus the then obscure Vietnamese revolutionary Nguyen Ai Quoc, who would later take the name Ho Chi Minh, was allegedly moved to declare that "a nation which has such citizens will never surrender." Similarly, Jawaharlal Nehru later reflected that MacSwiney's—and Roger Casement's—courage in the face of death was proof of Ireland's exemplary status as a "brave and irrepressible country" in which the "iron resolve of a handful of men" prevailed over "all the might of the British Empire." And lest we forget, leaders of the African diaspora such as Marcus Garvey and Cyril Briggs also saw in Mac-Swiney's martyrdom further vindication of their belief that Irish nationalism represented a model—indeed, *the* model—for their own struggles for freedom and the unity of the African race. According to Briggs, MacSwiney was "as great a patriot as any of the brilliant array of men and women who have died for their race and country."[75]

It is ironic, then, that at the very moment when the attention of much of the world was riveted on Ireland, de Valera issued an "appeal to the conscience of the United States" in which he pleaded Ireland's case on the grounds that "Ireland is now the last white nation that is deprived of its liberty."[76] This language was not altogether new, for him or for Irish nationalism. As we have seen, Sinn Féin publicist Erskine Childers frequently invoked the theme of white entitlement in making the case for Irish independence. Seán T. Ó Ceallaigh, who worked closely with Childers in Paris to publicize Ireland's cause, pleaded with Pope Benedict XV to recognize that "our aim is to achieve that independence which every other white race in the world has already won." "Ireland alone of all white nations," he repeated for good measure, "is denied the universally accepted right of self-determination." George Gavan Duffy, who would become Sinn Féin's minister of foreign affairs and a close associate of both Childers and Ó Ceallaigh, told his constituents in South County Dublin that the fundamental question in the general election of December 1918 was whether Ireland, "alone of the white race," would be denied its claim to self-determination.[77]

Even the *Irish World*, with its long record of support for the cause of racial equality, fell into line with this argument. Robert E. Ford, who had succeeded his father, the legendary Patrick Ford, as editor of the *Irish World* in 1913, proudly identified himself in a letter to Marcus Garvey as "the son of an abolishioner who worked while a young boy in the printing office of [William] Lloyd Garrison." Under Robert Ford's editorial direction, the *Irish World* supported the UNIA's insistence that "the principles of democracy, of which we hear so much these days, should be applied to the men and women of [the Negro] race. A democracy that makes a distinction on account of the color of a person's skin is not true democracy," the *Irish World* proclaimed in November 1918. "It is a sham and a fraud." But less than a year later the *World* printed an article by Childers under the prominent headline "Irish, Only White People Denied Self-Government," without so much as a hint of criticism.[78]

The timing of de Valera's remark at the end of October 1920 raises questions about his understanding of the meaning and significance of events that were breaking all around him, events in which some of his closest coworkers were deeply involved. Three months earlier, Marcus Garvey had sent de Valera a telegram from the convention of the Universal Negro Improvement Association at Madison Square Garden, declaring, "Please accept sympathy of Negroes of the world for your cause. We believe Ireland should be free even as Africa shall be free for the Negroes of the world."[79] Garvey was, to be sure, a lightning rod for controversy and, often, ridicule. But at that very moment, on the streets of Harlem, his followers were marching, by the thousands, in elaborately choreographed parades that became impressive demonstrations of Pan-African consciousness and racial pride. Helen and Peter Golden lived within a few blocks of Harlem and must have been familiar with the scale of these demonstrations. According to Claude McKay, they became "the dramatic occasion that made the City of New York fully aware of the movement in Harlem."[80]

The UNIA convention and its accompanying pageantry were succeeded by the Irish Patriotic Strike, with which de Valera was intimately familiar. After all, on July 31, when he accompanied Archbishop Mannix to the sailing of the *SS Baltic*, he had been very much a part of the electric atmosphere on Pier 60. According to Harry Boland's diary, Dev's momentary presence aboard the ship "cause[d] a mild sensation among the *Baltic* crew and officers"; it apparently caused a major sensation among the longshoremen. Boland appears to have been the principal architect of the chain of events that became the Irish Patriotic Strike, and he was involved, on a daily basis, in the events surrounding the boycott of British shipping. Helen Golden played a leading role in the mobilization of women pickets on the docks that set the boycott in motion, and de Valera himself spoke at a packed rally at the Lexington Opera House on the first night of the walkout. The *Sun and New York Herald* described the rally as "one of the wildest and most enthusiastic [mass meetings] the Irish have ever held in New York," and the *Irish World* characterized Dev's speech as "the most impassioned address he ever delivered."[81]

Surely de Valera knew, then, that one of the most extraordinary features of the Irish Patriotic Strike was its multinational and multiracial character. It was initiated by "American women of Irish birth," according to Eileen Curran, a member of the American Women Pickets who may have merited that description.[82] Its first key moment came when "British" seamen (members of the engine room crew of the *Baltic*, who were almost certainly Irish) came ashore in response to the women's exhortations. Then the longshoremen—especially the large numbers of Irishmen employed on the piers of the Cunard and White Star lines—walked out en masse.[83] By and large the Italians and "Austrians" (a catchall term for Germans and other central and eastern European dockworkers) did not participate in the walkout. There had been antagonism between the Irish and the Italians for several decades, and like their Italian counterparts, the "Austrians" felt little sympathy for the Irish, who had long defended their relatively privileged enclaves on the West Side waterfront with a heavy hand. But black longshoremen did join the strike, and in significant numbers. In the racially polarized world of the New York waterfront, this was an astonishing development. African Americans could find employment on only a few of the Chelsea piers at this time, usually in the most menial occupations. But when picketers approached the docks where several hundred black longshoremen were working, they walked off the ships and fell in with the line of march. When the boycott spread to the Brooklyn waterfront, rank-and-file spokesman Patrick McGovern told a mass meeting of strikers that "three thousand stalwart men have stopped work to force . . . British troops out of Ireland. It's the Irish spirit—no use—England can't kill it." But McGovern went on to add, "It's not simply an Irishman's fight. It is the fight of labor all over the world." The veteran labor activist Leonora O'Reilly, a member of the Irish Progressive League, also spoke at the meeting and made the same point. "They can no longer divide us on religious lines or on lines of nationality," she declared. "Labor is labor, the same the world over."[84]

But it's unlikely that hundreds of black longshoremen would have responded so enthusiastically to a struggle presented as "the fight of labor all over the world." Not that they were altogether lacking in class consciousness. But given the paltry rewards that had been their lot on the New York waterfront for more than a generation, they were likely to regard appeals to labor solidarity as a cover for the interests of white—especially Irish— longshoremen. Hence the entirely plausible response of Claude McKay's fictional character Jake to the entreaties of a white labor organizer: "I won't scab, but I ain't a joiner kind of a fellah. . . . When I longshored in Philly I was a good union man. But when I made New York I done finds out that they gived the colored mens the worser piers and holds the bes'n a' them foh the Irishmen. No, pardner, keep you' union card."[85]

There must have been another "hook" to pull black longshoremen out on an illegal strike with Irish longshoremen in the vanguard, and the hook appears to have been black nationalism and the involvement of leaders of the UNIA, including Garvey himself, in the boycott. It appears that some, perhaps many, of these longshoremen were attracted to Garveyism; the *New York World* reported that they shouted "Free Africa" as they walked off the ships. Remarkably enough, the boycott seems to have evolved into a joint enterprise between Irish and black workers, for the *Journal of Commerce* reported that four days into the conflict, loading and unloading of vessels was "going on very slowly. A few small forces were at work, but they were Italians and Americans, and it was said not a single man of Irish blood could be found among them." Moreover, according to the *Journal*, all of the streets along the Chelsea waterfront "were noticeably abandoned by the crowds of negroes who usually serve as stevedores and longshoremen's helpers."[86]

But in the complex world of American labor, black workers became involved as strikebreakers as well as strikers in this conflict. Two weeks into the boycott, hundreds of black workers were brought in from other areas of the port. They were union members, recruited by the shipowners with the full support of the union's Irish American leadership. But acts of interracial solidarity continued. In an attempt to turn back the strikebreakers, Helen Golden and her coworkers persuaded a number of black women to stand at the head of Pier 60 and carry signs that read "Ireland for the Irish. Africa for the Africans" and "Brothers, if you scab Ireland, you scab our race." Garvey himself sent one of his lieutenants down to the struck piers, and he "urge[d] all the Negro longshoremen not to load British ships." When a delegation of Irish longshoremen and their allies, led by Dudley Field Malone, ventured forth to Liberty Hall to seek a closer working relationship with the UNIA, an undercover agent who was monitoring the UNIA's activities for the federal government reported that "they spoke in high terms of Garvey and his movement and pledged their support." Garvey, in turn, assured them of his goodwill and affirmed that the quest for "liberty was common to all mankind, irrespective of creed or color."[87]

This was an important part of the context in which de Valera made his "appeal to the conscience of America." Whereas in her negotiations with UNIA representatives, Helen Golden had emphasized that the Irish and African peoples were engaged in a "Common fight for Liberty," the president of the Irish Republic tried to make his case to the American people on the basis of white entitlement. This was not the first time de Valera had made such a declaration. In his initial press statement, delivered at the Waldorf-Astoria in June 1919, he had called Ireland "the one remaining white nation in the slavery of alien rule."[88] But from the standpoint of de Valera's experience during his mission to America, October 1920 should have been different from June 1919. By October 1920 he had publicly declared his solidarity with the peoples of India, Egypt, and Persia, and some of his closest associates—Harry Boland, Liam Mellows, Frank Walsh, and Helen Golden—had participated (indeed, *he* had participated) in a momentous event that became an extraordinary demonstration of interracial solidarity on the New York waterfront.

Was all of this mere hypocrisy? Or, rather, does it suggest that the "two poles" of Irish nationalist sensibility identified by Declan Kiberd—the "anticolonial" and the "white triumphalist"—did not distinguish one group from another so much as they were entwined *within* individuals and the groups they represented? Irish republicans and home rulers had a long and honorable tradition of supporting the rights of India and other colonized nations, and it was natural, especially in the context of 1920, when nationalist insurgency was a global phenomenon, that de Valera would emphasize the ties that bound Ireland and India together. But the sense of white entitlement also had a long, if less openly celebrated, history in Ireland, and it was one of the foundation stones of Irish American identity. Is it unreasonable to suggest that when de Valera moved from one venue to another—from a meeting of the Friends of Freedom for India to an appeal to the "conscience of the United States"—he quite naturally gave expression to the contradictory sensibilities that existed within himself and the movement he led?

But there had to be an element of calculation on de Valera's part as well. In the context of the Great Migration, the New Negro movement, and the ferocious backlash they provoked among white Americans, his subordinates operated under the radar, so to speak. It was one thing for them to hold a summit meeting with UNIA leaders at Harlem's Liberty Hall during the Irish Patriotic Strike. Apart from the government undercover operative who was taking it all in, who noticed?[89] It would have been quite another thing for Dev to speak out publicly in support of the democratic rights of African Americans. Such an act could have meant no political gain for the cause of Irish independence. And yet it would be difficult to conclude that circumstances required him to play the race card. At the very least, he could have chosen to avoid the issue. Significant numbers of Anglo-American Protestants continued to resent the Catholicism, ethnic cohesion, and political clout of the American Irish.[90] But except among an especially bigoted minority, their whiteness was no longer in question. Among Irish Americans, moreover, it was a given that Ireland was a "white nation." *They* surely needed no reminder of that fact. Nonetheless, after nearly eighteen months in the United States, de Valera had failed to win the American government to Ireland's side. Perhaps at a moment when the forces of white supremacy were so stridently in the ascendant, he felt that the claim to white entitlement offered the last opportunity to secure the prize that had eluded him.

There is no evidence that Hubert Harrison, the Afro-Caribbean émigré who became famous in his own time as the "Father of Harlem Radicalism," was aware of de Valera's dubious "appeal to the conscience of the United States" in which he played the "white card" on Ireland's behalf. But it would not have surprised him, for over time experience had taught him that no matter how radical their platform and universal their claims, "white men" were likely to put "race first." Autodidact, educator, and newspaper editor; freethinker, socialist, and black nationalist, Harrison was, in Jeffrey Perry's memorable words, the "most class-conscious of the race radicals and the most race-conscious of the class radicals," the precursor of Marcus Garvey's visionary black nationalism and of Cyril Briggs's revolutionary Marxism. In Harrison's evolution from "class first" socialism to the internationalism of the "darker races," we can learn much about the trajectory of race and the bonds and boundaries of solidarity in the early twentieth century.[91]

Harrison arrived in the United States from Saint Croix in 1900, compiled an outstanding record at two evening high schools in New York City, and—like many educated and intellectually gifted blacks—worked at the U.S. Post Office before becoming a "street" educator and perhaps the greatest soapboxer of his time. After his untimely death in 1927, an editorial in the *New York Amsterdam News* recalled that "one of the most familiar sights of Harlem was Hubert Harrison on a soapbox on Seventh [A]venue. . . . he drew hundreds of hearers by the force of his ideas and passed his erudition on to them. . . . No one on the street asked him to speak, but once he was started no one wanted him to stop." Henry Miller, the novelist and icon of the cultural avant-garde, offered an even more striking observation. He recalled "the great sculptured head which [Harrison] carried on his shoulders like a lion" and remembered him as "a man who electrified one by his mere presence. Beside him, the other speakers, the white ones, looked like pygmies, not only physically, but culturally, spiritually."[92]

8.3. Hubert Harrison, ca. 1920 (courtesy of the Hubert Harrison family and Jeffrey B. Perry)

Harrison quickly gravitated toward the Socialist Party (SP), and for several years much of his soapboxing was on behalf of socialism and the SP's agenda. He also embraced the revolutionary Industrial Workers of the World and worked closely with Wobbly heroes such as Big Bill Haywood and Elizabeth Gurley Flynn. But by 1914 he had concluded that because most socialists and trade unionists put whiteness first and "class after," it was necessary for the people of the African diaspora to develop a "Race First" political perspective.[93] He claimed that part of the inspiration for this belief came from the example of the Irish Parliamentary Party. In an article published in September 1917, he argued that "the new Negro race in America will not achieve political self-respect until it is in a position to organize itself as a political party and follow the example of the Irish Home Rulers." By this time, the influence of the Irish home rulers was very much on the wane, as Sinn Féin and the resurgent Irish Volunteers had come to the fore in the aftermath of the Easter Rising. But for Harrison, the forces contending for leadership of the Irish nationalist movement mattered less than the slogan he derived from their common example. He concluded that for the "darker races" of the world, as for the Irish, the politics of freedom could not be based upon a wider sense of loyalty. Rather, it required allegiance to "ourselves first."[94]

Already, by 1917, Harrison was characterizing the Great War as the "White War" and dismissing the Wilsonian rhetoric of democracy and self-determination as a sham when used by the statesmen of Europe and the United States. "We deplore the agony and blood-shed [of the war]," he wrote,

> But we find consolation in the hope that when this white world shall have been washed clean by its baptism of blood, the white race shall be less able to thrust the strong hand of its sovereign will down the throats of the other races. We look for a free India and an independent Egypt; *for nationalities in Africa flying their own flags and dictating their own internal and foreign policies.* This is what we understand by "making the world safe for democracy."[95]

By 1921 his belief in the urgent need for a black alternative to Garveyism, and his apprehension at communist attempts to co-opt black radicals, had moved Harrison to call for the development of a "Colored International." Remarkably, he appealed once again to the Irish example, arguing that "we must . . . learn a lesson from those who suffer evils similar to ours, . . . whether it be Sinn Féin or Swadesha." But he made it clear that his goal was to mobilize the "darker races." "Today," he concluded, "the great world majority, made up of black, brown and yellow peoples, are stretching out their hands to each other and developing a 'consciousness of kind.' They are seeking to establish their own . . . internationalism. . . . The darker peoples of the world have begun to realize that their first duty is to themselves."[96]

As early as 1915, W.E.B. Du Bois had reluctantly predicted a "War of the Color Line." Sounding a variation on the same theme, Marcus Garvey declared in 1920 that "the bloodiest and greatest war of all times is yet to come—the war when Asia shall match her strength against Europe for 'the survival of the fittest,' for the dominance of Oriental or Occidental civilization." Even Cyril Briggs had stated in 1918 that in the United States, "before [the] problem of black and white all others sink into pale insignificance." But for Briggs, Garvey, Claude McKay, and A. Philip Randolph, Ireland's escalating struggle for independence—exemplified by the Easter Rising, the execution of the martyrs of 1916, the hunger strike of Terence MacSwiney, and the Irish Patriotic Strike on the New York waterfront—gave rise not only to a strong sense of international solidarity but also to a broader and more complex sense of racial affinity. Thus, at the very moment he predicted a cataclysmic race war between Asia and Europe, Garvey could also say: "We believe in the principles of Justice and of Equity. That is why we are in sympathy with Ireland. That is why we are in sympathy with the Zionist movement. That is why we are in sympathy with the Nationalist movement of Egypt, and of India. We believe all men should be free." And in February 1921, only a few months before Harrison's call for a Colored International, Briggs could argue that the peoples of the Irish and African diasporas "are in the same boat and [are] both the victims of the same Anglo-Saxon race."[97]

Over time, however, this more complex sense of race, and of the basis for racial affinity, would fall by the wayside and be replaced by a simpler, color-coded variant that would predominate in framing the discourse of race for many years to come. Although it was black nationalists who in 1900 predicted that the "color line" would become "the problem of the twentieth century," they were responding, in large measure, to what Du Bois would soon characterize as the "new religion of whiteness," which appeared to be sweeping the world. Born out of a sense of imminent danger to "white men's rights"—out of the fear that "slowly and irresistibly the yellow and the black races, the Chinaman and the negro, will crowd the higher races out"—this new "religion" not only framed race in terms of an unending conflict between "whites" and "nonwhites," it also in effect demanded that "nonwhite" intellectuals do the same.[98] Thus, if Hubert Harrison was aware of de Valera's embrace of whiteness as the basis of Ireland's entitlement to full independence, it can have only quickened his sense that "Race First" was indeed the wave of the future. "In sheer self-defense," he continued to believe, "we too must put race very high on our list of necessities."[99]

Epilogue:
The Ordeal of the Irish Republic

> The peace of the world . . . is possible only as a result of some . . . reconciliation of the nationalist and internationalist ideals of the human race.
>
> —Robert Lynd, 1917

> This fight of ours has been essentially a spiritual fight; it has been a fight of right against wrong, a fight of a small people struggling for a spiritual ideal against a mighty rapacious and material Empire.
>
> —Mary MacSwiney, December 1921

ON DECEMBER 6, 1921, AFTER MONTHS of arduous negotiations in London, five delegates representing the Irish Republican government signed the Anglo-Irish Treaty, which granted Ireland dominion status but stopped far short of recognizing the "isolated Republic" that the members of Dáil Éireann and the Irish Republican Army had sworn a solemn oath to uphold. Almost immediately, the treaty divided the republican movement, and by the time it was ratified by a narrow margin in early January 1922, Ireland was drifting toward civil war.[1]

The acrimonious treaty debate, the descent into fratricidal warfare that pitted former comrades against each other, the gratuitous violence that took the lives of leading republicans such as Michael Collins, Harry Boland, Erskine Childers, and Liam Mellows—all of this left an indelible imprint on the Irish psyche and affected politics in Ireland for much of the twentieth century. It is fair to say that from the moment the treaty was signed, the republican movement was engulfed by an internal crisis of direction and morale from which it never fully recovered.

In part, the crisis reinforced Irish nationalists' long-standing tendency to look inward and to see Ireland as the "most cruelly and sorely oppressed of all the world's nations."[2] The publication of *The Story of the Irish Race* in 1921 served only to accentuate this notion of the Irish as unique—in their suffering, their identity, and their destiny. The book's principal author was Seumas MacManus, a folklorist from Donegal and lecturer at the University of Notre Dame who had long been an active cultural and political nationalist. In compiling his 713-page text (which went through numerous editions over the years and is still in print), MacManus was assisted by a number of Irish scholars, including Aodh de Blacam, an outspoken republican, Gaelic enthusiast, and convert to Catholicism who had become a leading publicist for Sinn Féin. De Blacam believed that the Irish story began to turn decisively toward redemption with the founding of the Gaelic League in 1893. It was then that "the centre of gravity in national life changed from the anglicised towns to the rural population, sturdy, unspoilt, patriotic, virile, the offspring and living representative of the traditional Gael." It was then, too, that "Irish politics began . . . to reflect the mind of the real Irish race." De Blacam himself had not been a member of the "real Irish race," which was, by definition, rural, Gaelic, and Catholic. The son of emigrants from Ulster, he was born Hugh Blackham in London and raised in an evangelical Protestant family. As a young man he embraced socialism, but eventually he found it incompatible with his Catholic faith and his romantic vision of rural Irish society. His chapters on Sinn Féin and the Easter Rising in *The Story of the Irish Race* no doubt resonated with many delegates on both sides of the treaty debate. Like him, they were committed to the recovery of an authentic Gaelic civilization that was the antithesis of English values and mores. Mary MacSwiney stated the matter in characteristically stark terms when she asserted in the treaty debate that "this fight of ours has been essentially a spiritual fight, . . . a fight of a small people struggling for a spiritual ideal against a mighty rapacious and material Empire."[3]

Although radical nationalists shared a narrative of Irish suffering and regeneration, there was no consensus about what form the Irish Republic would take or about how it would resolve the recurring conflict between classes and interest groups in Irish society. Even among the much-maligned "idealists" and "militarists" who took the Republican side in the war against the Free State, there was no fundamental agreement beyond the belief that the Anglo-Irish Treaty fell far short of achieving the independence movement's most essential demands.[4] Although Republican ideology was complex and multifaceted, we can shine a light on its poles of identity and belief by focusing again on the lives of Peter Golden and Liam Mellows—two men who had worked together for years in New York City, often under the umbrella of the Irish Progressive League. In the context of Ireland's civil war, both became unrepentant Republicans, but their understanding of republicanism, and of the essential character of the Irish Revolution, was ultimately quite different.

With the signing of the Anglo-Irish Treaty in December 1921, it was perhaps foreordained that Peter Golden would take the antitreaty side. By that time he was serving as national secretary of de Valera's American Association for the Recognition of the Irish Republic and was firmly enmeshed in a network that was deeply committed to the achievement of complete independence from Britain. In 1919 he had told a friend that "if we but stick as one in an uncompromising body we'll win," but "if we waver or compromise in the least all is lost."[5] This theme of "no compromise" had found an especially eloquent proponent in Golden's second cousin Terence MacSwiney, who had declared, as his life ebbed away, "Thank God there will be no more compromises now." In dying, the lord mayor of Cork believed that his own sacrifice would show the way forward for his fellow republicans, and Mary MacSwiney reminded de Valera that her brother's hunger strike "would never have been endured to the end for anything less than absolute and total separation." This meant that "there must be no link [with Britain] formal or otherwise; no allegiance to anything but the Republic; no flag to fly in our country but the flag of that Republic."[6]

Golden managed to return home to Ireland for two months in the summer of 1922.[7] He arrived shortly after one of the decisive developments in the civil war—the fall of Limerick to Free State forces—and he had been there only ten days when Cork also fell.[8] Soon thereafter, he recorded his observations in a book entitled *Impressions of Ireland*. For him, the conflict dividing the Irish nation was marked by a set of stark polarities: "simplicity" versus "subtlety," "things of the mind and . . . spirit" versus a crass and narrow materialism; in the civil war, an "army of volunteers fighting for liberty" versus an "army of mercenaries fighting for money"; and, in regard to the treaty itself, "absolutely uncompromising . . . Republican principles" versus a fatally flawed "compromise . . . which left England supreme." The heroes of his story were Mary and Annie MacSwiney, Erskine Childers, Liam Lynch, and Eamon de Valera. "Mary Mac" was a veteran educator; she and her sister Annie ran a girls' school, Saint Ita's, in Cork. She was also the chief custodian of her brother's legacy as a uniquely heroic warrior for Ireland's independence. Childers, the leading Republican publicist, was, in Golden's rendering, a "gentle, childlike, almost Christlike soul" who "sees a great Light and will not be sw[ay]ed from following it at whatever cost." For this very reason he became the target of "Satanic hatred" and was soon "captured by the King's Irish troops and shot by the King's Irish executioners." Lynch, the chief of staff of the Republican military forces, was "very simple," "quiet," "almost shy," but "simple with the simplicity . . . of Pearse and MacSwiney." This was a quality Golden found in virtually all of the Republican soldiers he encountered. He marveled at their youth, at their eager faces, at the "great light shining from their eyes"; above all, at "their simplicity and their utter freedom from what one might call 'swank.'" The Free State soldiers, by way of contrast, were "mercenaries," driven by material want, characterized by drunkenness, indiscipline, and, perhaps worst of all, "English accents and English ways."[9]

And then there was Dev, the president of the Irish Republic, who was now a fugitive in his own country. Golden had worked closely with de Valera during his mission to the United States and was struck by the contrast between his status in America—where "thousands clamor[ed] to see him, to hear him, to get near enough to touch his hand"—and his reputation in the Free State, where he was reviled as a "wild-eyed . . . fanatic . . . eager for his fellow's blood." But Golden found him "a man heartsick and distraught at all the terrible things that have come to the nation and its people," a man who preached not death but "life" and "forgiveness." His description of his encounter with the Chief, at a "little house . . . on a lonely hillside," resonates with the Christian and Gaelic

E.1. Peter Golden (courtesy of the John J. Burns Library, Boston College)

mysticism that often permeated class-unconscious republicanism. As Golden entered the yard, he heard "borne to me on the night air what I think is the most beautifully musical sound I have ever listened to—the kind of sound one hears but once in a lifetime, and, having heard it, holds and hoards it in one's memory for all time—it is the rise and fall of the voices of Irish peasants saying the rosary in Gaelic." Among these peasants, kneeling and saying the rosary with them on the floor of their "neatly kept kitchen[,] . . . was Ireland's hunted but faithful Chief, De Valera."[10]

In New York, Peter Golden had often rubbed shoulders with socialists and had sought to link Ireland's struggle for independence with a wide array of progressive social movements. But in *Impressions of Ireland*, there is no sense of a wider solidarity, no hint of socialism, no reference to the social question in any form. True, the author alluded once to the "slum-bitten and impoverished" children he encountered in Cork City, but not to condemn slums or poverty or to suggest the possibility that such a condition could be altered by the conscious intervention of republican men and women. On the contrary, it was the distinctive "music" of the children's voices that captured his attention and inspired the declaration that he would "gladly travel across the ocean any time to hear [this] music" as the children played on the streets. Insofar as Golden embraced a vision of a transformed Ireland, it had no socioeconomic dimension. Rather, he recalled "the light in [Liam Lynch's] face as he unfolded all the things that were in store for Ireland—things of the mind and of the spirit." According to Golden, Lynch was "fighting against terrible odds for the liberation of his country so that it might again be the centre of culture and learning even as it had been many centuries before"; fighting, that is, to recover and regenerate the island of saints and scholars.[11]

In September 1922 Golden returned to New York to continue his fight for the cause he cherished. He and his allies, whose ranks included Terence Mac-Swiney's widow, Muriel, and brother Peter, faced enormous odds. Several years of fratricidal warfare had drained much of the energy from the movement and had served to marginalize the hard-core antitreatyites in the United States. Thus the American Association for the Recognition of the Irish Republic, which had enrolled about 700,000 members in 1921, declined precipitously and by 1925 had a membership of fewer than 14,000.[12]

Against all odds, Golden was determined to remain active in the movement, but his health was becoming an insuperable obstacle to further activity. For years his life had alternated between great bursts of activity and recurring bouts of illness. As early as 1917, he had written to his friend Joe McGarrity, "I've been a sick man these past two weeks—had one of my lungs terribly congested." In December 1921, after two grueling years during which he visited at least twenty-six states, he informed Harry Boland, "I have not been well for a long time and the Doctor simply insists that I stop work for a while or . . . I'll be sure to go under."[13] Finally, in early 1926 he suffered a "nervous breakdown," and he and his family set out for Southern California by train in search of a healthier climate and a more restful environment. According to the Associated Press, he was stricken while in transit and taken to Denver's Mercy Hospital, where he died.[14]

At a solemn requiem mass in Denver, Father Francis Walsh paid Golden the ultimate compliment by linking him to Terence MacSwiney and to the martyrs of Easter 1916. Even more effusive praise came from Father Peter Magennis, the superior general of the Carmelite order, who had worked closely with Golden, Mellows, and other Irish republican exiles in New York City during and after the Great War.[15] Magennis's heartfelt eulogy for Peter Golden in the pages of the *Catholic Bulletin* is a quintessential example of romantic nationalism in the service of Republican ideals. In this rendering, Ireland's history became a morality play in which the faithful sons of Dark Rosaleen, mystical mother of the Irish Nation, tried without success to stem the tide of opportunism and betrayal among their "countrymen," and Golden himself became a Christ figure, but one—it seemed—for whom crucifixion was not followed by resurrection. In a passage reminiscent of *Impressions of Ireland*, Magennis declared that "Peter's friends are nearly all laid to rest on the hillsides of Ireland," whereas "his enemies are wallowing in the flesh-pots." He portrayed Golden and his fellow martyr Erskine Childers as alike in many essential ways: "Cultured both of them; dreamers both of them; lovers of Dark Rosaleen both of them; maligned by friends; hated intensely by the enemy of the Irish people; dreaded by the Saxon foe; done to death by their own countrymen."[16]

And here was the final tragedy. The Irishmen who had executed Childers and driven Golden to a premature death had won, and for the foreseeable future, it appeared, their position was unassailable. Thus Golden had "died of a broken heart," for "no Irishman of his years had seen more treachery to Ireland, more unfaithfulness in her people." Adding insult to injury, he had been buried in an "exile's grave." But somehow Magennnis found this fitting. "It is better that it should be so," he argued, "for how could he, the Lover, the Dreamer, ever rest in peace in a land that has lost its vision and is covered with the mist and the shadows of death?"[17]

Peter Golden, Peter Magennis, and Mary MacSwiney not only articulated the Republican ideal of "no compromise" but also served as quintessential advocates of a republic that was often understood mainly in terms of symbols and simple binaries. According to Golden, it was "things of the mind and of the spirit" that mattered. In *Poems of the Irish Republic*, he declared,

> We of the Gael—we have the spirit things
> Whose wings are star dust—dust that shall endure
> Down all the arches of eternity.

For Mary MacSwiney as well, the quest for the Irish Republic was "spiritual" and a "fight of right against wrong." Father Magennis focused in on the contrast between "heat and cold, light and darkness, trickery and honesty." His republic was the abode of "the Lover, the Dreamer," the scholar, and the poet, and he reminded his readers that Peter Golden was a "Poet of the right kind."[18] For Aodh de Blacam, the republic embodied all of these qualities, but he was more explicit in placing it in a rural, agricultural context in which a commitment to Catholic devotionalism and to the maintenance of social cohesion and harmony took precedence over commerce and the accumulation of wealth. In fact, he regarded the pursuit of wealth and the modern culture of consumption as destabilizing and spoke up instead for de Valera's vision of Ireland as "the home of a people who valued material wealth only as a basis for right living, of a people who, satisfied with frugal comfort, devoted their leisure to the things of the spirit."[19]

Supporters of the treaty were quick to condemn their Republican rivals as impractical idealists who were incapable of adapting to the opportunities and imperatives that the emerging new order provided. In the treaty debate, Piaras Béaslaí endeavored to throw a "douche of cold water on the idealists and on the unrealities of the formulists." He claimed that "those who vote for the Treaty . . . are the true idealists. They have the vision and the imagination to sense the nation that is trying to be born."[20] Many historians have agreed and have tended to see the split over the treaty as a conflict between dogmatism and pragmatism, even dictatorship and democracy. Their narrative pits the "practical nationalism" of Michael Collins and his allies against the devious word splitting of Eamon de Valera, the Republican fundamentalism of Mary MacSwiney, and the militarism of Rory O'Connor.[21]

The problem with this argument is that it tends to flatten out and oversimplify a complex historical landscape. It is true that Republicans often articulated the issues at hand in Manichaean terms. But there were many different Republican voices. Sean MacEntee, for one, reminded supporters of the treaty that in 1916 Pearse and Connolly had "brought back the soul to a nation." "These are not dead phrases for which they spoke," he declared in the treaty debate, "and these are not mummy phrases for which we stand. They are the life and soul of this nation." Although these words implied that MacEntee, like many IRA cadres, was imbued with the "mysticism of the Celt," his daughter, Maire Cruise O'Brien, characterized him as "thoroughly a man of the twentieth century"—a former socialist who had been radicalized by James Connolly, an engineering graduate who managed to pursue a career in his chosen field between bouts in prison, a published poet who would become the minister for finance in the first Fianna Fáil government.[22] Even Mary MacSwiney, by reputation the most dogmatic of the dogmatists, eventually expressed openness to de Valera's attempt at resolving the treaty debate by means of a grand compromise (his famous Document No. 2); indeed, she argued that "the difference between [Document No. 2] and the Treaty was worth dying for." Moreover, in the midst of the civil war, she announced her commitment to the creation of "an entirely different economic and social system, which I can see coming and which I believe the history of the past twelve months is hastening. I do not believe in Communism as its so-called supporters define it, but I think that a co-operative Commonwealth can be worked out and must be worked out as the only means of salvation and reconstruction."[23]

Mary MacSwiney went on to become one of the best-known and most volatile of the Republican political prisoners during the civil war. One of her hunger strikes lasted twenty-four days. It ended only because the authorities agreed to release her from prison at a time when she was in a state of physical collapse and apparently near death. As she regained her health, she again took up the fight for the republic. Asked on one occasion if she was a "Communist or a Socialist," she replied, "I am either or both insofar as they do not controvert Christian teaching and common sense and there is no reason why rightly interpreted they should do either." Over the years, however, as the Republican movement declined and fragmented, she came to oppose any organization that, in her words, "sought to divide the people of Ireland on a class basis."[24]

The individual who argued most forcefully that republicanism required the creation of a cooperative commonwealth and the empowerment of the Irish laboring masses was Liam Mellows; and Mellows had the charisma, the credentials, and the organizational skill to forge an impressive cohort of like-minded activists around himself. But tragically, his life was cut short by a Free State firing squad, and much of the energy and theoretical debate that he had sparked dissipated during the antitreatyites' steady slide toward defeat and humiliation in the civil war. Even so, his life opens a window on another, and radically different, vision of the Irish Republic.

Mellows returned to Ireland in October 1920, after nearly four years in the United States. With the signing of the Anglo-Irish Treaty he quickly entered the antitreaty camp. In fact, only three days later, he and Cathal Brugha began touring parts of Ireland in a motorcar, visiting IRA units and pledging them to "maintain the existing Republic." Apparently, on their journey, the two men conducted their own debate, with Brugha insisting on the absolute supremacy of the national question in the struggle for independence and Mellows asserting the "close connection" between the "national and socialist revolutions."[25]

It was an article of faith for Mellows that the Irish Republic was not a mere aspiration, something to be achieved in the distant future. In the debate on the treaty in Dáil Éireann, he called the republic "a living tangible thing, something for which men gave their lives, for which men were hanged, for which men are in jail . . . [and] are still prepared to give their lives." His only major intervention in the debate came on January 4, when in spite of his declaration that he had "very little to say on this subject," he spoke at length and stated at the outset, "I stand definitely against this so-called Treaty and the arguments in favor of . . . compromise, of departing from the straight road, of going off . . . the only path that I believe this country can travel to its freedom."[26]

E.2. Mary MacSwiney and Muriel MacSwiney, 1922 (Hulton Archive/Topical Press Agency/Getty Images)

All of this reflected the Republican stance that emerged in the course of the treaty debate: no compromise; uphold the existing republic; and risk a renewal of war with Britain in order to achieve the independence that Ireland had been fighting for since 1919, or 1916, or "for 750 years."[27] What made Mellows's contribution to the debate distinctive was his internationalism and anti-imperialism, a stance that flowed from his restless, inquiring mind, his reading of Connolly, and his experience in the Irish Progressive League. "We have always in this country protested against being included within the British Empire," he reminded his audience.

> The British Empire represents to me nothing but the concentrated tyranny of ages.... [It is] the thing that has crushed this country; yet we are told that we are going into it now with our heads up. We are going into the British Empire now to participate in the Empire's shame . . . to participate in . . . the crucifixion of India and the degradation of Egypt. Is that what the Irish people fought for freedom for?[28]

There were a few other deputies who spoke in the same vein—most notably, Countess Markievicz, a member of the Irish Citizen Army, participant in the 1916 Rising, and minister for labor in the first Dáil Cabinet, whose active sympathy for the Dublin poor had become legendary. On January 3 she too spoke at length and startled some of the more conservative deputies by declaring that she stood for "James Connolly's ideal of a Workers' Republic." (A "Soviet Republic," one deputy cried out; a "cooperative commonwealth," she responded.) She also attacked the empire. "If we pledge . . . our allegiance to this thing," she warned, "whether you call it Empire or Commonwealth of Nations, [then we acquiesce in] treading down the people of Egypt and of India."[29]

In the aftermath of the treaty split, Mellows and his allies in the IRA moved to solidify the Republican commitment of the majority of Irish Volunteers. They faced a formidable obstacle in Michael Collins, who could count on the undeviating support of most members of the Irish Republican Brotherhood. In general, the leaders of the general headquarters staff in Dublin and many IRB men, whatever their location, were strong supporters of the treaty. But in the provinces there was a decided tendency not only to oppose the agreement but also to believe that "soldiers" rather than "politicians" should determine the outcome of the struggle. The most extreme manifestation of this way of thinking came at a press conference in March, when Rory O'Connor, perhaps the most intransigent of the dissident IRA officers, declared that "if a Government goes wrong it must take the consequences" and pointed out that "the army had overthrown the Government in many countries." When asked if his comments meant the coming of a military dictatorship, he responded, "You can take it that way if you like."[30]

Although Mellows was very much a soldier and leader of the Irish Republican Army, he was not a militarist. In fact, he became increasingly preoccupied with reclaiming the "existing Republic," not only via military action but also by developing a social program that could win the allegiance of the laboring masses. The collapse of law and order that accompanied the treaty split and the retreat of British authority in the new Free State offered opportunities for workers, small farmers, and agricultural laborers to take radical action. In the countryside, there were land seizures and cattle drives, sometimes under the auspices of the venerable "Captain Moonlight." In the cities and towns, especially in Munster, there were strikes, workplace occupations, and mass demonstrations. Many of those who occupied factories and creameries created "soviets" and deployed red flags to symbolize their militancy. Sometimes their goal was not to shut down the workplace but to keep it functioning, managed by the workers themselves. Much of this was a reprise of activity that had taken place during the War of Independence, but it was no less alarming to Free State officials for its familiarity. As early as April, Patrick Hogan, minister for agriculture in the Provisional Government, warned of the reality of "class war" and the danger that "the house of every large farmer and land owner will be burned and agrarian outrage . . . will be rampant for the next few years." Even earlier, Kevin O'Higgins had perceived a fundamental danger to state and society. "To the frenzied tune of 'the existing Republic,'" he declared in March, "this sorely tried land is drifting into anarchy. . . . The very social fabric is threatened."[31]

Mellows was a leading participant in the Republican seizure of Dublin's Four Courts in April, as well as in the battle there in late June that marked the beginning of the civil war and a major victory for the Free State military forces over their antitreaty adversaries. He acknowledged that in the final showdown at the Four Courts, "the workers weren't with us." From his cell in Mountjoy jail, where many leaders of the Republican movement were imprisoned in the aftermath of their defeat, he set out to change that. More than ever before, his charisma, keen intellect, and leadership ability came to the fore at Mountjoy. According to his friend and fellow socialist Peadar O'Donnell, the younger prisoners idolized him, and the older ones "melted their quarrels in his presence." He organized classes, concerts, and games and initiated the publication of a jail journal that he called the *Book of Cells*. He also spearheaded the formation of a group who undertook systematic study and debate about the way forward for the Republican movement. Its members included O'Donnell and Seamus Breslin, both of whom had been organizers for the Irish Transport and General Workers' Union; Richard Barrett and Joe McKelvey, who were leading members of the IRA; and Walter Carpenter, one of the few members of the Communist Party of Ireland (CPI) who had enlisted in the Republican military forces.[32]

In late August Mellows smuggled drafts of a radical republican manifesto out of prison. In his "Notes from Mountjoy," as the document became known, he focused on three vital themes that are worthy of further consideration. First, land. Here he drew directly on a recent editorial from the *Workers' Republic*, the voice of the CPI, which declared that "the lands of the aristocracy—who live in luxury in London, and at a distance support the Free State—will be seized and divided amongst those who will and can operate it [*sic*] for the nation's good— among the landless workers, the working farmers, the small farmers." He also insisted on the implementation of the famed Democratic Programme of 1919, which was "essential," he argued, "if the great body of workers are to be kept on the side of Independence." Since the commercial and financial interests were "on the side of the Treaty," the Republicans had no recourse but to follow Wolfe Tone in "relying on that great body 'the men of no property.'"[33]

Mellows also raised the issue of imperialism, although more briefly in this instance than in his speech during the treaty debate. He argued that Republicans must come to understand "what Ireland's connection with Imperialism . . . means to her future. No use freeing Ireland to set her up as a State following the footsteps of all the rotten nations of Europe today." Implicitly, he was again expressing solidarity with Indian and Egyptian nationalists while distancing Ireland from "the rotten nations of Europe today." Earlier, in New York, he had spoken out on behalf of Africa as well. Such a stance was bound to clash with that of nationalists who saw the treaty as an instrument for affirming the status of the Irish as "white." "Give us anything that will stamp us as white men and women," Deputy MacCabe of Sligo had declared during the treaty debate, "but for Heaven's sake don't give us a Central American Republic."[34]

Finally, Mellows raised an equally volatile issue—the relationship of the Roman Catholic hierarchy to Ireland's struggle for independence. Mellows was a devout Catholic. During his sojourn in the United States, he had drawn sustenance from his relationship with the Carmelite Fathers at their priory in New York City.[35] But now, with the church hierarchy siding with the Provisional Government, he pointed out that most of its members had "invariably [been] wrong in Ireland in their political outlook." They were against the men of 1798; against Robert Emmet, Young Ireland, the Fenians, and the Irish Volunteers; and, of course, against the Easter Rising. In supporting England in the Great War, moreover, they were "morally to blame for the deaths of thousands of Irish youths in France, Flanders, Mesopotamia, Gallipoli, Macedonia, etc." "Nothing," Mellows said, "can condone this. [The] European War [was] a hideous holocaust on the altar of Mammon." With such a record, it could hardly have been a surprise that the bishops supported the treaty. He bitterly denounced "their exaltation of defeat and hypocrisy" and their attempt to reduce the struggle for the Irish Republic to the "level of putrid politics."[36]

In the context of a guerrilla war that led to more killing and destruction, the bishops struck back with a pastoral letter that served as an unequivocal proscription of the Republicans. They denounced the "warfare now being carried on [by] the Irregulars" as "without moral sanction," which meant that "the killing of National soldiers is murder before God, the seizing of public and private property is robbery, the breaking of roads, bridges and railways is criminal." As a consequence of this declaration, Republican prisoners were denied the sacraments. According to Desmond Greaves, some of them "suffered in silence. Others became bitterly anti-clerical, even professing atheism."[37]

In September the *Irish Independent* secured a draft of Mellows's "Notes from Mountjoy" and published the document, leading to widespread allegations that its author was a communist. More astutely, the *Independent* accused Mellows of being an opportunist who spoke the language of labor only to use Irish workers as "'political cannon fodder' for the Republican cause." This charge must have stung most of all, but it spoke to an inconvenient truth. Mellows had been a full-time servant of the Irish Republic for virtually all of his adult life. He had no ties to the labor movement, no experience of working-class insurgency. His critics, then and now, have charged that he was "mainly concerned with how to co-opt the working class for the [R]epublicans."[38] But in spite of these accusations, he continued what was clearly a sustained and serious effort—dating back to 1918—to reconcile the class and national questions. He attacked the leadership of Irish labor, which had sided with the Free State, for "betray[ing] not only the Irish Republic but the Labour movement in Ireland and the cause of the workers and peasants throughout the world." He also warned that "if the Irish people do not control Irish industries, transport, money and the soil of the country, then foreign or domestic capitalists will."[39]

But Mellows and his radical network in Mountjoy remained isolated from the larger struggle, and as much as he was liked and respected in Republican circles, he could not provide a counterweight to the militarism of the IRA or an alternative to de Valera's earnest but futile efforts to forge a compromise political solution to the conflict. Increasingly his voice was drowned out by the spiral of violence that accompanied guerrilla warfare on the Republican side and the use of military tribunals by the Provisional Government. It was such a body that found Erskine Childers guilty in November and executed him on the twenty-fourth of the month, while his appeal was pending. The Republicans struck back on December 7, the day after the formal initiation of the Free State, killing Deputy Seán Hales and wounding Deputy Patrick O'Malley as the two were leaving a hotel in Dublin. That night the Free State cabinet met, and its members decided to execute four imprisoned Republicans in reprisal. They chose Richard Barrett, Joe McKelvey, Liam Mellows, and Rory O'Connor—all of whom had been imprisoned in Mountjoy since the end of June.[40] None of them could have been guilty of the assassination of Hales and the wounding of O'Malley; nor were they tried for this or any other offense. Instead, they were informed at 3 a.m. on December 8 that they would be shot at dawn. Mellows took the time to write a letter to his mother and one to his friends John and Eileen Hearn, who had often provided a welcome respite for him during his sojourn in the United States. "Let no thought of revenge or reprisals animate Republicans because of our deaths," he wrote. "We die for the truth. Vindication will come." Repeating a fundamental article of faith that he had articulated during the treaty debate, he assured his mother that "the Republic lives; our deaths make it a certainty." At nine o'clock that morning, the four men were executed by a Free State firing squad, and the cruelest atrocity of a remorseless civil war was consummated.[41]

A year earlier Rory O'Connor had been the best man at Kevin O'Higgins's wedding, but apparently neither O'Higgins nor any of his colleagues in the government showed any remorse. One member of the Free State political elite acknowledged that "in a way I'm glad that Mellows and O'Connor are gone, particularly the former as he was an irreconcilable."[42] On the other side, there was shock and outrage. In New York, Mellows's friends gathered at the Carmelite priory to memorialize their fallen hero. Father Magennis chaired the meeting and called Mellows "the noblest soul I have ever known." He recalled the first time he had encountered him, at a mass meeting in Manhattan. Mellows had not been scheduled to speak, but "the body of the hall wanted him, and [demanded that] he should come forth. . . . I remember his springing up two steps at a time. . . . I looked at him," Magennis said. "There was nothing very amazing in his figure, he seemed quite common-place, until you saw his wonderful head, his magnificent brow, the keen look in his eyes, and when he spoke, I knew why the people wanted to hear him—he spoke straight to their hearts." The journalist and Republican sympathizer Una Ford also spoke at the memorial meeting. She was the only participant who made even an oblique reference to his "Notes from Mountjoy." "He knew what Ireland needed economically," she told her audience, "and he evolved a great scheme that some of you may have read."

The most poignant assessment came from Gertrude Kelly, the veteran nationalist, socialist, and legendary medical doctor. She recalled Mellows's extraordinary courage in the face of police intimidation in New York, and also remembered an iconic moment from his trial

> in the Federal courts, where we all spent a good many days during the war, where our people were prosecuted from Big Jim Larkin to little Liam Mellowes. Liam was supposed to have entered this land of the free and home of the brave with a false passport. He was on trial for this terrible crime. All the windows were very dirty—they generally are dirty in the Federal courts—but in through one of those dirty windows came a solitary ray of sunlight and struck, as with a crown, his golden head. An old friend of mine whom I have known since I was a little girl said to his daughter: "When Ireland is free, her first duty will be to see that Liam Mellowes is sanctified." I can say one thing, as one of the unredeemed pagan Irish, that he needs no prayers, he needs no halo. It was long ago put on his head by every woman in Ireland, and Liam is a saint, Church or no Church.[43]

It is not for historians to decide whether their subjects are worthy of sainthood. But the life and death of Liam Mellows does illuminate a dimension of Irish nationalism that expressed itself with power and eloquence at critical moments in Irish history. Over the years, the tendency of many architects and custodians of the nationalist tradition was to present it as an enclosed, and exclusive, phenomenon. For them Irish nationalism was about the character and destiny of the peasant, the Catholic, and the Gael. It was about a sacred island whose people had little in common with other nations and movements that were fighting against oppression. They were, at best, nervous about socialists and apoplectic about anyone who made the fatal error of placing the social question on the same plane as the national question. As Arthur Griffith put it, "The man who declared he wanted National freedom in order to promote social reform, did not know the meaning of the nation."[44]

Liam Mellows stands as an affront and a challenge to this orthodoxy, although his upbringing and early expressions of nationalism very much reflected it. He was nurtured in the republican youth movement Fianna Éireann and then in the IRB. When he led the 1916 Rising in Galway, he was a conventional republican who demonstrated little or no sympathy for the social radicalism that was a significant factor in Connacht's recurring land wars. According to Fergus Campbell, his views at the time were "relatively conservative."[45] In New York, where he took refuge at the end of 1916, he felt no immediate sense of kinship with the insurgent movements that were a prominent feature of the city's political culture. But his politics changed dramatically over the next several years. He met Frank Robbins, Nora Connolly, and other Irish socialists; he read the work of James Connolly; he shared platforms with members of the American Socialist Party and interacted with Indian and African diaspora nationalists. Soon John Devoy's circle was denouncing him as a "Socialist and Anarchist," and even a friend and admirer such as Eamon de Valera would acknowledge, "I cannot think . . . as Liam Mellows thinks."[46]

Mellows's death was undeniably tragic. One can argue that as it approached, he was increasingly caught up in suffocating Marxist formulas as they were expressed by the tiny Communist Party of Ireland or that he was grappling with complex questions of historical and social analysis and groping toward a creative synthesis.[47] In any case, he was not alone. He stood on a foundation constructed not only by James Connolly but also by an eclectic array of nationalists and internationalists, suffragists and socialists, labor radicals and land reformers, who were seeking, in Robert Lynd's words, to reconcile the "nationalist and internationalist ideals of the human race" and who dared to believe that to struggle for the emancipation of Ireland was to stand for the oppressed of the whole world.[48] There were major differences—of class background and even of political outlook and agenda—among the men and women who shaped this tradition and articulated its ideals. O'Connell, for example, came from the Catholic gentry, whereas Davitt was born to poverty and experienced the calamity of eviction and migration at a very young age. O'Connell believed in the commercialization of Irish society; Davitt stood for land nationalization and the rights of "industrial humanity." And yet, in Carla King's words, both men were nationalists whose "evolving outlook . . . also presupposes and requires internationalism." Both refused to turn their backs on human suffering beyond Ireland's borders. As O'Connell told Frederick Douglass in 1845, "My sympathy with distress is not confined within the narrow bounds of my own green island. . . . It extends itself to every corner of the earth."[49] For all their differences, then, O'Connell and Davitt can stand as twin pillars of a generous, inclusive Irish nationalism that reached back to the United Irishmen of the 1790s and forward to James Connolly and Liam Mellows. When Mellows declared, on

Saint Patrick's Day 1918, that "we will be rebels . . . to any form of injustice in any country the world over," he was speaking in the context of revolutionary upheaval on a global scale. But he was also giving expression to a discourse that could claim an honorable place in the long tradition of making race and nation, in Ireland and in the "Greater Ireland" across the seas.

Notes

PROLOGUE: ARGUING ABOUT (THE IRISH) RACE

1. The first epigraph is from Disraeli's *Sybil; or, The Two Nations* (1845; repr., London: M. Walter Dunne, 1904), 2:191. The second is from Kwame Anthony Appiah, *In My Father's House: Africa in the Philosophy of Culture (New York: Oxford University Press, 1992), 45*.

2. In writing this book I have learned much about race in many of its complex and contradictory dimensions from Reginald Horsman, *Race and Manifest Destiny: The Origins of American Racial Anglo-Saxonism* (Cambridge, MA: Harvard University Press, 1981); Appiah, *In My Father's House*; Peter H. Wood, "Race," in Mary Kupiec Cayton, Elliott J. Gorn, and Peter W. Williams, eds., *The Encyclopedia of American Social History* (New York: Scribner, 1993), 437–50; Paul Gilroy, "Diaspora and the Detours of Identity," in Kathryn Woodward, ed., *Identity and Difference* (London: Sage, 1997), 299–343; Thomas F. Gossett, *Race: The History of an Idea in America*, new ed. (New York: Oxford University Press, 1997); Matthew Frye Jacobson, *Whiteness of a Different Color: European Immigrants and the Alchemy of Race* (Cambridge, MA: Harvard University Press, 1998); Thomas C. Holt, *The Problem of Race in the Twenty-first Century* (Cambridge, MA: Harvard University Press, 2000); George M. Frederickson, *Racism: A Short History* (Princeton, NJ: Princeton University Press, 2002); Nikhil Pal Singh, *Black Is a Country: Race and the Unfinished Struggle for Democracy* (Cambridge, MA: Harvard University Press, 2004); Anthony Appiah, "Race: An Interpretation," in Kwame Anthony Appiah and Henry Louis Gates Jr. eds., *Africana: The Encyclopedia of the African and African American Experience* (1999; repr., Oxford: Oxford University Press, 2005), 4:476–82; and, most recently, Nell Irvin Painter, *The History of White People* (New York: W. W. Norton, 2010).

3. Walter White, *A Man Called White: The Autobiography of Walter White* (New York: Viking Press, 1948), 3; Winston James, *Holding Aloft the Banner of Ethiopia: Caribbean Radicalism in Early Twentieth-Century America* (London: Verso, 1998), 157–59; Robert A. Hill, "Introduction: Racial and Radical; Cyril V. Briggs, the *Crusader* Magazine, and the African Blood Brotherhood, 1918–1922," in Hill, ed., *The Crusader*, vol. 1, *September 1918–August 1919* (New York: Garland Publishing, 1987), quoted on vi.

4. For pioneering studies of racial "in-betweenness," see Robert Orsi, "The Religious Boundaries of an Inbetween People: Street Feste and the Problem of the Dark-Skinned 'Other' in Italian Harlem, 1920–1990," *American Quarterly* 44 (September 1992), 313–47; James R. Barrett and David Roediger, "Inbetween Peoples: Race, Nationality and the 'New Immigrant' Working Class," *Journal of American Ethnic History* 16 (Spring 1997), 3–44.

5. Wood, "Race," quoted on 437.

6. Kerby A. Miller, "'Scotch-Irish' Myths and 'Irish' Identities in Eighteenth- and Nineteenth-Century America," in Charles Fanning, ed., *New Perspectives on the Irish Diaspora* (Carbondale: Southern Illinois University Press, 2000), 81. This generalization applies to other forms of identity as well. In recent years scholars in many fields have concluded that class, gender, ethnic, national, and sexual identities are also subjective,

situational, and variable and can be understood adequately only in particular historical settings. See, for example, Benedict Anderson, *Imagined Communities: Reflections on the Origin and Spread of Nationalism*, rev. ed. (London: Verso, 1991); Eric Hobsbawm and Terence Ranger, eds., *The Invention of Tradition* (Cambridge: Cambridge University Press, 1983); Kathleen Neils Conzen, David A. Gerber, Ewa Morawska, George E. Pozzetta, and Rudolph J. Vecoli, "The Invention of Ethnicity: A Perspective from the U.S.A.," *Journal of American Ethnic History* 12 (Fall 1992), 3–41; Barrett and Roediger, "Inbetween Peoples."

7. Saul Dubow, *Scientific Racism in Modern South Africa* (Cambridge: Cambridge University Press, 1995), 4–5, quoted on 5.

8. Disraeli, *Sybil*, 2:191.

9. Green, quoted in L. Perry Curtis Jr., *Anglo-Saxons and Celts: A Study of Anti-Irish Prejudice in Victorian England* (Bridgeport, CT: Conference on British Studies, University of Bridgeport, 1968), 6–7, 9, 11. See also Gossett, *Race*, 84–122, and Horsman, *Race and Manifest Destiny*, 7–77.

10. The full title of Charles Darwin's magnum opus, which appeared in 1859, is *On the Origin of Species by Means of Natural Selection; or, The Preservation of Favoured Races in the Struggle for Life*.

11. George M. Fredrickson, *White Supremacy: A Comparative Study in American and South African History* (New York: Oxford University Press, 1981), 195.

12. Matthew Frye Jacobson, *Special Sorrows: The Diasporic Imagination of Irish, Polish, and Jewish Immigrants in the United States* (Cambridge, MA: Harvard University Press, 1995), 186.

13. See Dubow, *Scientific Racism in Modern South Africa*, 17, where the author asserts that until the 1920s "the word 'race' . . . was often used as a synonym for 'nation' . . . rather than as a means of distinguishing between blacks and whites"; and Appiah, "Race: An Interpretation," 1580.

14. Dubow, *Scientific Racism in Modern South Africa*, quoted on 21.

15. Michael de Nie, *The Eternal Paddy: Irish Identity and the British Press, 1798–1882* (Madison: University of Wisconsin Press, 2004); Steve Garner, *Racism in the Irish Experience* (London: Pluto Press, 2004).

16. See John Gillingham, "The Beginnings of English Imperialism," *Journal of Historical Sociology* 5 (December 1992), 392–409, and "The English Invasion of Ireland," in Brendan Bradshaw, Andrew Hadfield, and Willy Maley, eds., *Representing Ireland: Literature and the Origins of Conflict, 1534–1660* (Cambridge: Cambridge University Press, 1993), 24–42.

17. Curtis, *Anglo-Saxons and Celts*, quoted on 50–51.

18. Ibid., 15.

19. Robert Knox, *The Races of Men: A Fragment* (Philadelphia: Lea and Blanchard, 1850), 39, 212, 211.

20. John Beddoe, *The Races of Britain: A Contribution to the Anthropology of Western Europe* (Bristol, UK: Arrowsmith, 1885); Madison Grant, *The Passing of the Great Race; or, The Racial Basis of European History* (New York: Charles Scribner's Sons, 1916).

21. Wallace Stegner, "Who Persecutes Boston?" *Atlantic Monthly* 174 (July 1944), 45–52, quoted on 47, 48.

22. Jonathan Schneer, *London 1900: The Imperial Metropolis* (New Haven, CT: Yale University Press, 1999), 213–26; David Levering Lewis, *W.E.B. Du Bois*, vol. 1, *Biography of a Race, 1868–1919* (New York: Henry Holt, 1993), 248–51, quoted on 251.

23. Ruth Benedict and Gene Weltfish, *The Races of Mankind* (1943; repr., New York: Public Affairs Committee, 1946), quoted on 11, 13.

24. Ibid., quoted on 10; Lois W. Banner, *Intertwined Lives: Margaret Mead, Ruth Benedict, and Their Circle* (New York: Alfred A. Knopf, 2003), 384–90, quoted on 388; Ruth Benedict, *Patterns of Culture* (1934; repr., Boston: Houghton Mifflin, 1959), quoted on 11; Painter, *History of White People*, quoted on 337.

25. Wallace Stegner and the editors of *Look*, *One Nation* (Boston: Houghton Mifflin, 1945), quoted on 197, 169, 320, 3.

26. See Arnold R. Hirsch, *Making the Second Ghetto: Race and Housing in Chicago, 1940–1960* (New York: Cambridge University Press, 1983), quoted on 187; Hirsch, "Massive Resistance in the Urban North: Trumbull Park, Chicago, 1953–1966," *Journal of American History* 82 (September 1995), 522–50; Thomas J. Sugrue, "Crabgrass-Roots Politics: Race, Rights, and the Reaction against Liberalism in the Urban North, 1940–1964," *ibid.*, 551–78; Sugrue, *The Origins of the Urban Crisis: Race and Inequality in Postwar Detroit* (Princeton, NJ: Princeton University Press, 1996); Bruce Nelson, *Divided We Stand: American Workers and the Struggle for Black Equality* (Princeton, NJ: Princeton University Press, 2001); Robert O. Self, *American Babylon: Race and the Struggle for Postwar Oakland* (Princeton, NJ: Princeton University Press, 2003); David R. Roediger, *Working toward Whiteness: How America's Immigrants Became White* (New York: Basic Books, 2005).

27. John W. Blassingame, ed., *The Frederick Douglass Papers*, ser. 1, *Speeches, Debates, and Interviews*, vol. 2, *1847–1854* (New Haven, CT: Yale University Press, 1982), quoted on 164–65.

28. David R. Roediger, *The Wages of Whiteness: Race and the Making of the American Working Class* (London: Verso, 1991), 134; Graham Hodges, "'Desirable Companions and Lovers': Irish and African Americans in the Sixth Ward, 1830–1870," in Ronald H. Bayor and Timothy J. Meagher, eds., *The New York Irish* (Baltimore: Johns Hopkins University Press, 1996), 107–24.

29. L. Perry Curtis Jr., *Apes and Angels: The Irishman in Victorian Caricature*, rev. ed. (Washington, DC: Smithsonian Institution Press, 1997). Curtis has many critics; he has been attacked from several standpoints. But generally his critics accuse him of overemphasizing the negative dimension of British press portraits of the Irish in the nineteenth century, and they argue that his choice of race as an explanatory category is at best overstated and at worst misguided. See, especially, Sheridan Gilley, "English Attitudes to the Irish in England, 1780–1900," in Colin Holmes, ed., *Immigrants and Minorities in British Society* (London: Allen & Unwin, 1978), 81–110; D. G. Paz, "Anti-Catholicism, Anti-Irish Stereotyping, and Anti-Celtic Racism in Mid-Victorian Working-Class Periodicals," *Albion* 18 (Winter 1986), 601–16; R. F. Foster, "Paddy and Mr. Punch," in *Paddy and Mr. Punch: Connections in Irish and English History* (London: Allen Lane, 1993), 171–94; G. K. Peatling, "The Whiteness of Ireland under and after the Union," *Journal of British Studies* 44 (January 2005), 115–33. Curtis has answered his critics at length in the revised edition of *Apes and Angels* and more briefly in his rejoinder to G. K. Peatling (and others): L. Perry Curtis Jr., "Comment: The Return of Revisionism," *Journal of British Studies* 44 (January 2005), 134–45.

30. The debate about how, or whether, the Irish "became white" has been particularly fierce. See Roediger, *Wages of Whiteness*; Theodore Allen, *The Invention of the White Race: Racial Oppression and Social Control* (London: Verso, 1994); Noel Ignatiev, *How*

262 • Notes to Prologue

the Irish Became White (New York: Routledge, 1995); Jacobson, *Whiteness of a Different Color*; Matthew Pratt Guterl, *The Color of Race in America, 1900–1940* (Cambridge, MA: Harvard University Press, 2001); Nelson, *Divided We Stand*; Eric Arnesen, "Whiteness and the Historians' Imagination," *International Labor and Working-Class History* 61 (Fall 2001), 3–32; Peter Kolchin, "Whiteness Studies: The New History of Race in America," *Journal of American History* 89 (June 2002), 154–73; Thomas A. Guglielmo, *White on Arrival: Italians, Race, Color, and Power in Chicago, 1890–1945* (New York: Oxford University Press, 2003).

31. George E. Cunningham, "The Italian, a Hindrance to White Solidarity in Louisiana, 1890–1898," *Journal of Negro History* 50 (January 1965), 22–36, quoted on 34; Orsi, "Religious Boundaries of an Inbetween People," 317–18; *Irish World*, June 11, Sept. 10, 1898; Jacobson, *Whiteness of a Different Color*, quoted on 209.

32. Douglas C. Riach, "Blacks and Blackface on the Irish Stage, 1830–60," *Journal of American Studies* 7 (December 1973), 231–41; W.E.B. Du Bois, "Bleeding Ireland," *Crisis* 21 (March 1921), 200. According to Michael Holmes, "Irish soldiers [in India, in particular] . . . had something of a reputation for being even more racist toward the native population than their British colleagues." Michael Holmes, "The Irish and India: Imperialism, Nationalism and Internationalism," in Andy Bielenberg, ed., *The Irish Diaspora* (Harlow, UK: Longman/Pearson, 2000), 241–42.

33. Terence Brown, *Ireland: A Social and Cultural History, 1922–1985* (London: Fontana, 1985), 146.

34. On the Irish diaspora, see Patrick O'Sullivan, ed., *The Irish World Wide*, 6 vols. (Leicester, UK: Leicester University Press, 1992–97); Bielenberg, ed., *Irish Diaspora*; Kevin Kenny, "Diaspora and Comparison: The Global Irish as a Case Study," *Journal of American History* 90 (June 2003), 134–62.

35. Timothy W. Guinnane, *The Vanishing Irish: Household, Migration, and the Rural Economy in Ireland, 1850–1914* (Princeton, NJ: Princeton University Press, 1997), 101, 104 (quoted).

36. For a powerful (but controversial) evocation of the cultural and psychological dimensions of the experience of emigration, see Kerby A. Miller, "Paddy's Paradox: Emigration to America in Irish Imagination and Rhetoric," in *Ireland and Irish America: Culture, Class, and Transatlantic Migration* (Dublin: Field Day, 2008), 100–121, and Miller's classic: *Emigrants and Exiles: Ireland and the Irish Exodus to North America* (New York: Oxford University Press, 1985). For a sharply worded critique of Miller's work, see Donald Harman Akenson, "The Historiography of the Irish in the United States," in O'Sullivan, ed., *Irish World Wide*, vol. 2, *The Irish in the New Communities* (Leicester, UK: Leicester University Press, 1992), 99–126.

37. John Millington Synge, *The Aran Islands* (1907; repr., Oxford: Oxford University Press, 1962), 16.

38. Miller, "Paddy's Paradox," 112.

39. McCormack, who was born in Athlone, County Westmeath, in 1884, became famous throughout the Irish diaspora for his renditions of P. J. O'Reilly's "Ireland, Mother Ireland," which included the words "Oh perfect loving mother / Your exiled children all / Across the sund'ring seas to you / In fond devotion call: / If you sigh, we hear you / If you weep, we weep / In your hours of gladness / How our pulses leap." See Gordon T. Ledbetter, *The Great Irish Tenor* (New York: Charles Scribner's Sons, 1977). See also William H. A. Williams, *'Twas Only an Irishman's Dream: The Image of Ireland and the Irish in American Popular Song Lyrics, 1800–1920* (Urbana: University of Illinois Press, 1996).

40. F. Hugh O'Donnell, *A History of the Irish Parliamentary Party* (London: Longmans, Green, 1910), 279. O'Donnell claimed that he had often encountered an "almost superhuman loathing of [England] in many Irishmen from America."

41. Friedrich Engels to Karl Marx, Dec. 9, 1869, quoted in Joost Augusteijn, ed., *The Irish Revolution* (New York: Palgrave, 2002), 6.

42. Kerby A. Miller, "Class, Culture, and Immigrant Group Identity in the United States: The Case of Irish-American Ethnicity," in Virginia Yans-McLaughlin, ed., *Immigration Reconsidered* (New York: Oxford University Press, 1990), 114.

43. David Emmons, "Faction Fights: The Irish Worlds of Butte, Montana, 1875–1917," in O'Sullivan, ed., *Irish in the New Communities*, 87.

44. "Letters to Antislavery Workers and Agencies," pt. 1,"Frederick Douglass," *Journal of Negro History* 10 (October 1925), 662.

45. *Liberator*, June 9, 1843.

46. Blassingame, ed., *Frederick Douglass Papers*, ser. 1, vol. 2, quoted on 60.

47. Michael Davitt, *The Fall of Feudalism in Ireland; or, The Story of the Land League Revolution* (London: Harper & Brothers, 1904), 724; Davitt, quoted in Roger Casement, *The Crime against Europe: A Possible Outcome of the War of 1914* (Philadelphia: Celtic Press, 1915), 13.

48. "The Peril of Irish Partition," *Irish Independent*, July 29, 1919, clipping in file 7825b, Erskine and Mary Childers Papers, Manuscripts and Archives Research Library, Trinity College Dublin.

49. For a recent summary of historians' opinions on this question, see Augusteijn, ed., *Irish Revolution*.

50. Jeffrey B. Perry, ed., *A Hubert Harrison Reader* (Middletown, CT: Wesleyan University Press, 2001); Cyril V. Briggs, "Heroic Ireland," *Crusader* 3 (February 1921), 5.

51. Guterl, *Color of Race in America*, 68–69.

52. *Boston Pilot*, Oct. 30, 1920.

53. Irish Progressive League, "The Irish Are for Hillquit" (flyer), n.d. [October 1917], folder 2, ms. 13,141, Peter Golden Papers, National Library of Ireland (NLI); C. Desmond Greaves, *Liam Mellows and the Irish Revolution* (London: Lawrence and Wishart, 1971), quoted on 155.

54. Fergus Campbell, *Land and Revolution: Nationalist Politics in the West of Ireland, 1891–1921* (Oxford: Oxford University Press, 2005), quoted on 255. Cathal Brugha served as minister for defense in the Irish government organized by Dáil Éireann in 1919. He also served in Eamon de Valera's cabinet and joined de Valera in opposing the Anglo-Irish Treaty. He was killed in Dublin on July 7, 1922, an early casualty of the fighting between pro- and antitreaty forces during the Irish Civil War.

55. Roger Casement, quoted in Séamas Ó Síocháin, "Roger Casement's Vision of Freedom," in Mary E. Daly, ed., *Roger Casement in Irish and World History* (Dublin: Royal Irish Academy, 2005), 4.

CHAPTER 1. ". . . THE BLOOD OF AN IRISHMAN"

1. Joep Leerssen, *Mere Irish and Fíor-Ghael: Studies in the Idea of Irish Nationality, Its Development and Literary Expression prior to the Nineteenth Century* (1986; repr., Cork: Cork University Press, in association with Field Day, 1996), quoted on 35, 36; Hiram Morgan, "Giraldus Cambrensis and the Tudor Conquest of Ireland," in Morgan,

ed., *Political Ideology in Ireland, 1541–1641* (Dublin: Four Courts Press, 1999), quoted on 24; L. Perry Curtis Jr., *Anglo-Saxons and Celts: A Study of Anti-Irish Prejudice in Victorian England* (Bridgeport, CT: Conference on British Studies, University of Bridgeport, 1968), quoted on 124n1. The quote in the chapter title is from Michael de Nie, *The Eternal Paddy: Irish Identity and the British Press, 1798–1882* (Madison: University of Wisconsin Press, 2004), 70. The epigraph is from Declan Kiberd, *Inventing Ireland: The Literature of the Modern Nation* (London: Hutchinson, 1995), 9.

2. R. F. Foster, *Modern Ireland, 1600–1972* (London: Allen Lane, 1988), 25–27; Christopher Maginn, "O'Neill, Shane (c. 1530–1567)," in H.C.G. Matthew and Brian Harrison, eds., *Oxford Dictionary of National Biography* (Oxford: Oxford University Press, 2004); online ed., ed. Lawrence Goldman, January 2008, http://www.oxforddnb.com/view/article/20785 (accessed Nov. 13, 2009).

3. Leerssen, *Mere Irish and Fíor-Ghael*, 67–76, quoted on 71.

4. Nicholas P. Canny, "The Ideology of English Colonization: From Ireland to America," *William and Mary Quarterly*, 3rd ser., 30 (October 1973), 576; William J. Smyth, *Map-Making, Landscapes and Memory: A Geography of Colonial and Early Modern Ireland, c. 1530–1750* (Cork: Cork University Press, in association with Field Day, 2006), 45.

5. Smyth, *Map-Making, Landscapes and Memory*, 47.

6. Canny, "Ideology of English Colonization," 583, quoted on 588, 592; David Beers Quinn, *The Elizabethans and the Irish* (Ithaca, NY: Cornell University Press, 1966), 71, 76; Sheila T. Cavanagh, "'The fatal destiny of that land': Elizabethan Views of Ireland," in Brendan Bradshaw, Andrew Hadfield, and Willy Maley, eds., *Representing Ireland: Literature and the Origins of Conflict, 1534–1660* (Cambridge: Cambridge University Press, 1993), quoted on 118, 119; Foster, *Modern Ireland*, 27; Leerssen, *Mere Irish and Fíor-Ghael*, 32–49.

7. Jane H. Ohlmeyer, "'Civilizinge of those Rude Partes': Colonization within Britain and Ireland, 1580s–1640s," in Nicholas Canny, ed., *The Oxford History of the British Empire*, vol. 1, *The Origins of Empire* (New York: Oxford University Press, 1998), 124–46, quoted on 132.

8. For a detailed summary of these arguments, see S. J. Connolly, *Contested Island: Ireland, 1460–1630* (Oxford: Oxford University Press, 2007), 264–68.

9. David Edwards, "The Escalation of Violence in Sixteenth-century Ireland," in Edwards, Pádraig Lenihan, and Clodagh Tait, eds., *Age of Atrocity: Violence and Political Conflict in Early Modern Ireland* (Dublin: Four Courts Press, 2007), 34–77, quoted on 69, 77; Quinn, *The Elizabethans and the Irish*, 123–42; Smyth, *Map-Making, Landscapes and Memory*, 45–47, quoted on 45; Colm Lennon, *Sixteenth-Century Ireland: The Incomplete Conquest* (New York: St. Martin's Press, 1995), 227–28; Nicholas Canny, *Making Ireland British, 1580–1650* (Oxford: Oxford University Press, 2001), quoted on 50; Andrew Hadfield, "Spenser, Edmund (1552?–1599)," in Matthew and Harrison, eds., *Oxford Dictionary of National Biography*; online ed., ed. Lawrence Goldman, January 2008, http://www.oxforddnb.com/view/article/26145 (accessed Oct. 24, 2009).

10. Nicholas Canny, "O'Neill, Hugh, Second Earl of Tyrone (c. 1550–1616)," in Matthew and Harrison, eds., *Oxford Dictionary of National Biography*; online ed., ed. Lawrence Goldman, January 2008, http://www.oxforddnb.com/view/article/20775 (accessed Nov. 16, 2009).

11. Canny, *Making Ireland British*, 66; Smyth, *Map-Making, Landscapes and Memory*, 44, 49–51; John McGurk, "The Pacification of Ulster, 1600–3," in Edwards, Lenihan, and

Tait, eds., *Age of Atrocity*, quoted on 122; Quinn, *The Elizabethans and the Irish*, quoted on 140; M. Perceval-Maxwell, *The Scottish Migration to Ulster in the Reign of James I* (1973; repr., Belfast: Ulster Historical Foundation Publications, 1990), 17–18.

12. Canny, "Ideology of English Colonization," 585.

13. Vincent Carey, "'What pen can paint or tears atone?': Mountjoy's Scorched Earth Campaign," in Hiram Morgan, ed., *The Battle of Kinsale* (Bray, Ireland: Wordwell, 2004), 209; McGurk, "Pacification of Ulster," quoted on 123.

14. Leerssen, *Mere Irish and Fíor-Ghael*, quoted on 35; James Lydon, *The Making of Ireland: From Ancient Times to the Present* (London: Routledge, 1998), 150.

15. McGurk, "Pacification of Ulster," quoted on 122.

16. Colm Lennon, *Sixteenth-century Ireland: The Incomplete Conquest* (New York: St. Martin's Press, 1995).

17. The full title of Temple's book is *The Irish Rebellion; or, An history of the beginnings and first progress of the general rebellion raised within the Kingdom of Ireland, upon the three and twentieth day of October, in the Year 1641, together with the barbarous cruelties and bloody massacres which ensued thereupon*. On the polemics generated by the rebellion, see Smyth, *Map-Making, Landscapes and Memory*, 116–18; Canny, *Making Ireland British*, 461–64; Kathleen M. Noonan, "'Martyrs in Flames': Sir John Temple and the Conception of the Irish in English Martyrologies," *Albion* 36 (Summer 2004), 223–55.

18. Hilary Simms, "Violence in County Armagh, 1641," in Brian Mac Cuarta, SJ, ed., *Ulster 1641: Aspects of the Rising* (Belfast: Institute of Irish Studies, Queen's University Belfast, 1993), 123–38; Marianne Elliott, *The Catholics of Ulster: A History* (London: Allen Lane, 2000), 101.

19. Brian Mac Cuarta, "Religious Violence against Settlers in South Ulster, 1641-2," in Edwards, Lenihan, and Tait, eds., *Age of Atrocity*, 154–75; Smyth, *Map-Making, Landscapes and Memory*, 128–30; Kathleen M. Noonan, "'The Cruell Pressure of an Enraged, Barbarous People': Irish and English Identity in Seventeenth-Century Policy and Propaganda," *Historical Journal* 41 (March 1998), quoted on 163.

20. John Morrill, "The Drogheda Massacre in Cromwellian Context," in Edwards, Lenihan, and Tait, eds., *Age of Atrocity*, 243–65, quoted on 263; Pádraig Lenihan, *Consolidating Conquest: Ireland, 1603–1727* (Harlow, UK: Longman/Pearson, 2007), quoted on 128. See also Jason McElligott, "Cromwell, Drogheda, and the Abuse of Irish History," *Bullán* 6 (Summer–Fall 2001), 109–32.

21. Patrick J. Corish, "The Cromwellian Regime, 1650–60," in T. W. Moody, F. X. Martin, and F. J. Byrne, eds., *A New History of Ireland*, vol. 3, *Early Modern Ireland, 1534–1691* (Oxford: Clarendon Press, 1976), 380–86, quoted on 382. By the late 1650s, a number of priests and bishops had returned to Ireland and were beginning to rebuild the infrastructure of Catholic worship.

22. Ibid., 361, 369–74; Samuel R. Gardiner, "The Transplantation to Connaught," *English Historical Review* 14 (October 1899), 700–34, quoted on 730; Smyth, *Map-Making, Landscape and Memory*, 377.

23. D. W. Hayton, "The Williamite Revolution in Ireland, 1688–91," in Jonathan I. Israel, ed., *The Anglo-Dutch Moment: Essays on the Glorious Revolution and Its World Impact* (Cambridge: Cambridge University Press, 1991), 188.

24. Ibid., quoted on 192, 196.

25. Lenihan, *Consolidating Conquest*, quoted on 186, 188.

26. Hayton, "Williamite Revolution in Ireland," 186.

27. Ibid., 209–10; "penal laws," in S. J. Connolly, ed., *The Oxford Companion to Irish History* (Oxford: Oxford University Press, 1998), quoted on 438. The fullest treatment of the penal laws and their impact over more than a century is Thomas Bartlett's *The Fall and Rise of the Irish Nation: The Catholic Question, 1690–1830* (Dublin: Gill and Macmillan, 1992).

28. Ian McBride, *Scripture Politics: Ulster Presbyterians and Irish Radicalism in the Late Eighteenth Century* (Oxford: Clarendon Press, 1998), 15, 24; Jonathan Swift, "An Answer to Several Letters sent me from unknown Hands (Written in the Year 1729)," in Herbert Davis, ed., *The Prose of Jonathan Swift*, vol. 12, *Irish Tracts, 1728–1733* (Oxford: Basil Blackwell, 1955), 89; Leerssen, *Mere Irish and Fíor-Ghael*, quoted on 310.

29. Leerssen, *Mere Irish and Fíor-Ghael*, quoted on 326 (emphasis in original); Sarah Butler, *Irish Tales; or, Instructive Histories for the Happy Conduct of Life*, ed. Ian Campbell Ross, Aileen Douglas, and Anne Markey (Dublin: Four Courts Press, 2010).

30. Leerssen, *Mere Irish and Fíor-Ghael*, 72.

31. Swift, "Answer to Several Letters," 89; Leerssen, *Mere Irish and Fíor-Ghael*, quoted on 320, 303, 305, 340; John Pinkerton, *A Dissertation on the Origins and Progress of the Scythians or Goths: Being an Introduction to the Ancient and Modern History of Europe* (London: George Nichol, 1787), 92.

32. "Patriot and Patriotism," in Connolly ed., *Oxford Companion to Irish History*, quoted on 435.

33. Maurice J. Bric, "Ireland, America and the Reassessment of a Special Relationship, 1760–1783," *Eighteenth-Century Ireland* 11 (1996), 88–119, quoted on 89; Kevin Whelan, "The Green Atlantic: Radical Reciprocities between Ireland and America in the Long Eighteenth Century," in Kathleen Wilson, ed., *A New Imperial History: Culture, Identity, and Modernity in Britain and the Empire, 1660–1840* (Cambridge: Cambridge University Press, 2004), 216–38.

34. Ian McBride, "'The common name of Irishman': Protestantism and Patriotism in Eighteenth-Century Ireland," in Tony Claydon and Ian McBride, eds., *Protestantism and National Identity: Britain and Ireland, c. 1650–c. 1850* (Cambridge: Cambridge University Press, 1998), 237; Jim Smyth, "Introduction: The 1798 Rebellion in Its Eighteenth-Century Contexts," in Smyth, ed., *Revolution, Counter-Revolution and Union: Ireland in the 1790s* (Cambridge: Cambridge University Press, 2000), 12.

35. Ian McBride, "Presbyterians in the Penal Era," *Bullán* 1 (Autumn 1994), quoted on 80; Jim Smyth, *The Men of No Property: Irish Radicals and Popular Politics in the Late Eighteenth Century* (New York: St. Martin's Press, 1992), quoted on 55.

36. Thomas Bartlett, "Tone, Theobald Wolfe," in James McGuire and James Quinn, eds., *Dictionary of Irish Biography* (Cambridge: Cambridge University Press, 2009), http://dib.cambridge.org/viewReadPage.do?articleId=a8590 (accessed March 30, 2010); Marianne Elliott, *Wolfe Tone: Prophet of Irish Independence* (New Haven, CT: Yale University Press, 1989).

37. Kevin Whelan, *The Tree of Liberty: Radicalism, Catholicism and the Construction of Irish Identity, 1760–1830* (Cork: Cork University Press, 1996), quoted on 101; McBride, "'Common name of Irishman,'" 238. David Wilson argues that "Catholic emancipation, from this viewpoint, really meant emancipation *from* Catholicism." David A. Wilson, *United Irishmen, United States: Immigrant Radicals in the Early Republic* (Ithaca, NY: Cornell University Press, 1998), 14 (emphasis in original).

38. Smyth, *Men of No Property*, 54–66, quoted on 66. On the rapid growth of the Catholic middle class in the eighteenth century, see Kevin Whelan, "The Catholic Church in County Tipperary, 1700–1900," in William Nolan and Thomas G. McGrath, eds., *Tipperary: History and Society* (Dublin: Geography Publications, 1985), 215–18.

39. Harman Murtagh, "General Humbert's Futile Campaign," in Thomas Bartlett, David Dickson, Dáire Keogh, and Kevin Whelan, eds., *1798: A Bicentenary Perspective* (Dublin: Four Courts Press, 2003), 174–87. For a more traditional perspective on 1798, which emphasizes its sectarian dimensions, see Tom Dunne, *Rebellions: Memoir, Memory and 1798* (Dublin: Lilliput Press, 2004), especially 130–48.

40. Nancy J. Curtin, *The United Irishmen: Popular Politics in Ulster and Dublin, 1791–1798* (Oxford: Clarendon Press, 1994), 260–81.

41. Daniel Gahan, "Class, Religion and Rebellion: Wexford in 1798," in Smyth, ed. *Revolution, Counter-Revolution and Union*, 83–98, quoted on 84, 92.

42. Daniel Gahan, "The Rebellion of 1798 in South Leinster," in Bartlett, Dickson, Keogh, and Whelan, eds., *1798*, 104–21.

43. Kevin Whelan, "Introduction to Section IV," in Bartlett, Dickson, Keogh, and Whelan, eds., *1798*, quoted on 300.

44. See, for example, L. M. Cullen, "The United Irishmen in Wexford," in Dáire Keogh and Nicholas Furlong, eds., *The Mighty Wave: The 1798 Rebellion in Wexford* (Dublin: Four Courts Press, 1996), 48–64; Kevin Whelan, "Reinterpreting the 1798 Rebellion in County Wexford," ibid., 9–36; Gahan, "Class, Religion and Rebellion" and "The Rebellion of 1798 in South Leinster."

45. Daniel Gahan, "The Scullabogue Massacre, 1798," *History Ireland* 4 (Autumn 1996), 27–31.

46. Thomas Bartlett, *Ireland: A History* (Cambridge: Cambridge University Press, 2010), 224.

47. Thomas Bartlett, "Clemency and Compensation: The Treatment of Defeated Rebels and Suffering Loyalists after the 1798 Rebellion," in Smyth, ed., *Revolution, Counter-Revolution and Union*, 99–127, quoted on 102. See also Michael Durey, "Marquess Cornwallis and the Fate of Rebel Prisoners in the Aftermath of the 1798 Rebellion," ibid., 128–45, especially 129 (table 8.1).

48. See Whelan, *Tree of Liberty*, 133–75, quoted on 148, and de Nie, *Eternal Paddy*, 36–81.

49. Whelan, *Tree of Liberty*, quoted on 134; James Kelly, " 'We were all to have been massacred': Irish Protestants and the Experience of Rebellion," in Bartlett et al., eds., *1798*, 312–30.

50. Jim Smyth, "Anti-Catholicism, Conservatism, and Conspiracy: Sir Richard Musgrave's Memoirs of the Different Rebellions in Ireland," *Eighteenth-Century Life* 22 (November 1998), 62–73, quoted on 62, 65; James Kelly, *Sir Richard Musgrave, 1746–1818: Ultra-Protestant Ideologue* (Dublin: Four Courts Press, 2009), 11–64; David Dickson, foreword to Sir Richard Musgrave's *Memoirs of the Different Rebellions in Ireland, from the Arrival of the English: Also, a Particular Detail of That Which Broke Out the 23rd of May, 1798; With the History of the Conspiracy Which Preceded It*, 4th ed., ed. Steven W. Myers and Delores E. McKnight (Fort Wayne, IN: Round Tower Books, 1995), i–xi.

51. Whelan, *Tree of Liberty*, 135–45, quoted on 139, 138, 141; Kelly, " 'We were all to have been massacred,' " quoted on 325.

52. James J. Sack, *From Jacobite to Conservative: Reaction and Orthodoxy in Britain, c. 1760–1832* (Cambridge: Cambridge University Press, 1993), 96–97, 240–43; de Nie, *Eternal Paddy*, quoted on 70.

CHAPTER 2. CELTS, HOTTENTOTS, AND "WHITE CHIMPANZEES"

1. Peter Gray, *The Irish Famine* (London: Thames and Hudson, 1995), 13–29, quoted on 27; James S. Donnelly Jr., *The Great Irish Potato Famine* (Stroud, UK: Sutton Publishing, 2001), 1–11; Kerby A. Miller, *Emigrants and Exiles: Ireland and the Irish Exodus to North America* (New York: Oxford University Press, 1985), 32–35. The epigraphs are from the following: Robert Knox, *The Races of Men: A Fragment* (Philadelphia: Lea & Blanchard, 1850), 13; Goldwin Smith, *Irish History and the Irish Question* (Toronto: Morang, 1905), 3; and Captain Hugh Pollard, a British intelligence officer at Dublin Castle, writing in 1922, quoted in L. Perry Curtis Jr., *Apes and Angels: The Irishman in Victorian Caricature*, rev. ed. (Washington, DC: Smithsonian Institution Press, 1997), 192n199.

2. De Beaumont, quoted in Gray, *Irish Famine*, 13.

3. Richard Ned Lebow, *White Britain and Black Ireland: The Influence of Stereotypes on Colonial Policy* (Philadelphia: Institute for the Study of Human Issues, 1976), 35–43, quoted on 40; Kevin Whelan, "Bitter Harvest," *Boston College Magazine* 55 (Winter 1996), 20–25, quoted on 23, 22; Knox, *Races of Men*, 214; Michael de Nie, *The Eternal Paddy: Irish Identity and the British Press, 1798–1882* (Madison: University of Wisconsin Press, 2004), 36–81, 129.

4. De Nie, *Eternal Paddy*, quoted on 24; Matthew Arnold, *On the Study of Celtic Literature* (London: Smith, Elder, 1867); Terence Brown, "Saxon and Celt: The Stereotype," in *Ireland's Literature: Selected Essays* (Mullingar: Lilliput Press, 1988), quoted on 7, 8; L. Perry Curtis Jr., *Anglo-Saxons and Celts: A Study of Anti-Irish Prejudice in Victorian England* (Bridgeport, CT: Conference on British Studies, University of Bridgeport, 1968), 40, 134n40.

5. The name "Fenian" derived from the Irish word "*Fianna*," which signified a warrior band in Gaelic Ireland and, in Irish mythology, the group who followed the legendary hero *Fionn mac Cumhaill*. For a provocative interpretation of Fenianism as a "circum-Atlantic and internationalist liberation movement," see Amy E. Martin, "Fenian Fever: Circum-Atlantic Insurgency and the Modern State," in Peter D. O'Neill and David Lloyd, eds., *The Black and Green Atlantic: Cross-Currents of the African and Irish Diasporas* (Basingstoke, UK: Palgrave Macmillan, 2009), 21–32, quoted on 31.

6. On Whiteboyism in the nineteenth century, see Michael Beames, *Peasants and Power: The Whiteboy Movements and Their Control in Pre-famine Ireland* (Sussex, UK: Harvester Press, 1983); Paul E. W. Roberts, "Caravats and Shanavests: Whiteboyism and Faction Fighting in East Munster, 1802–11," in Samuel Clark and James S. Donnelly Jr., eds., *Irish Peasants: Violence and Political Unrest, 1780–1914* (Madison: University of Wisconsin Press, 1983), 64–101; James S. Donnelly Jr., "Pastorini and Captain Rock: Millenarianism and Sectarianism in the Rockite Movement of 1821–4," ibid., 102–39; Donnelly, *Captain Rock: The Irish Agrarian Rebellion of 1821–1824* (Madison: University of Wisconsin Press, 2009); C.H.E. Philpin, ed., *Nationalism and Popular Protest in Ireland*

(Cambridge: Cambridge University Press, 1987); Kevin Kenny, *Making Sense of the Molly Maguires* (New York: Oxford University Press, 1998), 13–44.

7. Lebow, *White Britain and Black Ireland*, quoted on 43, 46; Thomas Crofton Croker, *Researches in the South of Ireland, Illustrative of the Scenery, Architectural Remains, and the Manners and Superstitions of the Peasantry* (London: John Murray, 1824); de Nie, *Eternal Paddy*, quoted on 120; Knox, *Races of Men*, 27.

8. Gray, *Irish Famine*; Cormac Ó Gráda, *Black '47 and Beyond: The Great Famine in History, Economy, and Memory* (Princeton, NJ: Princeton University Press, 1999); Donnelly, *Great Irish Potato Famine*, and on British policy in particular, Peter Gray, *Famine, Land and Politics: British Government and Irish Society, 1843–1850* (Dublin: Irish Academic Press, 1999).

9. Peter Gray estimates 1.8 million emigrants in the decade after 1845; James Donnelly suggests 2.1 million in the eleven years from 1845 through 1855. But Donnelly also offers an important qualification: "A significant portion of those who departed . . . would undoubtedly have left even if there had been no famine, for the emigrant stream had been swelling in the decade immediately before 1845." Gray, *Irish Famine*, 97; Donnelly, *Great Irish Potato Famine*, 178.

10. Donnelly, *Great Irish Potato Famine*, quoted on 27.

11. Ibid., quoted on 29; Christine Kinealy, *This Great Calamity: The Irish Famine, 1845–1852* (Dublin: Gill and Macmillan, 1994), 342–59.

12. Lebow, *White Britain and Black Ireland*, quoted on 41; Donnelly, *Great Irish Potato Famine*, 20, 31, 127–30; *(London) Times*, Sept. 22, 1846, reprinted in Gray, *Irish Famine*, 154–55, quoted on 155; de Nie, *Eternal Paddy*, quoted on 109.

13. Donnelly, *Great Irish Potato Famine*, quoted on 131; Gray, *Famine, Land and Politics*, quoted on 309; Whelan, "Bitter Harvest," quoted on 23.

14. Knox, *Races of Men*, 253–54 (emphasis in original), 27; Gray, *Irish Famine*, 88, 79 (quoted); Donnelly, *Great Irish Potato Famine*, 160.

15. Gray, *Famine, Land and Politics*, 180–83; Robert James Scally, *The End of Hidden Ireland: Rebellion, Famine, and Emigration* (New York: Oxford University Press, 1995), 38–40; Peter Duffy, *The Killing of Major Denis Mahon: A Mystery of Old Ireland* (New York: HarperCollins, 2007), x, quoted on 159, 161.

16. De Nie, *Eternal Paddy*, quoted on 121.

17. Curtis, *Apes and Angels*, 44, 43, quoted on 101.

18. Seán McConville, *Irish Political Prisoners, 1848–1922: Theatres of War* (London: Routledge, 2003), 136–38; and see: http://en.wikipedia.org/wiki/Fenian_dynamite_campaign (accessed Jan. 5, 2011).

19. Matthew Frye Jacobson, *Special Sorrows: The Diasporic Imagination of Irish, Polish, and Jewish Immigrants in the United States* (Cambridge, MA: Harvard University Press, 1995), quoted on 13.

20. Knox, *Races of Men*, quoted on 14, 147; Douglas Lorimer, "Race, Science and Culture: Historical Continuities and Discontinuities, 1850–1914," in Shearer West, ed., *The Victorians and Race* (Aldershot, UK: Ashgate, 1996), 12–33, especially 15. Whereas Lorimer identifies Knox as a "founding father of modern racism," George Stocking pays relatively little attention to Knox in his comprehensive study of Victorian anthropology. But Stocking does point out that James Hunt, who was a major intellectual force in the emergence of modern scientific racism, acknowledged that he had "imbibed" his racial

views "from the late Dr. Knox." George W. Stocking Jr., *Victorian Anthropology* (New York: Free Press, 1987), 247.

21. I. MacLaren, "Robert Knox MD, FRCSEd, FRSEd, 1791–1862: The First Conservator of the College Museum," *Journal of the Royal College of Surgeons of Edinburgh* 45 (December 2000), 392–97; Knox, *Races of Men*, quoted on 254.

22. Knox, *Races of Men*, quoted on 77, 61.

23. Ibid., quoted on 43, 41, 26, 214, 217. Surely it cannot be a coincidence that Knox singled out Derrynane as the lowest abode of "civilized man," for Derrynane was the family home of Daniel O'Connell. To self-proclaimed "Saxons" such as Knox, O'Connell represented the worst that Celtic civilization had to offer. Knox was undoubtedly familiar with Thomas Campbell Foster's letters to the *Times* in 1845 and 1846, in which the author claimed that "on the estates of O'Connell are to be found the most wretched tenants . . . in all Ireland." Thomas Campbell Foster, *Letters on the Condition of the People of Ireland* (London: Chapman and Hall, 1846), quoted on 457–58.

24. Knox, *Races of Men*, quoted on 27, 226.

25. F.P.C. [Frances Power Cobbe], "The Celt of Wales and the Celt of Ireland," *Cornhill Magazine* 36 (December 1877), 661–78, quoted on 666; Sally Mitchell, *Frances Power Cobbe: Victorian Feminist, Journalist, Reformer* (Charlottesville: University of Virginia Press, 2004).

26. J. W. Jackson, "The Race Question in Ireland," *Anthropological Review* 7 (January 1869), 54–76, quoted on 69, 58.

27. Hector MacLean, "On the Comparative Anthropology of Scotland," ibid., 4 (July 1866), 209–26, quoted on 218–19.

28. Elazar Barkan, *The Retreat of Scientific Racism: Changing Concepts of Race in Britain and the United States between the World Wars* (Cambridge: Cambridge University Press, 1992); 22–23, 25–26; Angelique Richardson, "Beddoe, John (1826–1911)," in H.C.G. Matthew and Brian Harrison, eds., *Oxford Dictionary of National Biography* (Oxford: Oxford University Press, 2004), http://www.oxforddnb.com/view/article/30666 (accessed Jan. 21, 2010).

29. John Beddoe, *The Races of Britain: A Contribution to the Anthropology of Western Europe* (Bristol, UK: Arrowsmith, 1885), 18, 261–68, quoted on 265, 262; Beddoe, *The Anthropological History of Europe: Being the Rhind Lectures for 1891* (Paisley, UK: Alexander Gardner, 1893), quoted on 117.

30. Beddoe, *Races of Britain*, 261–68, quoted on 136, 25, 266, 267, 5, 10, 12, 11.

31. Ibid., 17; R. M. Douglas, "Anglo-Saxons and Attacotti: The Racialization of Irishness in Britain between the World Wars," *Ethnic and Racial Studies* 25 (January 2002), 40–63, quoted on 41, 46.

32. Bruce Nelson, *Divided We Stand: American Workers and the Struggle for Black Equality* (Princeton, NJ: Princeton University Press, 2001), xxxvii–xxxviii; Dale T. Knobel, *Paddy and the Republic: Ethnicity and Nationality in Antebellum America* (Middletown, CT: Wesleyan University Press, 1986), 68–103; Matthew Frye Jacobson, *Whiteness of a Different Color: European Immigrants and the Alchemy of Race* (Cambridge, MA: Harvard University Press, 1998), 48; Curtis, *Apes and Angels*, 100.

33. Thomas F. Gossett, *Race: The History of an Idea in America*, new ed. (New York: Oxford University Press, 1997), quoted on 109, 110; Curtis, *Apes and Angels*, quoted on 63; Curtis, *Anglo-Saxons and Celts*, quoted on 63; John Barnes and David Nicholson, eds., *The Leo Amery Diaries*, vol. 1, *1896–1929* (London: Hutchinson, 1980), 515.

34. Robert Orsi, "The Religious Boundaries of an Inbetween People: Street Feste and the Problem of the Dark-Skinned 'Other' in Italian Harlem, 1920–1990," *American Quarterly* 44 (September 1992), 313–47; James R. Barrett and David Roediger, "Inbetween Peoples: Race, Nationality and the 'New Immigrant' Working Class," *Journal of American Ethnic History* 16 (Spring 1997), 3–44.

35. Nelson, *Divided We Stand*, xxxviii; *Charles Kingsley: His Letters and Memories of His Life*, "Edited by His Wife," 13th abridged ed. (London: Kegan Paul, Trench, 1883), 2:111–12; Curtis, *Anglo-Saxons and Celts*, quoted on 85; Curtis, *Apes and Angels*, quoted on 100; Thomas Carlyle, "The Repeal of the Union," in Percy Newberry, ed., *Rescued Essays of Thomas Carlyle* (London: Leadenhall Press, n.d.), 50–52; Thomas C. Holt, *The Problem of Freedom: Race, Labor, and Politics in Jamaica and Britain, 1832–1938* (Baltimore: Johns Hopkins University Press, 1992), quoted on 308. On Carlyle's racist views, and his fear that Jamaica would become a "Black Ireland," see Holt, *Problem of Freedom*, 280–84.

36. James Bryce, *The American Commonwealth*, 3rd ed. (London: Macmillan, 1893), 496.

37. Terence Denman, "The Catholic Irish Soldier in the First World War: The 'Racial Environment,'" *Irish Historical Studies* 27 (November 1991), 352–65, quoted on 353, 357, 359, 364; Wilson Jeremiah Moses, *The Golden Age of Black Nationalism, 1850–1925* (Hamden, CT: Archon Books, 1978), quoted on 239. See also Tyler Stovall, *Paris Noir: African Americans in the City of Light* (Boston: Houghton Mifflin, 1996), 19–20.

38. Fiske, quoted in Barbara Miller Solomon, *Ancestors and Immigrants: A Changing New England Tradition* (Cambridge, MA: Harvard University Press, 1956), 59; Freeman, quoted in Marilyn Lake and Henry Reynolds, *Drawing the Global Colour Line: White Men's Countries and the International Challenge of Racial Equality* (Cambridge: Cambridge University Press, 2008), 52.

39. Lake and Reynolds, *Drawing the Global Colour Line*, 2–3, 9 (quoted), 23–32; Alexander Saxton, *The Indispensable Enemy: Labor and the Anti-Chinese Movement in California* (Berkeley: University of California Press, 1971), especially 117–26; Charles Wentworth Dilke, *Greater Britain: A Record of Travel in English-Speaking Countries during 1866 and 1867* (Philadelphia: J. B. Lippincott, 1869), 2:65–75, quoted on 71, 69. See also Kornel Chang, "Circulating Race and Empire: Transnational Labor Activism and the Politics of Anti-Asian Agitation in the Anglo-American Pacific World, 1880–1910," *Journal of American History* 96 (December 2009), 678–701.

40. Curtis, *Anglo-Saxons and Celts*, 45–47; Dilke, *Greater Britain*, 1:33–39 (quoted on 38, 37), 2:69–71, 346–48.

41. L. Perry Curtis Jr., "Comment: The Return of Revisionism," *Journal of British Studies* 44 (January 2005), 134–45.

42. De Nie, *Eternal Paddy*, 119.

43. Curtis, *Apes and Angels*, 155–74, quoted on 163–64. Curtis has examined Irish portrayals of Hibernia in the late nineteenth century in L. Perry Curtis Jr., *Images of Erin in the Age of Parnell* (Dublin: National Library of Ireland, 2000).

44. Michael de Nie, "'A Medly Mob of Irish-American Plotters and Irish Dupes': The British Press and Transatlantic Fenianism," *Journal of British Studies* 40 (April 2001), 213–40, quoted on 239; de Nie, *Eternal Paddy*, 3–35, especially 23, 27 (quoted), 35.

45. James Anthony Froude, "Romanism and the Irish Race in the United States," pt. 1, *North American Review* 129 (December 1879), 522.

46. Joep Leerssen, *Mere Irish and Fíor-Ghael: Studies in the Idea of Irish Nationality, Its Development and Literary Expression prior to the Nineteenth Century* (1986; repr., Cork: Cork University Press, in association with Field Day, 1996), 254–87, quoted on 276.

47. *Nation*, Nov. 11, 1842, Dec. 9, 1843.

48. F. Hugh O'Donnell, *A History of the Irish Parliamentary Party* (London: Longmans, Green, 1910), vol. 1, quoted on 274; Douglas Hyde, "The Necessity for De-Anglicising Ireland," in Charles Gavan Duffy, George Sigerson, and Douglas Hyde, *The Revival of Irish Literature and Other Addresses* (London: T. Fisher Unwin, 1894), 159.

49. Lady Gregory, *Selected Writings*, ed. Lucy McDiarmid and Maureen Waters (London: Penguin Books, 1995), 47–48; Hyde, "Necessity for De-Anglicising Ireland," 159 (emphasis in original).

50. Paul Delaney, "D. P. Moran and the *Leader*: Writing an Irish Ireland through Partition," *Éire-Ireland* 38 (Fall–Winter 2003), 189–211, quoted on 190.

51. P. J. Mathews, *Revival: The Abbey Theatre, Sinn Féin, the Gaelic League and the Co-operative Movement* (Cork: Cork University Press, 2003), 95–98; Conor Cruise O'Brien, *Ancestral Voices: Religion and Nationalism in Ireland* (Dublin: Poolbeg, 1994), quoted on 59; Patrick Maume, *D. P. Moran* (Dundalk, Ireland: Dundalgan Press, 1995), quoted on 3, 23; Tom Garvin, *Nationalist Revolutionaries in Ireland, 1858–1928* (1987; repr., Dublin: Gill and Macmillan, 2005), 57–77.

52. *United Irishman*, June 3, 1899, quoted in R. F. Foster, *W. B. Yeats: A Life*, vol. 1, *The Apprentice Mage, 1865–1914* (Oxford: Oxford University Press, 1997), 220.

53. [Arthur Griffith,] "Death of Frederick Ryan," *Sinn Féin*, April 12, 1913; [Griffith,] "Nationalists and Internationalists," ibid., April 26, 1913. These two articles are reprinted (the latter as "Response to Sheehy Skeffington") in Seamus Deane, ed., *The Field Day Anthology of Irish Writing* (Derry, Ireland: Field Day, 1991), 2:1002–4. On Frederick Ryan, see Terry Eagleton, "The Ryan Line," in *Crazy John and the Bishop and Other Essays on Irish Culture* (Notre Dame, IN: University of Notre Dame Press, 1998), 249–72.

54. [Griffith], "Nationalists and Internationalists"; Padraic Colum, *Arthur Griffith* (Dublin: Browne and Nolan, 1959), 31–41, quoted on 34; Brian Maye, *Arthur Griffith* (Dublin: Griffith College Publications, 1997), 11–12.

55. *United Irishman*, Sept. 16, Oct. 14, Nov. 11, 1899; Maye, *Arthur Griffith*, 366.

56. *United Irishman*, Sept. 23, 1899.

57. Foster, *W. B. Yeats*, 1:190.

58. O'Donnell frequently wrote inflammatory articles in the *United Irishman* under the pseudonym "The Foreign Secretary." According to Patrick Maume, "O'Donnell encouraged Griffith's anti-Semitism." But it was Griffith who chose to give O'Donnell large amounts of space—much of it front-page space—in the *United Irishman* and who then airily dismissed the accusation of anti-Semitism when others—notably, Frederick Ryan—protested. Patrick Maume, *The Long Gestation: Irish Nationalist Life, 1891–1918* (Dublin: Gill and Macmillan, 1999), 51–52; Maye, *Arthur Griffith*, 362–72; Frederick Ryan, "Militarism" (letter to the editor), *United Irishman*, Aug. 26, 1899. Ryan asked, "What do you think [Wolfe] Tone would have thought could he have seen a paper, allied with his memory, filling its columns with 'anti-Semitic' ravings?" Griffith replied, simply, "All Mr. Ryan's assertions about THE UNITED IRISHMAN are untrue." Ibid.

59. Maye, *Arthur Griffith*, 368. On the Limerick pogrom, see Dermot Keogh, *Jews in Twentieth-Century Ireland: Refugees, Anti-Semitism and the Holocaust* (Cork: Cork University Press, 1998), 27–53.

60. Maume, *Long Gestation*, 49; Arthur Griffith, "Preface to 1913 Edition," in John Mitchel, *Jail Journal* (1913; repr., Dublin: University Press of Ireland, 1982), 370, 371.

61. Ben Novick, *Conceiving Revolution: Irish Nationalist Propaganda during the First World War* (Dublin: Four Courts Press, 2001), 115.

62. Ibid., 103, 113–20, quoted on 113–14, 119.

63. For classic examples of revisionist historiography, see Conor Cruise O'Brien, *States of Ireland* (London: Hutchinson, 1972), and O'Brien, *Ancestral Voices*; F.S.L. Lyons, *Culture and Anarchy in Ireland, 1890–1939* (Oxford: Oxford University Press, 1979); Garvin, *Nationalist Revolutionaries in Ireland*; R. F. Foster, *Modern Ireland, 1600–1972* (London: Allen Lane, 1988). For anthologies and surveys, see Ciaran Brady, ed., *Interpreting Irish History: The Debate on Historical Revisionism, 1938–1994* (Dublin: Irish Academic Press, 1994); D. George Boyce and Alan O'Day, eds., *The Making of Modern Irish History: Revisionism and the Revisionist Controversy* (London: Routledge, 1996); Boyce, *Nationalism in Ireland*, 3rd ed. (London: Routledge, 1995); Richard English, *Irish Freedom: The History of Nationalism in Ireland* (London: Macmillan, 2006); Paul Bew, *Ireland: The Politics of Enmity, 1789–2006* (Oxford: Oxford University Press, 2007). Revisionism's reach in Ireland extends far beyond academia. It has become a forceful presence in multiple arenas. For two examples, by a leading journalist and public intellectual and a renowned novelist, see Fintan O'Toole, *The Lie of the Land: Irish Identities* (London: Verso, 1998), and Roddy Doyle, *A Star Called Henry* (London: Jonathan Cape, 1999).

64. See, especially, Tom Garvin, *1922: The Birth of Irish Democracy* (Dublin: Gill and Macmillan, 1996).

65. For outstanding examples of postrevisionist scholarship, see Luke Gibbons, "Constructing the Canon: Versions of National Identity," in Deane, ed., *Field Day Anthology of Irish Writing*, 2:950–55, and Gibbons, "Challenging the Canon: Revisionism and Cultural Criticism," ibid., 3:561–68; Kevin Whelan, *The Tree of Liberty: Radicalism, Catholicism and the Construction of Irish Identity, 1760–1830* (Cork: Cork University Press, 1996); P. J. Mathews, "A Battle or Two Civilizations? D. P. Moran and William Rooney," *Irish Review* 29 (Autumn 2002), 22–37, and Mathews, *Revival*; Fergus Campbell, *Land and Revolution: Nationalist Politics in the West of Ireland, 1891–1921* (Oxford: Oxford University Press, 2005); Kerby A. Miller, *Ireland and Irish America: Culture, Class, and Transatlantic Migration* (Dublin: Field Day, 2008). I have also learned much from the brief but trenchant critiques of revisionist historiography in Jason McElligott, "Cromwell, Drogheda, and the Abuse of Irish History," *Bullán* 6 (Summer–Fall 2001), 109–32; Kevin Whelan, "The Revisionist Debate in Ireland," *boundary 2*, 31 (Spring 2004), 179–205; Donnelly, *Great Irish Potato Famine*, 11–32; Brendan O'Leary, "Cuttlefish, Cholesterol and Saoirse," *Field Day Review* 3 (2007), 187–203 (a review of *English's Irish Freedom*); and Kerby A. Miller, "Re-imagining Irish and Irish Migration History," in Miller, *Ireland and Irish America*, 370–85.

66. Theobald Wolfe Tone, *The Life of Theobald Wolfe Tone*, ed. Thomas Bartlett (Dublin: Lilliput Press, 1998), 46.

67. Bruce Nelson, "'Come out of such a land, you Irishmen': Daniel O'Connell, American Slavery, and the Making of the 'Irish Race,'" *Éire-Ireland* 42 (Spring/Summer

2007), 58–81; Nelson, " 'My Countrymen Are All Mankind,' " *Field Day Review* 4 (2008), 260–73.

68. James Paul Rodechko, *Patrick Ford and His Search for America: A Case Study of Irish-American Journalism, 1870–1913* (New York: Arno Press, 1976), quoted on 187; Carla King, introduction to King, ed., *Michael Davitt: Collected Writings, 1868–1906*, vol. 1, *Pamphlets, Speeches, and Articles, 1889–1906* (London: Thoemmes Press, 2001; Tokyo: Edition Synapse, 2001), xxviii.

69. Colum, *Arthur Griffith*, 17, 19–28, 32, quoted on 26; Mathews, "Battle of Two Civilizations?" 29; Maume, *Long Gestation*, 49.

70. Mathews, *Revival*, 98–103, quoted on 101, 100 (emphasis added); Mathews, "Battle of Two Civilizations?" 22–37.

71. Brian Inglis, *Roger Casement* (1973; repr., London: Penguin Books, 2002), 364.

72. Roger Casement, *The Crime against Europe: A Possible Outcome of the War of 1914* (Philadelphia: Celtic Press, 1915), quoted on 14. For contrasting views of Casement's attitude toward imperialism, see Andrew Porter, "Sir Roger Casement and the International Humanitarian Movement," in Mary E. Daly, ed., *Roger Casement in Irish and World History* (Dublin: Royal Irish Academy, 2005), 11–25; Margaret O'Callaghan, " ' With the Eyes of Another Race, of a People Once Hunted Themselves': Casement, Colonialism and a Remembered Past," ibid., 46–63; and Angus Mitchell, "Roger Casement: The Evolution of an Enemy of Empire—I," in Eóin Flannery and Angus Mitchell, eds., *Enemies of Empire: New Perspectives on Imperialism, Literature and Historiography* (Dublin: Four Courts Press, 2007), 40–57.

73. James Connolly, "On German Militarism," *Irish Worker*, Aug. 22, 1914.

74. C. Desmond Greaves, *Liam Mellows and the Irish Revolution* (London: Lawrence and Wishart, 1971), quoted on 189–90. Although Maclean's statement may seem preposterous in retrospect, given the conservative regime that developed in the aftermath of Ireland's war for independence and civil war, one cannot fully understand the Irish Revolution without coming to terms with the parallel upheaval that took place at the "point of production" during the revolutionary era. See Emmet O'Connor, *Syndicalism in Ireland, 1917–1923* (Cork: Cork University Press, 1988); O'Connor, "Agrarian Unrest and the Labour Movement in County Waterford, 1917–1923," *Saothar* 6 (1980), 40–58; Conor Kostick, *Revolution in Ireland: Popular Militancy, 1917–1923* (London: Pluto Press, 1996); and Campbell, *Land and Revolution*. On Maclean, see Gavin Foster, " 'Scotsmen, stand by Ireland': John Maclean and the Irish Revolution," *History Ireland* 16 (January/February 2008), 32–37.

75. Cyril V. Briggs, "Heroic Ireland," *Crusader* 3 (February 1921), 5.

CHAPTER 3. "COME OUT OF SUCH A LAND, YOU IRISHMEN"

1. Parts of this chapter appeared, in a somewhat different form, in Bruce Nelson, " 'Come out of such a land, you Irishmen': Daniel O'Connell, American Slavery, and the Making of the 'Irish Race,' " *Éire-Ireland* 42 (Spring/Summer 2007), 58–81, and Bruce Nelson, " 'My Countrymen Are All Mankind,' " *Field Day Review* 4 (2008), 260–73. The epigraphs are from the following: Walter M. Merrill, ed., *The Letters of William Lloyd Garrison*, vol. 3, *No Union with Slaveholders, 1841–1849* (Cambridge, MA: Belknap Press

of Harvard University Press, 1973), 63; *Liberator*, June 9, 1843; and Benjamin Quarles, *Black Abolitionists* (New York: Oxford University Press, 1969), 133.

2. *Liberator*, Oct. 16, 1840; Louis Ruchames, ed., *The Letters of William Lloyd Garrison*, vol. 2, *A House Divided against Itself, 1836–1840* (Cambridge, MA: Belknap Press of Harvard University Press, 1971), 669, 655.

3. Donal McCartney, "The World of Daniel O'Connell," in McCartney, ed., *The World of Daniel O'Connell* (Dublin: Mercier Press, 1980), 3; Sean McGraw and Kevin Whelan, "Daniel O'Connell in Comparative Perspective, 1800–50," *Éire-Ireland* 40 (Spring/Summer 2005), quoted on 70, 69. The starting point for the study of O'Connell must be Oliver MacDonagh's two-volume biography: *The Hereditary Bondsman: Daniel O'Connell, 1775–1829* (New York: St. Martin's Press, 1988), and *The Emancipist: Daniel O'Connell, 1830–47* (New York: St. Martin's Press, 1989). I have also learned much from the essays in McCartney, ed., *World of Daniel O'Connell*; Kevin B. Nowlan and Maurice R. O'Connell, eds., *Daniel O'Connell: Portrait of a Radical* (Belfast: Appletree Press, 1984); K. Theodore Hoppen, "Riding a Tiger: Daniel O'Connell, Reform, and Popular Politics in Ireland, 1800–1847," in T.C.W. Blanning and Peter Wende, eds., *Reform in Great Britain and Germany, 1750–1950* (Oxford: Oxford University Press, 1999), 121–43; and especially from McGraw and Whelan, "Daniel O'Connell in Comparative Perspective."

4. MacDonagh, *Emancipist*, 228–30, Macaulay quoted on 250; Gary Owens, "Nationalism without Words: Symbolism and Ritual Behaviour in the Repeal 'Monster Meetings' of 1843–5," in James S. Donnelly Jr. and Kerby A. Miller, eds., *Irish Popular Culture, 1650–1850* (Dublin: Irish Academic Press, 1998), 242–69, especially 245–46. While reaffirming their political significance, Owens brilliantly deconstructs the legend of O'Connell's monster meetings.

5. Denis Gwynn, *Daniel O'Connell*, rev. centenary ed. (Cork: Cork University Press, 1947), 9; McGraw and Whelan, "Daniel O'Connell in Comparative Perspective," 66, 78, 80–81; *Daniel O'Connell upon American Slavery, with Other Irish Testimonies* (New York: American Anti-Slavery Society, 1860), 12; Gillian M. Doherty, *The Irish Ordnance Survey: History, Culture and Memory* (Dublin: Four Courts Press, 2004), quoted on 27.

6. Oliver MacDonagh, "O'Connell's Ideology," in Laurence Brockliss and David Eastwood, eds., *A Union of Multiple Identities: The British Isles, c. 1750–c. 1850* (Manchester: Manchester University Press, 1997), 160; R. V. Comerford, "O'Connell, Daniel (1775–1847)," in H.C.G. Matthew and Brian Harrison, eds., *Oxford Dictionary of National Biography* (Oxford: Oxford University Press, 2004); http://www.oxforddnb.com/view/article/20501 (accessed Aug. 10, 2006).

7. The literature on O'Connell (and, more broadly, on Ireland), slavery, and abolition is also extensive. The pioneering articles and essays are Gilbert Osofsky, "Abolitionists, Irish Immigrants, and the Dilemmas of Romantic Nationalism," *American Historical Review* 80 (October 1975), 889–912; Douglas C. Riach, "Daniel O'Connell and American Anti-slavery," *Irish Historical Studies* 20 (March 1976), 3–25; and Riach, "O'Connell and Slavery," in McCartney, ed., *World of Daniel O'Connell*, 175–85. For more recent scholarship, see, especially, John F. Quinn, " 'Three Cheers for the Abolitionist Pope!': American Reaction to Gregory XVI's Condemnation of the Slave Trade, 1840–1860," *Catholic Historical Review* 90 (January 2004), 67–93; Quinn, "The Rise and Fall of Repeal: Slavery and Irish Nationalism in Antebellum Philadelphia," *Pennsylvania Magazine of History and Biography* 130 (January 2006), 45–78; Maurice J. Bric, "Daniel O'Connell and the

Debate on Anti-slavery, 1820–50," in Tom Dunne and Laurence M. Geary, eds., *History and the Public Sphere: Essays in Honour of John A. Murphy* (Cork: Cork University Press, 2005), 69–82.

8. Loyal National Repeal Association, "To . . . [the] Executive Committee of the Cincinnati Repeal Association" (Dublin, Oct. 11, 1843), 10 [hereafter, O'Connell, "To . . . the Cincinnati Repeal Association"]. See also Charles Gavan Duffy, *Young Ireland: A Fragment of Irish History, 1840–1850*, 2nd ed. (London: Cassell, Petter, Galpin, 1880), 201.

9. O'Connell, "To . . . the Cincinnati Repeal Association," 7; Doherty, *Irish Ordnance Survey*, 44–54; Burke, quoted in Theodore W. Allen, *The Invention of the White Race*, vol. 1, *Racial Oppression and Social Control* (London: Verso, 1994), 31.

10. Daniel O'Connell, *A Memoir on Ireland: Native and Saxon* (Dublin: printed for Charles Dolman of London, 1843), vii–viii, 8.

11. Ibid., 253–54; Daniel O'Connell, *A Memoir on Ireland: Native and Saxon*, 2nd ed. (New York: Greeley and McElrath, 1843), 65. There were numerous, and quite different, editions of the *Memoir*, ranging from the 406-page Dublin edition of 1843 to the 80-page New York edition of the same year.

12. *Liberator*, Aug. 7, 1840; O'Connell, *Memoir* (NY ed.), 65.

13. Fergus O'Ferrall, *Catholic Emancipation: Daniel O'Connell and the Birth of Irish Democracy, 1820–30* (Dublin: Gill and Macmillan, 1985), 144; Maurice R. O'Connell, ed., *The Correspondence of Daniel O'Connell*, 8 vols. (Dublin: Blackwater Press, 1972–80), 6:292 (quoted), 348; O'Connell, *Memoir* (Dublin ed.), 18, 137.

14. Richard Davis, *The Young Ireland Movement* (Dublin: Gill and Macmillan, 1987), 35.

15. *Liberator*, Aug. 7, 1840.

16. *Daniel O'Connell upon American Slavery*, 7, 17; "Letters to Antislavery Workers and Agencies," pt. 1, "Frederick Douglass," *Journal of Negro History* 10 (October 1925), 662.

17. Riach, "Daniel O'Connell and American Anti-slavery," 5; Riach, "O'Connell and Slavery," 176; Kenneth Charlton, "The State of Ireland in the 1820s: James Cropper's Plan," *Irish Historical Studies* 17 (March 1971), 320–39. On O'Connell's role in promoting the cause of antislavery in the British Parliament, see Izhak Gross, "The Abolition of Negro Slavery and British Parliamentary Politics, 1832–3," *Historical Journal* 23 (March 1980), 63–85.

18. *Daniel O'Connell upon American Slavery*, 8.

19. On the complex evolution of O'Connell's religious faith and spiritual life, see the excellent articles by James E. Guilfoyle: "The Religious Development of Daniel O'Connell," pt. 1, "From Deist to Roman Catholic," *New Hibernia Review* 2 (Autumn 1998), 89–101; and "The Religious Development of Daniel O'Connell," pt. 2, "The Making of a Devotional Catholic," ibid. (Winter 1998), 114–32. Guilfoyle does not, however, discuss O'Connell's religious beliefs in relation to slavery, where so many of his statements were characterized by a tone and spirit that paralleled the antislavery discourse of evangelical Protestants.

20. Joseph Lee, "The Social and Economic Ideas of O'Connell," in Nowlan and O'Connell, eds., *Daniel O'Connell*, 70–86, quoted on 82; O'Connell, "To . . . the Cincinnati Repeal Association," 3, 11; *Liberator*, June 9, 1843.

21. O'Connell, "To . . . the Cincinnati Repeal Association," 3; *Liberator*, Dec. 6, 1839; *Daniel O'Connell upon American Slavery*, 16.

22. Alexander Saxton, *The Rise and Fall of the White Republic: Class Politics and Mass Culture in Nineteenth-Century America* (London: Verso, 1995); Robert W. Johannsen, *To the Halls of the Montezumas: The Mexican War in the American Imagination* (New York: Oxford University Press, 1985), quoted on 293; *Daniel O'Connell upon American Slavery*, 5–6, 12, 14, 11, 15, 22, 24, 29.

23. *Daniel O'Connell upon American Slavery*, 9, 12 (quoted).

24. O'Connell, ed., *Correspondence of Daniel O'Connell*, 6:129; David T. Gleeson, *The Irish in the South, 1815–1877* (Chapel Hill: University of North Carolina Press, 2001), 68; Thomas F. Moriarty, "The Irish American Response to Catholic Emancipation," *Catholic Historical Review* 66 (July 1980), 353–73, especially 366, 370; Quinn, "Rise and Fall of Repeal," 47.

25. *Daniel O'Connell upon American Slavery*, 14–15; O'Connell, "To . . . the Cincinnati Repeal Association," 10.

26. *Liberator*, March 11, 1842. On Father Theobald Mathew, see Colm Kerrigan, *Father Mathew and the Irish Temperance Movement, 1838–1849* (Cork: Cork University Press, 1992), and John F. Quinn, *Father Mathew's Crusade: Temperance in Nineteenth-Century Ireland and Irish America* (Amherst: University of Massachusetts Press, 2002).

27. *Liberator*, Sept. 10, 1841; Osofsky, "Abolitionists, Irish Immigrants, and Romantic Nationalism," 895–98, quoted on 897. John F. Quinn maintains that the Irish Address was written by Haughton and Webb. If Allen was not one of its authors, he played an important role in setting it in motion. Quinn, "'Three Cheers for the Abolitionist Pope!'" 80.

28. Even before Remond returned to the United States, a copy of the Irish Address appeared in the *Colored American*, Oct. 2, 1841.

29. Merrill, ed., *Letters of William Lloyd Garrison*, 3:48; *Liberator*, Feb. 4, 1842.

30. Was James Cannings Fuller Irish? His words at Faneuil Hall and the *Liberator's* portrayal of him as a man with the "heart of an Irishman" suggest that he was. It is reasonable to assume, moreover, that the Garrisonians would have chosen an Irish expatriate to address an audience of Irish immigrants in the familiar terms that Fuller employed. However, when Fuller died in 1847, his obituary in the *Liberator* described him as "the only Englishman we know, of prominent standing, . . . who has been able to see through the hypocrisy and withstand the temptations of a new country, and act an English part on American soil." In addition, Walter Merrill, coeditor of the Garrison letters published by Harvard University Press, has identified Fuller as an "English Quaker who had settled in Skaneatles, New York, in 1834." *Liberator*, Feb. 4, April 8, 1842, Dec. 10, 1847 (obituary); Merrill, ed., *Letters of William Lloyd Garrison*, 3:47.

31. *Liberator*, March 11, 1842.

32. George M. Fredrickson, *The Black Image in the White Mind: The Debate on Afro-American Character and Destiny, 1817–1914* (1971; repr., Middletown, CT: Wesleyan University Press, 1987), 1–42; James Brewer Stewart, "The Emergence of Racial Modernity and the Rise of the White North, 1790–1840," *Journal of the Early Republic* 18 (Summer 1998), 181–217, quoted on 209.

33. Thomas More Madden, ed., *The Memoirs (Chiefly Autobiographical) from 1798 to 1886 of Richard Robert Madden* (London: Ward and Downey, 1891), 88.

34. Henry Mayer, *All on Fire: William Lloyd Garrison and the Abolition of Slavery* (New York: St. Martin's Press, 1998), 208; Clare Taylor, ed., *British and American Abolitionists: An Episode in Transatlantic Understanding* (Edinburgh: Edinburgh University Press, 1974), 207, 172.

35. Merrill, ed., *Letters of William Lloyd Garrison*, 3:53, 56, 62. On the religious dimension of Garrisonian abolitionism, especially its tendency toward "come-outerism," see Ronald G. Walters, *The Antislavery Appeal: American Abolitionism after 1830* (1978; repr., New York: W. W. Norton, 1984), 37–53; Lewis Perry, *Radical Abolitionism: Anarchy and the Government of God in Antislavery Thought* (1973; repr., Knoxville: University of Tennessee Press, 1995), 92–128; Peter F. Walker, *Moral Choices: Memory, Desire, and Imagination in Nineteenth-Century American Abolition* (Baton Rouge: Louisiana State University Press, 1978), 6–13; Mayer, *All on Fire*, 222–39, 300–329, quoted on 302. For a somewhat different interpretation of the Garrisonians' commitment to disunion, see W. Caleb McDaniel, "Repealing Unions: American Abolitionists, Irish Repeal, and the Origins of Garrisonian Disunionism," *Journal of the Early Republic* 28 (Summer 2008), 243–69.

36. Merrill, ed., *Letters of William Lloyd Garrison*, 3:92.

37. Maria Webb to the secretary of the Boston Female Antislavery Society, Nov. 2, 1846, quoted in Ellen M. Oldham, "Irish Support of the Abolitionist Movement," *Boston Public Library Quarterly* 10 (October 1958), 182.

38. All of these arguments are present, to one degree or another, in Osofsky, "Abolitionists, Irish Immigrants, and Romantic Nationalism," quoted on 889.

39. Kerby A. Miller, *Emigrants and Exiles: Ireland and the Irish Exodus to North America* (New York: Oxford University Press, 1985), 291; Ford, quoted in Thomas N. Brown, *Irish-American Nationalism, 1870–1890* (Philadelphia: Lippincott, 1966), 24. See also Richard Jensen, " 'No Irish Need Apply': A Myth of Victimization?" *Journal of Social History* 36 (Winter 2002), 405–29.

40. Cormac Ó Gráda, "The New York Irish in the 1850s," in *Ireland's Great Famine: Interdisciplinary Perspectives* (Dublin: University College Dublin Press, 2006), 143–74.

41. Ibid., 165–68, quoted on 165, 166; Cormac Ó Gráda, *Black '47 and Beyond: The Great Famine in History, Economy, and Memory* (Princeton, NJ: Princeton University Press, 1999), quoted on 108. For detailed data on Irish participation in the labor market and the kinds of jobs they held, see Ó Gráda, "New York Irish in the 1850s," 150, and Oscar Handlin, *Boston's Immigrants, 1790–1880: A Study in Acculturation*, rev. and enlarged ed. (Cambridge, MA: Belknap Press of Harvard University Press, 1991), 25–51.

42. Some historians have painted a more benign portrait of the experience of Irish immigrants, including the famine generation. See, for example, David Noel Doyle, "The Remaking of Irish America, 1845–80," in W. E. Vaughan, ed., *A New History of Ireland*, vol. 6, *Ireland under the Union, pt. 2, 1870–1921* (Oxford: Clarendon Press, 1996), 753; Tyler Anbinder, "From Famine to Five Points: Lord Lansdowne's Irish Tenants Encounter North America's Most Notorious Slum," *American Historical Review* 107 (April 2002), 351–87; and Joseph P. Ferrie, *"Yankeys Now": Immigrants in the Antebellum U.S., 1840–60* (New York: Oxford University Press, 1997). Ferrie acknowledges that the Irish were disadvantaged relative to German and British immigrants but argues that they made substantial gains over a twenty-year period.

43. David R. Roediger, *The Wages of Whiteness: Race and the Making of the American Working Class* (London: Verso, 1991), 134, 144–50; Graham Hodges, " 'Desirable Companions and Lovers': Irish and African Americans in the Sixth Ward, 1830–1870," in Ronald H. Bayor and Timothy J. Meagher, eds., *The New York Irish* (Baltimore: Johns Hopkins University Press, 1996), 107–24; Tyler Anbinder, *Five Points: The Nineteenth-Century New York City Neighborhood That Invented Tap Dance, Stole Elections, and*

Became the World's Most Notorious Slum (New York: Free Press, 2001); Leslie M. Harris, *In the Shadow of Slavery: African Americans in New York City, 1826–1863* (Chicago: University of Chicago Press, 2003), 240–62.

44. Bruce Nelson, *Divided We Stand: American Workers and the Struggle for Black Equality* (Princeton, NJ: Princeton University Press, 2001), xxxiv–xxxv, 12–21; Allen, *Invention of the White Race*, 1:192–98; C. Peter Ripley et al., eds., *The Black Abolitionist Papers*, vol. 3, *The United States, 1830–1846* (Chapel Hill: University of North Carolina Press, 1991), quoted on 275; Harris, *In the Shadow of Slavery*, quoted on 141.

45. Unlike most historians of Irish America, George Potter recognized this basic fact as early as the 1950s. See his chapter "The Anti-Abolitionist Irish" in his posthumously published *To the Golden Door: The Story of the Irish in Ireland and America* (Boston: Little, Brown, 1960), 371–87, especially 373.

46. Nelson, *Divided We Stand*, 15; Handlin, *Boston's Immigrants*, 251.

47. Albert von Frank, *The Trials of Anthony Burns: Freedom and Slavery in Emerson's Boston* (Cambridge, MA: Harvard University Press, 1998), 38; Hodges, "'Desirable Companions and Lovers,'" 110.

48. See Joel H. Silbey, *The Partisan Imperative: The Dynamics of American Politics before the Civil War* (New York: Oxford University Press, 1985), 87–115, quoted on 90; and the brief but superb chapter by Leonard L. Richards, "The Jacksonians and Slavery," in Lewis Perry and Michael Fellman, eds., *Antislavery Reconsidered: New Perspectives on the Abolitionists* (Baton Rouge: Louisiana State University Press, 1979), 99–118.

49. John T. McGreevy, *Catholicism and American Freedom: A History* (New York: W. W. Norton, 2003), 56–65; Taylor, ed., *British and American Abolitionists*, 200, 201, 224; Lee Jenkins, "'The Black O'Connell': Frederick Douglass and Ireland," *Nineteenth Century Studies* 13 (1999), 42n32; Riach, "Daniel O'Connell and American Anti-slavery," 9, 13 (quoted); O'Connell, "To . . . the Cincinnati Repeal Association," 10. While acknowledging "a deep strain of anti-Catholicism" among some abolitionists, Gilbert Osofsky argued that "the Garrisonians rarely slipped into a nativist stance. . . . In fact no more forceful attacks on nativism and Know-Nothingism came out of antebellum America than those of the Garrisonians." Osofsky, "Abolitionism, Irish Immigrants, and Romantic Nationalism," 908.

50. Donald M. Scott, "Abolition as a Sacred Vocation," in Perry and Fellman, eds., *Antislavery Reconsidered*, 51–74; Mayer, *All on Fire*, 299; Riach, "Daniel O'Connell and American Anti-slavery," 6–7; Burlingame, quoted in Tyler Anbinder, *Nativism and Slavery: The Northern Know Nothings and the Politics of the 1850s* (New York: Oxford University Press, 1992), 45.

51. *Letters of the Late Bishop England to the Hon. John Forsyth on the Subject of Domestic Slavery* (1844; repr., New York: Negro Universities Press, 1969), xi.

52. Ibid., xi, iv, v. The classic, and still valuable, study is Madeleine Hooke Rice's *American Catholic Opinion in the Slavery Controversy* (New York: Columbia University Press, 1944). I have learned much, as well, from Quinn, "'Three Cheers for the Abolitionist Pope!'"; Robert Emmett Curran, "Rome, the American Church, and Slavery," in Joseph C. Linck and Raymond J. Kupke, eds., *Building the Church in America* (Washington, DC: Catholic University of America Press, 1999), 30–49; and McGreevy, *Catholicism and American Freedom*.

53. Rice, *American Catholic Opinion*, quoted on 28; *Letters of the Late Bishop England*, 23.

54. *Letters of the Late Bishop England*, v; Potter, *To the Golden Door*, quoted on 375, 376; von Frank, *Trials of Anthony Burns*, 243–44; Rice, *American Catholic Opinion*, quoted on 64.

55. Quinn, "'Three Cheers for the Abolitionist Pope!'" quoted on 82.

56. *Liberator*, April 15, 1842. On Madden, see Madden, ed., *Memoirs*; León Ó Broin, "R. R. Madden, Historian of the United Irishmen," *Irish University Review* 2 (Spring 1972), 20–33; and Nini Rodgers, "Richard Robert Madden: An Irish Anti-slavery Activist in the Americas," in Oonagh Walsh, ed., *Ireland Abroad: Politics and Professions in the Nineteenth Century* (Dublin: Four Courts Press, 2003), 119–31.

57. Rodgers, "Richard Robert Madden," 127; Howard Jones, *Mutiny on the Amistad: The Saga of a Slave Revolt and Its Impact on American Abolition, Law, and Diplomacy* (New York: Oxford University Press, 1987), 99–110.

58. *Liberator*, April 15, 1842.

59. Ibid., June 24, 1842.

60. Quinn, "Rise and Fall of Repeal," 62–63; *Liberator*, Oct. 7, 1842, April 28, 1843.

61. *Daniel O'Connell upon American Slavery*, 5, 15.

62. Riach, "O'Connell and Slavery," 182; *Liberator*, Dec. 8, April 28, 1843, June 17, 1842; O'Connell, ed., *Correspondence of Daniel O'Connell*, 7:176.

63. Riach, "Daniel O'Connell and American Anti-slavery," quoted on 12; Merrill, ed., *Letters of William Lloyd Garrison*, 3:63; *Liberator*, June 9, 1843.

64. *Daniel O'Connell upon American Slavery*, 7, 17; O'Connell, "To . . . the Cincinnati Repeal Association," 8; *Liberator*, June 9, 1843.

65. Nelson, "'My Countrymen Are All Mankind,'" 260–73, especially 261–64; Orla Power, "The 'Quadripartite Concern' of St. Croix, 1751–1757: An Irish Catholic Plantation in the Danish West Indies" (paper presented at a conference on the Irish in the Atlantic World, College of Charleston, Charleston, SC, Feb. 27–March 2, 2007), quoted on 15; Nini Rodgers, *Ireland, Slavery and Anti-slavery, 1612–1865* (Basingstoke, UK: Palgrave Macmillan, 2007), quoted on 111. See also Donald Harman Akenson, *If the Irish Ruled the World: Montserrat, 1630–1730* (Liverpool: Liverpool University Press, 1997).

66. Nelson, "'My Countrymen Are All Mankind,'" 264; Rodgers, *Ireland, Slavery and Anti-slavery*, 113 (quoted), 121 (quoted), 160–61, 173–74, quoted on 173.

67. Maurice R. O'Connell, *Daniel O'Connell: The Man and His Politics* (Dublin: Irish Academic Press, 1990), 127–28.

68. O'Connell, "To . . . the Cincinnati Repeal Association," 2–3, 10–11, 4–5.

69. Ibid., 12, 2, 1 (emphasis added).

70. *Liberator*, April 22, 1842, July 14, 1843; Gleeson, *Irish in the South*, 121–32, quoted on 131. See also Kerby A. Miller, "'Scotch-Irish,' 'Black Irish' and 'Real Irish': Emigrants and Identities in the Old South," in Andy Bielenberg, ed., *The Irish Diaspora* (Harlow: Longman, 2000), 139–57.

71. Angela Murphy has challenged the conventional wisdom that O'Connell's anti-slavery stance, above all his demand that the Irish in America repudiate slavery, led to the dissolution of most Repeal associations in the southern United States in 1843. In fact, most of them survived for several more years. See Angela Murphy, "Slavery, Irish Nationalism, and Irish American Identity in the South, 1840–1845," in David T. Gleeson, ed., *The Irish in the Atlantic World* (Columbia: University of South Carolina Press, 2010), 129–53, quoted on 142.

72. Robert Ryal Miller, *Shamrock and Sword: The Saint Patrick's Battalion in the U.S.-Mexican War* (Norman: University of Oklahoma Press, 1989), 168; William W. Freehling, *The Road to Disunion*, vol. 1, *Secessionists at Bay, 1776–1854* (New York: Oxford University Press, 1990), 353–452, quoted on 414, 383; Harriet Smither, "English Abolitionism and the Annexation of Texas," *Southwestern Historical Quarterly* 32 (1929), 193–205, quoted on 200; Betty Fladeland, *Men and Brothers: Anglo-American Antislavery Cooperation* (Urbana: University of Illinois Press, 1972), 302–15.

73. Johannsen, *To the Halls of the Montezumas*, quoted on 293, 296; Reginald Horsman, *Race and Manifest Destiny: The Origins of American Racial Anglo-Saxonism* (Cambridge, MA: Harvard University Press, 1981), 208–48; Sam W. Haynes, "'But What Will England Say?'—Great Britain, the United States, and the War with Mexico," in Richard V. Francavilia and Douglas W. Richmond, eds., *Dueling Eagles: Reinterpreting the U.S.-Mexican War, 1846–1848* (Fort Worth: Texas Christian University Press, 2000), 19–39; Gleeson, *Irish in the South*, 134; Merrill, ed., *Letters of William Lloyd Garrison*, 3:284; Miller, *Shamrock and Sword*, 32–34, 156, 174, and "Appendix: Roster of Known San Patricios" (no page numbers).

74. Miller, *Shamrock and Sword*, 162–63; Peter F. Stevens, *The Rogue's March: John Riley and the Saint Patrick's Battalion* (Washington, DC: Brassey's, 1999), quoted on 221. I am much indebted to Abby Bender's exploration of the ways in which issues of race and nationality played out in the Mexican War, especially in relation to the San Patricio Battalion. See Abby Bender, "Irish-Mexican Solidarity and the San Patricio Battalion Flag," *Genre* 36 (Fall/Winter 2003), 271–93.

75. Fred Anderson and Andrew Clayton, *The Dominion of War: Empire and Liberty in North America, 1500–2000* (New York: Viking, 2005), quoted on 267; *Liberator*, Dec. 6, 1839, Aug. 7, 1840, May 2, 1845; O'Connell, ed., *Correspondence of Daniel O'Connell*, 6:282–83.

76. *Liberator*, June 13, 1845 (emphasis in original); Murphy, "Slavery, Irish Nationalism, and Irish American Identity in the South," 146–49. Murphy argues persuasively that it was O'Connell's "American Eagle" speech, more than his stance on slavery, that finally undermined the Repeal movement in the United States.

77. Maurice J. Bric, "O'Connell, Daniel, and America," in Michael Glazier, ed., *The Encyclopedia of the Irish in America* (Notre Dame, IN: University of Notre Dame Press, 1999), 714; Riach, "Daniel O'Connell and American Anti-slavery," 17–21.

78. On Young Ireland, especially on its adherents' attitude toward slavery, see Maurice R. O'Connell, "O'Connell, Young Ireland, and Negro Slavery: An Exercise in Romantic Nationalism," *Thought* 64 (June 1989), 130–36.

79. Ibid., quoted on 133, 132, 134 (emphasis in original).

80. L. Fogarty, *Father John Kenyon: A Patriot Priest of Forty-Eight* (Dublin: Mahon's Printing Works, 1921), quoted on 23, 25.

81. Potter, *To the Golden Door*, 386.

82. O'Connell, *Memoir* (NY ed.), 20.

83. Mitchel, quoted in Kevin Whelan, "The Revisionist Debate in Ireland," *boundary 2*, 31 (Spring 2004), 196.

84. Gwynn, *Daniel O'Connell*, 246.

85. *Letters of the Late Bishop England*, v; *Daniel O'Connell upon American Slavery*, 33.

86. Merrill, ed., *Letters of William Lloyd Garrison*, vol. 1, *I Will Be Heard! 1822–1835* (Cambridge, MA: Belknap Press of Harvard University Press, 1971), 133.

87. O'Connell, "To . . . the Cincinnati Repeal Association," 2; O'Connell, ed., *Correspondence of Daniel O'Connell*, vol. 6, quoted on 339–40; *Liberator*, May 2, 1845.

88. O'Connell, "To . . . the Cincinnati Repeal Association," 12, 8; *Liberator*, Nov. 24, 1843.

89. Gleeson, *Irish in the South*, 125–26, 129; Miller, " 'Scotch Irish,' 'Black Irish,' and 'Real Irish,' " 152.

90. See *Daniel O'Connell upon American Slavery*, 32. O'Connell was quoting Psalm 137, verses 5 and 6; he is quoted in Allen, *Invention of the White Race*, 1:170.

91. *Liberator*, Nov. 24, 1843. On Kossuth, see Louis Ruchames, ed., *Letters of William Lloyd Garrison*, vol. 4, *From Disunionism to the Brink of War, 1850–1860* (Cambridge, MA: Belknap Press of Harvard University Press, 1976), 97–199.

CHAPTER 4. "THE BLACK O'CONNELL OF THE UNITED STATES"

1. See, for example, Wendell Phillips, "Daniel O'Connell," an address delivered in 1875, the hundredth anniversary of O'Connell's birth, in Phillips, *Speeches, Lectures, and Letters*, 2nd ser. (Boston: Lee and Shepard, 1905), 384–417. The epigraphs are from the following: "Letters to Antislavery Workers and Agencies," pt. 1, "Frederick Douglass," *Journal of Negro History* 10 (October 1925), 656 (Douglass was writing to William Lloyd Garrison from Ireland on January 1, 1846), and Douglas C. Riach, "O'Connell and Slavery," in Donal McCartney, ed., *The World of Daniel O'Connell* (Dublin: Mercier Press, 1980), 176.

2. Parts of this chapter appeared, in a somewhat different form, in Bruce Nelson, " 'My Countrymen Are All Mankind,' " *Field Day Review* 4 (2008), 260–73.

3. Walter M. Merrill, ed., *The Letters of William Lloyd Garrison*, vol. 3, *No Union with Slaveholders, 1841–1849* (Cambridge, MA: Belknap Press of Harvard University Press, 1973), 56; Clare Taylor, ed., *British and American Abolitionists: An Episode in Transatlantic Understanding* (Edinburgh: Edinburgh University Press, 1974), 175.

4. William Edward Ward, "Charles Lenox Remond: Black Abolitionist, 1838–1873" (PhD diss., Clark University, 1977), 105–8, quoted on 105; Frederick Douglass, *My Bondage and My Freedom* (1855; repr., New York: Penguin Books, 2003), 15.

5. "Letters to Antislavery Workers and Agencies," 662.

6. W. A. Hart, "Africans in Eighteenth-Century Ireland," *Irish Historical Studies* 33 (May 2002), 19–32, quoted on 24; personal communication from William A. Hart, Oct. 31, 2006.

7. Nini Rodgers, "Ireland and the Black Atlantic in the Eighteenth Century," *Irish Historical Studies* 23 (November 2000), 188–89; Adam Hochschild, *Bury the Chains: Prophets and Rebels in the Fight to Free an Empire's Slaves* (Boston: Houghton Mifflin, 2005), 172.

8. Nini Rodgers, "Equiano in Belfast: A Study of the Anti-slavery Ethos in a Northern Town," *Slavery and Abolition* 18 (August 1997), 73–89; Olaudah Equiano, *The Interesting Narrative and Other Writings*, ed. Vincent Carretta (New York: Penguin Books, 1995); Vincent Carretta, *Equiano, the African: Biography of a Self-Made Man* (Athens: University of Georgia Press, 2005); Robin Blackburn, "The True Story of Equiano," *Nation* 281 (Nov. 21, 2005), 33–37.

9. Henry Louis Gates Jr. and William L. Andrews, eds., *Pioneers of the Black Atlantic: Five Slave Narratives from the Enlightenment, 1772–1815* (Washington, DC: Counterpoint, 1998).

10. Graham Russell Hodges, introduction to Hodges, ed., *Black Itinerants of the Gospel: The Narratives of John Jea and George White* (Madison, WI: Madison House, 1993), 18–27, quoted on 23.

11. See, especially, Irene Whelan, *The Bible War in Ireland: The "Second Reformation" and the Polarization of Protestant-Catholic Relations, 1800–1840* (Dublin: Lilliput Press, 2005), quoted on 94; and Stewart J. Brown, "The New Reformation Movement in the Church of Ireland, 1801–29," in Brown and David W. Miller, eds., *Piety and Power in Ireland, 1760–1960: Essays in Honor of Emmet Larkin* (Notre Dame, IN: University of Notre Dame Press, 2000), 180–208.

12. John Jea, "The Life, History, and Unparalleled Sufferings of John Jea, the African Preacher," in Hodges, ed., *Black Itinerants*, 89–163, especially 147–53, quoted on 149, 150.

13. According to Irene Whelan, "A deep-seated anti-Catholicism based on antagonism to the institutional forms and doctrinal beliefs of the Church of Rome" was "one of the central elements of the evangelical world view." Whelan, *Bible War in Ireland*, 129.

14. Over a period of many years, David Brion Davis has played a singular role in illuminating the relationship between Quakers and the antislavery impulse. See Davis, *The Problem of Slavery in the Age of Revolution, 1770–1823* (Ithaca, NY: Cornell University Press, 1975), 213–54. On Ireland, in particular, see Richard S. Harrison, "Irish Quaker Perspectives on the Anti-slavery Movement," *Journal of the Friends' Historical Society* 56 (1993), 106–25.

15. Richard S. Harrison, *Richard Davis Webb: Dublin Quaker Printer* (Skibbereen, Ireland: Red Barn Publishing, 1993), 2. An obituary published after Richard Davis Webb's death in 1872 maintained that "his ancestors, like those of most of the Irish Quakers, had come from England in the armies of Cromwell or William III (1650, 1690), and remained as farmers on confiscated lands." "The Late Richard D. Webb," unidentified press clipping, Boston, 1872, ms. 1745, Alfred Webb Miscellaneous, National Library of Ireland (NLI).

16. Hannah Maria Wigham, *A Christian Philanthropist of Dublin: A Memoir of Richard Allen* (London: Hodder and Stoughton, 1886), 9.

17. Anthony J. Barker, *Captain Charles Stuart: Anglo-American Abolitionist* (Baton Rouge: Louisiana State University Press, 1986), 46–48; Harrison, "Irish Quaker Perspectives," 112; Douglas Cameron Riach, "Ireland and the Campaign against American Slavery, 1830–1860"(PhD diss., University of Edinburgh, 1975), 39.

18. Barker, *Captain Charles Stuart*, 46.

19. Daniel O'Connell, "To the Ministers and Office-Bearers of the Wesleyan Methodist Societies in Manchester," London, July 6, 1839, in Daniel O'Connell, ed., *A Full Report of the Proceedings of the Great Meeting of the Catholics of London, Held at Freemason's Hall, on the Fifteenth Day of July, 1839, with an Address to the English People, and the Letters to the Wesleyan Methodists by Mr. O'Connell* (London: Thomas Jones, 1839), 40. See also D. N. Hempton, "The Methodist Crusade in Ireland, 1795–1845," *Irish Historical Studies* 22 (March 1980), 33–48. According to Hempton, "The true significance of Irish Methodism in the first half of the nineteenth century lay . . . in its front line position in the great evangelical crusade against Roman Catholicism." Ibid., 35.

20. Ward, "Charles Lenox Remond," 2, 6–8, quoted on 11, 12.

21. Ibid., 21–22, 27, quoted on 106; Robert C. Dick, *Black Protest: Issues and Tactics* (Westport, CT: Greenwood Press, 1974), 206–9, quoted on 208; Benjamin Quarles, *Black Abolitionists* (New York: Oxford University Press, 1969), quoted on 133.

22. Thompson, quoted in Barker, *Captain Charles Stuart*, 201. See also R.J.M. Blackett, "'And There Shall Be No More Sea': William Lloyd Garrison and the Transatlantic Abolitionist Movement" (unpublished paper, April 2006, in author's possession). Thompson, the son of a Methodist bank clerk in Liverpool, became the leading Garrisonian in Britain. His greatest impact was among Scottish abolitionists in Glasgow and Edinburgh.

23. Colver, quoted in John A. Collins, *Right and Wrong among the Abolitionists of the United States; or, The Objects, Principles, and Measures of the Original American Anti-Slavery Society, Unchanged* (Glasgow: George Gallie, 1841), 46; *Liberator*, May 21, 1841.

24. C. Peter Ripley et al., eds., *The Black Abolitionist Papers*, vol. 1, *The British Isles, 1830–1865* (Chapel Hill: University of North Carolina Press, 1985), 97; *Liberator*, Sept. 24, 1841.

25. "The Late Richard D. Webb"; Wendell Phillips Garrison and Francis Jackson Garrison, *William Lloyd Garrison, 1805–1879: The Story of His Life Told by His Children*, vol. 2, *1835–1840* (New York: Century, 1885), 403; Harrison, *Richard Davis Webb*, 26–27.

26. *Liberator*, Sept. 24, 1841.

27. Ibid., Sept. 10, Nov. 26, 1841.

28. James Clyde Sellman, "Douglass, Frederick," in Kwame Anthony Appiah and Henry Louis Gates Jr., eds., *Africana: The Encyclopedia of the African and African American Experience* (New York: Basic/Civitas Books, 1999), quoted on 627.

29. Douglass's coconspirator, the free Negro Anna Murray, had joined him in New York, and they were married there. During their forty-four years of marriage, she continued to live in relative obscurity, far from the glare of public life. Benjamin Quarles, *Frederick Douglass* (1948; repr., New York: Da Capo, 1997), 1–11; William S. McFeely, *Frederick Douglass* (New York: W. W. Norton, 1991), 3–73.

30. McFeely, *Frederick Douglass*, 77.

31. Ibid., 77–114; Quarles, *Frederick Douglass*, 11–30, quoted on 20, 27; John Stauffer, *The Black Hearts of Men: Radical Abolitionists and the Transformation of Race* (Cambridge, MA: Harvard University Press, 2001), quoted on 159.

32. Quarles, *Frederick Douglass*, 34–37; McFeely, *Frederick Douglass*, 114–18. "I am here . . . to avoid the scent of the blood hounds of America," Douglass told an audience in Cork in October 1845. John W. Blassingame, ed., *The Frederick Douglass Papers*, ser. 1, *Speeches, Debates, and Interviews*, vol. 1, *1841–46* (New Haven, CT: Yale University Press, 1979), 40.

33. Ellen M. Oldham, "Irish Support of the Abolitionist Movement," *Boston Public Library Quarterly* 10 (October 1958), quoted on 178; Blassingame, ed., *Frederick Douglass Papers*, ser. 1, 1:45, 37, 39.

34. Blassingame, ed., *Frederick Douglass Papers*, ser. 1, vol. 1, quoted on 42, 41, 44.

35. Ibid., 56; "Letters to Antislavery Workers and Agencies," 656–57. For an assessment of the significance of Douglass's experience abroad for his personal and political development, see Benjamin Soskis, "Heroic Exile: The Transatlantic Development of Frederick Douglass, 1845–1847" (senior honors thesis, Yale University, 1997), available online at http://www.Yale.edu/glc/soskis/cont.htm (accessed April 27, 2004).

36. Blassingame, ed., *Frederick Douglass Papers*, ser. 1, 1:222.

37. James. S. Donnelly Jr., *The Great Irish Potato Famine* (Phoenix Mill, UK: Sutton Publishing, 2001); Cormac Ó Gráda, *Black '47 and Beyond: The Great Irish Famine in History, Economy, and Memory* (Princeton, NJ: Princeton University Press, 1999); Peter Gray, *The Irish Famine* (London: Thames and Hudson, 1995).

38. "Letters to Antislavery Workers and Agencies," 673, 674, 675.

39. *Waterford Freeman*, Sept. 10, 1845, quoted in Blassingame, ed., *Frederick Douglass Papers*, ser. 1, 1:77n1.

40. John C. Cobden, *The White Slaves of England* (Auburn, NY: Derby and Miller, 1853), 284, 361–62.

41. "Letters to Antislavery Workers and Agencies," 672. On another occasion, however, he told Richard Webb that "my mission to this land is purely an Anti-Slavery one. . . . I only claim to be a man of one idea." Taylor, ed., *British and American Abolitionists*, 241.

42. Blassingame, ed., *Frederick Douglass Papers*, ser. 1, 1:77–78, 93.

43. McFeely, *Frederick Douglass*, 119–30; Douglas C. Riach, "Richard Davis Webb and Antislavery in Ireland," in Lewis Perry and Michael Fellman, eds., *Antislavery Reconsidered: New Perspectives on the Abolitionists* (Baton Rouge: Louisiana State University Press, 1979), 151; Douglas Charles Stange, *British Unitarians against American Slavery, 1833–65* (Rutherford, NJ: Fairleigh Dickinson University Press, 1984), 73; Alfred Webb, quoted in Wigham, *A Christian Philanthropist of Dublin*, 14. See Alfred Webb, *The Autobiography of a Quaker Nationalist*, ed. Marie-Louise Legg (Cork: Cork University Press, 1999), 17–32, for an evocative recollection of the world of the Dublin Quaker reformers.

44. Taylor, ed., *British and American Abolitionists*, 95, 97, 100, 113; Wigham, *A Christian Philanthropist of Dublin*, 17.

45. Merrill, ed., *Letters of William Lloyd Garrison,* 3:129–30; Wigham, *Christian Philanthropist of Dublin*, 39.

46. Maurice J. Wigham, *The Irish Quakers: A Short History of the Religious Society of Friends in Ireland* (Dublin: Historical Committee of the Religious Society of Friends in Ireland, 1992), 67–70, 80–84; Harrison, "Irish Quaker Perspectives," 107–10, 115–16; Riach, "Richard Davis Webb," 153–56; Frederick B. Tolles, introduction to Tolles, ed., *Slavery and "The Woman Question": Lucretia Mott's Diary of Her Visit to Great Britain to Attend the World's Anti-Slavery Convention of 1840* (Haverford, PA, and London: Friends' Historical Association [U.S.A.] and Friends' Historical Society [UK], 1952), 4–6, quoted on 4.

47. Harrison, "Irish Quaker Perspectives," 113; Taylor, ed., *British and American Abolitionists*, 120; Hannah Webb, quoted in Riach, "Richard Davis Webb," 156.

48. *A Letter from James Cannings Fuller to Joseph Gurney* (Dublin: Webb and Chapman, 1843), 10.

49. *Liberator*, Oct. 24, 1845; Harrison, "Irish Quaker Perspectives," 120; Riach, "Richard Davis Webb," 154–55; Taylor, ed., *British and American Abolitionists*, 530; Riach, "Ireland and the Campaign against American Slavery," 71.

50. *Liberator*, Sept. 10, 1841, Nov. 28, 1845; Blassingame, ed., *Frederick Douglass Papers,* ser. 1, 1:44; R.J.M. Blackett, *Building an Antislavery Wall: Black Americans in the Atlantic Abolitionist Movement* (Baton Rouge: Louisiana State University Press, 1983), 82–91, 95.

51. McFeely, *Frederick Douglass*, 124. Even though Father Mathew was unusually ecumenical in outlook and in his network of relationships, he was compelled to admit that

in spite of his strenuous efforts to attract Protestants to the cause, "the teetotalers of Ireland are a Roman Catholic body." John F. Quinn, *Father Mathew's Crusade: Temperance in Nineteenth-Century Ireland and Irish America* (Amherst: University of Massachusetts Press, 2002), 62 (quoted), 126; Colm Kerrigan, *Father Mathew and the Irish Temperance Movement, 1838–1849* (Cork: Cork University Press, 1992), 107.

52. *Limerick Reporter*, Nov. 11, 1845, quoted in Blassingame, ed., *Frederick Douglass Papers*, ser. 1, 1:77.

53. Alfred Webb, "An Important Letter upon an Important Subject," press clipping, 1893, ms. 1746, Alfred Webb Miscellaneous.

54. Ibid.

55. Blassingame, ed., *Frederick Douglass Papers*, ser. 1, 1:71; Blackett, *Building an Antislavery Wall*, 106; Blassingame, ed., *Frederick Douglass Papers, ser. 1, Speeches, Debates, and Interviews*, vol. 2, *1847–1854* (New Haven, CT: Yale University Press, 1982), 521.

56. "Letters to Antislavery Workers and Agencies," 675 (emphasis in original).

57. See Earl F. Niehaus, *The Irish in New Orleans, 1800–1860* (Baton Rouge: Louisiana State University Press, 1965), 48–49. Niehaus quotes a steamboat pilot who explained why slaves were not used as stokers on "worn-out" steamboats: "Every time a boiler bursts they would lose so many dollars'-worth-of-slaves; whereas by getting Irishmen at a dollar a-day they pay for the article as they get it, and if it is blown up, they get another."

58. Donnelly, *Great Irish Potato Famine*, 171, 178; Blassingame, ed., *Frederick Douglass Papers*, ser. 1, 2:258–59 (emphasis in original).

59. Ó Gráda, *Black '47 and Beyond*, 59–66, 87–89; Donnelly, *Great Irish Potato Famine*, 26, 144–56, 185; Ignatius Murphy, *A Starving People: Life and Death in West Clare, 1845–1851* (Dublin: Irish Academic Press, 1996), 48–76; Kevin Whelan, "Bitter Harvest," *Boston College Magazine* 55 (Winter 1996), 25.

60. Taylor, ed., *British and American Abolitionists*, 199; Donnelly, *Great Irish Potato Famine*, 202–7; Thomas Keneally, *The Great Shame: And the Triumph of the Irish in the English-Speaking World* (New York: Nan A. Talese/Doubleday, 1999), 141–79, quoted on 157.

61. James Brewer Stewart, "Boston, Abolition, and the Atlantic World, 1820–1861," in Donald M. Jacobs, ed., *Courage and Conscience: Black and White Abolitionists in Boston* (Bloomington: Indiana University Press, 1993), 101–25, quoted on 110; Hodges, introduction to Hodges, ed., *Black Itinerants*, 30.

62. Shane White, " 'It Was a Proud Day': African Americans, Festivals, and Parades in the North, 1741–1834," *Journal of American History* 81 (June 1994), 41; Hodges, introduction to Hodges, ed., *Black Itinerants*, 3–9, 29–30, quoted on 29.

63. Blassingame, ed., *Frederick Douglass Papers*, ser. 1, 2:48.

64. Robert James Scally, *The End of Hidden Ireland: Rebellion, Famine, and Emigration* (New York: Oxford University Press, 1995), 195–216, quoted on 205.

65. *Liberator*, Dec. 12, 1845; Blassingame, ed., *Frederick Douglass Papers*, ser. 1, 2:24–25, 27.

66. Riach, "Daniel O'Connell and American Anti-slavery," 19.

67. Blassingame, ed., *Frederick Douglass Papers*, ser. 1, 2:60.

68. L. Fogarty, *Father John Kenyon: A Patriot Priest of Forty-Eight* (Dublin: Mahon's Printing Works, 1921), 9, 23, 25, 87.

69. *Liberator*, July 25, May 2, 1845; Fogarty, *Father John Kenyon*, 73–74.

70. Keneally, *Great Shame*, 98–99, 142–48; P. A. Sillard, *Life and Letters of John Martin, with Sketches of Thomas Devin Reilly, Father Kenyon, and Other "Young Irelanders,"* 2nd ed. (Dublin: James Duffy, 1901), 41; P. S. O'Hegarty, *John Mitchel: An Appreciation, with Some Account of Young Ireland* (Dublin: Maunsel, 1917), 86.

71. Robert Kee, *The Green Flag: A History of Irish Nationalism* (1972; repr., London: Penguin Books, 2000), 192; *Liberator*, April 28, 1843; O'Hegarty, *John Mitchel*, 132; John Newsinger, "John Mitchel and Irish Nationalism," *Literature and History* 6 (1980), 182–200, quoted on 189; Oliver MacDonagh, *The Emancipist: Daniel O'Connell, 1830–47* (New York: St. Martin's Press, 1989), 19–22, quoted on 21; Kevin Whelan, "The Revisionist Debate in Ireland," *boundary 2*, 31 (Spring 2004), 195–97; Thomas Carlyle, "Occasional Discourse on the Negro Question," *Fraser's Magazine* 40 (February 1849), accessed online: *http://cepa.newschool.edu/het/texts/carlyle/carlodnq.htm (accessed April 29, 2004)*.

72. William Dillon, *Life of John Mitchel* (London: Kegan, Paul, Trench, 1888), 2:104–6, 112–13; O'Hegarty, *John Mitchel*, 85–86; Newsinger, "John Mitchel and Irish Nationalism," 184; Christopher Morash, *Writing the Irish Famine* (Oxford: Clarendon Press, 1995), 63–64; and, especially, James Quinn, "John Mitchel and the Rejection of the Nineteenth Century," *Éire-Ireland* 38 (Summer/Fall 2003), 90–108, quoted on 96.

73. Dillon, *Life of John Mitchel*, 2:54–55, 101–7, quoted on 105–6, 101.

74. Ibid., 43–44.

75. John Mitchel, *Jail Journal; or, Five Years in British Prisons* (New York: Published at the Office of the "Citizen," 1854), 170.

76. Carlyle, "Occasional Discourse on the Negro Question"; Julian Symons, *Thomas Carlyle: The Life and Ideas of a Prophet* (London: Victor Gollancz, 1952), 334–61, 370–71.

77. Mitchel, *Jail Journal*, 170, 175.

78. Keneally, *Great Shame*, 385, 391–92; Mitchel, quoted in Quinn, "John Mitchel," 102.

79. Charles Gavan Duffy, *Conversations with Carlyle*, new ed. (London: Cassell, 1896), 117. For a scholarly perspective on Duffy and his career, see Steve Knowlton, "The Enigma of Charles Gavan Duffy: Looking for Clues in Australia," *Éire-Ireland* 31 (Fall/Winter 1996), 189–208.

80. Richard Davis, *Revolutionary Imperialist: William Smith O'Brien, 1803–1864* (Dublin: Lilliput Press, 1998), 347n90.

81. William Smith O'Brien, *Principles of Government; or, Meditations in Exile* (Dublin: James Duffy, 1856), 2:167.

82. Davis, *Revolutionary Imperialist*, 344–48, 361; Keneally, *Great Shame*, 74.

83. R. R. Madden, "Necessity of Separating the Irish in America from the Sin of Slavery," in *Poems by a Slave in the Island of Cuba, Recently Liberated, translated from the Spanish by R. R. Madden, M.D.* (London: Thomas Ward, 1840), 137, 135–36; Nini Rodgers, "Richard Robert Madden: An Irish Anti-slavery Activist in the Americas," in Oonagh Walsh, ed., *Ireland Abroad: Politics and Professions in the Nineteenth Century* (Dublin: Four Courts Press, 2003), 129–30.

84. Madden, "Necessity of Separating the Irish," 136–37; R. R. Madden, "Memorial Addressed to the Catholic Archbishops and Bishops in Ireland, in Synod Assembled," in *Poems by a Slave in the Island of Cuba*, 146.

85. John F. Quinn, "'Three Cheers for the Abolitionist Pope!': American Reaction to Gregory XVI's Condemnation of the Slave Trade, 1840–1860," *Catholic Historical Review* 90 (January 2004), 67–93; Madden, "Memorial Addressed to the Catholic Archbishops and Bishops," 147.

86. Madden, "Necessity of Separating the Irish," 136; León Ó Broin, "R. R. Madden, Historian of the United Irishmen," *Irish University Review* 2 (Spring 1972), 20–33.

87. Oliver MacDonagh, *The Hereditary Bondsman: Daniel O'Connell, 1775–1829* (New York: St. Martin's Press, 1988), 125–31, quoted on 130; Whelan, *Bible War in Ireland*, quoted on 127.

88. Riach, "Richard Davis Webb," 162; Taylor, ed., *British and American Abolitionists*, 157; *Liberator*, March 18, 1842.

89. Emmet Larkin, "The Devotional Revolution in Ireland," *American Historical Review* 77 (June 1972), 625–52; Whelan, *Bible War in Ireland*.

90. John R. G. Hassard, *Life of John Hughes, First Archbishop of New York* (1866; repr., New York: Arno Press and the New York Times, 1966), 14, 18–20, 42–43, 215–16, 434–40; John T. McGreevy, *Catholicism and American Freedom: A History* (New York: W. W. Norton, 2003), quoted on 54; Charles R. Morris, *American Catholic: The Saints and Sinners Who Built America's Most Powerful Church* (New York: Times Books, 1997), 79. See also Albon P. Man Jr., "The Church and the New York City Draft Riots of 1863," *Records of the American Catholic Historical Society of Philadelphia* 62 (March 1951), 33–50.

91. Richard Shaw, *Dagger John: The Unquiet Life and Times of Archbishop John Hughes of New York* (New York: Paulist Press, 1977), 339; Hassard, *Life of John Hughes*, quoted on 437.

92. Shaw, *Dagger John*, 345–53, quoted on 352.

93. Emmet Larkin, *The Consolidation of the Roman Catholic Church in Ireland, 1860–1870* (Chapel Hill: University of North Carolina Press, 1987), Cullen quoted on 303, 150–51.

94. Samuel Haughton, *Memoir of James Haughton, with Extracts from His Private and Public Letters* (Dublin: Ponsonby, 1877), 80; Cobden, *White Slaves of England*, 6; Hassard, *Life of John Hughes*, 436.

95. Taylor, ed., *British and American Abolitionists*, 175; John T. Noonan Jr., "Development in Moral Doctrine," *Theological Studies* 54 (December 1993), 664–67, 673–75, quoted on 675.

96. Soskis, "Heroic Exile."

97. Edward T. O'Donnell, " 'The Scattered Debris of the Irish Nation': The Famine Irish and New York City, 1845–55," in E. Margaret Crawford, ed., *The Hungry Stream: Essays on Emigration and Famine* (Belfast: Institute of Irish Studies, Queens University of Belfast, 1997), 52; Donnelly, *Great Irish Potato Famine*, 182 (quoted); Merrill, ed., *Letters of William Lloyd Garrison*, 3:92.

98. Blassingame, ed., *Frederick Douglass Papers*, ser. 1, quoted on 2:241.

99. John W. Blassingame and John R. McKivigan, eds., *The Frederick Douglass Papers*, ser. 1, *Speeches, Debates, and Interviews*, vol. 4, *1864–80* (New Haven, CT: Yale University Press, 1991), 250; ibid., vol. 5, *1881–95* (New Haven, CT: Yale University Press, 1992), 116.

100. Ibid., 5:116, 273–78, quoted on 274–75, 276, 277; Douglass, *My Bondage and My Freedom*, 15.

101. Blassingame and McKivigan, eds., *Frederick Douglass Papers*, ser. 1, vol. 5, 277.

CHAPTER 5: "FROM THE CABINS OF CONNEMARA TO THE KRAALS OF KAFFIRLAND"

1. Parts of this chapter appeared, in a somewhat different form, in Bruce Nelson, "Irish Americans, Irish Nationalism, and the 'Social' Question, 1916–1923," *boundary 2,*

31 (Spring 2004), 147–78, and Bruce Nelson, " 'From the Cabins of Connemara to the Kraals of Kaffirland': Irish Nationalism, the British Empire, and the 'Boer Fight for Freedom,' " in David T. Gleeson, ed., *The Irish in the Atlantic World* (Columbia: University of South Carolina Press, 2010), 154–75. The epigraph is from "The West Awake!!!" (placard announcing the "Great Tenant Right Meeting in Irishtown," County Mayo, April 1879), in T. W. Moody, *Davitt and Irish Revolution, 1846–1882* (Oxford: Clarendon Press, 1981), 289.

    2. See Timothy Guinnane, *The Vanishing Irish: Households, Migration, and the Rural Economy in Ireland, 1850–1914* (Princeton, NJ: Princeton University Press, 1997), 101–4.

    3. Eric Stokes, "Milnerism," *Historical Journal* 5, no. 1 (1962), quoted on 48; John Benyon, " 'Intermediate' Imperialism and the Test of Empire: Milner's 'Excentric' High Commission in South Africa," in Donal Lowry, ed., *The South African War Reappraised* (Manchester, UK: Manchester University Press, 2000), quoted on 86.

    4. Conor Cruise O'Brien, *Parnell and His Party, 1880–90* (Oxford: Clarendon Press, 1957), 2–3, quoted on 2 (emphasis in original).

    5. *Irish World*, Oct. 14, 1916.

    6. Alvin Jackson, "Ireland, the Union, and the Empire, 1800–1960," in Kevin Kenny, ed., *Ireland and the British Empire* (Oxford: Oxford University Press, 2004), 123. See also Keith Jeffery, ed., *"An Irish Empire"? Aspects of Ireland and the British Empire* (Manchester, UK: Manchester University Press, 1996); Stephen Howe, *Ireland and Empire: Colonial Legacies in Irish History and Culture*, 2nd ed. (Oxford: Oxford University Press, 2002); Terence McDonough, ed., *Was Ireland a Colony? Economics, Politics and Culture in Nineteenth-Century Ireland* (Dublin: Irish Academic Press, 2005); William J. Smyth, *Map-Making, Landscapes and Memory: A Geography of Colonial and Early Modern Ireland, c. 1530–1750* (Cork: Cork University Press, 2006); the essays on Ireland in William Roger Louis et al., eds., *The Oxford History of the British Empire*, 5 vols. (Oxford: Oxford University Press, 1998–99), and in Kenny, ed., *Ireland and the British Empire*.

    7. Andrew S. Thompson, "The Language of Imperialism and the Meaning of Empire: Imperial Discourse in British Politics, 1895–1914," *Journal of British Studies* 36 (April 1997), 147–77, quoted on 174, 172.

    8. Daniel O'Connell, "Speech at a Meeting of the Aborigines Protection Society," *Liberator*, Aug. 7, 1840.

    9. At the time, and for generations thereafter, it was common to refer to the conflict as the Anglo-Boer War, or simply the Boer War. But historian Peter Warwick denies that it was only an "Anglo-Boer struggle." He argues that "in a real sense it was a 'South African war,' a conflict that directly touched the lives of hundreds of thousands of black people in whose midst the familiar dramas of the war unfolded. The war was fought in a region where whites made up only a fifth of the total population." Peter Warwick, *Black People and the South African War, 1899–1902* (Cambridge: Cambridge University Press, 1983), 4; and see his chapter "Myth of a White Man's War," in Warwick, ed., *The South African War: The Anglo-Boer War, 1899–1902* (Harlow, UK: Longman, 1980), 6–27.

    10. Scott B. Cook, "The Irish Raj: Social Origins and Careers of Irishmen in the Indian Civil Service, 1855–1914," *Journal of Social History* 20 (Spring 1987), 509.

    11. Peter Karsten, "Irish Soldiers in the British Army, 1792–1922: Suborned or Subordinate?" *Journal of Social History* 17 (Fall 1983), 36; Thomas Bartlett, "The Irish Soldier in India, 1750–1947," in Michael Holmes and Denis Holmes, eds., *Ireland and India: Connections, Comparisons, Contrasts* (Dublin: Folens, 1997), 16; Keith Jeffery, "The Irish Military Tradition and the British Empire," in Jeffery, ed., *"An Irish Empire"?* 94–95.

12. Cook, "Irish Raj," 520.

13. C. Desmond Greaves, *The Life and Times of James Connolly* (1961; repr., London: Lawrence and Wishart, 1986), 20; E. M. Spiers, "Army Organisation and Society in the Nineteenth Century," in Thomas Bartlett and Keith Jeffery, eds., *A Military History of Ireland* (Cambridge: Cambridge University Press, 1996), 335–57, especially 347 (photograph), 349.

14. Greaves, *Life and Times of James Connolly*, 17, 19–20, 24–25; Donal Nevin, *James Connolly: A Full Life* (Dublin: Gill and Macmillan, 2005), 5–7, 11–20.

15. Donal P. McCracken, *The Irish Pro-Boers, 1877–1902* (Johannesburg: Perskor, 1988), quoted on 38; Alan O'Day, "Butt, Isaac (1813–1879)," in H.C.G. Matthew and Brian Harrison, eds., *Oxford Dictionary of National Biography* (Oxford: Oxford University Press, 2004), http://www.oxforddnb.com/view/article/4222 (accessed Dec. 19, 2006); H. V. Brasted, "Irish Nationalism and the British Empire in the Late Nineteenth Century," in Oliver MacDonagh, W. F. Mandle, and Pauric Travers, eds., *Irish Culture and Nationalism, 1750–1950* (Dublin: Gill and Macmillan, 1983), 85. Brasted points out that Butt's view of Ireland's relationship to the empire lacked "any notion of universal liberty. The rights Butt appealed to were those of the conquerors."

16. Brasted, "Irish Nationalism and the British Empire," 85–88; Paul Townend, "Between Two Worlds: Irish Nationalism and Imperial Crisis, 1878–1880," *Past and Present* 194 (February 2007), 139–74, quoted on 172; Joseph P. Finnan, *John Redmond and Irish Unity, 1912–1918* (Syracuse, NY: Syracuse University Press, 2004), quoted on 159.

17. Finnan, *John Redmond and Irish Unity*, 167.

18. Jonathan Schneer, *London 1900: The Imperial Metropolis* (New Haven, CT: Yale University Press, 1999), 181–82; Angela Bourke, *The Burning of Bridget Cleary: A True Story* (London: Pimlico, 1999), 114–29, quoted on 115, 125; F.S.L. Lyons, *John Dillon: A Biography* (London: Routledge and Kegan Paul, 1968), quoted on 105; Finnan, *John Redmond and Irish Unity*, quoted on 162.

19. F. Hugh O'Donnell, *A History of the Irish Parliamentary Party* (London: Longmans, Green, 1910), 1:277–78; Howard Brasted, "Indian Nationalist Development and the Influence of Irish Home Rule, 1870–1886," *Modern Asian Studies* 14 (1980), 37–63.

20. Howe, *Ireland and Empire*, 43–49; Townend, "Between Two Worlds," 139–74.

21. Michael Davitt, "Synopsis of Data for an Autobiography" (Sept. 12, 1881), in Davitt, *Jottings in Solitary*, ed. Carla King (Dublin: University College Dublin Press, 2003), 6; Moody, *Davitt and Irish Revolution*, 8–9.

22. Moody, *Davitt and Irish Revolution*; Carla King, *Michael Davitt* (Dundalk, Ireland: Dundalgan Press, 1999); Donald E. Jordan Jr., *Land and Popular Politics in Ireland: County Mayo from the Plantation to the Land War* (Cambridge: Cambridge University Press, 1994), 199–229, quoted on 214; Edward T. O'Donnell, "'Though Not an Irishman': Henry George and the American Irish," *American Journal of Economics and Sociology* 56 (October 1997), 407–19, quoted on 416.

23. Ford founded the paper as the *Irish World* and changed its name to the *Irish World and American Industrial Liberator* in 1878.

24. Eric Foner, "Class, Ethnicity, and Radicalism in the Gilded Age: The Land League and Irish-America," in *Politics and Ideology in the Age of the Civil War* (New York: Oxford University Press, 1980), 150–200, quoted on 159, 161, 166; James Paul Rodechko, *Patrick Ford and His Search for America: A Case Study of Irish-American Journalism, 1870–1913* (New York: Arno Press, 1976), 186; *Irish World*, Jan. 8, 1881.

Fall River, Massachusetts, was a classic textile town with a large Irish immigrant population.

25. Although Henry George was neither Irish nor Irish American, his reform epic, *Progress and Poverty* (first published in 1879), had a major impact on Davitt and other Irish radicals. From October 1881 to October 1882, he lived and worked in Ireland as a correspondent for the *Irish World*. Altogether, he visited Ireland four times during the 1880s. See O'Donnell, "'Though Not an Irishman,'" and Fintan Lane, *The Origins of Modern Irish Socialism, 1881–1896* (Cork: Cork University Press, 1997), 65–90.

26. Rodechko, *Patrick Ford*, 187; and see David Brundage, "Irish Land and American Workers: Class and Ethnicity in Denver, Colorado," in Dirk Hoerder, ed., *"Struggle a Hard Battle": Essays on Working-Class Immigrants* (DeKalb: Northern Illinois University Press, 1986), 46–67.

27. Brasted, "Irish Nationalism and the British Empire," 88–89, 96–97; Niall Whelehan, "Skirmishing, the Irish World, and Empire, 1876–86," *Éire-Ireland* 42 (Spring/Summer 2007), 180–200, quoted on 192 (emphasis in original).

28. Foner, "Class, Ethnicity, and Radicalism," 163, 191, 167; Terry Golway, *Irish Rebel: John Devoy and America's Fight for Ireland's Freedom* (New York: St. Martin's Press, 1998), 1–12, 106, 107 (quoted), 143, 208; Rodechko, *Patrick Ford*, 84, 188–89. Although he remained an outspoken anti-imperialist, Ford's politics shifted to the right in the mid-1880s, especially in the aftermath of the Haymarket bombing of 1886 and the "red scare" it provoked. For a brief analysis, see Nelson, "Irish Americans, Irish Nationalism, and the 'Social' Question," 156–57.

29. Townend, "Between Two Worlds," quoted on 152; Moody, *Davitt and Irish Revolution*, 289.

30. Fintan Lane, "Michael Davitt and the Irish Working Class," in Fintan Lane and Andrew G. Newby, eds., *Michael Davitt: New Perspectives* (Dublin: Irish Academic Press, 2009), 79–98, quoted on 95; Moody, *Davitt and Irish Revolution*, 534–58, especially 546.

31. King, *Michael Davitt*, 45–47, 60–62, 70–72; Laurence Marley, *Michael Davitt: Freelance Radical and Frondeur* (Dublin: Four Courts Press, 2007), 222–65; T. W. Moody, "Michael Davitt and the British Labour Movement, 1882–1906," *Transactions of the Royal Historical Society*, 5th ser., 3 (1953), 53–76, quoted on 76.

32. Anne Kane, "Narratives of Nationalism: Constructing Irish National Identity during the Land War, 1879–82," *National Identities* 2 (November 2000), 258; Declan Kiberd, *Inventing Ireland: The Literature of the Modern Nation* (London: Jonathan Cape, 1995), 9–15.

33. Michael Davitt, "Davitt's Speech of Resignation from the House of Commons, 25 October 1899," in Davitt, *Collected Writings*, vol. 2, *Pamphlets, Speeches, and Articles, 1889–1906* (London: Thoemmes Press, 2001; Tokyo: Edition Synapse, 2001), 8; *Irish World*, Nov. 4, 1899.

34. See Bernard K. Mbenga, "Forced Labour in the Pilanesberg: The Flogging of Chief Kgamanyane by Commandant Paul Kruger, Saulspoort, April 1870," *Journal of Southern African Studies* 23 (March 1997), 127–40.

35. Preben Kaarsholm, "Pro-Boers," in Raphael Samuel, ed., *Patriotism: The Making and Unmaking of British National Identity* (London: Routledge, 1989), 1:110–26.

36. See Robert Ross, *Status and Respectability in the Cape Colony, 1750–1870* (Cambridge: Cambridge University Press, 1999), 55–60; Isabel Hofmeyr, "Building a Nation from Words: Afrikaans Language, Literature and Ethnic Identity, 1902–1924," in

Shula Marks and Stanley Trapido, eds., *The Politics of Race, Class and Nationalism in Twentieth-Century South Africa* (London: Longman, 1987), 95–123, especially 96; and Hermann Giliomee, *The Afrikaners: Biography of a People* (Charlottesville: University of Virginia Press, 2003), 52–53, 215–19. Speakers of "pure" Dutch regarded Afrikaans as the language of "the most uncivilised Hottentot and the meanest Negro." Thus the task of Afrikaner nationalists was to "whiten" Afrikaans, to rescue it from the colored "lower orders." Ross, *Status and Respectability in the Cape Colony*, quoted on 59; Achmat Davids, "The 'Coloured' Image of Afrikaans in Nineteenth Century Cape Town," *Kronos* 17, no. 1 (1990), 36–47.

37. Olive Schreiner, "The Wanderings of the Boer," in *Thoughts on South Africa* (1923; repr., Parklands, South Africa: A. D. Donker, 1992), 132–33. Schreiner wrote "The Wanderings of the Boer" in 1891.

38. Leonard Guelke, "Freehold Farmers and Frontier Settlers, 1652–1780," in Richard Elphick and Hermann Giliomee, eds., *The Shaping of South African Society, 1652–1840*, rev. ed. (Middletown, CT: Wesleyan University Press, 1988), 93–94; John Laband, *The Transvaal Rebellion: The First Boer War, 1880–1881* (Harlow, UK: Pearson/Longman, 2005), 13–14, 24, 37.

39. André Du Toit, "No Chosen People: The Myth of the Calvinist Origins of Afrikaner Nationalism and Racial Ideology," *American Historical Review* 88 (October 1983), 920–52, quoted on 923.

40. Susan Newton-King, "The Enemy Within," in Nigel Worden and Clifton Crais, eds., *Breaking the Chains: Slavery and Its Legacy in the Nineteenth-Century Cape Colony* (Johannesburg: Witwatersrand University Press, 1994), 225–70, and see the indispensable collection of essays in the revised edition of Elphick and Giliomee, eds., *Shaping of South African Society*.

41. George M. Fredrickson, *White Supremacy: A Comparative Study in American and South African History* (New York: Oxford University Press, 1981), 108–24, 162–77; Leonard Thompson, *A History of South Africa*, 3rd ed. (New Haven, CT: Yale University Press, 2001), xix, 1–69; W. M. Freund, "Race in the Social Structure of South Africa, 1652–1836," *Race and Class* 18, no. 1 (1976), 53–67; Giliomee, *Afrikaners*, 1–192.

42. Fredrickson, *White Supremacy*, 165; Du Toit, "No Chosen People," quoted on 937.

43. Clifton Crais, "Slavery and Emancipation in the Eastern Cape," in Worden and Crais, eds., *Breaking the Chains*, quoted on 278; Thompson, *A History of South Africa*, quoted on 88; Giliomee, *Afrikaners*, 151–52.

44. See Andrew Bank, "The Great Debate and the Origins of South African Historiography," *Journal of African History* 38 (July 1997), 274–79; Clifton C. Crais, "The Vacant Land: The Mythology of British Expansion in the Eastern Cape, South Africa," *Journal of Social History* 25 (Winter 1991), 255–75, quoted on 262, 265; and Crais, *White Supremacy and Black Resistance in Pre-industrial South Africa: The Making of the Colonial Order in the Eastern Cape, 1770–1865* (Cambridge: Cambridge University Press, 1992); Robert Ross, *A Concise History of South Africa* (Cambridge: Cambridge University Press, 1999), 38.

45. Giliomee, *Afrikaners*, 228–49; Thompson, *History of South Africa*, 134–41, quoted on 136; "Davitt's Speech of Resignation," 6; Christopher Saunders and Iain R. Smith, "Southern Africa, 1795–1910," in Andrew Porter, ed., *The Oxford History of the British Empire*, vol. 3, *The Nineteenth Century* (Oxford: Oxford University Press, 1999), 597–623, quoted on 617.

46. For many years the standard account of the war was Thomas Pakenham's *The Boer War* (New York: Random House, 1979). Bill Nasson provides a valuable, and much more up-to-date, overview in *The South African War, 1899–1902* (London: Arnold, 1999). In addition, three edited collections of essays offer easy and rewarding access to the tremendous outpouring of scholarship occasioned in part by the war's centennial. See Lowry, ed., *South African War Reappraised*; Greg Cuthbertson, Albert Grundlingh, and Mary-Lynn Suttie, eds., *Writing a Wider War: Rethinking Gender, Race, and Identity in the South African War, 1899–1902* (Athens: Ohio University Press, 2002); and David Omissi and Andrew S. Thompson, eds., *The Impact of the South African War* (Basingstoke, UK: Palgrave, 2002).

47. Limerick Borough Council resolution, quoted in Donal P. McCracken, *The Irish Pro-Boers, 1877–1902* (Johannesburg: Perskor, 1989), 47.

48. Hermann Giliomee estimates that the Boers had no more than 50,000 men under arms at any one time (Davitt claimed the number did not exceed 30,000), whereas the British forces peaked at 250,000. Leonard Thompson estimates a total British mobilization of 450,000 by the end of the war and a republican total of 88,000. Giliomee, *Afrikaners*, 250; Thompson, *History of South Africa*, 141–42; Michael Davitt, "Letter from South Africa," April 16, 1900, *Freeman's Journal*, June 11, 1900. Davitt's letters from South Africa are collected in file 9500, Letters to *Freeman's Journal* from South Africa, 1900, the Michael Davitt Papers, Manuscripts and Archives Research Library, Trinity College Dublin.

49. "The War and Its Lessons," *Quarterly Review* 195 (January 1902), 297.

50. See W. K. Hancock and Jean van der Poel, eds., *Selections from the Smuts Papers*, vol. 1, *June 1886–May 1902* (Cambridge: Cambridge University Press, 1966), 467–68; Emily Hobhouse, *The Brunt of the War and Where It Fell* (London: Methuen, 1902); Christiaan Rudolf de Wet, *Three Years War (October 1899–June 1902)* (London: Archibald Constable, 1903), quoted on 242–43. Helen Bradford points out that in spite of the many lamentations about the departure from the rules of civilized warfare, systematic cruelty and scorched earth had long been the norm on both sides—for the Boers, in their seemingly incessant warfare with indigenous peoples; for the British, in India, Afghanistan, Egypt, the Sudan, and other sites of imperial conflict, including South Africa. See Helen Bradford, "Gentlemen and Boers: Afrikaner Nationalism, Gender, and Colonial Warfare in the South African War," in Cuthbertson, Grundlingh, and Suttie, eds., *Writing a Wider War*, 38–44.

51. Greaves, *Life and Times of James Connolly*, 16–19; Nevin, *James Connolly*, 5–7, quoted on 141.

52. Gregory Dobbins, "Whenever Green Is Red: James Connolly and Postcolonial Theory," *Nepantla: Views from the South* 1 (2000), 605–48; David Lynch, *Radical Politics in Modern Ireland: The Irish Socialist Republican Party, 1896–1904* (Dublin: Irish Academic Press, 2005), 67–75, 105, 115–20; Robert Lynd, introduction to James Connolly, *Labour in Ireland* (Dublin: Maunsel, 1917), quoted on xxvi; James Connolly, "The South African War II," *Workers' Republic*, Nov. 18, 1899.

53. Margaret Ward, *Unmanageable Revolutionaries: Women and Irish Nationalism* (London: Pluto Press, 1995), quoted on 58; Nancy Cardozo, *Maud Gonne: Lucky Eyes and a High Heart* (London: Victor Gollancz, 1979), quoted on 52; Karen Steele, ed., *Maud Gonne's Irish Nationalist Writings, 1895–1946* (Dublin: Irish Academic Press, 2004), quoted on 77.

54. Historian Donal McCracken contends that "his African sojourn was central to Griffith's political development." Donal P. McCracken, *MacBride's Brigade: Irish Commandos in the Anglo-Boer War* (Dublin: Four Courts Press, 1999), 70; and see Patricia A. McCracken, "Arthur Griffith's South African Sabbatical," in Donal P. McCracken, ed., *Ireland and South Africa in Modern Times, Southern African–Irish Studies* 3 (1996), 227–62.

55. McCracken, *MacBride's Brigade*, 26. On South Africa's relatively small Irish emigrant community, see Donal P. McCracken, "Odd Man Out: The South African Experience," in Andy Bielenberg, ed., *The Irish Diaspora* (Harlow, UK: Longman, 2000), 251–71.

56. P. J. Mathews, "Stirring up Disloyalty: The Boer War, the Irish Literary Theatre and the Emergence of a New Separatism," *Irish University Review* 33 (Spring 2003), 99–116, especially 99–101; *United Irishman*, Oct. 7, 1899; *Irish World*, Oct. 21, 1899.

57. Louis Paul-Dubois, *Contemporary Ireland* (Dublin: Maunsel, 1908), 178; McCracken, *Irish Pro-Boers*, 46; Terence Denman, "'The red livery of shame': The Campaign against Army Recruitment in Ireland, 1899–1914," *Irish Historical Studies* 29 (November 1994), 208–33, quoted on 214, 212.

58. McCracken, *MacBride's Brigade*.

59. A. Norman Jeffares and Ann MacBride White, eds., *The Autobiography of Maud Gonne: A Servant of the Queen* (1938; repr., Chicago: University of Chicago Press, 1994), quoted on 267; Denman, "'Red livery of shame,'" quoted on 213.

60. Denman, "'Red livery of shame,'" 214, 216; O'Brien, quoted in McCracken, *Irish Pro-Boers*, 73; Paul-Dubois, *Contemporary Ireland*, 178.

61. F[rancis] Sheehy-Skeffington, *Michael Davitt: Revolutionary, Agitator and Labour Leader* (Boston: Dana Estes, 1909), 205–10; King, *Michael Davitt*, 66–67.

62. Colin Bundy, "Vagabond Hollanders and Runaway Englishmen: White Poverty in the Cape before Poor Whiteism," in William Beinart et al., eds., *Putting a Plough to the Ground: Accumulation and Dispossession in Rural South Africa, 1850–1930* (Johannesburg: Ravan Press, 1986), 101–27, quoted on 113; Bill Nasson, *Abraham Esau's War: A Black South African War in the Cape, 1899–1902* (Cambridge: Cambridge University Press, 1991), quoted on 9; Albert Grundlingh, "Collaborators in Boer Society," in Warwick, ed., *South African War*, 272–73; Hofmeyr, "Building a Nation from Words," 99–101; Giliomee, *Afrikaners*, 316–22, 251.

63. Michael Davitt, "Letter from South Africa," March 28, 1900, *Freeman's Journal*, June 19, 1900; "Letter from South Africa," April 14, 1900, ibid., June 8, 1900; "Letter from South Africa," April 28, 1900, ibid., June 30, 1900; "Commandant General Botha," ibid., July 10, 1900.

64. Michael Davitt, *The Boer Fight for Freedom* (New York: Funk and Wagnalls, 1902).

65. Edward Said, "Zionism from the Standpoint of Its Victims," in Moustafa Bayoumi and Andrew Rubin, eds., *The Edward Said Reader* (New York: Vintage Books, 2000), 123–27. The essay originally appeared in Edward Said, *The Question of Palestine* (New York: Times Books, 1979). See also Frantz Fanon, *The Wretched of the Earth* (New York: Grove Press, 1963), 51.

66. Sheehy-Skeffington, *Michael Davitt*, 165; Davitt, *Boer Fight for Freedom*, 3; Thompson, *History of South Africa*, 87–90.

67. Davitt, *Boer Fight for Freedom*, quoted on 3, 4, 5, 2.

68. V. G. Kiernan, *The Lords of Humankind: Black Mank, Yellow Man, and White Man in an Age of Empire* (Boston: Little Brown, 1969), 220–21; James Bryce, *Impressions*

of South Africa, 3rd ed. (New York: Century, 1900), 64. Bryce pointed out that "Kaffir" was adapted from the Arabic word "Kafir," which means "infidel" or, literally, "one who denies."

69. *Irish World*, Oct. 21, 1899.

70. Saunders and Smith, "Southern Africa," 609; Fredrickson, *White Supremacy*, 201–2, 210–11, 217–20; Ross, *Concise History of South Africa*, 66; Davitt, *Boer Fight for Freedom*, 12.

71. Hancock and van der Poel, eds., *Selections from the Smuts Papers*, 1:482.

72. Shula Marks, "White Masculinity: Jan Smuts, Race and the South African War," *Proceedings of the British Academy* 111 (2001), 219; Cronje, quoted in Brian Smith, "BBC Radio Retrospective on the Anglo-Boer War, 1899–1902," Sept. 29, 1999, World Socialist Web Site (*www.wsws.org*). Smuts failed to acknowledge that the Boers conscripted thousands of Africans and Coloureds to serve their commando units; at least some of them—usually the most loyal servants of individual Boer fighters—bore arms and participated in combat. Nasson, *Abraham Esau's War*, 94–95; Fransjohan Pretorius, "Boer Attitudes toward Africans in Wartime," in Lowry, ed., *South African War Reappraised*, 104–20.

73. Marks, "White Masculinity," 219–20, quoted on 220. See also Jeremy Krikler, *Revolution from Above, Rebellion from Below: The Agrarian Transvaal at the Turn of the Century* (Oxford: Clarendon Press, 1993), 14–23; Warwick, *Black People and the South African War*, especially 38–51; R. F. Morton, "Linchwe I and the Kgatla Campaign in the South African War, 1899–1902," *Journal of African History* 26 (1985), 169–91; Bernard Mbenga, "The Role of the Bakgatla of the Pilanesberg in the South African War," in Cuthbertson, Grundlingh, and Suttie, eds., *Writing a Wider War*, 84–114; Nasson, *Abraham Esau's War*; Bill Nasson, "Black Communities in Natal and the Cape," in Omissi and Thompson, eds., *Impact of the South African War*, 38–55.

74. Stanley Trapido, "Landlord and Tenant in a Colonial Economy: The Transvaal, 1880–1910," *Journal of Southern African Studies* 5 (October 1978), quoted on 45. See also Pretorius, "Boer Attitudes to Africans in Wartime," 111.

75. Hancock and van der Poel, eds., *Selections from the Smuts Papers*, 1:486.

76. Shula Marks, *Before "the white man was master and all white men's values prevailed"? Jan Smuts, Race and the South African War* (Vienna: Southern Africa Documentation and Cooperation Centre, 2000), quoted on 15–16n27.

77. Davitt, *Boer Fight for Freedom*, 72, 171–76, 501–2.

78. Moody, *Davitt and Irish Revolution*, 289; Robert Kee, *The Laurel and the Ivy: The Story of Charles Stewart Parnell and Irish Nationalism* (London: Hamish Hamilton, 1993), 187–88, 192; Townend, "Between Two Worlds," 161; Michael Davitt, "*Life and Progress in Australasia*," in *Collected Writings*, vol. 5, pt. 1, chap. 8, 34.

79. Davitt, "*Life and Progress in Australasia*," 35, 36.

80. Davitt, "Letter from South Africa," April 14, 1900.

81. In 1904 "Europeans" constituted 21.58 percent of South Africa's population; "Natives," 67.45 percent; "Coloureds," 8.60 percent; and "Asiatics," 2.37 percent. W. K. Hancock, *Smuts: The Sanguine Years* (Cambridge: Cambridge University Press, 1962), 219.

82. In his recent biography of Davitt, Laurence Marley characterizes his attitude toward black Africans during the South African War as "wilful naieveté [*sic*]." Insofar as Davitt envisioned a resolution of the conflict, Marley points out, "the indigenous black population did not figure at all in the political equation." Marley, *Michael Davitt*, 240–56, quoted on 251.

2

96 • Notes to Chapter 5

83. R. B. McDowell, *Alice Stopford Green: A Passionate Historian* (Dublin: Allen Figgis, 1967), 5–21.

84. Undated clipping [May 1900], *Freeman's Journal*, ms. 9932, Alice Stopford Green Papers, National Library of Ireland (NLI).

85. McDowell, *Alice Stopford Green*, 22–47; Sandra Holton, "Gender Difference, National Identity and Professing History: The Case of Alice Stopford Green," *History Workshop Journal* 53 (Spring 2002), 119–27, quoted on 125. See Green's public declaration of her "National faith," which appeared in the *Freeman's Journal* in May 1900. "Mrs. J. R. Green and Home Rule," *Freeman's Journal*, May 30, 1900, ms. 9932, Green Papers.

86. Alice Stopford Green to Jan Christian Smuts, March 30, 1917, in W. K. Hancock and Jean van der Poel, eds., *Selections from the Smuts Papers*, vol. 3, *June 1910–November 1918* (Cambridge: Cambridge University Press, 1966), 468; Alice Stopford Green, "Our Boer Prisoners—a Suggested Object-Lesson," *Nineteenth Century* 49 (May 1901), 755–71; Green, "A Visit to the Boer Prisoners at St. Helena," ibid. 48 (December 1900), 972–83; Green, "The Boer Character: A Personal Impression," Northern Press Syndicate, April 1901, clipping in folder 2, ms. 10,465, Green Papers.

87. Green, "Our Boer Prisoners," 755; Smuts, quoted in McDowell, *Alice Stopford Green*, 67. For a very different evaluation of Green, see Angus Mitchell, "Alice Stopford Green and the Origins of the African Society," *History Ireland* 14 (July/August 2006), 18–24.

88. Green, "Our Boer Prisoners," 767, 760. Significantly, this prisoner had expressed his willingness to sign an oath of neutrality if doing so would have allowed him to return to his family, a common stance among *bywoners*.

89. Alice Stopford Green, Diary, Deadwood Camp, Saint Helena, September 1900, ms. 421, Green Papers.

90. Jeffares and MacBride White, eds., *Autobiography of Maud Gonne*, 266; Maud Gonne, "The Boer Women," *United Irishman*, supplement, March 17, 1900.

91. Gonne, "Boer Women."

92. *Spectator*, May 4, 1901, clipping in folder 2, ms. 10,465, Green Papers.

93. Green, "The Boer Character"; Green, "Our Boer Prisoners," 759, 770.

94. *Irish World*, Oct. 21, 1899.

95. Mbenga, "Forced Labour in the Pilanesberg," 132; Fredrickson, *White Supremacy*, 186–90, Philip Curtin quoted on 190.

96. Fredrickson, *White Supremacy*, quoted on 193, 171.

97. Kiberd, *Inventing Ireland*, 481.

98. See Bourke, *Burning of Bridget Cleary*, especially 8–18, 44–61; Kiberd, *Inventing Ireland*, 171–88, 480–96; André Du Toit, "Puritans in Africa? Afrikaner 'Calvinism' and Kuyperian Neo-Calvinism in Late Nineteenth Century South Africa," *Comparative Studies in Society and History* 27 (April 1985), 216–17. Du Toit observes that in South Africa, "the rural communities of the 1890s were living in a totally different world from the *trekboer* and *Voortrekker* societies of two generations before" (217).

99. Maud Gonne, "The Famine Queen," *United Irishman*, April 7, 1900, reprinted in Steele, ed., *Maud Gonne's Irish Nationalist Writings*, quoted on 55–56.

100. Years later, in contemplating the peasantry of Connemara, Green acknowledged that they were "terribly poor," but she argued that they were nonetheless "unspoiled by the hardships of their lives" and were "far superior in qualities of mind and body to the slum dwellers of our great cities." McDowell, *Alice Stopford Green*, 95.

101. Green, "Boer Character."

102. Green, "Our Boer Prisoners," 757; Denman, " 'Red livery of shame,' " 217; *United Irishman*, Feb. 17, 1900.

103. *United Irishman*, March 4, 1899; Ward, *Unmanageable Revolutionaries*, quoted on 51; *Workers' Republic*, July 15, 1899.

104. Loren Kruger, "The Drama of the Country and City: Tribalization, Urbanization and Theatre under Apartheid," *Journal of Southern African Studies* 23 (December 1997), 565–84.

105. Richard Rive, ed., *Olive Schreiner Letters*, vol. 1, *1871–1899* (Oxford: Oxford University Press, 1988), 340, 344.

106. Hofmeyr, "Building a Nation from Words," 110.

107. Davitt, *Jottings in Solitary*, 31.

108. Ibid., 21–24, quoted on 24.

109. Davitt, "Letter from South Africa," April 14, March 31, April 5, March 28, 1900; Davitt, *Boer Fight for Freedom*, 98–99.

110. Francis Bernard Doyle, "South Africa," in Patrick J. Corish, ed., *A History of Irish Catholicism* (Dublin: Gill and Macmillan, 1971), 6:1–27, quoted on 7; McCracken, "Odd Man Out," 257, 264–65; *Irish World*, Dec. 23, 1899.

111. Donal Lowry, " 'Ireland shows the way': Irish-South African Relations and the British Empire/Commonwealth, c. 1902–61," in McCracken, ed., *Ireland and South Africa in Modern Times*, 89–135, quoted on 92, 91, 95; Deirdre McMahon, "Ireland and the Empire-Commonwealth, 1900–1948," in Judith M. Brown and William Roger Louis, eds., *The Oxford History of the British Empire*, vol. 4, *The Twentieth Century* (Oxford: Oxford University Press, 1999), 147; Michael Collins to General [Christian] de Wet, Sept. 21, 1921, ms. 33,916 (4), Piaras Béaslaí Papers, NLI; Æ [George Russell], *Thoughts for a Convention: Memorandum on the State of Ireland* (Dublin: Maunsel, 1917), 12.

112. Mathews, "Stirring up Disloyalty," quoted on 113; Schneer, *London 1900*, quoted on 257–58.

CHAPTER 6: "BECAUSE WE ARE WHITE MEN"

1. Jonathan Schneer, *London 1900: The Imperial Metropolis* (New Haven, CT: Yale University Press, 1999), 257–58. The quote in the chapter title is from John Dillon, quoted in F.S.L. Lyons, *John Dillon: A Biography* (London: Routledge and Kegan Paul, 1968), 105. The first epigraph comes from W. K. Hancock and Jean van der Poel, eds., *Selections from the Smuts Papers*, vol. 1, *June 1886–May 1902* (Cambridge: Cambridge University Press, 1966), 485, and the second from Erskine Childers, "To the Editor of the Times," *Times*, May 5, 1919, clipping in 7825b, Erskine and Mary Childers Papers, Manuscripts and Archives Research Library, Trinity College Dublin.

2. Andrew Boyle, *The Riddle of Erskine Childers* (London: Hutchinson, 1977); Jim Ring, *Erskine Childers* (London: John Murray, 1996); Martin Mansergh, "A Passionate Attachment to the Ideal: Erskine Childers," in *The Legacy of History: Lectures and Commemorative Addresses* (Cork: Mercier Press, 2003), 290–98, quoted on 294. On the Howth gunrunning, the most detailed and insightful treatment remains F. X. Martin, ed., *The Howth Gun-Running and the Kilcoole Gun-Running, 1914* (Dublin: Browne and

Nolan, 1964). For a concise portrait, see F.S.L. Lyons, *Ireland since the Famine* (London: Weidenfeld and Nicolson, 1971), 321–27.

3. Erskine Childers, "Might and Right in Ireland," *English Review* 28 (June 1919), 512–20, quoted on 512, 514.

4. W. K. Hancock's two-volume life of Smuts is biography in the grand tradition and in this case is indispensable. See W. K. Hancock, *Smuts*, vol. 1, *The Sanguine Years, 1870–1919* (Cambridge: Cambridge University Press, 1962), and vol. 2, *The Fields of Force, 1919–1950* (Cambridge: Cambridge University Press, 1968). I have also learned much from Shula Marks, "White Masculinity: Jan Smuts, Race and the South African War," *Proceedings of the British Academy* 111 (2001), 199–223.

5. Hancock and van der Poel, eds., *Selections from the Smuts Papers*, vol. 3, *June 1910–November 1918* (Cambridge: Cambridge University Press, 1966), 507; ibid., 1:478–81.

6. Hancock, *Smuts*, 2:57–58, 505–8; Ring, *Erskine Childers*, 239, 271–72, Churchill quoted on 283.

7. Smuts, quoted in Hancock, *Smuts*, 1:500.

8. Boyle, *Riddle of Erskine Childers*, 251; Frank Pakenham, *Peace by Ordeal: An Account, from First-Hand Sources, of the Negotiation and Signature of the Anglo-Irish Treaty, 1921* (London: Jonathan Cape, 1935), 99, 140–41, 257 (quoted).

9. Boyle, *Riddle of Erskine Childers*, 29–76, quoted on 37, 39; Ring, *Erskine Childers*, 21–44; Deborah Lavin, *From Empire to International Commonwealth: A Biography of Lionel Curtis* (Oxford: Clarendon Press, 1995), 8 (on Haileybury).

10. Erskine Childers, *In the Ranks of the CIV: A Narrative and Diary of Personal Experience with the CIV Battery (Honourable Artillery Company) in South Africa* (London: Smith, Elder, 1901), passim, quoted on 226, 28, 38; Erskine Childers, "Recent Speeches of Lord Milner," typescript, n.d. [1907?], 53, 7824, Childers Papers.

11. Childers, *In the Ranks of the CIV*, 296–97.

12. Milner, quoted in Hancock, *Smuts*, 1:74.

13. Erskine Childers, *The Framework of Home Rule* (London: Edward Arnold, 1911), 129; Erskine Childers, ed., *The Times History of the War in South Africa, 1899–1902* (London: Sampson, Low, Marston, 1907), 5:606. On the conflict between Kitchener and Milner, see Keith Surridge, "The Politics of War: Lord Kitchener and the Settlement of the South African War, 1901–1902," in Greg Cuthbertson, Albert Grundlingh, and Mary-Lynn Suttie, eds., *Writing a Wider War: Rethinking Gender, Race, and Identity in the South African War, 1899–1902* (Athens: Ohio University Press, 2002), 213–32.

14. Childers, "Recent Speeches of Lord Milner," 7; Childers, *Framework of Home Rule*, 126.

15. Childers, ed., *Times History of the War in South Africa*, 5:250–51; Childers, "Recent Speeches of Lord Milner," 29.

16. In 1900 the diplomat and historian James Bryce had argued that "what South Africa most needs is the reconcilement and ultimate fusion of the two white races." John Morley, a leading pro-Boer spokesman in Parliament, made essentially the same point. "The British and Dutch have got to live together in South Africa," he declared in 1899. "Do not say to one race, 'You are to be at the top and the other shall be at the bottom.' No. Let there be fusion." James Bryce, *Impressions of South Africa*, 3rd ed. (New York: Century, 1900), xli–xlii; Morley, quoted in *Irish World*, Sept. 30, 1899, 1.

17. Childers, *In the Ranks of the CIV*, 176–77, 184, 188–89, 192, 239–41; Childers, "Recent Speeches of Lord Milner," 41, 54; Childers, *Framework of Home Rule*, 128.

18. Hancock, *Smuts*, vol. 1, quoted on 110, 361; Childers, "Recent Speeches of Lord Milner," quoted on 65.

19. Leonard Thompson, *The Political Mythology of Apartheid* (New Haven, CT: Yale University Press, 1985), especially 25–104; Isabel Hofmeyr, "Building a Nation from Words: Afrikaans Language, Literature, and Ethnic Identity, 1912–1924," in Shula Marks and Stanley Trapido, eds., *The Politics of Race, Class and Nationalism in Twentieth-Century South Africa* (London: Longman, 1987), 95–123; Anne McClintock, *Imperial Leather: Race, Gender, and Sexuality in the Colonial Conquest* (New York: Routledge, 1995), 368–79.

20. Basil Williams, *Erskine Childers, 1870–1922: A Sketch* (London: Women's Printing Society, 1926), 16.

21. On the Irish Agricultural Organisation Society and its relationship to broader currents of Irish nationalism during the first decade of the twentieth century, see P. J. Mathews, *Revival: The Abbey Theatre, Sinn Féin, the Gaelic League and the Co-operative Movement* (Cork: Cork University Press, 2003), especially 29–34. On Plunkett's outlook and leadership, see Trevor West, *Horace Plunkett: Co-operation and Politics, an Irish Biography* (Gerards Cross, UK: Colin Smythe, 1986).

22. Erskine Childers, "Military Rule in Ireland" (draft typescript), n.d. [1920], 7833/24, Robert C. Barton Papers (part of the Childers Papers).

23. Ibid.; T. P. Gill to J. I. Macpherson, April 5, 1917, 7834/11/1, Barton Papers; Pakenham, *Peace by Ordeal*, 134.

24. Pakenham, *Peace by Ordeal*, 134; Childers, *Framework of Home Rule*, 148; Erskine Childers, *The Form and Purpose of Home Rule* (Dublin: E. Ponsonby, 1912), 30.

25. Childers, *Framework of Home Rule*, 150–87, quoted on 153, 164 (emphasis in original).

26. Ibid., quoted on 148–49.

27. Hibernicus, "Mr. Childers' Book," *Irish Independent*, June 10, 1912; "Fiscal Autonomy," ibid., March 4, 1912; *Dublin Review*, April 1912; Robert Lynd, "Home Rule," *Daily News*, Dec. 12, 1911, all in 7901, Childers Papers, which includes numerous other reviews.

28. John J. Horgan, *Parnell to Pearse: Some Recollections and Reflections* (Dublin: Browne and Nolan, 1948), quoted on 313; Darrell Figgis, *Recollections of the Irish War* (London: Ernest Benn, 1927), 23; MacLysaght, quoted in Boyle, *Riddle of Erskine Childers*, 233; Frank O'Connor, *The Big Fellow*, rev. ed. (Dublin: Clonmore & Reynolds, 1965), 138; Frank O'Connor, *An Only Child* (New York: Alfred A. Knopf, 1961), 212.

29. Burke Wilkinson, *The Zeal of the Convert* (Washington, DC: Robert B. Luce, 1976), 15; Boyle, *Riddle of Erskine Childers*, 62–63; Childers, *In the Ranks of the CIV*, 129, 226; Childers, *Framework of Home Rule*, passim; "Statement by Staff-Captain Erskine Childers at the Close of His Trial by a 'Military Court' on Nov. 17th, 1922," *Poblacht na hÉireann / War News*, no. 103, Nov. 29, 1922.

30. R. F. Foster, "Marginal Men and Micks on the Make: The Uses of Irish Exile, c. 1840–1922," in *Paddy and Mr. Punch: Connections in Irish and English History* (London: Allen Lane, 1993), 281–305, especially 302–3; Wilkinson, *Zeal of the Convert*, 18; Childers, *In the Ranks of the CIV*, 296–97; John J. Horgan to Erskine Childers, June 8, 1919, 7848/537, Childers Papers; Kevin O'Higgins, quoted in "O'Higgins Prepares the Ground," *Poblacht na hÉireann / War News*, no. 94, Nov. 17, 1922.

31. Brian Inglis, *Roger Casement* (1973; London: Penguin Books, 2002), 239–40, 251–54.

32. Robert Brennan, *Allegiance* (Dublin: Browne and Nolan, 1950), quoted on 248; Boyle, *Riddle of Erskine Childers*, 119–23, quoted on 119, 121; Ring, *Erskine Childers*, 80–96. For a portrait of Molly Childers, based mainly on correspondence from the 1950s and '60s, see Helen Landreth, *The Mind and Heart of Mary Childers* (privately printed, 1965).

33. Elizabeth Lazenby, *Ireland—a Catspaw* (New York: Charter Publishing, 1929), 27–28. Although Lazenby offered compelling portraits of some of the principals in Ireland's struggle for independence, her basic premise, that leading Irish republicans such as Erskine and Mary Childers were "the bridge-head for revolutionary activities outside Ireland, whose aim [was] the complete destruction and annihilation of the British Commonwealth," is not credible. What is remarkable is that a number of reputable students of Irish history have taken this claim more or less at face value. Ibid., 245–46. See Ulick O'Connor, *The Times I've Seen: Oliver St. John Gogarty, a Biography* (New York: Ivan Oblensky, 1963), 205, and Calton Younger, *Ireland's Civil War* (London: Frederick Muller, 1968), 480.

34. Robert C. Barton to "Darling" [Mary A. Childers], Nov. 24, 1932, 7833/74; Robert C. Barton to "Darling" [Mary A. Childers], n.d. [Nov. 1933?], 7833/75; Mary A. Childers to "Dearest Bob," June 17, 1921, 7833/47, all in Barton Papers.

35. Eamon de Valera to Mary A. Childers, Jan. 9, 1924, 7848/288, Childers Papers.

36. On Alice Stopford Green, her family, and her circle of friends and political associates, see León Ó Broin, *Protestant Nationalists in Revolutionary Ireland: The Stopford Connection* (Dublin: Gill and Macmillan, 1985).

37. Erskine Childers to Alice Stopford Green, Nov. 7, 1914, 7848/446, Childers Papers; Mary A. Childers to Alice Stopford Green, n.d. [July 1914], 7848/433–38, ibid.; Mary A. Childers to "Dearest Bob," June 17, 1921, ibid.

38. Ellis Archer Wasson, "Rice, Thomas Spring, First Baron Monteagle of Brandon (1790–1866)," in H.C.G. Matthew and Brian Harrison, eds., *Oxford Dictionary of National Biography* (Oxford: Oxford University Press, 2004), http://www.oxforddnb.com/view/article/26179 (accessed Aug. 12, 2005); "Monteagle of Brandon, Lord Thomas Spring-Rice," in Victor G. Plarr, *Men and Women of the Time: A Dictionary of Contemporaries* (London: George Routledge and Sons, 1899), 769; Thomas Hennessey, *Dividing Ireland: World War One and Partition* (London: Routledge, 1998), 192. In 1917 Lord Monteagle identified himself as one of "the moderate men who still believe in the principle of Union though they sadly recognise that it doesn't work in practice." Lord Monteagle to Maurice Moore, April 14, 1917, ms. 10,568, Maurice Moore Papers, NLI.

39. West, *Horace Plunkett*, 45, 23, 30; Ó Broin, *Protestant Nationalists in Revolutionary Ireland*, 139–40; Kit Ó Céirín and Cyril Ó Céirín , *Women of Ireland: A Biographic Dictionary* (Kinvara, Ireland: Tir Eolas / Irish Books and Media, 1996), 209–10; Donald Harman Akenson, *Conor: A Biography of Conor Cruise O'Brien*, vol. 1, *Narrative* (Montreal: McGill-Queen's University Press, 1994), 58, 61, 76–77. For Mary Spring-Rice's record of her sojourn aboard *Asgard*, see Mary Spring-Rice, "Log of the Gun-Running Cruise in the 'Asgard,' July 1914," 7841, Childers Papers. With remarkably little fanfare, Conor O'Brien landed a smaller cargo of weapons at Kilcoole, County Wexford, several days after the more heralded landing at Howth. Ring, *Erskine Childers*, 147.

40. Alvin Jackson, "The Larne Gun Running of 1914," *History Ireland* 1 (Spring 1993), 35–38; Jackson, *Sir Edward Carson* (Dublin: Historical Association of Ireland, 1993), 36–41; Jackson, *Home Rule: An Irish History* (New York: Oxford University Press, 2003), 132–37.

41. Michael Laffan, *The Resurrection of Ireland: The Sinn Fein Party, 1916–1923* (Cambridge: Cambridge University Press, 1999), 7. According to Laffan, when "the Conservative opposition and its unionist allies realized that they could no longer block home rule by constitutional means[,] they resorted to treason."

42. Martin, ed., *Howth Gun-Running*, passim, especially 57 and 67.

43. Mary A. Childers to Alice Stopford Green, n.d. [July 1914].

44. Mary A. Childers to Alice Stopford Green, n.d. [July 27?, 1914], 7848/433–38, Childers Papers.

45. Mary A. Childers to Alice Stopford Green, n.d. [July 1914]; Mary Spring-Rice to Mary A. Childers, July 29, [1914], 7851/1218, Childers Papers.

46. Mary Alden Childers, "Robert Erskine Childers," n.d. [1925?], 7851/1306A, ibid.

47. Robert Kee, *The Green Flag: A History of Irish Nationalism* (1972; repr., London: Penguin Books, 2000), 509–12.

48. Childers, *Framework of Home Rule*, 148–49; "The Baptism," *Irish Freedom*, no. 46 (August 1914), 1.

49. Ring, *Erskine Childers*, 147–48; Erskine Childers to Alice Stopford Green, Nov. 7, 1914.

50. Williams, *Erskine Childers*, 28.

51. Ring, *Erskine Childers*, quoted on 188; Erskine Childers to John J. Horgan, Oct. 28, 1917, file 7848/525, Childers Papers; West, *Horace Plunkett*, 157–76, quoted on 166. See also R. B. McDowell, *The Irish Convention, 1917–18* (London: Routledge and Kegan Paul, 1970); Jackson, *Home Rule*, 177–85; Nicholas Allen, "National Reconstruction: George Russell (Æ) and the Irish Convention," in D. George Boyce and Alan O'Day, eds., *Ireland in Transition, 1867–1921* (London: Routledge, 2004), 128–41.

52. Boyle, *Riddle of Erskine Childers*, 239.

53. "Statement by Staff-Captain Erskine Childers"; Ring, *Erskine Childers*, 195–96; Boyle, *Riddle of Erskine Childers*, 245.

54. Boyle, *Riddle of Erskine Childers*, 244–56; "The Peril of Irish Partition," *Irish Independent*, July 29, 1919, clipping in 7825b, Childers Papers; Erskine Childers, "To the Editor of the Times," *Times*, May 5, 1919, ibid.

55. Boyle, *Riddle of Erskine Childers*, quoted on 168; "Letter from Mr. Erskine Childers," *Irish Times*, Dec. 24, 1912, clipping in 7825b, Childers Papers.

56. L. F. Fitzhardinge, *William Morris Hughes: A Political Biography*, vol.1, *That Fiery Particle, 1862–1914* (Sydney: Angus and Robertson, 1964), 116–19, 128–29, 132–36, quoted on 136.

57. Margaret MacMillan, *Paris 1919: Six Months That Changed the World* (New York: Random House, 2001), 44, 48, 101–4, 319.

58. Ibid., Smuts quoted on 99.

59. Childers, *Framework of Home Rule*, 120.

60. Merriman, quoted in Hermann Giliomee, *The Afrikaners: Biography of a People* (Charlottesville: University of Virginia Press, 2003), 244.

61. Giliomee, *Afrikaners*, 249.

62. Hancock and van der Poel, eds., *Selections from the Smuts Papers*, 1:463, 467, 474, 479; Leonard Thompson, *A History of South Africa*, 3rd ed. (New Haven, CT: Yale University Press, 2000), 143. According to Christopher Saunders and Iain Smith, "Civilian deaths . . . amounted to about 10 per cent of the Boer population of the two republics." Christopher Saunders and Iain R. Smith, "Southern Africa, 1795–1910," in Andrew

Porter, ed., *The Oxford History of the British Empire*, vol. 3, *The Nineteenth Century* (New York: Oxford University Press, 1999), 618.

63. Hancock and van der Poel, eds., *Selections from the Smuts Papers*, 1:481, 494.

64. Ibid., 487; Giliomee, *Afrikaners*, 260–63, Smuts quoted on 262–63.

65. Giliomee, *Afrikaners*, 271; Hancock and van der Poel, eds., *Selections from the Smuts Papers*, 1:485; Hancock, *Smuts*, 1:221, 159; Marks, "White Masculinity," 210.

66. Hancock and van der Poel, eds., *Selections from the Smuts Papers*, 1:494; N. G. Garson, "'Het Volk': The Botha-Smuts Party in the Transvaal, 1904–11," *Historical Journal* 9, no. 1 (1966), 101–32; Giliomee, *Afrikaners*, 269–71, quoted on 269; Hofmeyr, "Building a Nation from Words"; Kenneth Ingham, *Jan Christian Smuts: The Conscience of a South African* (New York: St. Martin's Press, 1986), 77–80.

67. Hancock and van der Poel, eds., *Selections from the Smuts Papers*, vol. 3, quoted on 507, 508, 510–11, 512.

68. Hancock and van der Poel, eds., *Selections from the Smuts Papers*, vol. 4, *November 1918–August 1919* (Cambridge: Cambridge University Press, 1966), 273.

69. Donal Lowry, "New Ireland, Old Empire and the Outside World, 1922–49: The Strange Evolution of a 'Dictionary Republic,'" in Mike Cronin and John M. Regan, eds., *Ireland: The Politics of Independence, 1922–49* (Basingstoke, UK: Macmillan, 2000), quoted on 167; Hancock, *Smuts*, 2:50–54, quoted on 54; Pakenham, *Peace by Ordeal*, quoted on 77. Hancock claimed too great a role for Smuts in the drafting and specific language of the final text of the king's speech. According to Harold Nicolson, George V's biographer, "The speech as finally delivered may have borne but little relation to General Smuts' original 'declaration'; but its inception was undoubtedly due to the vision of that statesman and to the influence he possessed with the King and Government." Harold Nicolson, *King George the Fifth: His Life and Reign* (London: Constable, 1952), 349–54, quoted on 352; Thomas Jones, *Whitehall Diary*, vol. 3, *Ireland, 1918–1925*, ed. Keith Midlemass (London: Oxford University Press, 1971), 74–79, 247–48.

70. Hancock, *Smuts*, vol. 2, quoted on 55–56.

71. Jean van der Poel, ed., *Selections from the Smuts Papers*, vol. 5, *September 1919–November 1934* (Cambridge: Cambridge University Press, 1973), 96.

72. Hancock, *Smuts*, 1:56–58; van der Poel, ed., *Selections from the Smuts Papers*, 5:102, 104, 97.

73. Pakenham, *Peace by Ordeal*, 87; Ring, *Erskine Childers*, 239; Donal Lowry, "'Ireland shows the way': Irish-South African Relations and the British Empire/Commonwealth, c. 1902–61," in Donal P. McCracken, ed., *Ireland and South Africa in Modern Times*, Southern African–Irish Studies 3 (1996), 94; van der Poel, ed., *Selections from the Smuts Papers*, vol. 5, quoted on 39.

74. Ring, *Erskine Childers*, quoted on 212–13 (emphasis in original).

75. Deirdre McMahon, "Ireland and the Empire-Commonwealth, 1900–1948," in Judith M. Brown and William Roger Louis, eds., *The Oxford History of the British Empire*, vol. 4, *The Twentieth Century* (Oxford: Oxford University Press, 1999), 147–50; Boyle, *Riddle of Erskine Childers*, quoted on 252.

76. Desmond Ryan, *Remembering Sion: A Chronicle of Storm and Quiet* (London: Arthur Barker, 1934), quoted on 288–89. Ryan offered a sympathetic and insightful portrait of Childers as Irish Republican and principal target of the Free State propaganda machine, in *Remembering Sion*, 282–300.

77. Boyle, *Riddle of Erskine Childers*, 253–71.

78. McMahon, "Ireland and the Empire-Commonwealth," 151; Pakenham, *Peace by Ordeal*, 85–86; [Eamon de Valera] to David Lloyd George, Aug. 24, 1921, 7833/60, Childers Papers.

79. McMahon, "Ireland and the Empire-Commonwealth," 151–53; Pakenham, *Peace by Ordeal*, 110–19, quoted on 111, 112; Ring, *Erskine Childers*, quoted on 260, 264–65.

80. Ring, *Erskine Childers*, 267–82, quoted on 272, 271, 275; Brian Hanley, "The Rhetoric of Republican Legitimacy," in Fearghal McGarry, ed., *Republicanism in Modern Ireland* (Dublin: University College Dublin Press, 2003), 168; O'Connor, *An Only Child*, 214.

81. Pakenham, *Peace by Ordeal*, 342–44; Boyle, *Riddle of Erskine Childers*, 319, 22–27; Ring, *Erskine Childers*, 89, 283–89.

82. Ring, *Erskine Childers*, 289.

83. Childers, quoted in Pakenham, *Peace by Ordeal*, 233, 248.

84. Hancock, *Smuts*, 1:30; Hancock and van der Poel, eds., *Selections from the Smuts Papers*, 1:482; Marks, "White Masculinity," 219.

85. Derek Sayer, "British Reaction to the Amritsar Massacre, 1919–1920," *Past and Present*, no. 131 (May 1991), 130–64, quoted on 150, 153; McMahon, "Ireland and the Empire-Commonwealth," 146; Deirdre McMahon, "Ireland, the Empire, and the Commonwealth," in Kevin Kenny, ed., *Ireland and the British Empire* (Oxford: Oxford University Press, 2004), quoted on 209–10.

86. Williams, *Erskine Childers*, 28; Childers, "Might and Right in Ireland," 513.

87. Erskine Childers, Diary, July–August 1921, file 7813, Childers Papers; and see Brian P. Murphy, OSB, "Erskine Childers: The Evolution of an Enemy of Empire—II," in Eóin Flannery and Angus Mitchell, eds., *Enemies of Empire: New Perspectives on Imperialism, Literature and Historiography* (Dublin: Four Courts Press, 2007), 72–93.

88. Pakenham, *Peace by Ordeal*, quoted on 248; Mary Spring-Rice to Mary A. Childers, Nov. 25, 1922, 7851/1221, Childers Papers.

CHAPTER 7: NEGRO SINN FÉINERS AND BLACK FENIANS

1. Dáil Éireann, "Message to the Free Nations of the World," Jan. 21, 1919, in Ronan Fanning et al., eds., *Documents on Irish Foreign Policy*, vol. 1 (Dublin: Royal Irish Academy and Department of Foreign Affairs, 1998), 2. The term "Heroic Ireland" in the chapter title is from Cyril V. Briggs, "Heroic Ireland," *Crusader* 3 (February 1921), 5. The first epigraph is from Claude McKay, "How Black Sees Green and Red," *Liberator* 4 (June 1921), reprinted in Wayne F. Cooper, ed., *The Passion of Claude McKay: Selected Poetry and Prose, 1912–1948* (New York: Shocken Books, 1973), quoted on 59. The second is from Robert A. Hill, "Introduction: Racial and Radical; Cyril V. Briggs, *The Crusader Magazine*, and the African Blood Brotherhood, 1918–1922," in Hill, ed., *The Crusader*, vol. 1, *September 1918–August 1919* (New York: Garland Publishing, 1987), quoted on xxxii. Anselmo Jackson was a close friend of Cyril Briggs.

2. *Irish World*, June 9, 1917.

3. Lothrop Stoddard, *The Rising Tide of Color against White World Supremacy* (New York: Scribner's, 1920).

4. Richard P. Davis, *Arthur Griffith and Non-violent Sinn Féin* (Dublin: Anvil Books, 1974), 194n13; B. R. Nanda, *Jawaharlal Nehru: Rebel and Statesman* (Delhi: Oxford University Press, 1995), quoted on 9.

5. Robert A. Hill, ed., *The Marcus Garvey and Universal Negro Improvement Association Papers*, 9 vols. (1–7, 9–10) (Berkeley: University of California Press, 1983–2006), 1:21n2; Robert A. Hill, "General Introduction," ibid., quoted on lxxin115.

6. Davis, *Arthur Griffith and Non-violent Sinn Féin*, 194n13; Nanda, *Jawaharlal Nehru*, 9.

7. Frank P. Walsh, "Sinn Féin," 1920, box 32, Francis Patrick Walsh Papers, Manuscripts and Archives Division, New York Public Library; Robert Lynd, *Ireland a Nation* (New York: Dodd, Mead, 1920), 65.

8. Lynd, *Ireland a Nation*, 69–85; William Irwin Thompson, *The Imagination of an Insurrection: Dublin, Easter, 1916; A Study of an Ideological Movement* (New York: Oxford University Press, 1967); F. X. Martin, ed., *Leaders and Men of the Easter Rising: Dublin 1916* (London: Methuen, 1967); Charles Townshend, *Easter 1916: The Irish Rebellion* (London: Allen Lane, 2005); Clair Wills, *Dublin 1916: The Siege of the GPO* (Cambridge, MA: Harvard University Press, 2009); Fearghal McGarry, *The Rising: Ireland, Easter 1916* (New York: Oxford University Press, 2010).

9. Moira Regan participated in the Easter Rising and left Ireland for New York soon thereafter. She is quoted in Townshend, *Easter 1916*, 300.

10. Their ranks also included Arthur P. Hendricks, Otto Huiswood, Richard B. Moore, W. A. Domingo, and Grace Campbell, among many others. Hendricks, a theology student from British Guiana, was a left-wing socialist who died of tuberculosis in the spring of 1919. Huiswood, Hendricks's friend and fellow activist, was an immigrant from Suriname and the only person of African descent who participated in the founding of the American Communist Party in September 1919. Moore, from Barbados, was a brilliant orator who, along with Cyril Briggs, became one of Harlem's leading communists. Domingo trained as a tailor in Jamaica; in the United States, he was a journalist, small businessman, and tireless proponent of socialism. Campbell, whose father was from the Caribbean (probably Jamaica), was a civil servant and early member of the Communist Party. Mark Solomon, *The Cry Was Unity: Communists and African Americans, 1917–1936* (Jackson: University Press of Mississippi, 1998), 3–5; W. Burghardt Turner and Joyce Moore Turner, eds., *Richard B. Moore: Caribbean Militant in Harlem: Collected Writings, 1920–1972* (Bloomington: Indiana University Press, 1988); Robert A. Hill, "W. A. Domingo," in Hill, ed., *Marcus Garvey Papers*, 1:527–31; Winston James, *Holding Aloft the Banner of Ethiopia: Caribbean Radicalism in Early Twentieth-Century America* (London: Verso, 1998), 50–91 ("The Peculiarities of the Caribbeans"), and 173–77 (on Grace Campbell). For a polemical assault on the role Afro-Caribbean immigrants played in Harlem's political and cultural life, see Harold Cruse, *The Crisis of the Negro Intellectual* (New York: William Morrow, 1967), 115–46; and see the measured but ultimately devastating response by Winston James in *Holding Aloft the Banner of Ethiopia*, 262–91.

11. James, *Holding Aloft the Banner of Ethiopia*, quoted on 123, 122.

12. Ibid., quoted on 123.

13. McKay, "How Black Sees Green and Red," quoted on 59; Jeffrey B. Perry, *Hubert Harrison: The Voice of Harlem Radicalism, 1883–1918* (New York: Columbia University Press, 2009), quoted on 325.

14. Judith Stein, *The World of Marcus Garvey: Race and Class in Modern Society* (Baton Rouge: Louisiana State University Press, 1986), quoted on 53; James H. Sweet, "The Rhetoric of Nationalism: The Garvey Movement and Sinn Féin," *Journal of Caribbean Studies* 11 (1995), quoted on 124; Solomon, *The Cry Was Unity*, 5.

15. Basil Mathews, *The Clash of Colour: A Study in the Problem of Race* (1924; repr., Port Washington, NY: Kennikat Press, 1973), 29. Elsewhere in his book (on p. 26), Mathews appeared to include the Irish in his discussion of the "white European" while excluding the "bearded olive-faced Jew."

16. Hill, ed., *Marcus Garvey Papers*, 1:lxxvii; *Messenger* 2 (February 1920), 5. The *Messenger*, edited by A. Philip Randolph and Chandler Owen, proudly (but inaccurately) identified itself as "The Only Radical Negro Magazine in America."

17. McKay, "How Black Sees Green and Red," 59.

18. James Weldon Johnson, *Black Manhattan* (1930; repr., New York: Arno Press and the New York Times, 1968), 236–39; David Levering Lewis, *W.E.B. Du Bois*, vol. 1, *Biography of a Race, 1868–1919* (New York: Henry Holt, 1993), 536–37.

19. William M. Tuttle Jr., *Race Riot: Chicago in the Red Summer of 1919* (New York: Atheneum, 1970), 13–14; David Levering Lewis, *W.E.B. Du Bois*, vol. 2, *The Fight for Equality and the American Century, 1919–1963* (New York: Henry Holt, 2000), 8.

20. "If We Must Die" appeared in the *Liberator* 2 (July 1919), 21. See Wayne F. Cooper, *Claude McKay: Rebel Sojourner in the Harlem Renaissance; A Biography* (Baton Rouge: Louisiana State University Press, 1987), 99–100.

21. Peter Fryer, *Staying Power: The History of Black People in Britain* (London: Pluto Press, 1984), 298–316; Bruce Nelson, *Divided We Stand: American Workers and the Struggle for Black Equality* (Princeton, NJ: Princeton University Press, 2001), 33; Hill, ed., *Marcus Garvey Papers*, 2:43n2.

22. Robert C. Reinders, "Racialism on the Left: E. D. Morel and the 'Black Horror on the Rhine,'" *International Review of Social History* 13 (first quarter, 1968), 1–28, quoted on 1, 5; E. D. Morel, "Black Troops in Germany," *Foreign Affairs: A Journal of International Understanding* 2 (June 1920), special supplement, vii. For a sympathetic portrait of Morel, based on his Congo reform campaign and his antiwar stance, see Adam Hochschild, *King Leopold's Ghost: A Story of Greed, Terror, and Heroism in Colonial Africa* (Boston: Houghton Mifflin, 1998), 177–94, 209–24, 287–91.

23. Mathews, *Clash of Colour*; Stoddard, *Rising Tide of Color*.

24. Madison Grant, *The Passing of the Great Race; or, The Racial Basis of European History* (New York: Charles Scribner's Sons, 1916), 25. For portraits of Grant and summaries of his scholarly and popular writings, see Thomas F. Gosset, *Race: The History of an Idea in America*, new ed. (New York: Oxford University Press, 1997), 353–63; Matthew Pratt Guterl, *The Color of Race in America, 1900–1940* (Cambridge, MA: Harvard University Press, 2001), 27–48, 62–67; Nell Irvin Painter, *The History of White People* (New York: W. W. Norton, 2010), 305–17.

25. Barbara Miller Solomon, *Ancestors and Immigrants: A Changing New England Tradition* (Cambridge, MA: Harvard University Press, 1956), 102, 208, 205 (quoted); Gary Gerstle, *American Crucible: Race and Nation in the Twentieth Century* (Princeton, NJ: Princeton University Press, 2001), 94, 104–15.

26. Peggy Pascoe, "Miscegenation Law, Court Cases, and Ideologies of Race in Twentieth-Century America," *Journal of American History* 83 (June 1996), quoted on 54; Guterl, *Color of Race*, quoted on 8.

27. Guterl, *Color of Race*, 35; Gosset, *Race*, quoted on 356. In constructing his racial classifications, Grant was somewhat ambivalent about the Irish. He conceded that they were "as fully Nordic as the English." But he also recycled stereotypical portraits of the wild Irish that harked back to the work of John Beddoe and other British anthropologists.

Thus he observed that "ferocious gorilla-like living specimens of the Neanderthal man are found not infrequently on the west coast of Ireland, and are easily recognized by the great upper lip, bridgeless nose, beetling brow[,] . . . low growing hair, and wild and savage aspect." Grant, *Passing of the Great Race*, 59, 95–96.

28. Grant, *Passing of the Great Race*, 16; *Boston Herald*, quoted in Gerstle, *American Crucible*, 107; Gosset, *Race*, quoted on 361.

29. Guterl, *Color of Race*, quoted on 43; Marilyn Lake and Henry Reynolds, *Drawing the Global Colour Line: White Men's Countries and the International Challenge of Racial Equality* (Cambridge: Cambridge University Press, 2008).

30. Grant, quoted in Guterl, *Color of Race*, 43; Stoddard, quoted in Wilson Jeremiah Moses, *The Golden Age of Black Nationalism, 1850–1925* (1978; repr., New York: Oxford University Press, 1988), 251. For a portrait of Stoddard and overview of his work, see Gosset, *Race*, 390–98.

31. Stoddard, quoted in Moses, *Golden Age of Black Nationalism*, 252; Guterl, *Color of Race*, 35; Hubert Harrison, "The Rising Tide of Color against White World-Supremacy[,] by Lothrop Stoddard," *Negro World*, May 29, 1920, reprinted in Jeffrey B. Perry, ed., *A Hubert Harrison Reader* (Middletown, CT: Wesleyan University Press, 2001), 306–9, Stoddard quoted on 308.

32. Morel, "Black Troops in Germany," ix.

33. Moses, *Golden Age of Black Nationalism*, 252, 234, 235.

34. Alexander Crummell, "The Progress of Civilization along the West Coast of Africa," in Wilson Jeremiah Moses, ed., *Classical Black Nationalism: From the American Revolution to Marcus Garvey* (New York: New York University Press, 1996), 169–87, quoted on 171.

35. Equiano, quoted in Paul Gilroy, "Diaspora and the Detours of Identity," in Kathryn Woodward, ed., *Identity and Difference* (London: Sage Publications, in association with the Open University, 1997), 325.

36. Crummell, "Progress of Civilization," quoted on 182–83. On Crummell, and more broadly on black nationalism in the nineteenth century, see Moses, *Golden Age of Black Nationalism*, especially 59–82; and Wilson Jeremiah Moses, *Alexander Crummell: A Study of Civilization and Discontent* (New York: Oxford University Press, 1989).

37. Lewis, *W.E.B. Du Bois*, 1:161–70; W.E.B. Du Bois, "Of Alexander Crummell," in *The Souls of Black Folk* (1903; repr., New York: New American Library, 1969), 233–44, quoted on 234.

38. Jonathan Schneer, *London 1900: The Imperial Metropolis* (New Haven, CT: Yale University Press, 1999), 203–26, quoted on 226.

39. Winston James, *A Fierce Hatred of Injustice: Claude McKay's Jamaica and His Poetry of Rebellion* (London: Verso, 2000), quoted on 97, 95.

40. Ronald Schaffer, *America in the Great War: The Rise of the War Welfare State* (New York: Oxford University Press, 1991), 80, 86; James, *Holding Aloft the Banner of Ethiopia*, 50–69; Nelson, *Divided We Stand*, 33. Houston served in the all-black Ninety-second Division and later became the dean of Howard University Law School and principal architect of the NAACP's legal campaign against segregation in the United States.

41. Robert A. Hill, "General Introduction," in Hill, ed., *Marcus Garvey Papers*, 1:lxvii, lxviii (quoted).

42. W. A. Domingo, "The Tropics in New York," *Survey Graphic* 6 (March 1925), 648, 650 (quoted).

43. Hill, "W. A. Domingo"; James, *Holding Aloft the Banner of Ethiopia*, 283, 270; *Messenger* 2 (July 1919), 22.

44. Domingo, "Tropics in New York," quoted on 649, 650.

45. James, *Holding Aloft the Banner of Ethiopia*, 114, 123 (quoted), 124, 157; Perry, *Hubert Harrison*, 44, 56–57.

46. McKay titled his autobiography, published in 1937, *A Long Way from Home*. See Claude McKay, *A Long Way from Home* (1937; repr., New Brunswick, NJ: Rutgers University Press, 2007).

47. James, *Holding Aloft the Banner of Ethiopia*, 110–14, 89, 141–42 (quoted on 142); Hill, ed., *Marcus Garvey Papers*, 1:cx–cxi, 34–35 (quoted on 35).

48. Hill, ed., *Marcus Garvey Papers*, 1:3–5; Hill, "General Introduction," xxxvi–xxxvii; Tony Martin, "Garvey, Marcus Mosiah," in H.C.G. Matthew and Brian Harrison, eds., *Oxford Dictionary of National Biography* (Oxford: Oxford University Press, 2004); http://www.oxforddnb.com/view/article/60164 (accessed Aug. 25 2008).

49. *Negro World*, Nov. 30, 1918 (I thank Robert A. Hill for the source); Hill, ed., *Marcus Garvey Papers*, 2:411, 416, 94.

50. James, *Holding Aloft the Banner of Ethiopia*, 193.

51. Hill, ed., *Marcus Garvey Papers*, 2:416. On Garvey's "amazing audacity" (the term is Kelly Miller's), see James, *Holding Aloft the Banner of Ethiopia*, 192–93.

52. Hill, "General Introduction," lxx–lxxviii, quoted on lxx.

53. Hill, ed., *Marcus Garvey Papers*, 4:333.

54. Hill, "General Introduction," lxxii.

55. Hill, ed., *Marcus Garvey Papers*, 2:8, 1:354; Tony Martin, *Race First: The Ideological and Organizational Struggles of Marcus Garvey and the Universal Negro Improvement Association* (Westport, CT: Greenwood Press, 1976), quoted on 44. Garvey's identification of the red in the UNIA flag with the "Reds of the World" and the green with the Irish struggle for independence represented a momentary departure from the standard black nationalist interpretation of the flag's symbolism. According to the "Universal Negro Catechism," "Red is the color of the blood which men must shed for redemption and liberty; black is the color of the noble and distinguished race to which we belong; green is the color of the luxuriant vegetation of our Motherland." Hill, ed., *Marcus Garvey Papers*, 3:319.

56. Hill, ed., *Marcus Garvey Papers*, 2:90, 4:263, 85, 265, 266.

57. Robert A. Hill, "The First England Years and After, 1912–1916," in John Henrik Clarke, ed., with the assistance of Amy Jacques Garvey, *Marcus Garvey and the Vision of Africa* (New York: Vintage Books, 1974), 264 (emphasis in original).

58. Hill, ed., *Marcus Garvey Papers*, 3:16, 4:185.

59. Ibid., 4:259.

60. Dorothy Macardle, *The Irish Republic*, 4th ed. (Dublin: Irish Press, 1951), 382–83, 391–92, quoted on 391; Hill, ed., *Marcus Garvey Papers*, 4:259.

61. Hill, "General Introduction," lxxii; Hill, ed., *Marcus Garvey Papers*, 4:364, 490.

62. Hill, ed., *Marcus Garvey Papers*, 2:499; Hill, "General Introduction," lxxiv, lxxv.

63. Hill, ed., *Marcus Garvey Papers*, 4:259–60; Hill, "General Introduction," lxxviii.

64. Hill, ed., *Marcus Garvey Papers*, 4:336.

65. Ibid., 336, 5:363.

66. Imanuel Geiss refers to Garvey's "truly bewildering eclecticism," which led him to combine "reactionary, bourgeois-capitalist and (quasi) social revolutionary elements." Imanuel Geiss, *The Pan-African Movement* (London: Methuen, 1974), 281.

67. Hill, ed., *Marcus Garvey Papers*, 2:457, 4:79.

68. Ferris, quoted in George M. Fredrickson, *Black Liberation: A Comparative History of Black Ideologies in the United States and South Africa* (New York: Oxford University Press, 1995), 156. On Ferris, see Kevin K. Gaines, *Uplifting the Race: Black Leadership, Politics, and Culture in the Twentieth Century* (Chapel Hill: University of North Carolina Press, 1996), 100–127.

69. Hill, ed., *Marcus Garvey Papers*, 4:487.

70. Hill, "General Introduction," lxxii.

71. Hill, ed., *Marcus Garvey Papers*, 2:411. Geiss argues that Garvey was an "imperial" Pan-Africanist and believes that Garveyism's "chief trait is a curious predilection for the imperial idea." Geiss, *Pan-African Movement*, 263.

72. Hill, ed., *Marcus Garvey Papers*, 4:81, 1:375, 2:413.

73. Ibid., 4:335–37.

74. Ibid., 7:517.

75. Briggs, "Heroic Ireland." The indispensable sources on Briggs are James, *Holding Aloft the Banner of Ethiopia*, 155–68; Solomon, *The Cry Was Unity*, 5–29; and Hill, "Introduction: Racial and Radical," v–lxx. See also Robert A. Hill, "Cyril V. Briggs," in Hill, ed., *Marcus Garvey Papers*, 1:521–27; Theodore Draper, *American Communism and Soviet Russia: The Formative Period* (New York: Viking Press, 1960), 322–26 on Briggs and the African Blood Brotherhood and, more broadly, 315–56 on communists and the "Negro Question."

76. James, *Holding Aloft the Banner of Ethiopia*, 157–58, quoted on 158 (emphasis in original). In October 1921 three consecutive issues of the *Negro World* featured an advertisement declaring that Briggs was "a white man claiming to be a Negro for Convenience." Briggs immediately sued Garvey for libel and won. Hill, "Cyril V. Briggs," 524; and see Harry Haywood, *Black Bolshevik: Autobiography of an Afro-American Communist* (Chicago: Liberator Press, 1978), 126–27, 131–32, which reflects on the legendary animosity between Briggs and Garvey.

77. Hill, "Introduction: Racial and Radical," vi–xxiii, quoted on xvi, xxi, xxii.

78. Cyril V. Briggs, "Africa for the Africans," *Crusader* 1 (September 1918), 1–4, quoted on 4.

79. Remarkably, Briggs's recommendation to join the UNIA came after Garvey had forced Briggs's friend and political ally W. A. Domingo to resign as editor of the *Negro World*. Mark Naison, *Communists in Harlem during the Depression* (Urbana: University of Illinois Press, 1983), 7.

80. James, *Holding Aloft the Banner of Ethiopia*, 160.

81. Hill, "Introduction: Racial and Radical," quoted on xxv, xxviii; Naison, *Communists in Harlem during the Depression*, 13; Cyril V. Briggs, "The Salvation of the Negro," *Crusader* 4 (April 1921), 9; Solomon, *The Cry Was Unity*, quoted on 8, 14, 13.

82. Solomon, *The Cry Was Unity*, 9, 14; Hill, "Cyril V. Briggs," 523 (quoted); James, *Holding Aloft the Banner of Ethiopia*, 155–56; Briggs, quoted in Hill, "Introduction: Racial and Radical," xlvi.

83. Theodore Draper argued, half a century ago, that "the Brotherhood was organized in 1919 in complete independence of the Communist party." See Draper, *American Communism and Soviet Russia*, 322–26, quoted on 326; James, *Holding Aloft the Banner of Ethiopia*, 160–68; Solomon, *The Cry Was Unity*, 9, 10, 20. Draper, James, and Solomon agree that Briggs joined the Communist Party (CP) in 1921 or later and that the

ABB only gradually became an instrument of communist work among black radicals. Robert A. Hill believes that Briggs joined the CP in late 1919 and that the main purpose of the ABB, from the beginning, was to recruit black communists. See Hill, "Introduction: Racial and Radical," xxiv–xxviii.

84. Hill, "Introduction: Racial and Radical," xxvi, xxviii, xxix; Briggs, "Heroic Ireland," 5.

85. Hill, "Introduction: Racial and Radical," quoted on xxix; Haywood, *Black Bolshevik*, 122 (Haywood joined the brotherhood in 1922). For a historical perspective on blood rituals in a diasporic setting, see Michael Mullin, *Africa in America: Slave Acculturation and Resistance in the American South and the British Caribbean, 1736–1831* (Urbana: University of Illinois Press, 1992), 63, 67–68, 182, 184–85.

86. Briggs, "Heroic Ireland"; Hill, "Introduction: Racial and Radical," xxvii–xxxiii, quoted on xxxii; Cyril V. Briggs, "Lessons in Tactics for the Liberation Movement," *Crusader* 5 (November 1921), 15.

87. "MacSwiney," *Crusader* 3 (December 1920), 9; Hill, "Introduction: Racial and Radical," quoted on xxxii.

88. Briggs, "Heroic Ireland."

89. "Approaching Irish Success," *Crusader* 1 (August 1919), 8; Briggs, "Heroic Ireland." See also "The Irish Fight for Liberty," *Crusader* 2 (July 1920), 16, and "British Rule in Ireland," ibid. 3 (December 1920), 10; "The Irish Boycott on British Goods," ibid. 4 (March 1921), 9–10.

90. Claude McKay, *My Green Hills of Jamaica and Five Jamaican Short Stories* (Kingston, Jamaica: Heinemann Educational Books [Caribbean], 1979), 12, 24.

91. Winston James, "Becoming the People's Poet: Claude McKay's Jamaican Years, 1889–1912," *Small Axe* 13 (March 2003), 28–30, quoted on 30.

92. Ibid., quoted on 28. See also James, *Fierce Hatred of Injustice*, the most detailed and important source on McKay's Jamaican years.

93. Cooper, *Claude McKay*, 63–102.

94. *Liberator* 2 (July 1919), 21; Cooper, *Claude McKay*, 99–100.

95. Wayne Cooper and Robert C. Reinders, "A Black Briton Comes 'Home': Claude McKay in England, 1920," *Race* 9 (September 1967), 67–83, quoted on 79; McKay, "How Black Sees Green and Red," 59.

96. Cooper, *Claude McKay*, 103–33.

97. Ibid., 134–43; McKay, *Long Way from Home*, 131–34, quoted on 132.

98. Claude McKay, "Socialism and the Negro," *Workers' Dreadnought*, Jan. 31, 1920; "The Negro and Radical Thought," *Crisis* 22 (July 1921), 102; Cooper, *Claude McKay*, 178, 179.

99. McKay, "Socialism and the Negro"; McKay, "How Black Sees Green and Red," quoted on 59.

100. McKay, "Socialism and the Negro."

101. McKay, "How Black Sees Green and Red," 57, 58, 59.

102. Ibid., 61.

103. Cooper, *Claude McKay*, 110, 185.

104. Claude McKay, *Home to Harlem* (1928; repr., Boston: Northeastern University Press, 1987); McKay, *Banjo: A Story without a Plot* (1929; repr., San Diego: Harcourt Brace, 1957).

105. McKay, *Banjo*, 45.

106. Ibid., 201.

107. James, *Holding Aloft the Banner*, 172; McKay, *Banjo*, 165; McKay, *Home to Harlem*, 154 (quoted).

108. Cooper, *Claude McKay*, 215–16, 258–59, quoted on 259; Nick Nesbitt, "Négritude," in Kwame Anthony Appiah and Henry Louis Gates Jr., eds., *Africana: The Encyclopedia of the African and African-American Experience*, 2nd ed., Oxford African American Studies Center, http://www.oxfordaasc.com/article/opr/t0002/e2872 (accessed Aug. 25, 2008). Césaire, a poet and playwright, was also the leading figure in Martinican politics for half a century.

109. *Messenger* 2 (July 1919), 9. See the anguished reply by an Irishman: P. O. Huaithne, "The Irish and the Negro," ibid. (October 1919), 32. W.E.B. Du Bois, "Bleeding Ireland," *Crisis* 21 (March 1921), 200.

110. Theodore Kornweibel Jr., *No Crystal Stair: Black Life and the Messenger, 1917–1928* (Westport, CT: Greenwood Press, 1975), 3–4, 18–35, quoted on 4; Paula F. Pfeffer, *A. Philip Randolph, Pioneer of the Civil Rights Movement* (Baton Rouge: Louisiana State University Press, 1990), 1, 6, 7 (quoted); Jervis Anderson, *A. Philip Randolph: A Biographical Portrait* (1973; repr., Berkeley: University of California Press, 1986).

111. Anderson, *A. Philip Randolph*, 141–45.

112. *Messenger* 2 (September 1920), 90, 84; 1 (November 1917), 8; 2 (December 1920), 163; 2 (August 1919), 5.

113. Lewis, *W.E.B. Du Bois*, 1:20–25, quoted on 23; W.E.B. Du Bois, *The Autobiography of W.E.B. Du Bois* (New York: International Publishers, 1968), quoted on 64. Lewis's two-volume biography of Du Bois is the indispensable starting point for understanding his life and thought.

114. Lewis, *W.E.B. Du Bois*, 1:13–15, 27 (quoted).

115. Ibid., 15–19, 26–55, quoted on 15, 26, 17, 31; Du Bois, *Autobiography of W.E.B. Du Bois*, 61–100, quoted on 82.

116. The admirer is Mary White Ovington, quoted in Lewis, *W.E.B. Du Bois*, 1:496.

117. W.E.B. Du Bois, "The African Roots of the War," *Atlantic Monthly* 115 (May 1915), 707–14, reprinted in David Levering Lewis, ed., *W.E.B. Du Bois: A Reader* (New York: Henry Holt, 1995), 642–51.

118. Du Bois, quoted in Lewis, *W.E.B. Du Bois*, 1:515, 556. Du Bois's Anglophilia would continue long after the end of the war. In June 1922, as Ireland continued to "bleed" and Egypt and India also tested the empire's mettle, he fretted about "the deep distrust of England by the masses of the hurt and disinherited, the world round." Acknowledging the empire's "blundering" and "double dealing," he exclaimed: "Milton! Thou shouldst be living at this hour: England hath need of thee!" "The World and Us," *Crisis* 24 (June 1922), 151.

119. "Sir Roger Casement—Patriot, Martyr," *Crisis* 12 (September 1916), 215–16; W.E.B. Du Bois, "[The] Negro at Paris," *Chronicle (Rochester, NY)*, May 4, 1919, reprinted in Herbert Aptheker, ed., *Writings by W.E.B. Du Bois in Periodicals Edited by Others*, vol. 2, *1919–1934* (Millwood, NY: Kraus-Thomson, 1982), 127.

120. "Ireland and India," *Crisis* 23 (January 1922), 104; "The World and Us," ibid. (February 1922), 151.

121. "Bleeding Ireland," ibid. 21 (March 1921), 200; "Ireland," ibid. 12 (August 1916), 167.

CHAPTER 8. "THE IRISH ARE FOR FREEDOM EVERYWHERE"

1. Niall Ferguson, *The Pity of War* (London: Penguin Books, 1998), 295; Margaret MacMillan, *Paris 1919: Six Months That Changed the World* (New York: Random House, 2001); Alan Sharp, "The Genie That Would Not Go Back into the Bottle: National Self-Determination and the Legacy of the First World War and the Peace Settlement," in Seamus Dunn and T. G. Fraser, eds., *Europe and Ethnicity: The First World War and Contemporary Ethnic Conflict* (London: Routledge, 1996), 10–29. According to Ferguson's estimate, there were 9.45 million deaths among military personnel and a grand total of 32,722,826 casualties (dead, wounded, and prisoners of war). These figures do not include civilian casualties.

Parts of this chapter appeared, in a somewhat different form, in Bruce Nelson, "Irish Americans, Irish Nationalism, and the 'Social' Question, 1916–1923," *boundary 2*, 31 (Spring 2004), 147–78.The quotation in the chapter subtitle is from Irish Progressive League, "The Irish Are for Hillquit" (flyer), n.d. [October 1917], folder 2, ms. 13,141, Peter Golden Papers, National Library of Ireland (NLI). The first epigraph is from C. Desmond Greaves, *Liam Mellows and the Irish Revolution* (London: Lawrence and Wishart, 1971), 155, and the second from *Boston Pilot*, Oct. 30, 1920.

2. Patrick McCartan, "To the Citizens of the Republic of Ireland Who Are at Present Resident in the United States and Canada," Dec. 30, 1918, P150/1024, Eamon de Valera Papers, University College Dublin Archives; Patrick McCartan, *With de Valera in America* (Dublin: Fitzpatrick, 1932), 245–49.

3. McCartan, *With de Valera in America*, quoted on 245; William J.M.A. Maloney, "The Irish Issue in Its American Aspect," *America: A Catholic Review of the Week* 20 (Nov. 16, 1918), quoted on 132.

4. There is an extensive literature on de Valera's mission to the United States. Tim Pat Coogan's *De Valera: Long Fellow, Long Shadow* (London: Hutchinson, 1993), 135–96, is hostile but indispensable. Charles Callan Tansill's *America and the Fight for Irish Freedom, 1866–1922* (New York: Devin-Adair, 1957), 340–96, is even more hostile. It is dedicated to de Valera's two principal adversaries in the United States, Judge Daniel Cohalan and John Devoy, whom Tansill memorialized as "Valiant Fighters for Irish Freedom." The Earl of Longford and Thomas P. O'Neill's *Eamon de Valera* (London: Hutchinson, 1970) is favorable, as any authorized biography would be. Terry Golway's *Irish Rebel: John Devoy and America's Fight for Ireland's Freedom* (New York: St. Martin's Press, 1998) looks at Dev's visit mainly from the vantage point of Devoy and other leaders of Clan na Gael in New York City. David Fitzpatrick's *Harry Boland's Irish Revolution* (Cork: Cork University Press, 2003), 122–224, naturally concentrates far more on Boland than on de Valera, but it is an indispensable resource for understanding the network of relationships that surrounded Dev during his eighteen months in America. See also Donal McCartney, "De Valera's Mission to the United States, 1919–20," in Art Cosgrove and Donal McCartney, eds., *Studies in Irish History Presented to R. Dudley Edwards* (Dublin: University College Dublin, 1979), 304–23; F. M. Carroll, *American Opinion and the Irish Question, 1910–23* (Dublin: Gill and Macmillan, 1978), 149–62; McCartan, *With de Valera in America*; and a recent, and sympathetic, biography by Diarmaid Ferriter, *Judging Dev: A Reassessment of the Life and Legacy of Eamon de Valera* (Dublin: Royal Irish Academy, 2007).

5. Eamon de Valera, "Press Statement, New York, 23 June 1919," in Maurice Moynihan, ed., *Speeches and Statements by Eamon de Valera, 1917–73* (Dublin: Gill and Macmillan, 1980), 29–31.

6. Dáil Éireann, "Message to the Free Nations of the World," Jan. 21, 1919, in Ronan Fanning et al., eds., *Documents on Irish Foreign Policy*, vol. 1, *1919–1922* (Dublin: Royal Irish Academy and Department of Foreign Affairs, 1998), 2.

7. Wilson, quoted in Coogan, *De Valera*, 143; Lansing, quoted in Sharp, "The Genie That Would Not Go Back," 19. See also Allen Lynch, "Woodrow Wilson and the Principle of 'National Self-Determination': A Reconsideration," *Review of International Studies* 28 (2002), 419–36.

8. Fitzpatrick, *Harry Boland's Irish Revolution*, 136; McCartney, "De Valera's Mission to the United States," 307.

9. Coogan, *De Valera*, 3–10; T. Ryle Dwyer, *Eamon de Valera* (Dublin: Gill and Macmillan, 1980), quoted on 61.

10. Longford and O'Neill, *Eamon de Valera*, 1–2, quoted on 2; Coogan, *De Valera*, 7–8, 10–11; Dwyer, *Eamon de Valera*, quoted on 61.

11. Fitzpatrick, *Harry Boland's Irish Revolution*, quoted on 125; Tansill, *America and the Fight for Irish Freedom*, quoted on 361.

12. Golway, *Irish Rebel*, quoted on 280. Devoy's ally and friend John P. Grace, the mayor of Charleston, South Carolina, stopped short of such a sweeping condemnation but declared nonetheless, "De Valera's attitude was one of infallibility; he was right, everybody else was wrong, and he couldn't be wrong." Grace, quoted in Tansill, *America and the Fight for Irish Freedom*, 368.

13. J. J. Lee, *Ireland, 1912–1985: Politics and Society* (Cambridge: Cambridge University Press, 1989), 48–50; Lee, "De Valera's Use of Words: Three Case-Studies," *Radharc* 2 (November 2001), 75–100; Eamon de Valera to Mary MacSwiney, Sept. 11, 1922, P150/657, de Valera Papers.

14. Coogan, *De Valera*, 148.

15. Ibid., 173, 192–93.

16. Fitzpatrick, *Harry Boland's Irish Revolution*, 130–31; McCartan, *With de Valera in America*, vi (quoted), 141; Coogan, *De Valera*, 148–51.

17. William M. Tuttle Jr., *Race Riot: Chicago in the Red Summer of 1919* (1970; repr., New York Atheneum, 1978), 22–23, 29–30; David Levering Lewis, *W.E.B. Du Bois*, vol. 2, *The Fight for Equality and the American Century* (New York: Henry Holt, 2000), 7–8; Coogan, *De Valera*, 150.

18. Fitzpatrick, *Harry Boland's Irish Revolution*, quoted on 140.

19. "President de Valera at Bethlehem Iron Works," n.d. [July 1919], P150/787, de Valera Papers; "Speech of President de Valera at Labor Meeting, Butte, [Montana,] July 27, 1919," P150/800, ibid.

20. Brugha quoted in Fitzpatrick, *Harry Boland's Irish Revolution*, 107. On Cathal Brugha, see 263n54.

21. Joseph A. McCartin, *Labor's Great War: The Struggle for Industrial Democracy and the Origins of Modern American Labor Relations, 1912–1921* (Chapel Hill: University of North Carolina Press, 1997), quoted on 22, 197.

22. Timothy J. Meagher, *Inventing Irish America: Generation, Class, and Ethnic Identity in a New England City, 1880–1928* (Notre Dame, IN: University of Notre Dame Press, 2001), 324.

23. McCartin, *Labor's Great War*, 21; Dante Barton, "Frank P. Walsh," *Harper's Weekly* 88 (Sept. 27, 1913), 24.

24. McCartin, *Labor's Great War*, 21–23, quoted on 21, 22.

25. Ibid., quoted on 22; Shelton Stromquist, "Class Wars: Frank Walsh, the Reformers, and the Crisis of Progressivism," in Eric Arnesen et al., eds., *Labor Histories: Class, Politics, and the Working-Class Experience* (Urbana: University of Illinois Press, 1998), 97–124, quoted on 115.

26. Robert A. Hill, ed., *The Marcus Garvey and Universal Negro Improvement Association Papers*, 9 vols. (1–7, 9–10) (Berkeley: University of California Press, 1983–2006), 3:13–14n2. In a letter to Malone in September 1914, Wilson referred to "our close personal relationship which I so much prize." Arthur S. Link, *Wilson: The New Freedom* (Princeton, NJ: Princeton University Press, 1956), 171.

27. David Brundage has estimated that the league had a "core membership of about 150 people." David Brundage, "American Labour and the Irish Question, 1916–23," *Saothar* 24 (1999), quoted on 61.

28. Remarks by Peter Magennis, "Memorial Meeting to Liam Mellowes at the Carmelite Hall, January 28th, 1923," ms. 15,985, John J. Hearn Papers, NLI.

29. Francis M. Carroll, "Irish Progressive League," in Michael F. Funchion, ed., *Irish American Voluntary Organizations* (Westport, CT: Greenwood Press, 1983), 206–10, quoted on 207; McCartan, *With de Valera in America*, 40–41; Carroll, *American Opinion and the Irish Question*, 106–7; Greaves, *Liam Mellows*, 131, 149–65; Irish Progressive League, *Bulletin*, no. 4 (September 1919), quoted on 1, 4.

30. Irish Progressive League, "Irish Are for Hillquit"; Irish Progressive League, *Bulletin*, no. 2 (March 25, 1918), 1; Morris Hillquit, *Loose Leaves from a Busy Life* (New York: Macmillan, 1934), 180–210, quoted on 183, 202; John F. McClymer, "Of 'Mornin' Glories' and 'Fine Old Oaks': John Purroy Mitchell, Al Smith, and Reform as an Expression of Irish-American Aspiration," in Ronald H. Bayor and Timothy J. Meagher, eds., *The New York Irish* (Baltimore: Johns Hopkins University Press, 1996), 374–94; *New York Times*, Nov. 7, 1917.

31. Greaves, *Liam Mellows*, 30–117; Fitzpatrick, *Harry Boland's Irish Revolution*, 126.

32. If the U.S. Attorneys' Office had known that Mellows was seeking to secure passage on a merchant vessel traveling to Germany in order to negotiate the landing of German armaments in Ireland, it is unlikely that he would have been released from jail so quickly, if at all. Greaves, *Liam Mellows*, 118–34, quoted on 133. On the indictment of Elizabeth Gurley Flynn, see Elizabeth Gurley Finn, *The Rebel Girl: An Autobiography; My First Life (1906–1926)* (1955; repr., New York: International Publishers, 1973), 233; Helen C. Camp, *Iron in Her Soul: Elizabeth Gurley Flynn and the American Left* (Pullman: Washington State University Press, 1995), 76–77.

33. On the indictment of Jeremiah O'Leary, see Jeremiah A. O'Leary, *My Political Trial and Experiences* (New York: Jefferson Publishing, 1919), 49. Jeremiah O'Leary to Joseph McGarrity, June 27, 1918, folder 1, ms. 17,650, Joseph McGarrity Collection (Dr. William J. Maloney), NLI; Greaves, *Liam Mellows*, 129, 149–50, quoted on 150.

34. Liam Mellows to "My dear Mrs. Hearn," Jan. 24, 1919, ms. 15,986, Hearn Papers.

35. Remarks by Peter Magennis, "Memorial Meeting to Liam Mellowes"; Liam Mellows to Peter Golden, Aug. 8, 1918, folder 11, Golden Papers; Carroll, *American Opinion and the Irish Question*, 244n70.

36. McCartney, "De Valera's Mission to the United States," 312.

37. On April 9, 1921, Bishop Gallagher of Detroit, an ally of Cohalan and Devoy, charged that "President de Valera deliberately split the Irish movement in America, and all the energies of his followers have been wasted in the struggle to destroy, instead of being expended for Ireland's cause against the common enemy." Gallagher quoted in *Irish Times*, Feb. 1, 1964, and see Seán Nunan's defense of de Valera, *Irish Times*, Feb. 2, 1964, P150/1009, de Valera Papers.

38. Mellows to Peter Golden, Aug. 8, 1918; Liam Mellows to Patrick McCartan, Feb. 28, 1920, folder 2, ms. 17,674, Dr. Patrick McCartan Papers, NLI.

39. Greaves, *Liam Mellows*, quoted on 125, 158, 159; *New York Times*, May 21, 1918.

40. Greaves, *Liam Mellows*, 161–62 (quoted), 165, 219; Fitzpatrick, *Harry Boland's Irish Revolution*, quoted on 127.

41. Frank Robbins, *Under the Starry Plough: Recollections of the Irish Citizen Army* (Dublin: Academy Press, 1977), 167, 170.

42. Greaves, *Liam Mellows*, quoted on 154–55; Emmet Larkin, *James Larkin: Irish Labour Leader, 1876–1947* (Cambridge, MA: MIT Press, 1965), 223.

43. Jim Herlihy, *Peter Golden: The Voice of Ireland* (Cork: Peter Golden Commemoration Committee, 1994), 19, 21, 55, 58–59; P. E. Magennis, "Peter Golden: Orator—Poet—Patriot," *Catholic Bulletin* 16 (May 1926), 527–28; "Golden's Career Is Spectacular" (newspaper clipping, n.p., n.d. [February 1916]), in "Clippings about Peter Golden," folder 1-c, Golden Papers; Peter Golden, *Ballads of Rebellion* (n.p., 1914), quoted on 5; Peter Golden, *The Voice of Ireland* (New York: Press of M. A. O'Connor, n.d. [1916?]), 84–85, 109 (quoted).

44. Peter Golden to W. V. Delahunt, May 23, 1919, folder 2, Golden Papers; Peter Golden to Lincoln Colcord, Aug. 5, 1919, ibid.; "Wanted: 2,000 irish men and women and friends of the irish republic!" (New York, n.d. [1918]), folder 1-c, ibid.

45. Golden, *Ballads of Rebellion*, quoted on 6; *America* 20 (Nov. 9, 1918), quoted on 118; see flyers announcing Irish Progressive League mass meetings, folder 2, Golden Papers.

46. Peter Golden to W. V. Delahunt, May 23, 1919; Peter Golden to Patrick McCartan, March 24, 1919, ms. 17,668, McCartan Papers; Greaves, *Liam Mellows*, quoted on 198–99, 205.

47. Richard English, *Ernie O'Malley, IRA Intellectual* (Oxford: Clarendon Press, 1998), 34; Helen Golden to Mr. Welch, Sept. 19, 1920, folder 6, Golden Papers; Carroll, *American Opinion and the Irish Question*, 106–7, 239–40n45; *New York Times*, Feb. 17. 1934; Frank P. Walsh to Leonora O'Reilly, Aug. 2, 1920, box 28, Francis Patrick Walsh Papers, Manuscripts and Archives Division, New York Public Library.

48. *New York Times*, Feb. 17. 1934; remarks by Dr. Gertrude Kelly, "Memorial Meeting to Liam Mellowes." For a study of Gertrude Kelly's brother John Forrest Kelly, whose career was in some respects as extraordinary as hers, see Michael E. Chapman, " 'How to Smash the British Empire': John Forrest Kelly's Irish World and the Boycott of 1920–21," *Éire-Ireland* 43 (Fall/Winter 2008), 217–52.

49. *New York Times*, Feb. 17, 1934. On the "Boston marriage," see Margaret Ward, *Hanna Sheehy Skeffington: A Life* (Cork: Attic Press, 1997), 197.

50. David Krause, "The Conscience of Ireland: Lalor, Davitt, and Sheehy-Skeffington," *Éire-Ireland* 28 (Spring 1993), quoted on 10; Hanna Sheehy Skeffington, *Impressions of Sinn Féin in America* (Dublin: Davis Publishing, 1919); Ward, *Hanna Sheehy Skeffington*,

184–208, quoted on 193; Joanne Mooney Eichacker, *Irish Republican Women in America: Lecture Tours, 1916–1925* (Dublin: Irish Academic Press, 2003), 63–91, 215–18.

51. Sheehy Skeffington, *Impressions of Sinn Féin in America*, 7; Ward, *Hanna Sheehy Skeffington*, 196–201, quoted on 200; Carroll, *American Opinion and the Irish Question*, 86–87, 106–7; Hanna Sheehy Skeffington to Peter Golden, n.d., folder 11, Golden Papers; Eichacker, *Irish Republican Women in America*, 73–75, quoted on 74.

52. The indispensable source on Helen Golden and the American Women Pickets is Joe Doyle, "Striking for Ireland on the New York Docks," in Bayor and Meagher, eds., *New York Irish*, 360–63, 369, 371, 663n37, n38.

53. Herlihy, *Peter Golden*, 24–25, 55 (quoted); and see the photo, on page 45, of Helen Golden dressed as a longshoreman, with her hair tucked under a workman's cap, after boarding a British ship to urge support for the Irish Patriotic Strike. Peter Golden left his position as secretary of the Irish Progressive League because de Valera asked him to play a larger role in the nationalist movement. In April 1921 he became national secretary of de Valera's American Association for the Recognition of the Irish Republic. Peter Golden to Helen Golden, April 20, 1921, folder 1-c, Golden Papers.

54. Fitzpatrick, *Harry Boland's Irish Revolution*, quoted on 129, 18; Eamon de Valera to Arthur Griffith, Aug. 21, 1919, in Fanning et al., eds., *Documents on Irish Foreign Policy*, 1:43.

55. Fitzpatrick, *Harry Boland's Irish Revolution*, quoted on 180.

56. *Journal of Commerce*, Aug. 28, 1920; *Sun and New York Herald*, Aug. 28, 1920; *New York Tribune*, Aug. 28, 1920. For scholarly treatment of the Irish Patriotic Strike, see David Brundage, "The 1920 New York Dockers' Boycott: Class, Gender, Race, and Irish-American Nationalism" (paper presented at the Organization of American Historians' annual meeting, Chicago, April 1992); Doyle, "Striking for Ireland," 357–73; Bruce Nelson, *Divided We Stand: American Workers and the Struggle for Black Equality* (Princeton, NJ: Princeton University Press, 2001), 26–38.

57. *Evening Sun*, Sept. 3, 1920; *New York Times*, Sept. 3, 1920; *Irish World*, Sept. 11, 1920.

58. Nelson, *Divided We Stand*, 26–28; Doyle, "Striking for Ireland," 365–66; *New York Times*, Aug. 10, 28, 1920; *New York World*, Aug. 29, 1920; *New York Tribune*, Aug. 28, 1920.

59. Fitzpatrick, *Harry Boland's Irish Revolution*, quoted on 180, 179; and see untitled typescript, with the words "Fr[om] Father Shanley probably" at the head of the first page, P150/668, de Valera Papers. Whoever wrote the document maintained that Boland "appointed" the delegates who took the lead in mobilizing other members of the *Baltic*'s engine room crew.

60. McCartan, *With de Valera in America*, 5–6, quoted on 6; Piaras Béaslaí, *Michael Collins and the Making of a New Ireland* (London: George G. Harrap, 1926), 1:217–20, 2:98–99; Greaves, *Liam Mellows*, 224–26; Peter Hart, *The I.R.A. at War, 1916–1923* (Oxford: Oxford University Press, 2003), 141–77, quoted on 151. For a vivid description of the maritime network that helped Irish revolutionaries—most notably, Eamon de Valera—cross the Atlantic to build support in the United States, see "Deverant's Story," P150/668, de Valera Papers. Deverant, whose real name was Barney Downs, was the seaman who oversaw Dev's journey from Liverpool to New York and back as a stowaway.

61. Fitzpatrick, *Harry Boland's Irish Revolution*, 179 (quoted), 382n60.

62. Eamon de Valera, speech at the "great Labor Day celebration," New York City, Sept. 1, 1920, P150/826, de Valera Papers. On Connolly's sojourn in the United States, see Donal Nevin, *James Connolly: "A Full Life"* (Dublin: Gill and Macmillan, 2005), 225–322.

63. Emmet O'Connor, *A Labour History of Ireland* (Dublin: Gill and Macmillan, 1992), 105–6; Lee, *Ireland, 1912–1985*, quoted on 124; de Valera, speech at the "great Labor Day celebration."

64. Lee, *Ireland, 1912–1985*, quoted on 124.

65. *Boston Post*, Sept. 3, 1920.

66. Joan M. Jensen, *Passage from India: Asian Indian Immigrants in North America* (New Haven, CT: Yale University Press, 1988), 241–42; Janice R. MacKinnon and Stephen R. MacKinnon, *Agnes Smedley: The Life and Times of an American Radical* (Berkeley: University of California Press, 1986), 56; Michael Silvestri, "'An Assertion of Liberty Incarnate': Irish and Indian Nationalists in North America," in *Ireland and India: Nationalism, Empire and Memory* (Basingstoke, UK: Palgrave Macmillan, 2009), 13–45.

67. Jensen, *Passage from India*, 242; Declan Kiberd, *Inventing Ireland* (London: Jonathan Cape, 1995), 253–57, quoted on 254; Sarmila Bose and Eilis Ward, "'India's cause is Ireland's cause': Elite Links and Nationalist Politics," in Michael Holmes and Denis Holmes, eds., *Ireland and India: Connections, Comparisons, Contrasts* (Dublin: Folens, 1997), 58–59; Michael G. Malouf, "With Dev in America: Sinn Féin and Recognition Politics, 1919–21," *Interventions* 4 (April 2002), 22–34, quoted on 26.

68. Agnes Smedley to Eamon de Valera, March 9, 1920, P150/1053, de Valera Papers; Kiberd, *Inventing Ireland*, quoted on 255; *Irish World*, Feb. 28, 1920; Jensen, *Passage from India*, quoted on 242.

69. Fitzpatrick, *Harry Boland's Irish Revolution*, 140–42.

70. Kiberd, *Inventing Ireland*, quoted on 255; Eamon de Valera, "A Race That Has Never Ceased to Strive," in Moynihan, ed., *Speeches and Statements by Eamon de Valera*, 35, emphasis added.

71. Peter Hart, *The I.R.A. and Its Enemies: Violence and Community in Cork, 1916–1923* (Oxford: Oxford University Press, 1998), 78–79, 84–85; Francis J. Costello, *Enduring the Most: The Life and Death of Terence MacSwiney* (Dingle, Ireland: Brandon, 1995), 114–19, 139–53.

72. Moirin Chavasse, *Terence MacSwiney* (Dublin: Clonmore and Reynolds, 1961), quoted on 132, 133. See also "Mayor MacSwiney's Speech at the Trial [August 1920]," in "American Commission on Conditions in Ireland, Second Report:—Hearings in Washington, D.C., December 8 and 9, 1920, Testimony of Mrs. Terence MacSwiney and Miss Mary MacSwiney," *Nation* (December 22, 1920), sec. 2:753–54; and P. S. O'Hegarty, *A Short Memoir of Terence MacSwiney* (Dublin: Talbott Press, 1922), 76–79.

73. Eamon de Valera, "President's Speech at Lexington Theatre, Friday, August 27th, [1920]," P150/1042, de Valera Papers; McCartan, *With De Valera in America*, 199, 215; Eamon de Valera, "Death of Terence MacSwiney," in Moynihan, ed., *Speeches and Statements by Eamon de Valera*, 47; "Advance Extracts from President de Valera's Speech at Polo Grounds, New York, Sunday, Oct. 31, 1920," P150/1045, de Valera Papers. MacSwiney finally died in London's Brixton Prison. At nearly the same time, two other Irish republicans died on hunger strike in Cork: Michael Fitzgerald, on October 17; and Joseph Murphy, on October 25, only a few hours after MacSwiney succumbed. Costello, *Enduring the Most*, 180, 201; Chavasse, *Terence MacSwiney*, 141–42.

74. Chavasse, *Terence MacSwiney*, 171.

75. De Valera maintained, nearly forty years later, that because of Terence Mac-Swiney, "Ireland's Cause became the cause of every people rightly struggling to be free." Eamon de Valera, "Appeal for Subscriptions for Erection of Memorial Chapel to Traolach Mac Suibhne in Southwark Cathedral, London (Statement Recorded by Tao-iseach at Radio Eireann on 3rd February, 1958, for Broadcasting on 16 February, 1958)," P150/651, de Valera Papers; Ho Chi Minh, quoted in Bill Rolston and Michael Shannon, *Encounters: How Racism Came to Ireland* (Belfast: Beyond the Pale, 2002), 92; Nehru, quoted in Bose and Ward, "'India's cause is Ireland's cause,'" 63, 61; "MacSwiney," *Crusader* 3 (December 1920), 9.

76. *Boston Pilot*, Oct. 30, 1920.

77. "Memorandum by Seán T. Ó Ceallaigh to Pope Benedict XV," May 18, 1920, in Fanning et al., *Documents on Irish Foreign Policy*, 1:64; Gavan Duffy, quoted in Bill Kissane, *The Politics of the Irish Civil War* (Oxford: Oxford University Press, 2005), 52.

78. Hill, ed., *Marcus Garvey Papers*, 1:287, 289n9; *Irish World*, Nov. 16, 1918, Aug. 16, 1919. During his tenure as editor of the *Irish World*, Robert Ford suffered from recurring illnesses, culminating in a paralyzing stroke in September 1919 and his death three months later. He was succeeded by his brother Austin Ford, who was content to leave much of the editorial work of the paper to others, notably John Forrest Kelly. On changes at the *Irish World*, see Chapman, "'How to Smash the British Empire,'" 219, 222–23.

79. Hill, ed., *Marcus Garvey Papers*, 2:499.

80. E. David Cronon, *Black Moses: The Story of Marcus Garvey and the Universal Negro Improvement Association* (1955; repr., Madison: University of Wisconsin Press, 1969), 62–71; "Report of UNIA Parade, [New York, 3 August 1920,]" in Hill, ed., *Marcus Garvey Papers*, 2:490–94, especially 491; Fitzpatrick, *Harry Boland's Irish Revolution*, 382n60; Claude McKay, *Harlem: Negro Metropolis* (New York: E. P. Dutton, 1940), 153, 155 (quoted).

81. Fitzpatrick, *Harry Boland's Irish Revolution*, 179–80, quoted on 180; Doyle, "Striking for Ireland," 368–69; *Sun and New York Herald*, Aug. 28, 1920.

82. Eileen Curran played a leading role in the American Women Pickets. She was also a leader of the Celtic Players, an Irish theater group with ties to the Irish Progressive League that performed the works of John Millington Synge, Lady Gregory, William Butler Yeats, and other luminaries of the Irish Literary Revival in the United States. Doyle, "Striking for Ireland," 365; *Sun and New York Herald*, Aug. 28, 1920; *Journal of Commerce*, Aug. 28, 1920.

83. *New York Tribune*, Aug. 28, 1920; *Journal of Commerce*, Aug. 28, 1920; *New York Times*, Aug. 28, 1920.

84. Nelson, *Divided We Stand*, 12–26, 30–31; Brundage, "1920 New York Dockers' Boycott," 10–11; Doyle, "Striking for Ireland," 366–67, 370–71; *New York Times*, Aug. 28, Sept. 2, 3, 1920; *Sun and New York Herald*, Aug. 28, 1920; *New York World*, Aug. 29, 1920; *Irish World*, Sept. 11, 1920.

85. Claude McKay, *Home to Harlem* (1928; repr., Boston: Northeastern University Press, 1987), 45.

86. Doyle, "Striking for Ireland," 370; *New York World*, Aug. 29, 1920; *Journal of Commerce*, Aug. 31, 1920.

87. *New York Times*, Sept. 11, 1920; Doyle, "Striking for Ireland," 370, 665n71; Hill, ed., *Marcus Garvey Papers*, 3:12–14; "Decision of Colored Longshoremen Engaged in the

Breaking of the Irish Patriotic Strike," Sept. 13, 1920, folder 6, Golden Papers; Nelson, *Divided We Stand*, 30, 36.

88. De Valera, "Press Statement, New York, 23 June 1919," 31.

89. See "Report by Special Agent P-138," Sept. 20, 1920, in Hill, ed., *Marcus Garvey Papers*, 3:12–14.

90. For a vivid portrait of hostility to Irish Americans, and to de Valera himself, during his American tour, see David B. Franklin, "Bigotry in 'Bama: De Valera's Visit to Birmingham, Alabama, April 1920," *History Ireland* 12 (Winter 2004), 30–33. Birmingham was a hotbed of anti-Catholicism, which was the main source of the opposition to de Valera's visit. The city was also a bastion of white supremacy, and de Valera told his audience that Ireland was "the only white nation on earth still in the bonds of political slavery."

91. There are two outstanding sources on Harrison: Jeffrey B. Perry, ed., *A Hubert Harrison Reader* (Middletown, CT: Wesleyan University Press, 2001), and Perry, *Hubert Harrison: The Voice of Harlem Radicalism, 1883–1918* (New York: Columbia University Press, 2009), quoted on 394. Perry's extraordinarily thorough and insightful work on Harrison has finally rescued the "Father of Harlem Radicalism" from obscurity.

92. Perry, *Hubert Harrison*, 21–87, especially 49–51, 56–57, 83–87; Winston James, *Holding Aloft the Banner of Ethiopia: Caribbean Radicalism in Early Twentieth-Century America* (London: Verso, 1998), 123–34, Henry Miller quoted on 131, the *Amsterdam News* on 133.

93. Perry, introduction to Perry, ed., *Hubert Harrison Reader*, 4, 14–16.

94. Perry, ed., *Hubert Harrison Reader*, 139–40. In an article published in July 1917, Harrison declared, "We are not Republicans, Democrats or Socialists any longer. We are Negroes first. . . . All . . . rebuffs will make for manhood—if we are men—and will drive us to play in American politics the same role which the Irish party played in British politics." Ibid., 137–39.

95. Ibid., 202–3 (emphasis in original).

96. Ibid., 223–28, quoted on 225, 227.

97. W.E.B. Du Bois, "The African Roots of the War," *Atlantic Monthly* 115 (May 1915), 707–14, reprinted in David Levering Lewis, ed., *W.E.B. Du Bois: A Reader* (New York: Henry Holt, 1995), 642–51; Hill, ed., *Marcus Garvey Papers*, 2:501; Briggs (1918), quoted in Matthew Pratt Guterl, *The Color of Race in America, 1900–1940* (Cambridge, MA: Harvard University Press, 2001), 69; Cyril V. Briggs, "Heroic Ireland," *Crusader* 3 (February 1921), 5.

98. Marilyn Lake and Henry Reynolds, *Drawing the Global Colour Line: White Men's Countries and the International Challenge of Racial Equality* (Cambridge: Cambridge University Press, 2008), 1–2 (quoted), 9–10, 88 (quoted).

99. Perry, introduction to Perry, ed., *Hubert Harrison Reader*, 17.

EPILOGUE: THE ORDEAL OF THE IRISH REPUBLIC

1. Parts of this chapter appeared, in a somewhat different form, in Bruce Nelson, "Irish Americans, Irish Nationalism, and the 'Social' Question, 1916–1923," *boundary 2*, 31 (Spring 2004), 147–78. The first epigraph is from Robert Lynd, *If the Germans*

Conquered England and Other Essays (Dublin: Maunsel, 1917), xi, and the second from Statement of Miss M. MacSwiney, Dec. 21, 1921, in Parliamentary Debates, Dáil Éireann, "Debate on Treaty," http://historical-debates.oireachtas.ie/D/DT/D.T.192112210002.html (accessed Jan. 8, 2011).

2. A Son of Ireland, "Ireland's Despairing Cry for Liberty" (n.p.,n. d. [1920]), folder 68, box 9, Chicago Federation of Labor / John Fitzpatrick Papers, Chicago Historical Society.

3. Seumas MacManus, *The Story of the Irish Race: A Popular History of Ireland* (New York: Irish Publishing, 1921), 684–705, quoted on 685; Patrick Maume, "De Blacam, Aodh (Hugh Saunders Blackham, Aodh Sandrach de Blacam)," in James McGuire and James Quinn, eds., *Dictionary of Irish Biography* (Cambridge: Cambridge University Press, 2009), http://dib.cambridge.org/quicksearch.do# (accessed Dec. 8, 2010); Maume, "Anti-Machiavel: Three Ulster Nationalists in the Age of De Valera," *Irish Political Studies* 14 (1999), 43–63; Statement of Miss M. MacSwiney; Charlotte H. Fallon, *Soul of Fire: A Biography of Mary MacSwiney* (Cork: Mercier Press, 1986).

4. I capitalize "Republican" here and hereafter only to identify the antitreaty side in the Irish Civil War, which pitted protreaty (or Free State) forces against their antitreaty (or Republican) opponents. The opponents of the treaty claimed the term "Republican" for themselves, whereas their adversaries called them antitreatyites and referred to their military units as Irregulars.

5. Peter Golden to W. V. Delahunt, May 23, 1919, folder 2, Peter Golden Papers, National Library of Ireland (NLI).

6. Mary MacSwiney to Eamon de Valera, n.d. [October? 1921], P150/656, Eamon de Valera Papers, University College Dublin Archives.

7. Golden sailed from New York and arrived in Cobh (formerly Queenstown) on July 31, 1922. He departed from Cobh for New York on September 25, 1922. He listed his occupation as "Journalist and Lecturer." I thank Susan Bibeau for providing me with copies of the ships' registers.

8. Michael Hopkinson, *Green against Green: The Irish Civil War* (Dublin: Gill and Macmillan, 1988), 146–65.

9. Peter Golden, *Impressions of Ireland* (New York: Irish Industries Depot, n.d. [1924?]), 12, 14, 18, 19, 20, 22, 38, 39, 44, 75, 80, 89.

10. Ibid., 54.

11. C. Desmond Greaves, *Liam Mellows and the Irish Revolution* (London: Lawrence and Wishart, 1971), 198–99, 205; Golden, *Impressions of Ireland*, 34, 39.

12. Brian Hanley, "Irish Republicans in Interwar New York," *Irish Journal of American Studies* 1 (June 2009), http://www.ijasonline.com/BRIAN-HANLEY.html (accessed Nov. 30, 2010).

13. Peter Golden to Joseph McGarrity, n.d. [1917], Joseph McGarrity Collection (Dr. W. J. Maloney), NLI; Peter Golden to Harry Boland, Dec. 7, 1921, P150/1150, de Valera Papers.

14. Jim Herlihy, *Peter Golden: The Voice of Ireland* (Cork: Peter Golden Commemoration Committee, 1994), 69–72, quoted on 70; Associated Press dispatch, March 19, 1926, folder 16, Golden Papers. In an oral history interview many years later, Golden's daughter Eithne Sax reported that the family had been planning to settle, at least temporarily, in an artists' colony in Pasadena and that the cause of her father's death was Bright's disease (a severe kidney ailment). See interview with Eithne Merriam Golden

Sax, Nov. 2, 2006, Ireland House Oral History Collection, Archives of Irish America, New York University, http://www.nyu.edu/library/bobst/research/aia/collections/ ihoral/saxeg01.php (accessed Nov. 4, 2009).

15. "Peter Golden Lauded for Irish Patriotism at Funeral Mass," *Catholic Register (Denver)*, undated clipping, folder 16, Golden Papers; P. E. Magennis, "Peter Golden: Orator—Poet—Patriot," *Catholic Bulletin* 16 (May 1926), 527–33; Dermot Keogh, *Ireland and the Vatican: The Politics and Diplomacy of Church-State Relations, 1922–1960* (Cork: Cork University Press, 1995), 6.

16. Magennis, "Peter Golden," quoted on 526, 526–27, 532.

17. Ibid., quoted on 533. After the publication of Father Magennis's eulogy, Peter Golden's remains were taken to Ireland, and he was buried next to his cousin Terence MacSwiney in the republican cemetery in Cork. Herlihy, *Peter Golden*, 73–80.

18. Peter Golden, *Poems of the Irish Republic* (n.p., n.d.), no page numbers; Magennis, "Peter Golden," quoted on 527.

19. Maume, "De Blacam, Aodh" and "Anti-Machiavel," 55–58; Terence Brown, *Ireland: A Social and Cultural History, 1922–1985* (London: Fontana, 1985), de Valera quoted on 146. In "Anti-Machiavel," Maume claims that de Blacam influenced de Valera's famous "Dancing at the Crossroads" speech of 1943.

20. Statement of Mr. Piaras Béaslaí, Jan. 3, 1922, in Parliamentary Debates, Dáil Éireann, "Debate on Treaty," http://historical-debates.oireachtas.ie/D/DT/D.T.192201030002. html (accessed Jan. 4, 2011).

21. J. J. Lee, *Ireland, 1912–1985: Politics and Society* (Cambridge: Cambridge University Press, 1989), 67–69; Francis Costello, *The Irish Revolution and Its Aftermath, 1916–1923: Years of Revolt* (Dublin: Irish Academic Press, 2003), quoted on 294; Bruce Nelson, "The Dangerous Years," *Irish Literary Supplement* 23 (Fall 2003), 16–17. For persuasive critiques of the conventional wisdom that the treatyites were democrats and their antitreaty adversaries were prepared to resort to a military dictatorship, see Bill Kissane, *The Politics of the Irish Civil War* (Oxford: Oxford University Press, 2005), 207–9; John M. Regan, *The Irish Counter-Revolution, 1921–1936: Treatyite Politics and Settlement in Independent Ireland* (Dublin: Gill and Macmillan, 1999), 67–70; R. M. Douglas, "Antidemocratic Influences in Ireland, 1919–39," in *Architects of the Resurrection: Ailtirí na hAiséirghe and the Fascist "New Order" in Ireland* (Manchester, UK: Manchester University Press, 2009), 5–42, especially 16–22.

22. Statement of Mr. Sean MacEntee, Dec. 22, 1921, in Parliamentary Debates, Dáil Éireann, "Debate on Treaty," http://historical-debates.oireachtas.ie/D/DT/ D.T.192112220002.html (accessed Jan. 3, 2011); Eoghan Davis, "The Guerrilla Mind," in David Fitzpatrick, ed., *Revolution? Ireland, 1917–1923* (Dublin: Trinity College History Workshop, 1990), quoted on 47; Deirdre McMahon, "MacEntee, Sean (John) Francis," in McGuire and Quinn, eds., *Dictionary of Irish Biography*, http://dib.cambridge.org/ viewReadPage.do?articleId=a5202 (accessed Jan. 3, 2011).

23. Mary MacSwiney to "Southern Command," n.d. [Spring? 1923], P150/657, de Valera Papers.

24. Fallon, *Soul of Fire*, 89–93, 96–100, quoted on 115; Margaret Ward, *Unmanageable Revolutionaries: Women and Irish Nationalism* (1983; repr., London: Pluto Press, 1995), 214 (quoted), 225–26; Tom Garvin, *1922: The Birth of Irish Democracy* (Dublin: Gill and Macmillan, 1996), 151.

25. Greaves, *Liam Mellows*, quoted on 270.

26. Statement of Liam Mellowes, Jan. 4, 1922, in Parliamentary Debates, Dáil Éireann, "Debate on Treaty," http://historical-debates.oireachtas.ie/D/DT/D.T.192201040002.html (accessed Jan. 4, 2011).

27. Statement of Piaras Béaslaí.

28. Statement of Liam Mellowes.

29. Anne Haverty, *Constance Markievicz: An Independent Life* (London: Pandora, 1988); Statement of Madame Markievicz, Jan. 3, 1922, in Parliamentary Debates, Dáil Éireann, "Debate on Treaty," http://historical-debates.oireachtas.ie/D/DT/D.T.192201030002.html (accessed Jan. 4, 2011).

30. Hopkinson, *Green against Green*, 40–45, 58–69, quoted on 67.

31. D. R. O'Connor Lysaght, "County Tipperary: Class Struggle and National Struggle, 1916–1924," in William Nolan, ed., *Tipperary: History and Society* (Dublin: Geography Publications, 1985), 406–7; Emmet O'Connor, *Syndicalism in Ireland, 1917–1923* (Cork: Cork University Press, 1988), 104; Terence Dooley, "IRA Veterans and Land Division in Independent Ireland, 1923–48," in Fearghal McGarry, ed., *Republicanism in Modern Ireland* (Dublin: UCD Press, 2003), 86–107, quoted on 92; Regan, *Irish Counter-Revolution*, quoted on 86.

32. Greaves, *Liam Mellows*, 349, 350 (quoted), 362; Peadar O'Donnell, *The Gates Flew Open* (London: Jonathan Cape, 1932), 28–34, 50–52, quoted on 29; Donal Ó Drisceoil, *Peadar O'Donnell* (Cork: Cork University Press, 2001), 26–28.

33. Greaves, *Liam Mellows*, quoted on 358, 364–65.

34. Ibid., quoted on 365; *New York Times*, May 20, 1918; Statement of A. MacCabe, Jan. 4, 1922, in Parliamentary Debates, Dáil Éireann, "Debate on Treaty," http://historical-debates.oireachtas.ie/D/DT/D.T.192201040002.html (accessed Jan. 4, 2011).

35. See Mellows's letters to Eileen and John Hearn in ms. 15,986, John J. Hearn Papers, NLI. The Hearns lived in Westfield, Massachusetts, and often provided hospitality to Mellows during his sojourn in the United States. His letters to them are full of references to his religious beliefs and devotional activity.

36. Greaves, *Liam Mellows*, quoted on 365, 366.

37. Tim Pat Coogan, *De Valera: Long Fellow, Long Shadow* (London: Hutchinson, 1993), quoted on 344; Kissane, *Politics of the Irish Civil War*, 129, 153, 160; Greaves, *Liam Mellows*, quoted on 379.

38. Conor Kostick, *Revolution in Ireland: Popular Militancy, 1917–1923* (London: Pluto Press, 1996), quoted on 171. Greaves considers the merits of this accusation in *Liam Mellows*, 375.

39. Greaves, *Liam Mellows*, quoted on 384.

40. On why these four men were chosen, see Regan, *Irish Counter-Revolution*, 117–19.

41. Greaves, *Liam Mellows*, 386–90, quoted on 387; O'Donnell, *The Gates Flew Open*, 78–85; Statement of Liam Mellowes.

42. Regan, *Irish Counter-Revolution*, quoted on 116.

43. "Memorial Meeting to Liam Mellowes at the Carmelite Hall, January 28th, 1923," ms. 15,985, Hearn Papers.

44. [Arthur Griffith,] "Nationalists and Internationalists," *Sinn Féin*, April 26, 1913.

45. Fergus Campbell, *Land and Revolution: Nationalist Politics in the West of Ireland, 1891–1921* (Oxford: Oxford University Press, 2005), 200–218, quoted on 215.

46. Greaves, *Liam Mellows*, quoted on 162; Eamon de Valera to Mary MacSwiney, Sept. 11, 1922, P150/657, de Valera Papers.

47. For critical perspectives on socialist republicanism in twentieth-century Ireland, see Richard English, *Radicals and the Republic: Socialist Republicanism in the Irish Free State, 1925–1937* (Oxford: Clarendon Press, 1994), and Henry Patterson, *The Politics of Illusion: Republicanism and Socialism in Modern Ireland* (London: Hutchinson Radius, 1989).

48. Lynd was raised by devout Presbyterian parents in Belfast and educated at Queen's University. To his parents' dismay, he became a socialist and admirer of James Connolly, as well as a republican. See Sean McMahon, "Robert Lynd: An Introduction," in Robert Lynd, *Galway of the Races: Selected Essays* (Dublin: Lilliput Press, 1990), 1–44.

49. Carla King, introduction to Michael Davitt's *Collected Writings, 1868–1906*, ed. Carla King, vol. 1, *Pamphlets, Speeches, and Articles, 1889–1906* (London: Thoemmes Press, 2001; Tokyo: Edition Synapse, 2001), xxviii; "Letters to Antislavery Workers and Agencies," pt. 1, "Frederick Douglass," *Journal of Negro History* 10 (October 1925), 662.

Index

abolitionism (in Ireland), 65-66, 86, 88-92, 97, 99-102, 106, 113; and anti-Catholicism, 71-72, 89, 102. *See also* Religious Society of Friends; Webb, Richard Davis

abolitionism (in the United States): and anti-Catholicism, 65, 71-72, 78, 279n49; and "come-outerism," 67, 278n35; and Irish immigrants, 65, 67-69; and nativism, 67, 69, 72, 78, 279n49. *See also* Douglass Frederick; Garrison, William Lloyd; Remond, Charles Lenox

Aborigines' Protection Society, 60

Act of Settlement (1652), 22

Adams, President John Quincy, 79-80

"Address of the Irish People to Their Countrymen and Countrywomen in America" (Irish Address), 65-66, 67, 68, 73, 74, 86; origins of, 65-66; radicalism of, 66; signers of, 113-14; unveiled at Boston's Faneuil Hall, 66, 100

African Blood Brotherhood for African Liberation and Redemption (ABB), 54, 184, 199; character and purpose of, 201, 308-9n83; founding of, 200; and Irish Republican Brotherhood, 201

Allen, Richard, 65, 67, 68, 92, 99, 101, 112-13

American Anti-Slavery Society, 90, 117

American Association for the Recognition of the Irish Republic: ascent and decline of, 246; and Peter Golden, 243, 315n53

American Federation of Labor, 229, 230

American Land League, 126

American Legion, 231

American Negro Academy, 190

American Revolution: Irish views of, 24-25, 50, 113

American Women Pickets for the Enforcement of America's War Aims, 224, 226-27, 235

Amery, Leo, 42

Amritsar Massacre, 176

Anglo-Irish Committee, 158, 159, 160, 163

Anglo-Irish Treaty, 149, 173, 194, 196, 210, 242, 243, 249; and Catholic hierarchy in Ireland, 253

anti-Irish stereotypes, 9-10, 20, 24, 28-36, 38-43; evolution, and summary, of, 44-45; and Giraldus Cambrensis, 17-18, 19; and Irish nationalist response to, 44, 46-47, 53, 143-44. *See also* Beddoe, John; Carlyle, Thomas; Knox, Robert

Appiah, Kwame Anthony, 3

Arnold, Matthew, 31

Asgard: and the Howth gunrunning, 160-63

Bailey, Betsy, 93

Bailey, Frederick. *See* Douglass, Frederick

Barrett, Richard, 252, 254

Bartlett, Thomas, 25, 27

Barton, Agnes, 150

Barton, Charles, 150

Barton, Robert, 154, 158; and Anglo-Irish Treaty, 172-73; conversion to Irish nationalism of, 154-55; and Mary Childers, 159; portrait of, 154-55

Battle of Aughrim (1691), 23

Battle of the Boyne (1690), 23

Béaslaí, Piaras, 173, 248

Beddoe, John, 7, 39; author of *The Races of Britain* (1885), 40; on the "dark-complexioned aborigines" of the west of Ireland, 39-40; and Index of Nigrescence, 40; portrait of, 39

Benedict XV (pope), 234

Benedict, Ruth: coauthor of *The Races of Mankind* (1943), 8; on racial identity and discrimination, 8

Benyon, John, 121

Berkeley, Bishop George, 24

Black Star Line, 198

Blake, Colonel John, 134

Boers, 14; and black Africans, 130-31, 135-38, 142-43, 146; and Catholicism, 146-47; Great Trek of, 135-36; history of, 130-33; nationalism of, 153; and South African War, 132-33, 135, 137-38, 167

Boer War. *See* South African War (1899-1902)

Boland, Harry, 217, 218, 222, 230, 235, 242, 246; and acts of sabotage in the United States, 228-29; and Eamon de Valera, 226; and Irish Patriotic Strike, 228, 235, 237, 315n59; and Irish Republican Brotherhood, 228; portrait of, 226

Domingo, W. A (cont'd)
   of, 191-92, 200, 304n10; and socialism, 192,
   304n10
Douglass, Frederick, 61, 66, 70, 86, 256; and
   Anna Murray Douglass, 284n29; author of
   Narrative of the Life of Frederick Douglass
   (1845), 93, 95; and Daniel O'Connell, 86-87,
   118; on England as friend of freedom, 105;
   internationalism of, 14, 96, 118; in Ireland,
   13-14, 86-87, 92, 95-106; on the Irish in
   America, 9, 117-18; portrait of, 92-95; on
   slavery, 93, 95, 97, 101-2; as spokesman for
   Black America, 117; and the United States,
   14, 95-97, 101-2, 106; and the "white slaves"
   of Ireland, 97-98, 103-4
Dreyfus, Alfred, 48
Dublin Negro's Friend Society, 89
Du Bois, Alexander, 208
Du Bois, Alfred, 208
Du Bois, James, 207-8
Du Bois, Mary Silvina Burghardt, 208
Du Bois, William Edward Burghardt (W.E.B.),
   7, 15, 190, 192, 193, 206, 207; and Alexander
   Crummell, 190; as founder and editor of
   the *Crisis*, 209; on Ireland and the Irish, 11,
   15, 208, 210-11; portrait of, 207-11; on the
   "religion" of "whiteness," 241; and the "War
   of the Color Line," 210, 240
Duffy, Charles Gavan, 111
Duffy, George Gavan, 172, 234
Duggan, Charles, 161
Duggan, E. J., 172
Dyer, General Reginald, 176

Easter Rising (1916), 26, 52, 54, 134, 147, 148,
   154, 164, 182, 210, 222, 225, 226, 240, 243,
   251, 253; role of Irish Republican Brother-
   hood in, 183; and Sinn Féin, 183
East India Company, 123
Elizabeth I (queen of England), 18
Emancipation Day, 105
Emmet, Robert, 32, 145, 182, 196, 197, 253
Emmons, David, 12
Encumbered Estates Act (1849), 33
Engels, Friedrich, 12, 108
England, Bishop John, 73, 114
Equiano, Olaudah, 190; author of *The Interest-
   ing Narrative of the Life of Olaudah Equiano*
   (1789), 87; in Ireland, 87, and Methodism,
   105
Equi, Marie, 225-26

Fauset, Jessie, 192
Fenianism, 12, 32, 35, 156, 182, 268n5; and
   "black Fenianism," 201; and Catholic
   hierarchy in Ireland, 253; and Clerkenwell
   bombing, 35; and "The Fenian Guy Fawkes"
   (1867), 36; internationalism of, 268n5; trans-
   atlantic links of, 35, 37
Figgis, Darrell, 157
Finley, Father Tom, 154
Fiske, John, 43
Flynn, Elizabeth Gurley, 220, 239
Ford, Patrick, 10, 35, 37, 54, 69, 194, 234; editor
   of the *Irish World*, 51; internationalism of,
   127; portrait of, 126-27; retreat from radical-
   ism in the 1880s, 291n28
Ford, Robert E., 234, 317n78
Ford, Una, 255
Freeman, Edward Augustus, 42, 43-44
Friends of Freedom for India, 230-31, 232, 237
Friends of Irish Freedom, 207, 230
Friends of Negro Freedom, 207
Froude, James Anthony, 46; on the passion of
   the Celts, 31-32
Fuller, James Cannings, 66; and Dublin Quak-
   ers, 100-101; nationality of, 277n30

Gaelic American, 221, 222, 223
Gaelic League, 215; founding of, 243
Gahan, Daniel, 27
Gandhi, Mohandas K., 176, 182, 206, 231
Garner, Steve, 6
Garrison, William Lloyd, 57, 65, 66, 68, 90,
   93, 97, 98, 101, 102, 113, 126, 234; and Daniel
   O'Connell, 57, 75-76, 84; and Dublin Quaker
   reformers, 99-100; and Irish immigrants, 67-
   69, 80, 86; as Irish Repealer and American
   Repealer, 67-68
Garvey, Marcus Mosiah, 15, 184, 191-92, 199,
   207, 210, 233, 234, 238, 240-41, 307n66,
   308n71; on Africa as a "mighty nation," 198;
   and Eamon de Valera, 197-98; and Great War,
   193, 196; on Ireland and Irish nationalism,
   193-99, 234; and Irish Patriotic Strike, 236-37;
   portrait of, 192-93, 195; and racial separation,
   198; and social Darwinism, 198-99, 240; and
   soviet form of government, 195-96
Garvin, Tom, 49-50
George V (king of England), 170
George, Henry, 127, 225; influence of on Michael Davitt and Patrick Ford, 291n25
Ghose, Salindra, 231

Whiteboys, 32

Wilberforce, William, 98, 105

William of Orange (King William III of England), 22-23

Williams, Basil, 153

Wilson, David, 266n37

Wilson, President Woodrow, 176, 199, 213, 219, 313n26; criticized by Irish nationalists, 214; and the right of self-determination, 181, 186-87, 213, 240

Workers' Socialist Federation (WSF), 203, 204

World Anti-Slavery Convention (1840), 57, 64, 65, 90, 99, 100

World War I. *See* Great War

Yeats, William Butler, 46, 47, 48

Young, Arthur, 24

Young Ireland, 32, 213, 253; Anglophobic nationalism of, 105, 106; on English culture in Ireland, 46; and O'Connell, 82; and rising of 1848, 104; and slavery, 82, 109, 111; and the United States, 82, 106

Made in the USA
Lexington, KY
11 June 2015